Police and the Unarmed Black Male Crisis

Presenting both historical and contemporary discussions and coverage, this book provides an in-depth and critical analysis of police brutality and the killing of unarmed Black males in the USA. Within the book, contributors cover five key areas: the historical context and contemporary evidence of police brutality of unarmed Black people in the USA, the impact of police aggression on Blacks' well-being, novel strategies for prevention and intervention, the advancement of a cordial relationship between police and Black communities, and how best to equip the next generation of scholars and professionals. Each contributor provides a simple-to-understand, thought-provoking, and creative recommendation to address the perennial social ill of police brutality of Black males, making this book an excellent resource for students, scholars, and professionals across disciplinary spectrums.

This book was originally published as a special issue of the *Journal of Human Behavior in the Social Environment.*

Sharon E. Moore is Professor of Social Work in the Raymond A. Kent School of Social Work at the University of Louisville, Louisville, Kentucky, USA. Her primary research is related to African American faculty at predominantly White institutions, as well as issues that affect Black males. She is a national trainer on human diversity issues.

A. Christson Adedoyin is an associate professor of Social Work in the Department of Social Work at Samford University, Birmingham, Alabama, USA. His research interests include church-based social work; the integration of faith and learning; the nexus of religion/spirituality in addressing socioeconomic, educational, and health disparities among African Americans; and African immigrants.

Michael A. Robinson is an assistant professor in the School of Social Work at the University of Georgia, Athens, Georgia, USA. His research interests address the health and well-being of African Americans, and other underserved populations, particularly in relation to substance abuse and mental disorders.

Police and the Unarmed Black Male Crisis

Advancing Effective Prevention Strategies

Edited by
Sharon E. Moore, A. Christson Adedoyin, and Michael A. Robinson

Routledge
Taylor & Francis Group
LONDON AND NEW YORK

First published 2018 by Routledge

2 Park Square, Milton Park, Abingdon, Oxfordshire OX14 4RN
52 Vanderbilt Avenue, New York, NY 10017

Routledge is an imprint of the Taylor & Francis Group, an informa business

First issued in paperback 2019

British Library Cataloguing in Publication Data
A catalogue record for this book is available from the British Library

ISBN 13: 978-1-138-09532-8 (hbk)
ISBN 13: 978-0-367-23497-3 (pbk)

Typeset in Minion Pro
by diacriTech, Chennai

Publisher's Note
The publisher accepts responsibility for any inconsistencies that may have arisen during the conversion of this book from journal articles to book chapters, namely the possible inclusion of journal terminology.

Disclaimer
Every effort has been made to contact copyright holders for their permission to reprint material in this book. The publishers would be grateful to hear from any copyright holder who is not here acknowledged and will undertake to rectify any errors or omissions in future editions of this book.

Contents

Citation Information

The chapters in this book were originally published in the *Journal of Human Behavior in the Social Environment*, volume 26, issues 3–4 (2016). When citing this material, please use the original page numbering for each article, as follows:

Chapter 1
A death to justice (The shooting of Michael Brown—Summer 2014)
Sylvia Telafaro
Journal of Human Behavior in the Social Environment, volume 26, issues 3–4 (2016)
pp. 251–253

Chapter 2
From "brute" to "thug:" The demonization and criminalization of unarmed Black male victims in America
CalvinJohn Smiley and David Fakunle
Journal of Human Behavior in the Social Environment, volume 26, issues 3–4 (2016)
pp. 350–366

Chapter 3
Police shootings of unarmed African American males: A systematic review
George T. Patterson and Philip G. Swan
Journal of Human Behavior in the Social Environment, volume 26, issues 3–4 (2016)
pp. 267–278

Chapter 4
Police killings of unarmed Black people: Centering race and racism in human behavior and the social environment content
Willie F. Tolliver, Bernadette R. Hadden, Fabienne Snowden, and Robyn Brown-Manning
Journal of Human Behavior in the Social Environment, volume 26, issues 3–4 (2016)
pp. 279–286

Chapter 5
Parenting while powerless: Consequences of "the talk"
Tracy R. Whitaker and Cudore L. Snell
Journal of Human Behavior in the Social Environment, volume 26, issues 3–4 (2016)
pp. 303–309

Chapter 6

The nation's unprotected children and the ghost of Mike Brown, or the impact of national police killings on the health and social development of African American boys
Raja Staggers-Hakim
Journal of Human Behavior in the Social Environment, volume 26, issues 3–4 (2016)
pp. 390–399

Chapter 7

The death of Black males: The unmasking of cultural competence and oppressive practices in a micro-aggressive environment
Folusho Otuyelu, Warren Graham, and Shakira A. Kennedy
Journal of Human Behavior in the Social Environment, volume 26, issues 3–4 (2016)
pp. 430–436

Chapter 8

EVIP—Edutainment violence intervention/prevention model
Valerie Dorsey Allen and Phyllis Solomon
Journal of Human Behavior in the Social Environment, volume 26, issues 3–4 (2016)
pp. 325–335

Chapter 9

"Hands up, don't shoot" or shut up and play ball? Fan-generated media views of the Ferguson Five
Emmett L. Gill, Jr.
Journal of Human Behavior in the Social Environment, volume 26, issues 3–4 (2016)
pp. 400–412

Chapter 10

"Police took my homie I dedicate my life 2 his revenge": Twitter tensions between gang-involved youth and police in Chicago
Desmond Upton Patton, Patrick Leonard, Loren Cahill, Jamie Macbeth, Shantel Crosby, and Douglas-Wade Brunton
Journal of Human Behavior in the Social Environment, volume 26, issues 3–4 (2016)
pp. 310–324

Chapter 11

Law enforcement perceptions of their relationship with community: Law enforcement surveys and community focus groups
Juan J. Barthelemy, Cassandra Chaney, Elaine M. Maccio, and Wesley T. Church, II
Journal of Human Behavior in the Social Environment, volume 26, issues 3–4 (2016)
pp. 413–429

Chapter 12

An authentic discourse: Recentering race and racism as factors that contribute to police violence against unarmed Black or African American men
Bernadette R. Hadden, Willie F. Tolliver, Fabienne Snowden, and Robyn Brown-Manning
Journal of Human Behavior in the Social Environment, volume 26, issues 3–4 (2016)
pp. 336–349

Chapter 13

Vile vigilance: An integrated theoretical framework for understanding the state of Black surveillance
Whitney Sewell, Christina E. Horsford, Kanisha Coleman, and Charity S. Watkins
Journal of Human Behavior in the Social Environment, volume 26, issues 3–4 (2016)
pp. 287–302

Chapter 14

Police-involved homicide of unarmed Black males: Observations by Black scholars in the midst of the April 2015 Baltimore uprising
Natasha C. Pratt-Harris, Michael M. Sinclair, Cynthia Barbara Bragg, Nicole R. Williams, Kalfani Nyerere Ture, Belinda Davis Smith, Isiah Marshall Jr., and Lawrence Brown
Journal of Human Behavior in the Social Environment, volume 26, issues 3–4 (2016)
pp. 377–389

Chapter 15

"I can't breathe": A case study—Helping Black men cope with race-related trauma stemming from police killing and brutality
Samuel R. Aymer
Journal of Human Behavior in the Social Environment, volume 26, issues 3–4 (2016)
pp. 367–376

Chapter 16

Hands up—Don't shoot: Police shooting of young Black males: Implications for social work and human services
Sharon E. Moore, Michael A. Robinson, A. Christson Adedoyin, Michael Brooks, Dana K. Harmon, and Daniel Boamah
Journal of Human Behavior in the Social Environment, volume 26, issues 3–4 (2016)
pp. 254–266

Notes on Contributors

A. Christson Adedoyin is an associate professor of Social Work in the Department of Social Work at Samford University, Birmingham, Alabama, USA.

Samuel R. Aymer, Silberman School of Social Work, Hunter College, City University of New York, New York, USA.

Cynthia Barbara Bragg, Department of Sociology, Anthropology, and Criminal Justice, Morgan State University, Baltimore, Maryland, USA.

Juan J. Barthelemy, School of Social Work, Louisiana State University, Baton Rouge, Louisiana, USA.

Daniel Boamah, Raymond A. Kent School of Social Work, University of Louisville, Louisville, Kentucky, USA.

Michael Brooks, Human Development and Services, North Carolina Agricultural and Technical State University, Greensboro, North Carolina, USA.

Lawrence Brown, Morgan State University, Baltimore, Maryland, USA.

Robyn Brown-Manning, Silberman School of Social Work at Hunter College, City University of New York, New York, USA.

Douglas-Wade Brunton, Department of Communication Studies, University of Michigan, Ann Arbor, Michigan, USA.

Loren Cahill, School of Social Work, University of Michigan, Ann Arbor, Michigan, USA.

Cassandra Chaney, Department of Child and Family Studies, Louisiana State University, Baton Rouge, Louisiana, USA.

Wesley T. Church, II, School of Social Work, Louisiana State University, Baton Rouge, Louisiana, USA.

Kanisha Coleman, School of Social Work, University of North Carolina at Chapel Hill, Chapel Hill, North Carolina, USA.

Belinda Davis Smith, Morgan State University, Baltimore, Maryland, USA.

Valerie Dorsey Allen, African-American Resource Center, University of Pennsylvania, Philadelphia, Pennsylvania, USA.

David Fakunle, Drug Dependence Epidemiology Training Program, Department of Mental Health, Johns Hopkins Bloomberg School of Public Health, Baltimore, Maryland, USA.

Emmett L. Gill, Jr., Department of Social Work, College of Public Policy, University of Texas at San Antonio, San Antonio, Texas, USA.

Warren Graham, Graduate School of Social Work, Touro College, New York, New York, USA.

Bernadette R. Hadden, Silberman School of Social Work at Hunter College, City University of New York, New York, USA.

Dana K. Harmon, Department of Human Development and Family Studies, Child Development Research Center, The University of Alabama, Tuscaloosa, Alabama, USA.

Christina E. Horsford, School of Social Work, University of North Carolina at Chapel Hill, Chapel Hill, North Carolina, USA.

Shakira A. Kennedy, Graduate School of Social Work, Touro College, New York, New York, USA.

Patrick Leonard, School of Social Work, Columbia University, New York, New York, USA; and SAFE Lab, Columbia University, New York, USA.

Jamie Macbeth, School of Engineering, Fairfield University, Fairfield, Connecticut, USA.

Shantel Crosby, School of Social Work, Wayne State University, Detroit, Michigan, USA.

Elaine M. Maccio, School of Social Work and Women's and Gender Studies, Louisiana State University, Baton Rouge, Louisiana, USA.

Isiah Marshall Jr., Department of Sociology and Social Work, Daemen College, Amherst, New York, USA.

Sharon E. Moore is Professor of Social Work in the Raymond A. Kent School of Social Work at the University of Louisville, Louisville, Kentucky, USA.

Kalfani Nyerere Ture, Morgan State University, Baltimore, Maryland, USA.

Folusho Otuyelu, Graduate School of Social Work, Touro College, New York, New York, USA.

George T. Patterson, Silberman School of Social Work at Hunter College, City University of New York, New York, USA.

Natasha C. Pratt-Harris, Department of Sociology, Anthropology, and Criminal Justice, Morgan State University, Baltimore, Maryland, USA.

Michael A. Robinson is an assistant professor in the School of Social Work at the University of Georgia, Athens, Georgia, USA.

Whitney Sewell, George Warren Brown School of Social Work, Washington University in St. Louis, St. Louis, Missouri, USA.

Michael M. Sinclair, Department of Sociology, Anthropology, and Criminal Justice, Morgan State University, Baltimore, Maryland, USA.

CalvinJohn Smiley, Department of Justice Studies, Montclair State University, Montclair, New Jersey, USA.

Cudore L. Snell, School of Social Work, Howard University, Washington, DC, USA.

Fabienne Snowden, University of New York Graduate Center, New York, New York, USA.

Phyllis Solomon, School of Social Policy and Practice, University of Pennsylvania, Philadelphia, Pennsylvania, USA.

Raja Staggers-Hakim, Department of Health Science, College of Health Professions, Sacred Heart University, Fairfield, Connecticut, USA.

Philip G. Swan, Hunter College Libraries, City University of New York, New York, USA.

Sylvia Telafaro, School of Social Work, San Diego State University, San Diego, California, USA.

Willie F. Tolliver, Silberman School of Social Work at Hunter College, City University of New York, New York, USA.

Desmond Upton Patton, School of Social Work, Columbia University, New York, USA.

Charity S. Watkins, School of Social Work, University of North Carolina at Chapel Hill, Chapel Hill, North Carolina, USA.

Tracy R. Whitaker, School of Social Work, Howard University, Washington, DC, USA.

Nicole R. Williams, Department of Human Services, Anne Arundel Community College, Hanover, Maryland, USA.

Introduction

A discourse on police shooting of unarmed Black males: Advancing novel prevention and intervention strategies

Sharon E. Moore is Professor of Social Work in the Raymond A. Kent School of Social Work at the University of Louisville, Louisville, Kentucky, USA.
A. Christson Adedoyin is an associate professor of Social Work in the Department of Social Work at Samford University, Birmingham, Alabama, USA.
Michael A. Robinson is an assistant professor in the School of Social Work at the University of Georgia, Athens, Georgia, USA.

As the authors worked on this text, many Americans grieved for the lives that have been lost as a result of the unjust killing of unarmed African American males by police. This belief that the killings were unjust was evident by national movements (i.e. Black Lives Matter) that grew out of this inhumane treatment of African American men. These killings are, in part, a result of the outgrowth of a history of racism and marginalization of African American people by those in power. Moreover, many Americans are uncertain of their futures as a new political ideology assumed control of the government at the highest levels. This uncertainty was fueled by a presidential campaign that stirred up a tremendous amount of racial tension and social–economic divisions across the country. Just how much that rhetoric fuels new acts of racism against African American males remains to be seen. As you read the textbook, the authors want you to imagine how must it feel to be a Black male knowing that the at-large society blames you for many of society's ills, to be the recipient of mistrust, scapegoating, and to have laws established and implemented that are directly aimed at your demise. A subsequent question that warrants debate is: How long can police shootings of unarmed African American males with impunity continue? Since the publication of the special issue of the *Journal of Human Behavior in the Social Environment* (*JHBSE*) in 2016, several more unarmed African Americans have died during encounters with police.

When the call for the special edition was issued, the editors were inundated with manuscripts from across the country specifically focusing on unjust killing of African American men by police. This increased interest in this social problem prompted the journal editor to approve a double volume. The special issue continues to be one of the most read issues on police killings of unarmed African American men to date. The continued interest in the topic inspired the current editor of *JHBSE* to contact us to consider an edited textbook. The authors selected manuscripts that provide factual accounts of the killings from a variety of perspectives from scholars across the country. One of the goals of this text is to provide a forum for critical inquiry and discussion relative to theory that helps to explain what is occurring and why, give opportunity for analysis of the implications of these shootings at the micro, mezzo, and macro societal levels and, perhaps most importantly, provide solution-based recommendations for rectifying this problem. This edited textbook contains 16 manuscripts and 1 poem.

Chapter 1 opens with a poem written by Sylvia Telafaro, who wrote "A Death to Justice" in response to young Black males in the United States who grow up with different narratives about who they should be in a society that does not always love nor appreciate them. She believes that Black males are living in a world policed by people who fear them simply because of their skin tone. This fear is often perpetrated by negative messages in the corporate media, cementing the fear in the general population which sometimes leads to insecurity and isolation among this group that makes them feel invisible. According to the author of the poem, "A Death to Justice" is a cry for justice for all Black males being marginalized in the United States and abroad. This poem is a legacy for Michel J. Brown because his death has given a voice to many who had previously suffered in silence. It is a battle cry of "No Justice, No Peace!" reaffirming that unless we continue to fight for justice, it will become nonexistent. In Chapter 2, CalvinJohn Smiley and David Fakunle investigated the historical criminalization of Black males and its connection to contemporary unarmed victims of law enforcement in their chapter, "From 'brute' to 'thug:' The demonization and criminalization of unarmed Black male victims in America." Action research methodology in the data collection process was utilized to interpret how Black male victims are portrayed by traditional mass media in ways that marginalize and devictimize these individuals. The authors also elucidated a contemporary understanding of race relations, racism, and the plight of the Black male in a twenty-first-century "post-racial" America.

Chapter 3 is a research synthesis of police shootings of unarmed African American males by George T. Patterson and Philip G. Swan titled "Police shootings of unarmed African American males: A systematic review." Social work practice implications were gleaned from secondary data obtained from the coroner, medical examiner, toxicologists, and police reports, and experimental studies. Individual, community, and police departmental policy factors were most often reported to explain such shootings when excluding sources that examined armed African American males. In chapter 4, "Police killings of unarmed Black people: Centering race and racism in human behavior and the social environment content," Willie F. Tolliver, Bernadette R. Hadden, Fabienne Snowden, and Robyn Brown-Manning place police killings of unarmed Black people in a context that takes into consideration historical and contemporary evidence of the denigration of Black people in the United States. They specifically challenge the utility of diversity as a frame to prepare social work practitioners for practice with Blacks whose ancestral lineage traces back to people of African descent, and whose lived experiences in the United States occurred during slavery and/or legally sanctioned apartheid (Jim Crow). In chapter 5, Tracy R. Whitaker and Cudore L. Snell explore the new emphasis on African American parents having "the talk" with their children, particularly their sons in "Parenting while powerless: Consequences of 'the talk.'" "The talk" represents the "surviving interactions with police or other members of authority" discussion and is largely considered an essential rite of passage in African American homes. And, while the pretext for "the talk" is providing children with the rule book for survival from an authoritative source, the subtext for this conversation is the inherent powerlessness of African American parents and their *inability to protect* their children. Despite its necessity, "the talk" has an ugly underside that also manifests in disruptions to child development, families, and the larger community. These disruptions are particularly critical in an allegedly post-racial environment. Chapter 6 is a discussion of the preliminary findings of a pilot study conducted by Raja Staggers-Hakim titled "The nation's unprotected children and the ghost of Mike Brown. His study examines the impact of national police killings on the social development and health of African American boys" and indicates that a relationship exists between awareness of police killings on one hand, and the independent variables of mental health, social development, and parenting practices of African Americans.

Chapter 7, "The death of Black males: The unmasking of cultural competence and oppressive practices in a micro-aggressive environment," by Folusho Otuyelu, Warren Graham, and Shakira A. Kennedy, highlights the prevalence of racial micro aggressions within the social work and law enforcement environments. This chapter reinforces the need for awareness of micro aggressions among social work practitioners, which negatively impacts their clients of color, and also suggests ways in which social work practitioners and members of law enforcement agencies can address them. Valerie Dorsey Allen and Phyllis Solomon's Chapter 8 focuses on "EVIP—Edutainment violence intervention/prevention model." Solomon introduces an intervention and preventative tool that incorporates performance drama accompanied with intergroup dialogue, which allows adolescents to discuss police brutality and related trauma in an entertaining and engaging format. This tool is geared toward practical use in multiple settings with adolescents affected by trauma caused by police violence, and also promotes self-efficacy, positive social relationships, and pro-social behaviors and decisions. Chapter 9, written by Emmett L. Gill, Jr., "'Hands up, don't shoot' or shut up and play ball? Fan-generated media views of the Ferguson Five," discusses the prevalence of police violence and professional athletes' involvement in activism surrounding the "Black Lives Matter" movement. This chapter suggests that athletes have a huge impact on the specific movements they are part of and includes implications for future activism among professional athletes. In Chapter 10, "'Police took my homie I dedicate my life 2 his revenge': Twitter tensions between gang-involved youth and police in Chicago," Desmond Upton Patton, Patrick Leonard, Loren Cahill, Jamie Macbeth, Shantel Crosby, and Douglas-Wade Brunton leverage the policing literature to examine how the perpetual detestation between urban youth and police is expressed in physical and digital contexts (e.g. Twitter). They found that urban youth, particularly gang-involved youth, publicly articulate their disdain for law enforcement agents on Twitter. The young people in their study expressed chronic grief and anger after the fatal police shooting of a Southside Chicago gang member. Further, they expressed a strong desire to violently retaliate against the Chicago Police Department after their friend was killed. In fact, users on Twitter frequently posted the hashtag #CPDK—an acronym for Chicago Police Department Killer—shortly after this incident. The authors discuss the implications of using Twitter data to inform policing practices, as well as early intervention and prevention strategies for youth living in inner cities.

Juan J. Barthelemy, Cassandra Chaney, Elaine M. Maccio and Welsey T. Church's Chapter 11, "Law enforcement perceptions of their relationship with community: Law enforcement surveys and community focus groups," discusses a novel group violence reduction community–law enforcement partnership in the Baton Rouge, Louisiana, that was based on the Operation Ceasefire Gun Project that dramatically reduced violence in Boston, Massachusetts. This study also determined whether a relationship exists between law enforcement's involvement with the Baton Rouge Area Violence Elimination (BRAVE) project and community members' willingness to call police during times of need. The authors highlighted characteristics that make individuals in low-income communities more or less likely to work with police. The 2012 General Social Survey (GSS) dataset was analyzed in Chapter 12 by Bernadette R. Hadden, Willie Tolliver, Fabienne Snowden, and Robyn Brown Manning in their work titled "An authentic discourse: Re-centering racism as factors that contribute to police violence against unarmed Black or African American men" to examine beliefs about socioeconomic inequities, race differences in incarceration history, attitudes toward police aggression, and confidence in the criminal justice system. Chapter 13, "Vile vigilance: An integrated theoretical framework for understanding the state of Black surveillance" by Whitney Sewell, Christina E. Horsford, Kanisha Coleman, and Charity S. Watkins, reviews the Mundane Extreme Environmental Stress (MEES) model, racial socialization theory, and the Family Stress Model in the development of a theoretical framework for understanding the patterns of interactions between Blacks and law enforcement, the immediate and long-term effects of unjustified shootings on African American families and communities, and the response of sociopolitical systems. This theoretical framework is used to inform the work of human service providers and practitioners by identifying targets for interventions to improve relations and trust between Black communities and law enforcement institutions. A fresh perspective to this text is presented in Chapter 14 through the combination of the personal experiences and professional interpretations of Black scholars on police-involved homicides of unarmed Black males as articulated by Natasha C. Pratt-Harris, Michael M. Sinclair,, Cynthia Barbara Bragg, Nicole R. Williams, Kalfani Nyerere Ture, Belinda Davis Smith, Isiah Marshall Jr., and Lawrence Brown in their chapter titled "Police involved homicide of unarmed Black males: Observations by Black scholars in the midst of the April 2015 Baltimore uprising." Further, the authors explored Black homicide victims by law enforcement officers, specifically, as a public health crisis and examined a range of views—White supremacy, the ecological perspective, fears of parents and educators, perceptions of Black males, and the role of the Black church. Chapter 15, "'I Can't Breathe': Helping Black men cope with race-related trauma stemming from police killing and brutality" by Samuel R. Aymer, focuses on utilizing critical race theory (CRT) to analyze current events of police brutality and also highlights the lack of attention given to the race-based traumatic stress that is caused by "living while black" and police brutality. This chapter also suggests forms of psychotherapeutic treatment that may be useful in practice with clients dealing with race-based traumatic stress. Finally, in Chapter 16, "Hands up—Don't shoot: Police shooting of young Black males: Implications for social work and human services," Sharon E. Moore, Michael A. Robinson, A. Christson Adedoyin, Michael Brooks, Dana K. Harmon, and Daniel Boamah address areas that need to be attended to that relate to the historical context in which police relations with Black males exist that impact current police relations with this population, why the lives of young Black males are seemingly given less value by US society than their White counterparts, the role that spirituality and religiosity play in the lives of young Black males that may help to make connections between them and the police and the benefit of the Black church in fostering amicable police relations with young Black males.

Social work is a profession that values all people regardless of their race, ethnicity, gender, age, or ability; everyone has an inherent worth and a right to be treated with respect and dignity. When Black men die prematurely due to a socially unjust act, not only are the values of the social work profession cut short but so are the following potential impacts: (1) families that may have been formed by the deceased never are, (2) children who may have grown to be adults and who may have left indelible marks on society are never born, (3) Black boys and young men lose the benefit of mentors, and (4) society is at a loss as to the unique contribution that these men could have made to the world. It is hoped that this will foster a national and international discussion on how the lives of this group can be protected.

POETRY

A death to justice

(The shooting of Michael Brown—Summer 2014)

Sylvia Telafaro

School of Social Work, San Diego State University, San Diego, California, USA

Years ago,
I had "the talk" with my son,
before he was old enough to learn
that justice in our America
is not color blind.
He had to know;
how to act wherever he may go
how to walk, and never run,
how to speak and answer in
polite monotone,
how a violation of this
could become a deadly risk,
especially if he is
stopped and frisked.

I sternly told my son,
never bond with
a "gang style" crowd,
be careful how you express
your Black pride,
express your culture by staying alive.

My heart cries for other sons,
like Michael Brown,
who was gunned down in a
Missouri suburban town.
It wasn't that Michael
didn't hear the "talk,"
I'm sure he knew
what to say and how to talk
yet he ended up dead on a cold sidewalk.

My heart cries for a small
town, called Ferguson
filled with Black and Brown sons
that police now have a verdict
that allows them to
indiscriminately use their guns.

POLICE AND THE UNARMED BLACK MALE CRISIS

My heart cries for the
Michael Browns in every town
in an America that places
less value on lives
of young Black and Brown males,
either shooting them down
or filling up her jails.

My heart screams
at the injustice
that erupts from an imaginary sea
of anger and fear
as status quo waves scream out in retaliation,
"Black lives will never truly matter here
in this nation."

In retaliation to this,
my heart yearns for peace;
I wait to see
if the disruption and violence will cease,
drying my tears and channeling my frustration,
counting the ways I can help make positive change,
joining with like minds to protect our sons
from mass incarceration,
police brutality, institutionalized and systemic racism
and mental capitulation.

I wait for a better day
a day when all sons
are safe from being choked,
tased or walking and talking
while Black.

I wait for a day when police will not
react to a perceived threat
generated by skin tone,
or a cell phone,
mistaken for a gun.

I wait for a day when our sons are not
shot down simply because they decided to run.
I wait to participate in a
revolution that is brewing underground,
that helps invoke changes that
overhaul policies and practices that
perpetuate this national
crisis of discriminatory policing
against Blacks and Browns.

I wait for justice
"I can't breathe"

I wrote "A Death to Justice" because I feel that young Black males in our communities are growing up with criticism, discrimination, disrespect, and different narratives about not who they are but who they should be in a world that doesn't always love or appreciate them. Our men are living in a society policed by people who fear them simply because of their skin tone. This fear is often perpetrated by negative messages in the corporate media, cementing the fear in the general population that they are violent and dangerous. In my opinion, this leads to insecurity, fear, and isolation among our young Black males that not only makes them feel invisible, it often encourages them to act out in negative and sometimes a hostile manner.

"A Death to Justice" was inspired by one such Black male, Michael J. Brown, an unarmed teenager, who had been marginalized, shot, and killed on August 9, 2014. It was a reaction to the killing of Michael Brown by white police officer Darren Wilson in Ferguson, MO, and the aggressive and demeaning response of Ferguson's political and police leaders.

"A Death to Justice" is about more than Michael J. Brown; it is a cry for justice for all Black males being marginalized in the United States and abroad. It is a call to action to mothers, sisters, grandmothers, aunts, and the community at large that the lives of our men are being jeopardized by a systematic system still practicing Jim Crow ideology. "A Death to Justice" is a legacy for Michael J. Brown because his death has given a voice to many that had previously suffered in silence. It is a battle cry of "No Justice, No Peace!" reaffirming that unless we continue to fight for justice, it will become nonexistent.

From "brute" to "thug:" The demonization and criminalization of unarmed Black male victims in America

CalvinJohn Smiley[a] and David Fakunle[b]

[a]Department of Justice Studies, Montclair State University, Montclair, New Jersey, USA; [b]Drug Dependence Epidemiology Training Program, Department of Mental Health, Johns Hopkins Bloomberg School of Public Health, Baltimore, Maryland, USA

ABSTRACT

The synonymy of Blackness with criminality is not a new phenomenon in America. Documented historical accounts have shown how myths, stereotypes, and racist ideologies led to discriminatory policies and court rulings that fueled racial violence in the post-Reconstruction era and have culminated in the exponential increase of Black male incarceration today. Misconceptions and prejudices manufactured and disseminated through various channels such as the media included references to a "*brute*" image of Black males. In the 21st century, this negative imagery of Black males has frequently utilized the negative connotation of the terminology "*thug*." In recent years, law enforcement agencies have unreasonably used deadly force on Black males allegedly considered to be "suspects" or "persons of interest." The exploitation of these often-targeted victims' criminal records, physical appearances, or misperceived attributes has been used to justify their unlawful deaths. Despite the connection between disproportionate criminality and Black masculinity, little research has been done on how unarmed Black male victims, particularly but not exclusively at the hands of law enforcement, have been posthumously criminalized. This article investigates the historical criminalization of Black males and its connection to contemporary unarmed victims of law enforcement. Action research methodology in the data collection process is utilized to interpret how Black male victims are portrayed by traditional mass media, particularly through the use of language, in ways that marginalize and devictimize these individuals. This study also aims to elucidate a contemporary understanding of race relations, racism, and the plight of the Black male in a 21-century "postracial" America.

Introduction

On April 28, 2015, President Barack Obama referred to a collection of citizens from Baltimore, Maryland, as "criminals and thugs" in response to a question about the recent rebellion that broke following the death of Freddie Gray[1] while in police custody. The use of the term "thug" by President Obama became the zenith of the word's use to characterize primarily individuals and groups of Black males. In this specific case of the rebellion that began on April 25, 2015, public figures such as President Obama and Baltimore Mayor Stephanie Rawlings-Blake both used the term "thug" along with many news reporters and others on social media outlets such as Facebook, Twitter, and Instagram. During an interview with CNN, Baltimore councilman Carl Stokes, a Black male, rejected the notion of calling citizens "thugs" by the news anchor who pushed him to agree with the term to describe the occurrences of looting. Stokes responded by stating, "C'mon, so calling them thugs, just call them niggers, just call them niggers" (WorldStarHipHop, 2015). Councilman Stokes was calling attention to the use of coded language that is in some ways explicitly and other ways implicitly used as a substitute for personally mediated racism, specifically the term "nigger."

Over the last several years, the term "thug" has become a way to describe Black males who reject or do not rise to the standard of White America. For example, NFL football player Richard Sherman was called a "thug" for his postgame interview following the National Football Conference Championship game (Wagner, 2014). Although Sherman did not use vulgar language or express any feelings of violence or criminal action, his physical presence and loud voice was used to evoke the idea of "thuggery." Additionally, political adversaries of President Obama such as Michelle Bachmann, Karl Rove, and Rush Limbaugh have referred to him as a "political thug." This term has become the platform to dismiss Black life as less valuable and perpetuates a negative and criminal connotation in forms of micro-insults and micro-invalidations. Moreover, the recent killings of unarmed Black men have sparked discussion and discourse surrounding the term "thug" and how it is used in the context of reshaping perceptions of Black life broadly and Black males specifically.

This study investigates how language is used to describe Black men who have been killed by law enforcement in the past year (July 2014 to April 2015). Specifically, a demonizing process takes place that happens to unarmed Black men posthumously. Unlike earlier Black icons and figures, such as Dr. Martin Luther King, Jr., and Malcolm X, who were vilified while alive and then sanitized in death to be repackaged as an acceptable part of the U.S. historical narrative, these men are portrayed as thugs and criminals to seemingly justify their deaths while simultaneously shifting blame away from law enforcement. To illustrate, we examine six different unarmed Black men[2] who were killed by police in the United States to understand how media coverage addresses their deaths. By utilizing local, national, and international media coverage of these cases, we are able to find both overlapping and unique themes to each case that support the notion of posthumous demonization and criminalization of unarmed Black men.

To explore this notion of posthumous demonization and criminalization, we examine this inquiry in several ways. First, we look at the terms historically used to describe Black people in the United States. Second, it is important to connect the historical legacies of racial demonization to contemporary criminalization of Blackness, particularly in a Post-Obama America. Therefore, we utilize four major groups to categorize the language and imagery of the articles being investigated for this study: (1) behavior, (2) appearance, (3) location, and (4) lifestyle. These are used to specifically address both overt instances of racism as well as micro-insults and micro-invalidations. Moreover, we look at the cases of each unarmed Black male and how they are treated by media sources focusing particularly on the primacy effect, or the first impression media outlets create when describing these males posthumously that either justifies or negates their death by law enforcement. Finally, the article discusses the growing social movements of #BlackLivesMatter and the impact these collectives have on both national and international awareness of White privilege, White supremacy, and coded race-based language.

Literature review

Race is the most significant sociodemographic distinction in the United States. The social construction of contemporary racial ideology finds its birth in the period known as the Enlightenment (Eze, 1997). Enlightenment thinkers such as David Hume, Immanuel Kant, and Thomas Jefferson contributed to the literature and theory behind biological racial differences. Jefferson, a founding father of the United States, third U.S. president, and slave owner, wrote about the differences between the races in his essays *Notes on the State of Virginia*. In his writings he describes physical differences such as skin color and hair texture as the basis for scientific distinction, stating, "the difference is fixed in nature, and is as real as if its seat and causer were better known to us" (Jefferson, 1997, p. 97). Jefferson uses observable data—presumably his own slaves—to come to his conclusions, stating:

> Besides those of colour, figure, and hair, there are other physical distinctions proving a difference of race. They have less hair on the face and body. They secrete less by the kidneys, and more by the glands of the skin. ... They seem to require less sleep. ... They are at least as brave, and more adventuresome. ... They are more ardent after their female; but love seems with them to be more an eager desire, than a tender delicate mixture of sentiment and sensation. (Jefferson, 1997, p. 98)

These sentiments and ideologies were carried on to develop notions of race, and more specifically the racial dynamics of superiority and inferiority.

As slavery prevailed this dichotomy of racial superiority and inferiority metastasized because of the need for economic labor (Fields, 1990). The need for a surplus of cheap labor, which was acquired in Africa, was justified through racial distinction primarily set by law (Fields, 1990; Memmi, 2000). Separations were made clear through the passage of laws that determined the race of child via the matrilineal line and antimiscegenation laws, harsher punishments for Black runaway slaves, and the use of poor Whites as laborers to monitor and guard against slave rebellions. These legal distinctions coupled with economic need justified slavery and the growth of racial ideologies, to which Barbara Jeanne Fields (1990) states, "Racial ideology supplied the means of explaining slavery to people whose terrain was a republic founded on radical doctrines of liberty and natural rights; and, more important, a republic in which those doctrines seemed to represent accurately the world in which all but a minority lived" (p. 114). In other words, through the repetitive and daily routine, these social constructions take on meaning over time and become seen and internalized as truth.

This "truth" of racial ideology spawned racism, which is practiced at both the institutional and individual level in American society. However, we must be cognizant of other sociodemographic variables such as social class and gender and the authority they play in influencing the dynamics of the superiority and inferiority dyad. Therefore, to understand racism in the 21st century we must look at the intersectionality (Crenshaw, 1989) of these variables in how it relates to the use of excessive and deadly force by law enforcement on unarmed Black males and its relationship to historic views of race, class, and gender. Specifically, there must be an understanding of the shift from the "brute" that demonized Black males in the 19th and early 20th century to the "thug" that brought about criminalization in the late 20th and early 21st century.

From "brute" to "thug"

During the institution of slavery, the image of Black people, specifically Black males, was of a docile character. The images of buffoonery, blissful ignorance, and juvenile angst were seen as the primary traits of enslaved Blacks. This is characterized in several portrayals of Black males of this time. The use of Blackface—a type of performance that generally used White actors wearing black make-up to portray Black people in stereotypes—became popular in the 19th century. White actors popularized minstrel shows, depicting stereotypes of Black life as foolish, messy, and overall comedic at the expense of Black culture (Lhamon, 2000; Strausbaugh, 2006). In addition, other popular literature and media characterized antebellum enslaved Blacks as content with their place in society. In literature, the character of Uncle Tom in *Uncle Tom's Cabin* is portrayed as an older Black slave who is faithful and dutiful to his White master. The film *Gone with the Wind* depicts content slaves, specifically the role of Mammy who even fends off freedmen. Finally, the Disney film *Song of the South* depicts Uncle Remus as an elderly Black freedman who was satisfied with his place in society, singing the famous happy song "Zip-a-Dee-Doo-Dah."

These depictions of Blackness as docile and manageable reflected the ability to control the Black body and mind, creating the idea that slavery was the best position for Black people. This status of inferiority is echoed in W. E. B. DuBois's writing of how Whites viewed freedom as a way to "spoil" and "ruin" Black people (DuBois, 1903). Additionally, according to David Pilgram:

> These portrayals were pragmatic and instrumental. Proponents of slavery created and promoted images of blacks that justified slavery and soothed white consciences. If slaves were childlike, for example, then a paternalistic institution where masters acted as quasi-parents to their slaves was [*sic*] humane, even morally

> right. More importantly, slaves were rarely depicted as brutes because that portrayal might have become a self-fulfilling prophecy. (2012)

However, this image of Blackness ended after the American Civil War. During the period of Reconstruction (1865–1877), newly freed Blacks began to obtain social, economic, and political rights with the passage of the 13th, 14th, and 15th Amendments to the Constitution. This growth was seen in the building of Black communities such as Greenwood in Tulsa, Oklahoma, which was referred to as "Black Wall Street" (Pickens, 2013), the building of schools now known as Historically Black College and Universities, and the election of the first two Black U.S. senators in Hiram Revels and Blanche Bruce.

This growth in power challenged White supremacy and created White fear of Black mobility. Particularly, wealthy Whites were fearful of political power newly freed Black people could acquire via voting, whereas poor Whites saw Blacks as competition in the labor force. Thus the rise of the Jim Crow era began, which was solidified by the Supreme Court ruling of *Plessy v. Ferguson* that stated "separate but equal is constitutional." This fear was met with a shift from Black people being viewed as compliant and submissive servants to savages and brute monsters.

Media portrayals of this mythical Black brute began to grow using the same initial science Jefferson and other Enlightenment-era theorists proclaimed, which was based on inaccurate anthropological and biological factors. This time, the argument was that Blacks were naturally more prone to violence and other aggressive behaviors. Charles H. Smith wrote in 1893, "A bad Negro is the most horrible creature upon the earth, the most brutal and merciless" (p. 181). This myth of cruelty and vicious disposition was directed toward White women. As the myth grew and stories spread about the savage Black brute, so did the occurrences of lynching. Lynching—the extrajudicial punishment—was ritualistic and struck fear into Black residents throughout the United States (Litwack, 2004). The most prevalent accusation was the rape or sexual assault of a White woman by a Black male. This allegation would have reverberating effects throughout entire communities. In Tulsa, Oklahoma, a young White woman accused a Black male of sexual assault and roughly 300 Black people were killed, and more than 9,000 people were left homeless after White mobs destroyed the Greenwood community (Pickens, 2013). Regardless of producing evidence or facts, White mobs would seize Black defendants or attack Black neighborhoods to seek revenge for this crime.

The case of Sam Hose is an example of how different and various versions of the truth were reported. Hose killed his employer in self-defense after being threatened with a pistol. However, newspapers wrote that "a monster in human form" emerged, which detailed Hose as cold-blooded, killing his employer, and savagely raping his employer's wife. The report drove White fear to lynch Hose (Litwack, 2004). In reality, these charges were mere excuses to exercise exorbitant amounts of violence on Black people. The lynching of a Black body became a form of ritualistic violence where limbs and other body parts were taken as souvenirs. Litwack wrote:

> After stripping Hose of his clothes and chaining him to a tree, the self-appointed executioners stacked kerosene-soaked wood high around him ... they cut off his ears, fingers, and genitals, and skinned his face ... the contortions of Sam Hose's body as the flames rose, distorting his features, causing his eyes to bulge out their sockets. ... Before Hose's body had even cooled, his heart and liver were removed and cut into several pieces and his bones were crushed into small particles. The crowd fought over these souvenirs. (2004, p. 123)

This overkill of the Black body became part of the racist ideology that was used to justify these acts of violence. This mythical act of Black savagery was situated in this idea of Black brutality and criminality that had no other recourse but death. A prominent Georgia woman wrote about the Sam Hose lynching, "The premeditated outrage on Mrs. Cranford was infinitely more intolerable than the murder of her husband" (Litwack, 2004). Hence, uncontrollable desires of Black males were illegal and criminal and needed to be stopped through the use of physical force. Therefore, this justified vigilante justice in the name of keeping White womanhood pure.

The brute image of Black men became significant moving into the early 20th century, when fear was reinforced with depictions of Black men as harmful. The film *Birth of a Nation*, made in 1915, shows Black men as savages trying to attack White women. Their brutality is met with propaganda depicting the

Ku Klux Klan as heroic and honorable. The result was Blackness becoming closely associated with criminalization. The criminalization of Blackness (Alexander, 2010; Davis, 1998; Muhammad, 2010) allowed for White supremacy to use Black bodies as their scapegoat for all problems, real or fictional. The driving forces behind Black criminality as savage and unmanageable were structurally reinforced by passage of stricter sentencing guidelines in prison and the expansion of the War on Drugs in the second half of the 20th century (Mauer, 2002). These programs and stricter prison guidelines exponentially grew the American prison system by 700% (Pew Charitable Trusts, 2007). During this time campaigns for "tough on crime" policy emerged as the soundboard for elected officials. For example, George H. W. Bush's presidential run used a smear campaign tactic, famously known as the "Willie Horton" ad, where a Black prisoner's face was used to talk about his heinous crimes and Bush's opponent's soft-on-crime policy. While the ad overtly discusses a single Black man, the subliminal and larger takeaway is Willie Horton's face became synonymous with all Blackness. In short, the mythical brute became the realistic thug via the process of criminalization.

The image of Black men as brutes in society has a long legacy that begins with the social construction of race and brings us to the current period of mass incarceration. In the United States, Black men are six times as likely to go to jail or prison as White men (Gao, 2014). This disproportionate and unequal number indicates the skewed representation of Black men in U.S. prisons. However, the argument is shifted to no longer being about race but about crime and community safety. This negation of understanding the historical link between "brute" and "thug" marginalizes the significant role race plays.

Last, a prime example of how the brute image still thrives in society is the April 2008 *Vogue* magazine cover of professional basketball player LeBron James holding supermodel Gisele Bündchen. The image of LeBron giving a menacing look while Gisele is in his arms bears a strikingly eerily similarity to a World War I poster that depicts a gorilla holding a White woman with the title "Destroy This Mad Brute" (Shea, 2008). These types of images that draw on past racial stereotypes and myths reinforce this criminalization and are now coded with terms such as "thug" today. Although historically in America overt racist language was socially acceptable, there has been a cultural shift of social intolerance to this blatant racist behavior. This does not mean that racism or discriminatory actions have been eradicated but rather driven beneath the surface and reemerged as coded language, gestures, signs, and symbols to indicate difference. Terms such as "thug," "ghetto," "hood," "sketchy," and "shady" are all examples of coded language that are used to refer to or speak of Blackness without overtly sounding racially prejudiced. Fraternities on college campuses throw "Pimps and Hos" parties where stereotypes of Black people as pimps or prostitutes, exemplifying characters from the film *Superfly* (1972), also lack the language of race but show in physical gesture and imagery the racism encoded in the details.

Over the last several years with the proliferation of social media, many more events are documented and shared via social networking sites (Smiley, 2015; Yar, 2012). Some of these events captured on video are cases involving unarmed Black males being killed by law enforcement agents. Although some videos show the disturbing death, such as Eric Garner, others show the aftermath like that of Michael Brown's body in the street. These deaths and others have sparked outrage across communities looking for justice and accountability of law enforcement's excessive force when dealing with Black people.

Furthermore, this article looks at how these Black males who are killed by law enforcement are turned into a "thug" (the modern-day "brute"), which seemingly tries to justify their death or personal contribution to their demise. Beyond this, a "blame game" effect occurs that shifts culpability from the perpetrator to the victim. In this case, the blame moves from law enforcement agents to the Black males who have been killed.

Methods

Content analysis

For this study, media coverage of the deaths of six unarmed Black males resulting from law enforcement interaction were investigated. Specifically, the portrayal of the incidents and the victims involved via newspaper articles were examined. Newspaper articles were chosen as the modality for investigations because of the understanding that all published articles go through a vetting process. As a result, the articles, including the perceptions created, are an organizational decision. The cases garnered significant national and international coverage for a notable period, leading to a considerable database from which to select samples. The incidents chosen for analysis are as follows, listed in chronological order from earliest to latest:

- Eric Garner—43 years old, died July 17, 2014, due to "compression of neck (choke hold), compression of chest and prone positioning during physical restraint by police" after altercation with New York Police Department officers Daniel Pantaleo and Justin Damico in Staten Island, New York.
- Michael Brown, Jr.—18 years old, died August 9, 2014, due to multiple gunshot wounds after altercation with Ferguson Police Department officer Darren Wilson in Ferguson, Missouri.
- Akai Gurley—28 years old, died November 20, 2014, due to single gunshot wound after interaction with New York Police Department officer Peter Liang in Brooklyn, New York.
- Tamir Rice—12 years old, died November 22, 2014, due to single gunshot wound after interaction with Cleveland Police Department officers Timothy Loehmann and Frank Garmback in Cleveland, Ohio.
- Tony Robinson—19 years old, died March 6, 2015, due to multiple gunshot wounds after altercation with Madison Police Department officer Matt Kenny in Madison, Wisconsin.
- Freddie Gray—25 years old, died April 19, 2015, due to various injuries, including three fractured vertebrae, damage to the voice box, and spine 80% severed at the neck, after altercation with Baltimore Police Department officers Caesar Goodson, Garret Miller, Edward Nero, William Porter, Brian Rice, and Alicia White in Baltimore, Maryland.

Analytical plan

For each incident 10 news articles, each published no more than 30 days after the victim's death, were selected. The time range allowed for an accurate capturing of the newspapers' initial portrayals of the victims, underlining the influence of the primacy effect (Holbert, Lambe, Dudo, & Carlton, 2007), as well as minimized the coverage of tangential events to the incident such as protests and legal proceedings. All newspaper articles were retrieved from LexisNexis using only the names of the victims. An effort was made to select an equal number of articles from national and international outlets if possible, and particular attention was paid to articles from news outlets in the cities where the deaths occurred. Analysis of the articles were based on the concept of autoethnography, which allowed the authors to utilize personal knowledge of and experience with racial profiling, harassment, negative interactions with law enforcement, and involvement in protests stemming from a number of police brutality cases, as a primary foundation of expertise and evidence.

Autoethnography

Although this article is an exercise in academic writing about current and social issues, for the authors—both of whom identify as Black males—the intersections of race, police brutality, and harassment are part of the lived experience that contextualize our social milieu. The relevance and urgency in creating a discourse around state violence, particularly law enforcement, upon the Black community, specifically unarmed Black males, is not at a distance but an immediate threat to the health and livelihood of the authors. Therefore, autoethnography becomes an important and useful methodology to include in this work because it relies on the narrators' credibility of using memory as legitimate data (Byfield, 2014; Ellis, Adams, & Bochner, 2011; Wall, 2006). In other words, as Blacks in America experiencing racism through forms of overt speech and actions, as well as through micro-insults and micro-invalidations (Sue et al., 2007), we believe our own experiences are relevant and valid toward assessing the results and conclusions of this article.

There has been a precedent set by scholars using autoethnography. Natalie Byfield (2014) utilized autoethnography methodology in her study of media coverage of the "Central Park Five" case, where five young men of color were tried and convicted for the rape and attempted murder of a White female jogger in New York City. Byfield, who is a Black woman and a reporter for the *New York Daily News* at the time of the event, covered the case from the arrest, trial, and conviction and then followed up when another person admitted to the crime. Byfield wrote, "Autoethnography seemed an ideal methodology for me to incorporate into this study because it is a technique that allows the researcher to also be a subject in a study" (Violence in war and peace: An anthology 2014, p. 20). Furthermore, while not articulated through the term "autoethnography," various Black historical figures have utilized this methodology to bring to light their experiences of racism and social justice. People such as Frederick Douglass, Sojourner Truth, and Malcolm X elucidated their narratives of being victimized by state violence, and their memories and experiences validated their claims.

Our personal encounters with harassment by law enforcement become a way in which we corroborate the narratives of unarmed Black males being killed by law enforcement. For example, the first author of this article has been stopped by New York City police and has been questioned by all-White officers if he "was the one screaming nigger down the street?" The second author, although having no notable instance of harassment by law enforcement, has lived much of his adult life combatting the perception of being an intimidating, menacing Black male due to his large size, long locked hair, goateed facial profile, and propensity to wear urban attire. Additionally, he has experienced the physical and social manifestations of anger and pain due to the death of an unarmed Black male by law enforcement as a lifelong resident and participant in protests surrounding Freddie Gray's death in Baltimore, Maryland. These are just a couple of illustrations of law enforcement's abuse of power through micro-aggressions, believing the police were looking for a hostile reaction in order to escalate the situation. Overall,

> Autoethnography is characterized by personal experience narratives, auto-observation, personal ethnography, lived experience, self-ethnography, reflexive ethnography, emotionalism, experiential texts, and autobiographical ethnography. Thus autoethnographic accounts are characterized by a move from a broad lens focus on individual situatedness within the cultural and social context, to a focus on the inner vulnerable and often resistant self. (Boyle & Parry, 2007, p. 186)

Results

Research suggests that race and racism is still a relevant and determinant factor in the United States (Advisory Board to the President's Initiative on Race, 1998; Haney-Lopez, 2010; Thompson & Neville, 1999). The election of Barack Obama as the 44th President of the United States and the first Black president led many to believe that America achieved racial equality. The term "postracial" America was coined to validate this notion of racial parity, while simultaneously negating issues of racism as somehow irrelevant in this new era of American history. Despite this idea of being postracial, several cultural critics and scholars point out that this racial equity has not been reached or achieved (Tesler & Sears, 2010; Wise, 2010). Further research indicates the widening gap in racial inequality in this postracial era include the following: Education research shows racial segregation has grown in the last 40 years, and policy makers have abandoned policies to create efforts for integration (Kucsera & Orfield, 2014; Rothstein, 2013); housing examinations determine that Black and White citizens still live in racially segregated communities (Crowder, Pais, & South, 2012; Desmond, 2012); health disparities indicate the vast differences in health care determined by race (Dressler, Oths, & Gravlee, 2005; LaVeist, 2005); employment opportunities starkly contrast by racial differences favoring White potential employees over their Black counterparts (Pager, 2007; Western, 2006); voting rights have been shown to play a significant difference in changing election results and denying Black citizens through disenfranchisement laws (Harvey, 1994; Manza & Uggen, 2006; Uggen, Manza, & Thompson, 2006); and incarceration has been shown to be unequally distributed across racial lines (Alexander, 2010; Wacquant, 2002; Western, 2007).

Despite the abundance of research specifying stark differences by race and creating enormous racial disparities, White Americans believe racial differences are declining (Sue et al., 2007). In addition, many White Americans view themselves as good, moral, and believe in equality, which would refute ideas of prejudice or discrimination (Sue, 2004). Therefore, racism in a postracial America is much more covert and implicit as opposed to earlier forms of overt and explicit forms of racial aggression. Scholarship indicates that new forms of racism have emerged via micro-aggressions that imply traditional racist ideology without having to be explicit in using race but now use other traditional American values (e.g., self-reliance) as a reason why individuals or groups are unsuccessful.

Operational definitions

The sample of news articles fell under two operational classifications, both derived from the concept of racial micro-aggressions. The first classification is the micro-insult, which is defined as "verbal and nonverbal communication that subtly conveys rudeness and insensitivity as well as demeaning a person's racial identity and heritage" (Sue et al., 2007). The second classification is the micro-invalidation, defined as "communication that subtly excludes, negates, or nullifies the thoughts, feelings, or experiential reality of a person of color" (Sue et al., 2007). A number of examples demonstrated aspects of both micro-insults and micro-invalidations, suggesting that the two are not mutually exclusive.

Key themes

In addition to the two operational classifications, the portrayals of the victims fell under four major recurring themes:

- Behavior—the actions of the victim at the time of their death. Also found were actions of the victim prior to their death that could be considered correlational to the interaction with law enforcement. This included but was not limited to past criminality.
- Appearance—the look of the victim at the time of their death. This included both their physical composition as well as the style of apparel worn.
- Location—the geographical area in which the victim's death occurred. Also found were references to the area in which the victim lived and references to the area(s) in which the victim frequented for social engagement.
- Lifestyle—the culture(s) with which the victim was associated. Family usually provided friends, this information, or close associates of the victim.

Eric Garner

Eric Garner's representation in newspapers primarily featured micro-invalidations revolved around his physical composition. Specifically, Garner's health and size, as he was a particularly tall and large individual with a number of preexisting medical conditions, were among the first pieces of information introduced in many of the articles:

> The 350-pound man, about to be arrested on charges of illegally selling cigarettes, was arguing with the police. (Goldstein & Schweber, 2014)

> But the 350-pound Garner's poor health, including "acute and chronic bronchial asthma; obesity; hypertensive cardiovascular disease," were also "contributing conditions" to his death, it added. (Schram, Bain, & Fredericks, 2014)

> A 400-pound asthmatic Staten Island dad died Thursday after a cop put him in a chokehold and other officers appeared to slam his head against the sidewalk, video of the incident shows. (Murray et al., 2014)

The prominent references related to Garner's physical attributes were micro-invalidations and micro-insults regarding his behavior at the time of his death, which involved Garner vehemently defending his role in breaking up an altercation. In addition were the micro-invalidations related to his past actions and lifestyle. This included criminality and the perception of being a "hustler" due to his propensity to sell single cigarettes, which is illegal yet not a felony in New York:

> The encounter between Mr. Garner and plainclothes officers, from the 120th Precinct, began after the officers accused Mr. Garner of illegally selling cigarettes, an accusation he was familiar with. He had been arrested more than 30 times, often accused of selling loose cigarettes bought outside the state, a common hustle designed to avoid state and city tobacco taxes. In March and again in May, he was arrested on charges of illegally selling cigarettes on the sidewalk. (Goldstein & Schweber, 2014)

> The pending cases, which have now been dismissed and sealed, included selling untaxed cigarettes, driving without a license, and possession of marijuana, said a law enforcement official. (Fox, 2014)

> Police suspected that Garner, who was African American, was selling untaxed cigarettes—a charge that he had faced numerous times before. (Blakely, 2014)

Michael Brown

The representation of Michael Brown in the media immediately following his death surrounded issues of behavior and appearance. The incident between Michael Brown and Officer Darren Wilson was wrapped in opaque details with various eyewitness testimonies contradicting each other. On one hand some witnesses, including Brown's friend, indicated that he had his hands raised in the air when Wilson opened fire. On the other hand, others, including Officer Wilson, said that Brown lunged at the officer and physically assaulted him.

Brown's death ignited the "Hands Up, Don't Shoot" chant in subsequent protests around the country. Within days, articles appeared that implicated Brown in a robbery moments before his death:

> Police on Friday said that Darren Wilson, the officer who shot and killed Michael Brown last weekend, confronted Brown after the teenager was identified as the main suspect in a convenience store robbery that occurred Saturday morning. (Berman & Lowery, 2014)

> Almost a week after 18-year-old Michael Brown was killed in Ferguson, the police department identified the officer involved as six-year veteran Darren Wilson. At a press conference at 9 a.m. this morning, police chief Tom Jackson said Wilson, who has no disciplinary history, was responding to a robbery at a nearby convenience store when he encountered the teenager. The police also released video stills that appeared to show Brown threatening the convenience store owner, and a detailed report on the incident. (Coscarelli, 2014)

These reports became micro-insults and micro-invalidations to Brown's death as this report of him robbing a convenience store took precedent to the overall narrative of an unarmed young Black male being shot several times by a police officer. In addition, there were contradictions in news reports about the relevancy of the robbery and the stop of Brown by Officer Wilson. *The Huffington Post* reported Ferguson Police Chief Tom Jackson said, "the initial contact between 18-year-old Michael Brown and police officer Darren Wilson was not related to a convenience store robbery" (Lavender & Cadet, 2014). Despite the opposing stories, the larger theme of associating the posthumous Michael Brown with robbery became the broader narrative.

Beyond the theme of behavior was that of Brown's physical presence. Images released by the media showed Michael Brown's physical size:

> Brown certainly was a giant, as surveillance footage seems to prove, showing his 6′4″, nearly 300-pound self towering over a petrified convenience-store employee, who got manhandled and intimidated for having the temerity to object to his store being robbed. (Duke, 2014)

> Shortly before his encounter with Officer Wilson, the police say he was caught on a security camera stealing a box of cigars, pushing the clerk of a convenience store into a display case. He lived in a community that had

> rough patches, and he dabbled in drugs and alcohol. He had taken to rapping in recent months, producing lyrics that were by turns contemplative and vulgar. He got into at least one scuffle with a neighbour. … He was hit at least six times, twice in the head. His 6-foot-4 frame lay face down in the middle of the warm pavement for hours, a stream of blood flowing down the street. (Eligon, 2014)

Very much married to the theme of the convenience store robbery, descriptions of his physical presence and lifestyle, including the coupling of rapping, has a negative connotation of both Brown's physical appearance and lifestyle. This larger-than-life description of Michael Brown is supported by Officer Wilson's description of Brown in a media interview given in November 2014. Wilson stated:

> When I grabbed him, the only way I can describe it is I felt like a five-year-old holding onto Hulk Hogan … and then after he did that, he looked up at me and had the most intense aggressive face. The only way I can describe it, it looks like a demon, that's how angry he looked. (Sanburn, 2014)

While Wilson's description of Brown gave the impression of Brown being a colossal or more than human figure, it should be noted this imagery of Brown became another justification of the use of excessive and lethal force. However, what was very much downplayed was the fact that Wilson and Brown were of the same relative size. Sanburn writes, "Wilson, who is 6′4″ and 210 lbs., said of Brown, who was 6′4″ and 292 lbs. at the time of his death" (2014). In any professional boxing match or mixed martial arts fight, Wilson and Brown would fall into the same weight class, heavyweight. In other words, Wilson's imagery makes him the victim while simultaneously perpetuates Brown's criminalization.

Akai Gurley

The shooting death of Akai Gurley was immediately spun in the media, mainly by police press conferences as a "tragic accident" by a rookie officer. Despite the concerned effort to make this story not about police brutality or conscious excessive force, this case presented Gurley in several ways including his appearance and location as indications of micro-insults and micro-invalidations, which devictimized him.

Akai Gurley's death gained coverage because of its timing of happening within days of the grand juries in both the Michael Brown and Eric Garner cases declining to indict the officers involved. Many images of Akai were used in news articles. The most flagrant image of his mug shot was used by at least two international media sources. The United Kingdom's *Daily Mail* published a story with a double entendre title: "NYPD rookie officer shot 'innocent' unarmed father dead in Brooklyn stairwell by 'accident' as girlfriend watched in horror." The interesting part of this is they put innocent and accident in quotes as if to question if Akai Gurley was actually innocent, which would then imply that his death was not an accident but valid if he was not innocent. The *Daily Mail* went a step further and published a mug shot photo saying, "Akai Gurley, 28, (pictured left and right in an old booking photo) was shot and killed by rookie cop Peter Liang as he entered a stairwell in a public housing project in Brooklyn" (Robinson, 2014). Beyond the use of mug shots, many of the images published of Gurley show him wearing urban fashion styles: cornrow hairstyle, flat brimmed hats, sunglasses, and visible neck tattoos (Corcoran, 2014; Goodman, 2014). All of these images are associated with Blackness specifically, which are in turn linked to this idea of criminality (Davis, 1998; Muhammad, 2010).

In addition to Gurley's appearance is the location of his death. He was killed leaving his girlfriend's apartment located in the New York City Housing Authority Pink Houses located in East New York, Brooklyn. The East New York section of Brooklyn is associated with violence and according to DNAinfo.com, East New York holds some of the highest crime rates in all five boroughs. Fagan, West, and Holland (2002) have indicated that more than 70 percent of all New York state prison inmates come from New York City. Moreover the majority of those being incarcerated from New York City come from one of seven neighborhoods, East New York being one of them. Beyond just the environment of East New York, the location of Gurley's death at the

Pink Houses is also relevant. The Pink Houses is a notorious New York City public housing complex making several online sites' worst housing projects (Ettelson, 2009). *The New York Post* published an article two days after Akai Gurley's death entitled "Living in Fear at the Dark & Deadly Hellhole Houses" (Feuerherd, Mongelli, & Rosenbaum, 2014). The article discusses the collapse and neglect of the Pink Houses, particularly the lack of proper lighting in the hallways and uncleanliness of the environment. In addition, the article makes reference to violence saying, "The Pink Houses are among the most dangerous projects in the city, and their stairwells are the most dangerous places in the projects" (Feuerherd et al., 2014). Although the article is addressing real concerns of environmental justice and public safety issues, the timing of its release becomes an issue. From the beginning the NYPD claimed this shooting to be an accident because of lack of lighting in the hallways, which once again shifts the blame from the NYPD officer who killed Gurley to city government. In addition, the theme of continually expressing how violent the Pink Houses are does two things: (1) Again, shifts the blame from the officer who did not use proper training tactics and (2) negates Gurley's death as a victim because he is associated with the Pink Houses, which are linked to violence, therefore implicating Gurley as a criminal or violent. The micro-insults and micro-invalidations of Akai Gurley come out in a particular manner of subversive text and imagery to take the focus off the particular case of excessive police violence but rather focus on the physical character and appearance of Gurley and the location and environment of the event.

Tamir Rice

Tamir Rice's death was met with questions of lifestyle and behavior. However, the themes of micro-insults and micro-invalidations were expanded to include Rice's mother as part of his death. The first and most shocking theme that emerged out of this case of a twelve-year-old child being shot and killed by law enforcement was the discussion of who was to blame. Initially, the city of Cleveland, Ohio announced that Rice caused his own death:

> The city of Cleveland's response to a lawsuit filed by the family of Tamir Rice says the 12-year-old boy is to blame for his own death by police. ... The family's suit filed in December said Tamir 'suffered terror and fear' at the hands of Loehmann [police officer] before his shooting death—claims the city says Tamir and his family are at fault for. It states Tamir's death was "directly and proximately caused by their own acts." (Hensley, 2015)
>
> In papers filed in federal court Friday, the city said Tamir was responsible for his own death and said the injuries, losses and damages were "directly and proximately caused by the failure of [Tamir] to exercise due care to avoid injury." (Muskal & Raab, 2015)
>
> The city also stated in their response, obtained by Cleveland.com, that Tamir died because of "the conduct of individuals or entities other than Defendant." ... The Defendant is police officer Timothy Loehmann. (Spargo, 2015).

This blaming of a child for his own demise by a professional law enforcement agent is a micro-invalidation of his death. It puts the ownership on the victim rather than the perpetrator.

Other forms of micro-insults toward the death of Tamir Rice were in the form of blame and lifestyle of his mother. Many on social media outlets were pondering and posing the question: Why did his mother allow Tamir Rice to play with a realistic-looking fake gun? Again, this is a micro-insult, which implies Tamir's mother was not a good parent and did not exercise good parenting skills. This also reinforces micro-invalidation of Tamir's life because it implies his fault that he was shot for playing with this gun. Tamir Rice's mother, Samaria Rice's, character became the focus. An article on Cleveland.com entitled "Lawyer Representing Tamir Rice's Family Defended Boy's Mom in Drug Trafficking Case" (Blackwell, 2014) explains that the mother's lawyer from an earlier drug charge would be representing her in her son's death case. This irrelevant connection to a previous drug charge becomes a way to invalidate and negate Tamir's death and his mother's credibility as a parent. More recently, Samaria Rice has moved into a homeless shelter, which would also give a negative connotation of her unfit parenting and ability provide for her children, therefore to blame for Tamir's unsupervised playing with a toy gun. Like other cases, this case shifts the focus from excessive force by law enforcement and puts blame on the victim and victim's family.

Tony Robinson

The perception of Tony Robinson was overwhelming concentrated on the behavior that immediately preceded his death, prompting a number of micro-invalidations and micro-insults based on presumed criminality:

> Authorities have said Robinson, who was unarmed, was shot multiple times after he assaulted Officer Matt Kenny, punching him in the head and knocking him off balance. (Savidge, 2015)

> Anthony Robinson, 19, was killed about 6:30 P.M. as police responded to multiple reports of a disturbance, Koval said. Officers were told a man was jumping in and out of traffic and was suspected of committing battery before he ran into an apartment, he said. An officer forced his way inside after hearing sounds of a disturbance, where Robinson struck the officer in the head, Koval said. The officer then fired his weapon. (Frankel, 2015)

> Robinson was shot after Officer Matt Kenny responded to calls about a man dodging cars in traffic who had allegedly battered another person, according to police officials. They said Kenny fired after Robinson attacked him. (O'Brien, 2015)

One newspaper, a local outlet, highlighted Robinson's past behavior that included criminality:

> Wisconsin court records show that Mr. Robinson pleaded guilty to armed robbery last year and received a probated six-month sentence. Chief Koval declined to comment on Mr. Robinson's record. (Brooks, 2015)

Freddie Gray

Much of the narrative surrounding Freddie Gray focused on the behavior immediately prior to his arrest. Many considered his behavior suspicious and thereby warranted a presumption of criminality, resulting in examples of micro-insults:

> Four bicycle officers tried to stop Gray about 9 A.M. on April 12 in the 1600 block of W. North Ave. for an alleged violation that police have not disclosed. He ran, police said, and the officers caught him and restrained him on the ground while awaiting backup. (Sherman, Kaltenbach, & Campbell, 2015)

> In a police report filed with the court, Officer Garrett Miller wrote that Gray was stopped after fleeing "unprovoked upon noticing police presence." Miller said a knife was found clipped to Gray's pants pocket and he was arrested. (Johnson & Eversley, 2015)

Also notable in Gray's posthumous portrayal were micro-invalidation, which emphasized both where he lived, known to be one of the more impoverished and crime-heavy neighborhoods in Baltimore, and also his prior interactions with law enforcement and the criminal justice system. A few newspaper outlets included his physical composition:

> Gray was a 25-year-old resident of the neighborhood around the Gilmor Homes, a Baltimore Housing Authority project. He stood 5 feet 8 and weighed 145 pounds. He had a police record, mainly on drug charges and minor crimes, according to court records reported by the Baltimore Sun. (Muskal, 2015)

> Court records indicate that Gray's arrests were mostly for drug charges and minor crimes, and sometimes were not prosecuted. He had several cases scheduled for trial in the coming months. One case, involving charges for second-degree assault and malicious destruction of property, was scheduled for a June trial. He also faced drug charges that were scheduled for trial in April and May. He has been found guilty of drug charges in the past; his sentences were unclear from court records. (Rector & Marbella, 2015)

Discussion

Although media depictions of Black bodies have remained compliant to White supremacist structures using body type, negative images (e.g., picture of victim in mug shot), previous criminal convictions or charges, and allegations of criminal behavior, it is important to realize that individual reporters do not need to be consciously racist. The purpose of this study is not to accuse any individual of holding those values but to recognize how White privilege and other forms of privilege allow journalists and other media outlets to report on these cases the way they do, without self-reflection of how the words, images, and storylines are disseminated. These narratives play a role in the initial assumption of the victim and can shift the perspective of how these victims are viewed.

In this last section, we discuss the overall movement that has grown in wake of these deaths, #BlackLivesMatter. It is important to recognize social movements and their usefulness in gaining equality. It is also important to recognize and understand why this movement uses the language of "Black Lives Matter."

#BlackLivesMatter

In the wake of the deaths of Michael Brown and Eric Garner, which occurred less than a month apart in the summer of 2014, activists, students, and many groups of various racial, class, and social backgrounds came together to protest the ways in which law enforcement handled these situations. In New York City, an organic rally emerged using the slogan "hands up, don't shoot!" which was also being chanted in Ferguson, Missouri. Other cities around the country took notice and joined in solidarity. Fast forward to November 2014, when both the Eric Garner and Michael Brown cases were dismissed because grand juries decided to not indict either officer involved in these cases. The first decision came in the Brown case. Contradictory testimony from eyewitnesses, racial tension in the community of Ferguson, and a prosecutor who seemed to not do his job dictated this case. However, the main argument was that there was no video evidence that confirmed either side's story. Conversely, a week later, a grand jury in Staten Island, New York, put forth a nonindictment verdict for the officer who was implicated in killing Eric Garner. The main difference in this case from Ferguson was the video evidence.

Over the next several days and weeks leading into the holiday season, mass movements began to emerge across U.S. cities shutting down highways, practicing forms of civil disobedience, and chanting "Black Lives Matter." #BlackLivesMatter has become a recognizable hashtag on social media, which has been used to connect individuals and organizations in solidarity against police brutality, excessive force by law enforcement, and racial profiling. Critics of the #BlackLivesMatter movement argue that equality is about "all" lives and therefore saying "Black" lives is limiting and a form of racism. The answer is simple: Those who have issue with the term "Black" do not recognize their own privilege and why there is both a historical and systemic need to focus on the brutality the Black community has faced throughout America's existence. If Black lives mattered in the United States, we would not see such disproportional rates of poverty, incarceration, school dropouts, lack of secure housing and other socially significant factors. To not recognize racism as an ongoing problem only exacerbates the issue, silences and marginalizes those affected by it, and does not start the process of discourse on how to change cultural and social paradigms in society that only see young Black men as thugs.

Responsibility of media

As previously mentioned, the aim of this study is not to accuse the selected newspaper outlets of intentionally perpetuating a negative or insensitive racialized portrayal of any of the aforementioned victims of police brutality. We cannot ascertain the mind-sets of either the authors or the editorial staffs who finalized the articles' publication, so to make such assumptions would be highly flawed and unethical. However, this study aims to highlight that the White-dominated media, newspapers included, is operated under the perspective of White privilege. Among its many aspects, White privilege incorporates an assumed naïveté as to the negative implications of perceived innocuous verbal and nonverbal behaviors committed by Whites against people of color. Simply put, it is not their obligation to understand, let alone acknowledge, that what they believe to be a compliment, a term of endearment, a simple observation, or even the presentation of facts is anything but what they intended it to be.

Relative to the horrors of lynching and mob "justice" carried out against people of color on a regular basis during the 19th and 20th centuries, personally mediated racism is rarely committed via overt acts of violence today. For as much as it seems that little progress has been made in the efforts to promote true racial equality, such blatant expressions of racial hatred are usually met with the highest levels of condemnation in American society. The resulting adjustments made are that an individual who aims to exert their White supremacy over a person of color is socially inclined to do so via coded language—micro-aggressions, as previously detailed—as its subtlety limits mainstream detection. Additionally, the nature of micro-aggressions has evolved to include tangential facets and characteristics historically linked to people of color such as socioeconomic status and culture (Clark, Anderson, Clark, & Williams, 1999). What occurs with the inclusion of tangential facets and characteristics to race is that the line of demarcation between entities that are intentional in their racial disrespect and insensitivity and entities that have no ill will are blurred. Therefore even honest reporting of an incident carries the risk of creating a negative persona for the victim, and that is what the selected newspaper articles exemplify.

A reasonable question can be raised when considering the potential influence of micro-aggressions in media: Should an outlet sacrifice journalistic integrity for the sake of a heightened sensitivity to racialized language? The simple answer is a resounding no. Rather, outlets must be more judicious in the information that they decide to present regarding any incident, let alone deaths involving unarmed Black males and law enforcement. The situations previously examined provide many teachable moments. For example, how necessary was it that the audience knew Eric Garner was 6′3″, 400 pounds, and had preexisting medical conditions (Goldstein & Schweber, 2014)? What greater clarity was achieved by readers in knowing that Tony Robinson was previously convicted for armed robbery (Brooks, 2015)? How does knowing that he lived in a housing project and had an extensive police record promote a better understanding of why Freddie Gray died (Muskal, 2015)? Relative to the facts of each incident, these pieces of information were peripheral at best. The only contributions they potentially provide are a triggering of negative misconceptions that will be unconsciously and unjustifiably attached to these individuals. What is worse is that because this potential triggering is done in the immediacy following their deaths, when all information is novel, the perception created is very difficult to alter even in the face of more sound, debunking information. The growing number of fatal law enforcement interactions involving unarmed individuals, especially Black males, warrants greater cognizance of the images created by the media of the victims. Simply regurgitating all information provided, most of which comes from the same law enforcement agencies involved in the altercations and could possibly contain an agenda, is no longer acceptable. True understanding of the power of racialized language, both overt and covert, should be the new standard of journalistic integrity.

Notes

1. Freddie Gray, 25, was an African-American male who was arrested by Baltimore City police on April 12, 2015. Gray died on April 19, 2015, stemming from neck and head injuries he suffered while in police custody. On May 2, 2015, Baltimore City's State Attorney, Marilyn Mosby, ruled the death a homicide and charged six officers involved in Gray's death.
2. Eric Garner (NY); Michael Brown (MO); Akai Gurley (NY); Tamir Rice (OH); Tony Robinson (WI); and Freddie Gray (MD).

Funding

This study was funded by the National Institute on Drug Abuse grant number T32DA007292.

References

Advisory Board to the President's Initiative on Race. (1998). *One America in the 21st century: Forging a new future.* Washington, DC: U.S. Government Printing Office.

Alexander, M. (2010). *The new Jim Crow: Mass incarceration in the age of colorblindness.* New York, NY: New Press.

Berman, M., & Lowery, W. (2014, August 15). Ferguson police say Michael Brown was a robbery suspect, identify Darren Wilson as officer who shot him. *Washington Post.* Retrieved from http://www.washingtonpost.com/news/post-nation/wp/2014/08/15/ferguson-police-releasing-name-of-officer-who-shot-michael-brown/

Blackwell, B. (2014, November 24). Lawyer representing Tamir Rice's family defended boy's mom in drug trafficking case. *Cleveland.com.* Retrieved from http://www.cleveland.com/metro/index.ssf/2014/11/lawyer_representing_tamir_rice.html

Blakely, R. (2014, July 24). NYPD cop who choked man to death sued twice before. *The Times* (London), p. 33.

Boyle, M., & Parry, K. (2007). Telling the whole story: The case for organizational autoethnography. *Culture and Organization, 13*(3), 185–190. doi:10.1080/14759550701486480

Brooks, K. (2015, March 9). Activists decry black teen's death: Wisconsin capital marked by 3rd day of protests after police shooting. *Pittsburgh Post-Gazette,* p. A6.

Byfield, N. (2014). *Savage portrayals: Race, media and the central park jogger story.* Philadelphia, PA: Temple University Press.

Clark, R., Anderson, N. B., Clark, V. R., & Williams, D. R. (1999). Racism as a stressor for African Americans. *American Psychologist, 54,* 805–816. doi:10.1037/0003-066X.54.10.805

Corcoran, K. (2014, November 22). 'I miss my daddy': Tears of girl, 2, whose unarmed father was 'accidentally' shot dead in housing project by rookie NYPD officer, as family vow to fight for justice. *Daily Mail.* Retrieved from http://www.dailymail.co.uk/news/article-2845029/Family-NYC-man-killed-police-seek-answers.html

Coscarelli, J. (2014, August 15). Ferguson police officer Darren Wilson shot and killed Michael Brown after alleged robbery. *New York Magazine.* Retrieved from http://nymag.com/daily/intelligencer/2014/08/darren-wilson-shot-and-killed-michael-brown.html

Crenshaw, K. (1989). Demarginalizing the intersection of race and sex: A black feminist critique of antidiscrimination doctrine, feminist theory and antiracist politics. *University of Chicago Legal Forum, 140,* 139–167.

Crowder, K., Pais, J., & South, S. J. (2012). Neighborhood diversity, metropolitan constraints, and household migration. *American Sociological Review, 77*(3), 325–353. doi:10.1177/0003122412441791

Davis, A. Y. (1998). Race and criminalization: Black Americans and the punishment industry. In J. Jones (Ed.), *The Angela Y. Davis reader* (pp. 61–73). Malden, MA: Blackwell Publishing.

Desmond, M. (2012). Eviction and the reproduction of urban poverty. *American Journal of Sociology, 118*(1), 88–133. doi:10.1086/666082

Dressler, W. W., Oths, K. S., & Gravlee, C. C. (2005). Race and ethnicity in public health research: Models to explain health disparities. *Annual Review of Anthropology, 34,* 231–252. doi:10.1146/annurev.anthro.34.081804.120505

DuBois, W. E. B. (1903). *The souls of black folk.* New York, NY: Barnes & Noble Classics.

Duke, S. (2014, August 19). Ferguson's Michael Brown: The tall tale of the "gentle giant." *New American.* Retrieved from http://www.thenewamerican.com/usnews/crime/item/18943-ferguson-s-michael-brown-the-tall-tale-of-the-gentle-giant

Eligon, J. (2014, August 24). Michael Brown spent last weeks grappling with problems and promise. *New York Times.* Retrieved from http://www.nytimes.com/2014/08/25/us/michael-brown-spent-last-weeks-grappling-with-lifes-mysteries.html?_r=0

Ellis, C., Adams, T., & Bochner, A. (2011). Autoethnography: An overview. Forum. *Qualitative Social Research, 12,* 1, article 10.

Ettelson, R. (2009). The Unkut guide to hip-hop's most notorious projects—Part 1. *Unkut.com.* Retrieved from http://www.unkut.com/2009/03/the-unkut-guide-to-hip-hops-most-notorious-projects-part-1/

Eze, E. (1997). *Race and the enlightenment: A reader.* Malden, MA: Wiley-Blackwell.

Fagan, J., West, V., & Holland, J. (2002). Reciprocal effects of crime and incarceration in New York City neighborhoods. *Fordham Urban Law Journal, 30*(5), 1551–1599.

Fields, B. J. (1990). Slavery, race and ideology in the United States of America. *New Left Review, 181*(1), 95–118.

Fox, A. (2014, July 23). Open cases dismissed against Eric Garner, Staten Island man who died in police custody. *amNewYork.* Retrieved from http://www.amny.com/news/eric-garner-staten-island-man-who-died-in-police-custody-has-open-cases-dismissed-1.8875188

Frankel, T. C. (2015, March 8). Fatal shooting of black man by Wis. officer sparks protests. *Washington Post,* p. A3.

Feuerherd, B., Mongelli, L, & Rosenbaum, S. (2014, November 22). Living in fear at the dark & deadly hellhole houses. *New York Post.* Retrieved from http://nypost.com/2014/11/22/tenants-live-in-fear-at-the-notorious-pink-houses/

Gao, G. (2014, July 18). Chart of the week: The black-white gap in incarceration rates. *Pew Research Center*. Retrieved from http://www.pewresearch.org/fact-tank/2014/07/18/chart-of-the-week-the-black-white-gap-in-incarceration-rates/

Goldstein, J., & Schweber, N. (2014, July 19). Man's death after chokehold raises old issue for the police. *New York Times*. Retrieved from http://www.nytimes.com/2014/07/19/nyregion/staten-island-man-dies-after-he-is-put-in-chokehold-during-arrest.html.

Goodman, J. D. (2014, November 23). In Brooklyn, 2 young men, a dark stairwell and a gunshot. *New York Times*. Retrieved from http://www.nytimes.com/2014/11/24/nyregion/police-tactic-scrutinized-after-accidental-shooting.html

Haney-Lopez, I. (2010). Post-racial racism: Racial stratification and mass incarceration in the age of Obama. *California Law Review*, *98*(3), 1023–1074.

Harvey, A. (1994). Ex-felon disenfranchisement and its influence on the Black vote: The need for a second look. *University of Pennsylvania Law Review*, *142*(3), 1145–1189. doi:10.2307/3312504

Hensley, N. (2015, February 28). City of Cleveland says Tamir Rice was at fault for his police shooting death. *New York Daily News*. Retrieved from http://www.nydailynews.com/news/national/city-cleveland-tamir-rice-death-fault-article-1.2132922

Holbert, R. L., Lambe, J. L., Dudo, A. D., & Carlton, K. A. (2007). Primacy effects of The Daily Show and national TV news viewing: Young viewers, political gratifications, and internal political self-efficacy. *Journal of Broadcasting & Electronic Media*, *51*(1), 20–38. doi:10.1080/08838150701308002

Jefferson, T. (1787 [1997]). Notes on the state of Virginia. In E. Eze (Ed.), *Race and the enlightenment: A reader* (pp. 95–103). Malden, MA: Wiley-Blackwell.

Johnson, K., & Eversley, M. (2015, April 22). Justice Department to investigate Baltimore death. *USA Today*. Retrieved from http://www.usatoday.com/story/news/nation/2015/04/21/justice-department-freddie-gray/26139375/

Kucsera, J., & Orfield, G. (2014). *New York state's extreme school segregation: Inequality, inaction and a damaged future*. New York, NY: Civil Rights Project/Proyecto Derechos Civiles.

LaVeist, T. (2005). *Minority populations and health: An introduction to health disparities in the U.S.* San Francisco, CA: Jossey-Bass.

Lavender, P., & Cadet, D. (2014, August 15). Ferguson police chief: Darren Wilson did not know Michael Brown was suspect in 'strong-armed' robbery. *Huffington Post*. Retrieved from http://www.huffingtonpost.com/2014/08/15/tom-jackson-michael-brown_n_5682762.html

Lhamon, W. T., Jr. (2000). *Raising Cain: Blackface performance from Jim Crow to hip hop*. Cambridge, MA: Harvard University Press.

Litwack, L. F. (2004). Hellhounds. In N. Scheper-Hughes & P. Bourgois (Eds.), *Violence in war and peace: An Anthology* (pp. 123–128). Malden, MA: Blackwell Publishing.

Manza, J., & Uggen, C. (2006). *Locked out: Felon disenfranchisement and American democracy*. New York, NY: Oxford University Press.

Mauer, M. (2002). Mass imprisonment and the disappearing votes. In *Invisible punishment: The collateral consequences of mass imprisonment*. New York, NY: New Press.

Memmi, A. (2000). *Racism*. Minneapolis, MN: University of Minnesota Press.

Muhammad, K. (2010). *The condemnation of Blackness: Race, crime, and the making of modern urban America*. Cambridge, MA: Harvard University Press.

Murray, K., Burke, K., Marcius, C. R., Parascandola, R., McCarron, P., & Hutchinson, B. (2014, July 18). 'I can't breathe ... I can't breathe ...' Officers slam 400-lb. 'illegal cig seller' to sidewalk: Kin demand 'justice' after Staten Island death. *New York Daily News*, p. 10.

Muskal, M. (2015, April 23). Back story: A mystery in Baltimore: What we know, and don't know, about a man's death in police custody. *Los Angeles Times*, p. A2.

Muskal, M., & Raab, L. (2015, March 2). Cleveland blames Tamir Rice, 12, for his own death, then apologizes. *LA Times*. Retrieved from http://www.latimes.com/nation/la-na-tamir-rice-lawsuit-blame-cleveland-20150302-story.html

O'Brien, B. (2015, March 12). Madison police shooting forces liberal city to look at race gap. *Reuters*. Retrieved from http://www.reuters.com/article/2015/03/10/us-usa-police-wisconsin-race-idUSKBN0M62HN20150310.

Pager, D. (2007). *Marked: Race, crime, and finding work in an era of mass incarceration*. Chicago, IL: University of Chicago Press.

Pew Charitable Trusts. (2007). *Public safety, public spending: Forecasting America's prison population 2007–2011*. Washington, DC.

Pickens, J. (2013). The destruction of Black Wall Street: The events that destroyed a thriving Black Oklahoma community 92 years ago were much more than a 'race riot'. *Ebony*. Retrieved from http://www.ebony.com/black-history/the-destruction-of-black-wall-street-405#axzz3ciwo5htv

Pilgram, D. (2012). The brute caricature. *Jim Crow museum*. Retrieved from http://www.ferris.edu/jimcrow/brute/

Rector, K., & Marbella, J. (2015, April 21). Injuries in van ride focus of city probe. *Baltimore Sun*, p. 1A.

Robinson, W. (2014, November 21). NYPD rookie officer shot 'innocent' unarmed father dead in Brooklyn stairwell by 'accident' as girlfriend watched in horror. *Daily Mail.* Retrieved from http://www.dailymail.co.uk/news/article-2844570/NYPD-rookie-officer-shot-innocent-unarmed-father-dead-Brooklyn-stairwell-accident-girlfriend-watched-horror.html

Rothstein, R. (2013). *For public schools, segregation then, segregation since: Education and the unfinished march.* Washington, DC: Economic Policy Institute.

Sanburn, J. (2014, November 25). All the ways Darren Wilson described being afraid of Michael Brown. *Time.* Retrieved from http://time.com/3605346/darren-wilson-michael-brown-demon/

Savidge, N. (2015, 3 April). Landlord seeking nearly $2,000 from tenants at home where Tony Robinson was shot. *Wisconsin State Journal.* Retrieved from http://host.madison.com/wsj/news/local/crime_and_courts/landlord-seeking-nearly-from-tenants-at-home-where-tony-robinson/article_49778fab-13ab-571e-a410-f04be33e0a3e.html

Schram, J., Bain, J., & Fredericks, B. (2014, August 2). Taken out by 'killer' clutch, NYPD choke death ruled a homicide. *New York Post,* p. 7.

Shea, D. (2008, April 5). Uncovered: Possible inspiration for controversial LeBron James Vogue cover. *Huffington Post.* Retrieved from http://www.huffingtonpost.com/2008/03/28/uncovered-possible-inspir_n_93944.html

Sherman, N., Kaltenbach, C., & Campbell, C. (2015, April 20). Gray dies a week after his arrest; He was injured while police had him in custody. *Baltimore Sun,* p. 1A.

Smiley, C. (2015). From silence to propagation: Understanding the relationship between "Stop Snitchin" and "YOLO." *Deviant Behavior, 36*(1), 1–16. doi:10.1080/01639625.2014.883888

Smith, C. H. (1893). Have Negroes too much liberty? *Forum, 16*(Oct.), 176–181.

Spargo, C. (2015, March 1). Family of Cleveland boy, 12, shot dead by police while brandishing a 'fake gun' is told he was to blame for his own death. *Daily Mail.* Retrieved from http://www.dailymail.co.uk/news/article-2973970/City-Cleveland-tells-family-Tamir-Rice-blame-death-despite-fact-boy-12-holding-fake-gun-shot-dead-police-officer.html

Strausbaugh, J. (2006). *Black like you: Blackface, Whiteface, insult & imitation in American popular culture.* New York, NY: Tarcher.

Sue, D. W. (2004). Whiteness and ethnocentric monoculturalism: Making the "invisible" visible. *American Psychologist, 59,* 759–769. doi:10.1037/0003-066X.62.4.271

Sue, D. W., Capodilupo, C. M., Torino, G. C., Bucceri, J. M., Holder, A., Nadal, K. L., & Esquilin, M. (2007). Racial microaggressions in everyday life: Implications for clinical practice. *American Psychologist, 62*(4), 271–286. doi:10.1037/0003-066X.62.4.271

Tesler, M., & Sears, D. O. (2010). *Obama's race: The 2008 election and the dream of a post-racial America.* Chicago, IL: University of Chicago Press.

Thompson, C. E., & Neville, H. A. (1999). Racism, mental health, and mental health practice. *Counseling Psychologist, 27,* 155–223. doi:10.1177/0011000099272001

Uggen, C., Manza, J., & Thompson, M. (2006). Democracy, and the civic reintegration of criminal offenders. *Annals of the American Academy of Political and Social Science, 605,* 281–310. doi:10.1177/0002716206286898

Wacquant, L. (2002). From slavery to mass incarceration: Rethinking the "race question" in the US. *New Left Review, 13,* 41–60.

Wagner, K. (2014). The word "thug" was uttered 625 times on TV on Monday. That's a lot. *Regressing.* Retrieved from http://regressing.deadspin.com/the-word-thug-was-uttered-625-times-on-tv-yesterday-1506098319

Wall, S. (2006). An autoethnography on learning about autoethnography. *International Journal of Qualitative Methods, 5*(2), 146–160.

Western, B. (2006). *Punishment and inequality in America.* New York, NY: Russell Sage Foundation.

Western, B. (2007). Mass imprisonment and economic inequality. *Social Research, 74*(2), 509–532.

Wise, T. (2010). *Colorblind: The rise of post-racial politics and the retreat from racial equity.* San Francisco, CA: City Lights Books.

WorldStarHipHop. (2015, April 30). Baltimore councilman goes off on news reporter "Just Call Them Ni**ers"! *WorldStarHipHop.* Retrieved from http://www.worldstarhiphop.com/videos/video.php?v=wshh0JEl7ztvUzc10aiU.

Yar, M. (2012). Crime, media and the will-to-representation: Reconsidering relationships in the new media age. *Crime Media Culture, 8*(3), 245–260. doi:10.1177/1741659012443227

Appendix: Data Extraction Sheet

Variable POLHITOK: EVER APPROVE OF POLICE STRIKING CITIZEN

Literal Question

232. Are there any situations you can imagine in which you would approve of a policeman striking an adult male citizen?

Descriptive Text

In 1973 and 1975, those replying "no" to POLHITOK (punch 2, Col. 896) were not asked POLABUSE, POLMURDR, POLESCAP, and POLATTAK. Since 1975, all respondents were asked POLABUSE, POLMURDR, POLESCAP, and POLATTAK regardless of response to POLHITOK. See Appendix T, GSS Methodological Report No. 10. If planning to perform trend analysis with these variables, please consult GSS Methodological Report No. 56.

Values	Categories
1	YES
2	NO
0	NAP
8	DK
9	NA

Variable POLABUSE: CITIZEN SAID VULGAR OR OBSCENE THINGS

Pre-Question Text

Would you approve of a policeman striking a citizen who:

Literal Question

A. Had said vulgar and obscene things to the policeman?

Descriptive Text

In 1973 and 1975, those replying "no" to POLHITOK (punch 2, Col. 896) were not asked POLABUSE, POLMURDR, POLESCAP, and POLATTAK. Since 1975, all respondents were asked POLABUSE, POLMURDR, POLESCAP, and POLATTAK regardless of response to POLHITOK. See Appendix T, GSS Methodological Report No. 10. If planning to perform trend analysis with these variables, please consult GSS Methodological Report No. 56.

Values	Categories
1	YES
2	NO
0	NAP
8	DK
9	NA

Variable POLMURDR: CITIZEN QUESTIONED AS MURDER SUSPECT

Pre-Question Text

Would you approve of a policeman striking a citizen who:

Literal Question

B. Was being questioned as a suspect in a murder case?

Descriptive Text

In 1973 and 1975, those replying "no" to POLHITOK (punch 2, Col. 896) were not asked POLABUSE, POLMURDR, POLESCAP, and POLATTAK. Since 1975, all respondents were asked POLABUSE, POLMURDR, POLESCAP, and POLATTAK regardless of response to POLHITOK. See Appendix T, GSS Methodological Report No. 10. If planning to perform trend analysis with these variables, please consult GSS Methodological Report No. 56.

Values	Categories
1	YES
2	NO
0	NAP
8	DK
9	NA

Variable POLESCAP: CITIZEN ATTEMPTING TO ESCAPE CUSTODY

Pre-Question Text

Would you approve of a policeman striking a citizen who:

Literal Question

C. Was attempting to escape from custody?

Descriptive Text

In 1973 and 1975, those replying "no" to POLHITOK (punch 2, Col. 896) were not asked POLABUSE, POLMURDR, POLESCAP, and POLATTAK. Since 1975, all respondents were asked POLABUSE, POLMURDR, POLESCAP, and POLATTAK regardless of response to POLHITOK. See Appendix T, GSS Methodological Report No. 10. If planning to perform trend analysis with these variables, please consult GSS Methodological Report No. 56.

Values	Categories
1	YES
2	NO
0	NAP
8	DK
9	NA

Variable POLATTAK: CITIZEN ATTACKING POLICEMAN WITH FISTS

Pre-Question Text

Would you approve of a policeman striking a citizen who:

Literal Question

D. Was attacking the policeman with his fists?

Descriptive Text

In 1973 and 1975, those replying "no" to POLHITOK (punch 2, Col. 896) were not asked POLABUSE, POLMURDR, POLESCAP, and POLATTAK. Since 1975, all respondents were asked POLABUSE, POLMURDR, POLESCAP, and POLATTAK regardless of response to POLHITOK. See Appendix T, GSS Methodological Report No. 10. If planning to perform trend analysis with these variables, please consult GSS Methodological Report No. 56.

Values	Categories
1	YES
2	NO
0	NAP
8	DK
9	NA

Variable RACE: RACE OF RESPONDENT

Literal Question

24. CODE WITHOUT ASKING ONLY IF THERE IS NO DOUBT IN YOUR MIND. What race do you consider yourself? RECORD VERBATIM AND CODE.

Descriptive Text

Interviewer coded except in cases where question suggested was asked. Punch 3 in Col. 110 (Other SPECIFY) included 1 Aleut, 154 American Indian, 1 Arab, 139 Asian, 1 Chamorro, 24 Chinese, 1 Chinese/Japanese, 1 Creole, 2 Cuban, 1 Dominican, 1 Egyptian, 38 Filipino, 1 Guyanese, 6 Hawaiian, 6 Hindu, 267 Hispanic, 1 Hmong, 4 Human, 31 Indian (Asian), 1 Indonesian, 1 Israelite, 3 Iranian, 1 Jamaican, 29 Japanese, 11 Korean, 3 Laos, 4 Latin, 3 Latino, 2 Lebanese, 1 Malaysian, 2 Mestizo, 59 Mexican, 3 Mulatto, 18 Native American, 49 Oriental, 5 Pacific Islander, 3 Polynesian, 22 Puerto Rican, 30 Spanish, 2 Thai, 3 Vietnamese, 1 West Indies, 8 "Mixed," 1 "mixed bag," 1 "person of color," "1/2 American Indian, 1/2 Hispanic," 1 "halfbreed," 5 "Brown," and 3 "Yellow," 2 "Amerasian," 2 "Biracial," 1 "Black and Asian," and 1 "Black and White," 1 "Black, American Indian, and Spanish," 1 "Asian Pacific Islander," 1 "White Indian American," and 1 "American Indian/White," 1 "Euro-Asian," 1 "don't have one, just me," 1 "White+Mexican," 2 "1/2 Caucasian, 1/2 Philippines," 1 "African Cherokee," 1 "Mexican and Indian," 1 "American/Bangdi" and 1 "wheat color." If planning to perform trend analysis with this variable, please consult GSS Methodological Report No. 56. In 2000 RACE was based on RACESEE, RACEDBTF, and RACESELF. RACE was asked as indicated above from 1972 to 2000. Starting in 2002 RACE was replaced by RACECEN1, RACECEN2, RACECEN3 and RACE was imputted based on these and other variables. See Appendix D: Recodes. See RACECEN1,2,3 (Qs 1462A-C) for the new race variables first used in 2000. See GSS Methodological Reports 85 and 89. Intent of Recode: In 2002 the GSS switched from asking race in this three-category format and adopted an item based on the new Census race questions (RACECEN1,2,3). For 2002 onwards RACE is imputed based on RACECEN1,2,3; ETHNIC, ETH1, ETH2, ETH3, and HISPANIC so researchers have one race variable covering all years. Method of Recode: In 2000 both RACE and RACECEN1,2,3 were asked on the GSS. Along with other racial and ethnicity variables (ETHNIC, ETH1,2,3, HISPANIC), RACECEN1,2,3 were used to reproduce the racial classification produced by RACE. This same procedure has since been used to create RACE in 2002 onwards.

Values	Categories
1	White
2	Black
3	Other
0	Not applicable

Variable RACECEN1: WHAT IS RS RACE 1ST MENTION

Pre-Question Text

IF RACE CODED IN Q.1349A DISAGREES WITH Q.1349C, ANSWER Q.1351A-Q.1352C. IF RACE CODED IN Q.1349A AND Q.1349C AGREE, SKIP TO Q.1353. 1351. What is your race? Indicate one or more races that you consider yourself to be.

Literal Question

A. First mention

Descriptive Text

Hand card IV contained response options 1–15 and prompts for options 3,10,14, and 15.

Values	Categories
1	WHITE
2	BLACK OR AFRICAN AMERICAN
3	AMERICAN INDIAN OR ALASKA NATIVE
4	ASIAN INDIAN
5	CHINESE
6	FILIPINO
7	JAPANESE
8	KOREAN
9	VIETNAMESE
10	OTHER ASIAN
11	NATIVE HAWAIIAN
12	GUAMANIAN OR CHAMORRO
13	SAMOAN
14	OTHER PACIFIC ISLANDER
15	SOME OTHER RACE
16	HISPANIC
0	NAP
98	DK
99	NA

Variable ETHNIC: COUNTRY OF FAMILY ORIGIN

Pre-Question Text

1345. From what countries or part of the world did your ancestors come? IF SINGLE COUNTRY IS NAMED, REFER TO NATIONAL CODES BELOW AND ENTER CODE NUMBER IN BOXES: IF MORE THAN ONE COUNTRY IS NAMED, REFER TO NATIONAL CODES BELOW, CODE UP TO 3 RESPONSES AND THEN ASK A: FIRST MENTION SECOND MENTION THIRD MENTION

Literal Question

A. IF MORE THAN ONE COUNTRY NAMED: Which one of these countries do you feel closer to? IF ONE COUNTRY NAMED, REFER TO CODES BELOW, AND ENTER CODE NUMBER IN BOXES: IF CAN'T DECIDE ON ONE COUNTRY, ENTER CODE 88.

Descriptive Text

Question was recoded so that the summary ethnicity of the respondent appears in ETHNIC, whether obtained in ETHNIC, ETH1, ETH2, or ETH3. See Appendix D: Recodes, for details. Content of Punch 29 (Other SPECIFY) available from NORC. See Appendix N for changes across surveys. See Appendix T, GSS Methodological Reports Nos. 6, 12, and 18. Codes 40 and 41 were used starting in 1994. If planning to perform trend analysis with ETHNIC, please consult GSS Methodological Report No. 56.

Values	Categories
1	AFRICA
2	AUSTRIA
3	FRENCH CANADA
4	OTHER CANADA
5	CHINA
6	CZECHOSLOVAKIA
7	DENMARK
8	ENGLAND & WALES
9	FINLAND
10	FRANCE
11	GERMANY
12	GREECE
13	HUNGARY
14	IRELAND
15	ITALY
16	JAPAN
17	MEXICO
18	NETHERLANDS
19	NORWAY
20	PHILIPPINES
21	POLAND
22	PUERTO RICO
23	RUSSIA
24	SCOTLAND
25	SPAIN
26	SWEDEN
27	SWITZERLAND
28	WEST INDIES
29	OTHER
30	AMERICAN INDIAN
31	INDIA
32	PORTUGAL
33	LITHUANIA
34	YUGOSLAVIA
35	RUMANIA
36	BELGIUM
37	ARABIC
38	OTHER SPANISH
39	NON-SPAN WINDIES
40	OTHER ASIAN
41	OTHER EUROPEAN
97	AMERICAN ONLY
0	UNCODEABLE
98	NO ETH MENTIONED
99	NA

Variable ETH1: 1ST MENTIONED COUNTRY OF ORIGIN

Literal Question

765. Now I'd like you to imagine a neighborhood that had an ethnic and racial mix you personally would feel most comfortable in. Here is a blank neighborhood card, which depicts some houses that surround your own. Using the letters A for Asian, B for Black, H for Hispanic or Latin American and W for White, please put a letter in each of these houses to represent your preferred neighborhood where you would most like to live. Please be sure to fill in all of the houses.

Descriptive Text

Question was recoded so that the summary ethnicity of the respondent appears in ETHNIC, whether obtained in ETHNIC, ETH1, ETH2, or ETH3. See Appendix D: Recodes, for details. Content of Punch 29 (Other SPECIFY) available from NORC. See Appendix N for changes across surveys. See Appendix T, GSS Methodological Reports Nos. 6, 12, and 18. Codes 40 and 41 were used starting in 1994. If planning to perform trend analysis with ETHNIC, please consult GSS Methodological Report No. 56.

Values	Categories
1	AFRICA
2	AUSTRIA
3	FRENCH CANADA
4	OTHER CANADA
5	CHINA
6	CZECHOSLOVAKIA
7	DENMARK
8	ENGLAND & WALES
9	FINLAND
10	FRANCE
11	GERMANY
12	GREECE
13	HUNGARY
14	IRELAND
15	ITALY
16	JAPAN
17	MEXICO
18	NETHERLANDS
19	NORWAY
20	PHILIPPINES
21	POLAND
22	PUERTO RICO
23	RUSSIA
24	SCOTLAND
25	SPAIN
26	SWEDEN
27	SWITZERLAND
28	WEST INDIES
29	OTHER
30	AMERICAN INDIAN
31	INDIA
32	PORTUGAL
33	LITHUANIA
34	YUGOSLAVIA
35	RUMANIA
36	BELGIUM

Values	Categories
37	ARABIC
38	OTHER SPANISH
39	NON-SPAN WINDIES
40	OTHER ASIAN
41	OTHER EUROPEAN
97	AMERICAN ONLY
0	NAP
98	NO ETH MENTIONED
99	NA

Variable HISPANIC: HISPANIC SPECIFIED

Literal Question

1350. IF R IS FEMALE, READ LATINA; IF MALE, READ LATINO. Are you Spanish, Hispanic, or Latino/Latina? IF YES: Which group are you from?

Descriptive Text

The two questions above were asked sequentially of the respondent. Hand Card IU was given to Latino respondents and had response options 2–4 plus "Other Hispanic, specify." See Recodes, Appendix D.

Values	Categories
1	NOT HISPANIC
2	MEXICAN, MEXICAN AMERICAN, CHICANO/A
3	PUERTO RICAN
4	CUBAN
5	SALVADORIAN
6	GUATEMALAN
7	PANAMANIAN
8	NICARAGUAN
9	COSTA RICAN
10	CENTRAL AMERICAN
11	HONDURAN
15	DOMINICAN
16	WEST INDIAN
20	PERUVIAN
21	EQUADORIAN
22	COLUMBIAN
23	VENEZUELAN
24	ARGENTINIAN
30	SPANISH
31	BASQUE
35	FILIPINO/A
40	LATIN AMERICAN
41	SOUTH AMERICAN
45	LATIN
46	LATINO/A
47	HISPANIC
50	OTHER, NOT SPECIFIED
0	NAP
98	DK
99	NA

Variable RACDIF1: DIFFERENCES DUE TO DISCRIMINATION

Pre-Question Text

266. On the average (Negroes/Blacks/African-Americans) have worse jobs, income, and housing than white people.

Do you think these differences are …

Literal Question

A. Mainly due to discrimination?

Descriptive Text

Asked of non-Blacks only in 1977. See Appendix N for changes in wording across surveys.

Values	Categories
1	YES
2	NO
0	NAP
8	DK
9	NA

Variable RACDIF2: DIFFERENCES DUE TO INBORN DISABILITY

Pre-Question Text

266. On the average (Negroes/Blacks/African-Americans) have worse jobs, income, and housing than white people.

Do you think these differences are …

Literal Question

B. Because most (Negroes/Blacks/African-Americans) have less in-born ability to learn?

Descriptive Text

Asked of non-Blacks only in 1977. See Appendix N for changes in wording across surveys.

Values	Categories
1	YES
2	NO
0	NAP
8	DK
9	NA

Variable RACDIF3 : DIFFERENCES DUE TO LACK OF EDUCATION

Pre-Question Text

266. On the average (Negroes/Blacks/African-Americans) have worse jobs, income, and housing than white people.

Do you think these differences are . . .

Literal Question

C. Because most (Negroes/Blacks/African-Americans) don't have the chance for education that it takes to rise out of poverty?

Descriptive Text

Asked of non-Blacks only in 1977. See Appendix N for changes in wording across surveys.

Values	Categories
1	YES
2	NO
0	NAP
8	DK
9	NA

Variable RACDIF4: DIFFERENCES DUE TO LACK OF WILL

Pre-Question Text

266. On the average (Negroes/Blacks/African-Americans) have worse jobs, income, and housing than white people.

Do you think these differences are . . .

Literal Question

D. Because most (Negroes/Blacks/African-Americans) just don't have the motivation or will power to pull themselves up out of poverty?

Descriptive Text

Asked of non-Blacks only in 1977. See Appendix N for changes in wording across surveys.

Values	Categories
1	YES
2	NO
0	NAP
8	DK
9	NA

Variable MARBLK : CLOSE RELATIVE MARRY BLACK

Pre-Question Text

405. What about having a close relative marry a Jewish person? Would you be very in favor of it happening, somewhat in favor, neither in favor nor opposed to it happening, somewhat opposed, or very opposed to it happening?

Literal Question

B. How about having a close relative or family member marry a black person?

Values	Categories
1	STRONGLY FAVOR
2	FAVOR
3	NEITHER FAVOR NOR OPPOSE
4	OPPOSE
5	STRONGLY OPPOSE
0	NAP
8	DONT KNOW
9	NA

Variable EDUC: HIGHEST YEAR OF SCHOOL COMPLETED

Literal Question

Now just a few more background questions.

15–22. ASK ALL PARTS OF QUESTION ABOUT RESPONDENT BEFORE GOING ON TO ASK ABOUT R'S FATHER; AND THEN R'S MOTHER; THEN R'S SPOUSE, IF R IS CURRENTLY MARRIED.

A. What is the highest grade in elementary school or high school that (you/your father/your mother/your [husband/wife]) finished and got credit for? CODE EXACT GRADE.
B. IF FINISHED 9th–12th GRADE OR DK*: Did (you/he/she) ever get a high school diploma or a GED certificate? [SEE D BELOW.]
C. Did (you/he/she) complete one or more years of college for credit—not including schooling such as business college, technical or vocational school? IF YES: How many years did (you/he/she) complete?

Descriptive Text

See Appendix D: Recodes, for a discussion of original format of EDUC, PAEDUC, MAEDUC, and SPEDUC. See Appendix N for changes across surveys.

Values	Categories
0	
1	
2	
3	
4	
5	
6	
7	
8	
9	
10	
11	
12	
13	
14	
15	
16	
17	
18	
19	
20	
97	Not applicable
98	Don't know
99	No answer

Variable AGE: AGE OF RESPONDENT

Descriptive Text

Date of birth has been recoded into actual age in Cols. 92 and 93. See Appendix D: Recodes. See Appendix E: Age Distributions, for detailed responses. The distribution for the first digit, Col. 92 is given below. See Appendix N for changes across surveys. The response categories have been collapsed for convenience of display.

Values	Categories
18	
19	
20	
21	
22	
23	
24	
25	
26	
27	
28	
29	
30	
31	
32	
33	
34	
35	
36	
37	
38	
39	
40	
41	
42	
43	
44	
45	
46	
47	
48	
49	
50	
51	
52	
53	
54	
55	
56	
57	
58	
59	
60	
61	
62	
63	
64	
65	
66	

Values	Categories
67	
68	
69	
70	
71	
72	
73	
74	
75	
76	
77	
78	
79	
80	
81	
82	
83	
84	
85	
86	
87	
88	
89	89 or older
98	Don't know
99	No answer

Variable INCOME: TOTAL FAMILY INCOME

Literal Question

37. In which of these groups did your total family income, from all sources, fall last year, before taxes, that is? Just tell me the letter.

Descriptive Text

Card D contained responses for Punches 01–12 only. See RINCOME, INCOME72, INCOME77, INCOME82, INCOME86, INCOME91, and INCOME06 for comparable questions in 1972 and 1977+. For 1972, 1977, 1978, 1980, and 1982–2006 income has been recoded from these questions to match the categories in INCOME. If planning to perform trend analysis with this variable, please consult GSS Methodological Report No. 56.

Values	Categories
1	Under $1000
2	$1000 to 2999
3	$3000 to 3999
4	$4000 to 4999
5	$5000 to 5999
6	$6000 to 6999
7	$7000 to 7999
8	$8000 to 9999
9	$10000 to 14999

Values	Categories
10	$15000 to 19999
11	$20000 to 24999
12	$25000 or over
13	Refused
0	Not applicable
98	Don't know
99	No answer

Variable SEX: RESPONDENTS SEX

Literal Question

CODE RESPONDENT'S SEX

Descriptive Text

Interviewer coded. See Appendix T, GSS Methodological Report No. 9. If planning to perform trend analysis with this variable, please consult GSS Methodological Report No. 56.

Values	Categories
1	Male
2	Female

Variable WRKSTAT: LABOR FORCE STATUS

Literal Question

1. Last week were you working full time, part time, going to school, keeping house, or what?
   CIRCLE ONE CODE ONLY. IF MORE THAN ONE RESPONSE, GIVE PREFERENCE TO SMALLEST CODE NUMBER THAT APPLIES.

Values	Categories
1	Working full time
2	Working part time
3	With a job, but not at work because of temporary illness, vacation, strike
4	Unemployed, laid off, looking for work
5	Retired
6	In school
7	Keeping house
8	Other
9	No answer

Variable MARITAL: MARITAL STATUS

Literal Question

4. Are you currently married, widowed, divorced, separated, or have you never been married?

Values	Categories
1	Married
2	Widowed
3	Divorced
4	Separated
5	Never married
9	No answer

Variable RELIG: RS RELIGIOUS PREFERENCE

Literal Question

104. What is your religious preference? Is it Protestant, Catholic, Jewish, some other religion, or no religion?

Values	Categories
1	PROTESTANT
2	CATHOLIC
3	JEWISH
4	NONE
5	OTHER (SPECIFY)
6	BUDDHISM
7	HINDUISM
8	OTHER EASTERN
9	MOSLEM/ISLAM
10	ORTHODOX-CHRISTIAN
11	CHRISTIAN
12	NATIVE AMERICAN
13	INTER-NONDENOMINATIONAL
0	NAP
98	DK
99	NA

Variable PARTYID: POLITICAL PARTY AFFILIATION

Literal Question

56. Generally speaking, do you usually think of yourself as a Republican, Democrat, Independent, or what?

Descriptive Text

See Appendix D: Recodes, for original question format and method of recoding. See Appendix N for changes across surveys. If planning to perform trend analysis with this variable, please consult GSS Methodological Report No. 56.

Values	Categories
0	STRONG DEMOCRAT
1	NOT STR DEMOCRAT
2	IND,NEAR DEM
3	INDEPENDENT
4	IND,NEAR REP
5	NOT STR REPUBLICAN
6	STRONG REPUBLICAN
7	OTHER PARTY
8	DK
9	NA

Variable CHILD: NUMBER OF CHILDREN

Literal Question

12. How many children have you ever had? Please count all that were born alive at any time (including any you had from a previous marriage).

Values	Categories
0	
1	
2	
3	
4	
5	
6	
7	
8	Eight or more
9	No answer, don't know

Variable HOMPOP: NUMBER OF PERSONS IN HOUSEHOLD

Literal Question

34. Household Size and Composition

Descriptive Text

See Appendix D: Recodes, for information about these variables

Values	Categories
98	Don't know
99	No answer

Police shootings of unarmed African American males: A systematic review

George T. Patterson[a] and Philip G. Swan[b]

[a]Silberman School of Social Work at Hunter College, City University of New York, New York, New York, USA; [b]Hunter College Libraries, City University of New York, New York, New York, USA

ABSTRACT

This article describes the results of a systematic review examining police shootings of unarmed African American males. Each source was evaluated by two reviewers and coded based on topic relevance and inclusion criteria. Because of the weak external validity found among the experimental studies, the authors made a substantive decision not to synthesize studies in a meta-analysis. Social work practice implications are gleaned from secondary data obtained from coroner, medical examiner, toxicology, police reports, and the experimental studies included in the systematic review. Individual, community, and police departmental policy factors were most often reported to explain such shootings when excluding sources that examined armed African American males. Implications for micro and macro-social work practice are summarized as individual, community, and police departmental policy factors.

Introduction

In October 1974 Edward Garner, a 15-year-old unarmed African American male, was shot and killed by a police officer in Memphis, Tennessee. Police officers were responding to a burglary call when Garner was located at the scene and considered a suspect. The police officer assumed that he was unarmed and 17–18 years old. After Garner did not obey the officer's commands to halt he was shot and killed. On March 27, 1985, in *Tennessee v. Garner* the Supreme Court ruled that in situations in which deadly force is used by a police officer to prevent a felony suspect from fleeing "such force may not be used unless it is necessary to prevent the escape and the officer has probable cause to believe that the suspect poses a significant threat of death or serious physical injury to the officer or others" (*Tennessee v. Garner*, 471 U.S 1 (1985), p. 1).

Prior to this ruling state and police departmental policies were inconsistent and ranged from authorizing police to use any means necessary to stop a felony suspect from fleeing to allowing the use of deadly force only when necessary to protect the life of others (Tennenbaum, 1994). Nearly 10 years after the Supreme Court's ruling, Tennenbaum investigated whether *Tennessee v. Garner* had an effect on the number of police homicides. Results show that police homicides of fleeing felony suspects decreased nationwide by 16% following the decision and overall police shootings also decreased.

Police use of firearms and homicides

At present a national database does not exist that summarizes statistics on police shootings. The lack of national data contributes to the difficulty in understanding police shootings of unarmed African

American males. A report prepared by the Bureau of Justice Statistics using data based on the number of complaints reported by community residents for police use of force suggests that in large police departments 6.6 complaints per 100 police officers occur, with 8% of these complaints resulting in discipline against an officer (National Institute of Justice, 2015). Indeed, it is difficult to obtain data quantifying police use of force including shootings that result in either injury or homicide. When police shootings and homicides of unarmed individuals do occur they are high-profile events. Following a police shooting public concerns often arise whether the shooting, particularly of an unarmed individual, was justified. Public calls for social justice and concerns about civil rights violations also often follow some of these events. Certainly, police use of deadly force including firearm use is a complex issue that requires split-second decisions with numerous factors involved related to officer training and experience, police departmental organizational policies, and citizens' compliance with police commands. Even the medical examiner's findings may be questioned (Gill & Pasquale-Styles, 2009).

Few data are available that describe police shootings that result in injury or homicide of unarmed African American males. Available evidence from the Centers for Disease Control (CDC) National Violent Death Reporting System (NVDRS) summarizes the number and percentage of deaths that occurred during 2007 when an individual was killed by a police officer, peace officer, or military police officer in the line of duty (Karch, Dahlberg, & Patel, 2010). The CDC NVDRS data describe victim's race and ethnicity, marital status, location of the event, and toxicology report results and were collected from death certificates, coroner's or medical examiner's reports, and police reports in 16 states (Alaska, Colorado, Georgia, Kentucky, Maryland, Massachusetts, North Carolina, New Jersey, New Mexico, Oklahoma, Oregon, Rhode Island, South Carolina, Utah, Virginia, and Wisconsin). Within the 16 states, 145 individuals were killed by officers authorized to use deadly force. Among these individuals, 66 (45.5%) were non-Hispanic whites and 51 (35.2%) were non-Hispanic Blacks. The age range for the majority of the victims was 20–54 years. Sixty-three (46.0%) were never married, 30 (21.9%) were married, and 31 (22.6%) were divorced. The majority of homicides occurred in a house (55, 37.9%) closely followed by a street or highway (46, 31.7%). Toxicology tests for blood alcohol content (BAC) were conducted on 127 (87.6%) of the victims and found that 38.6% tested positive for alcohol, 67.4% had a BAC greater than 0.08, 30.6% tested positive for marijuana, 21.6% for cocaine, 20.1% for amphetamines, 9.3% for opiates, and 5.1% tested positive for antidepressants. While the CDC NVDRS data are descriptive and informative, they were collected from less than half of the states and are subject to the limitations of secondary data analysis. Furthermore, these data do not inform concerns about police shootings of unarmed African American males because the data do not specify whether individuals were unarmed.

Gill and Pasquale-Styles (2009) examined police shooting homicides that occurred in New York City from 2003 to 2007. During this four-year period, 42 deaths were identified. Similar to the CDC NVDRS data, the authors reviewed medical examiner reports, and police and toxicology reports. They found the average age of the victims was 31 years. Among the victims there were 41 males and one female. Relatives identified victim's race as 26 Black, nine Hispanic, and seven white. Toxicology reports showed that alcohol and/or drugs were present among 78% of the victims; 15 tested positive for cannabis, 14 for alcohol, 10 for cocaine, and one for amphetamines. Additionally seven had a history of mental illness. Gill and Pasquale-Styles note that two of the homicides resulted in indictments; one police officer was indicted for pursuing an unarmed man, and the other was indicted for shooting at the driver of an automobile. Taken together, these studies describe numerous characteristics of the victims of police homicides but do not offer implications for social work practice interventions. Also, no national data are present that are representative of all the states. Finally, these data also do not explicate the factors present in the police shooting injury or homicide of unarmed African American males. Because of the lack of accurate data describing police shootings, the Federal Bureau of Investigation Bureau director announced on September 28, 2015 that as part of the Uniformed Crime Report (UCR) program data will be collected describing fatal and nonfatal police shootings (Tucker, 2015). However, law enforcement organizations voluntarily participate in the UCR program when reporting data.

Prior systematic reviews

A prior systematic review examined police use of improper force (Harris, 2009). The search period was from 1960 to 2006, and of the 357 retrieved abstracts, three studies were included in the review. The purpose of the review was to identify the characteristics of victims and police officers as well as the causes of police use of improper force. Although meta-analysis was not conducted, and Harris found the studies were low quality in terms of methodological rigor, Harris concluded that psychological variables (e.g., officers' attitudes toward their job and African Americans), situational variables (e.g., the nature of the offense and the individuals' behavior), and organizational variables (e.g., characteristics of the police department) affect the use of improper force. Further, young male officers with fewer years of police experience were more likely to be involved in the use of improper force, and victims tended to be hostile toward police, intoxicated, poor, and African American. These results are based on data collected from reports filed by citizens for complaints against police officers for improper use of force. Study implications suggest that police use of improper force has a negative effect on police community relations and community policing initiatives.

Mekawi and Bresin (2015) conducted a meta-analysis that examined the effects of racial shooter bias. The meta-analysis included 16 sources that reported results from 42 experimental studies. The following study participants were compared: undergraduate students were compared with police officers, community members with police officers, and undergraduate students and community members with police officers (N = 3,427). Separate analyses were not conducted for police officers only. Study outcomes included the following: (1) reaction time to shoot or not shoot an individual with or without a gun, (2) false alarms (shooting unarmed individuals), (3) shooting sensitivity, and (4) shooting threshold (bias toward shooting).

No significant effects for racial shooter bias were found between undergraduate students, community members, and police officers. A significant effect for reaction time was found such that all participants were more likely to shoot armed Black individuals sooner than armed White individuals, and slower to not shoot unarmed Black individuals than unarmed White individuals.

No significant effect was found for false alarms. In other words, false alarms for shooting either unarmed Black individuals or unarmed White individuals were not different. Likewise, no significant effect was found for shooting sensitivity such that all study participants' shooting sensitivity was no different for Black individuals or White individuals. A significant effect was found for shooting threshold such that less bias toward shooting Black individuals than White individuals was found. Thus, Mekawi and Bresin (2015) found that study participants demonstrated "a liberal shooting threshold" (p. 123) toward shooting Black individuals suggesting that participants took longer to shoot Black individuals.

The social work profession and police shootings

The social work profession has had a long-standing commitment to social justice; indeed, it is a core value of the field, with NASW declaring that social workers strive for social change and provide pertinent facts and information in the practice of social justice (National Association of Social Workers, 2008). Police shootings of unarmed African American males is a subject in which facts and information are greatly needed to guide the profession in social justice efforts. Consequently, a systematic review examining police shootings of unarmed African American males is warranted.

Objectives of the systematic review

The objective of this systematic review was to examine the factors present in police shootings of unarmed African American males. It was anticipated that meta-analysis results could provide implications for social work practice, defined broadly as clinical practice, policy, research, advocacy, or community organizing.

Methods

Inclusion criteria

Four criteria for study inclusion were used: (1) studies must utilize samples of participants who are police officers or police recruits; (2) separate quantitative outcome data are reported for police officers or recruits that can be synthesized in a meta-analysis; (3) random assignment is made to experimental or comparison conditions, or the use of methods that utilize a comparison group (i.e., Black/White, armed/unarmed); and (4) English language publications from any geographic location are used. Only studies utilizing random assignment or those utilizing experimental and control groups were included because these studies provide the "best evidence" (Lipsey & Wilson, p. 9).

Electronic search strategy

The Boolean search terms were Unarmed and (Black or "African American") and (police or "law enforcement") and (shot or shoot*) and "social work." As Table 1 shows 15 electronic databases were searched with and without the term "social work" to assess whether studies were specifically applicable to the profession.

The search and screening period was March 31, 2015, through October 22, 2015. Publication dates were limited to studies published between 2000 and 2015. These dates approximately cover the period after a Department of Justice report (Brown & Langan, 2001) found that between 1976 and 1998 there were approximately 400 justifiable killings of felons each year by police officers. During this 22-year period 8,578 felons were justifiably killed by police officers.

Data extraction

Retrieved studies were imported into Refworks for collection and storage. RefWorks is a web-based tool that is used to collect and store electronic sources. It can also be used to create citations and bibliographies (Refworks, 2009). The review team comprised two reviewers. Retrieved studies were coded based on (1) the utilization of police officer or recruit study participants, (2) utilization of a comparison group, (3) the shooting of an unarmed African American male, (4) the reporting of quantitative analysis, and (5) social work or interdisciplinary studies.

Table 1. Summary of Boolean search results.

Database	Number of hits without social work	Number of hits with social work
Academic One File	22	0
Academic Search Complete	16	0
Cochrane	1	0
Criminal Justice Abstracts*	8	0
Criminal Justice Collection	9	0
ProQuest Criminal Justice	121	5
Psych Articles	2	0
Psych Info	12	1
Sage Journals	49	29
Social Sciences full text	9	2
Social Work Abstracts	1	0
Sociological Abstracts	6	1
Soc Index	9	0
Springer Link	296	17
Social Sciences Citation Index	16	0

*The initial search query without the term "social work" yielded zero results. Using SmartText Searching, 24 results were found. To maintain consistency among all the databases SmartText Searching results are not reported.

Results

Electronic search strategy

Table 1 shows the 15 databases that were searched. The number of hits ranged from zero to more than 200. As also shown in Table 1, more hits were obtained in electronic databases when the term "social work" was omitted from the Boolean search strategy. This is a consistent pattern that was found throughout the search. As examples of this pattern, Academic Search Complete resulted in no hits when including the term "social work" and 16 hits when the term was omitted. Searching ProQuest Criminal Justice resulted in five hits when including the term "social work" and 100 hits when the term was excluded. As a final example, Social Work Abstracts resulted in zero hits when the term was included and one hit when it was omitted.

The screening process first involved a review of the retrieved titles. Those titles that did not appear relevant to the topic were excluded from further examination. Next, abstracts were obtained when they were not included with the title. Following this review full text studies were retrieved for review. To illustrate the screening process, some studies required retrieval for further examination because titles alone were not sufficient. For example, the study by Correll, Park, Judd and Wittenbrink (2002) titled *The police officer's dilemma: Using ethnicity to disambiguate potentially threatening individuals* contains the term "police officers" in the title, and although the abstract describes a shooting bias experiment the study participants are not identified. Moreover, some studies included law enforcement and non–law enforcement study participants.

The identification, screening, eligibility, and study inclusion process is illustrated in the PRISMA flow diagram found in Figure 1. As Figure 1 shows, a total of 632 titles and abstracts were retrieved and screened. After titles and abstracts were screened for duplicates and upon removing these 112 duplicates, 520 sources remained. A total of 17 full text studies were retrieved, screened applying the inclusion criteria, and assessed for inclusion.

This screening process resulted in the exclusion of 11 studies that utilized study participants who were college students (Correll, Park, Judd, & Wittenbrink, 2007; Correll, Urland, & Ito, 2006; Correll,

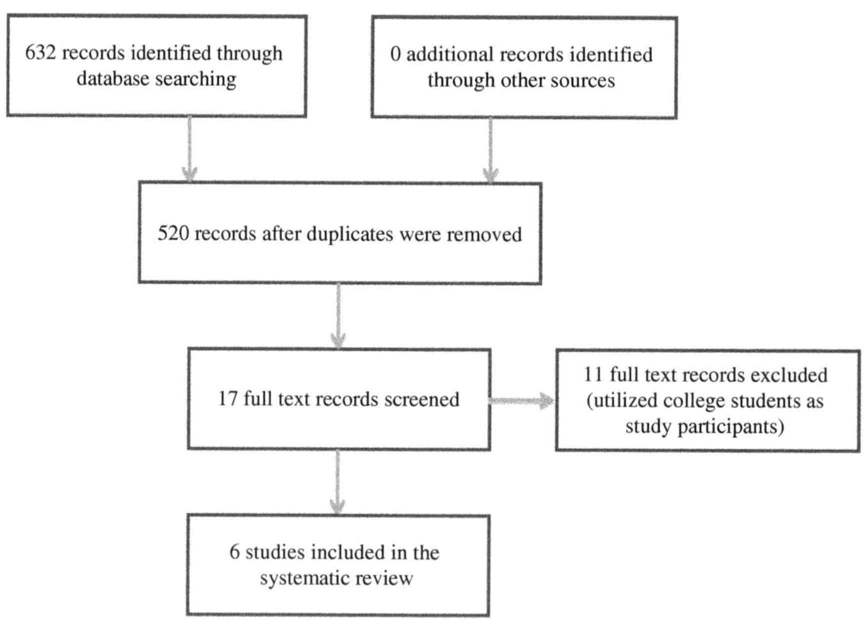

Figure 1. PRISMA flow diagram.

Note. Adapted from Moher, Liberati, Tetzlaff, and Altman (2009), p. 877.

Wittenbrink, Park, Judd, & Goyle, 2011; Correll et al., 2002; Greenwald, Oakes, & Hoffman, 2003; Kleider & Parrott, 2009; Ma & Correll, 2011; Park & Kim, 2015; Plant, Goplen, & Kunstman, 2011; Plant, Peruche, & Butz, 2005; Sadler, Correll, Park, & Judd, 2012).

Six studies met the inclusion criteria (Akinola & Mendes, 2012; James, Vila, & Daratha, 2013; Peruche & Plant, 2006; Plant & Peruche, 2005; Sim, Correll, & Sadler, 2013; Taylor, 2011). Two of the studies describe different components of the same study (Peruche & Plant, 2006; Plant & Peruche, 2005).

External validity issues

Although Plant and Peruche (2005) report that police officers are trained using computer-simulated scenarios, the review team made a substantive decision to not include the six experimental studies in a meta-analysis because of concerns about weak external validity and generalizability to real-world situations. Situations such as resisting arrest during an altercation or a fleeing felony suspect, among other events, do not appear to be shown in the experiments. Discussing the weaknesses of computer-simulated experiments for investigating racial bias associated with decisions to shoot individuals, James et al. (2013) note that most studies require participants to press a keyboard (although their experiments utilized high-fidelity deadly force simulators with realistic weapons), the scenarios are not interactive, allowing participants to change the outcome by using skills and training, the possibility to use other than deadly force is not an option, and repeated exposure to the armed/unarmed computer scenarios may result in an increased concerns about safety that do not occur in reality. Further, James et al. suggest that police officer participants' decisions to shoot or not shoot could have been affected by bias, desires to appear unbiased, or desires to appear socially acceptable.

Given the recent media coverage of police shootings of unarmed African American males, and the content of audio and video recordings that have emerged from bystanders' cameras or police vehicle dashboard cameras or body cameras, the authors agree with the views about first-person-shooter tasks (FPSTs) used in controlled laboratory experiments articulated by Sim et al. (2013):

> The FPST is an impoverished simulation of an actual police encounter. The images are static, bystanders are deliberately precluded, trials occur in rapid succession, and responses are made by pressing buttons (not pulling triggers). The task assesses bias in a split-second reaction that would ordinarily represent the final stage in police decision making. Perhaps most critically, the FPST takes place in the safety of a lab, and failure in the simulation poses no real threat. (p. 302)

Taken together, these external validity issues contributed to the review team making the decision to not include the computer-simulated and simulated shooting range experiments in a meta-analysis. However, these experiments are of such significance relative to a topic with little empirical data that it is important nonetheless to discuss their findings.

Characteristics of included studies

Table 2 provides a summary of the characteristics of the six studies that met the inclusion criteria. Of these six experimental studies, five reported results obtained from computer-simulated experiments and one from high-fidelity deadly force simulators with realistic weapons.

The aims of the Akinola and Mendes (2012) study were to examine the effects of neuroendocrine and testosterone levels on a videogame simulation of a shoot/don't shoot task. First, neuroendocrine and testosterone levels were assessed using saliva samples. Next, study participants participated in a high-stress role play involving a Black male actor who reported physical and verbal maltreatment by a police officer based on his race. After participating in this high-stress role play it was anticipated that neuroendocrine and testosterone levels would increase among the officers. Therefore, officers then completed the videogame simulation. Images of Black and White men were shown holding various guns and items that were not guns such as cell phones. Study participants were instructed to

Table 2. Characteristics of included studies.

Study	Sample characteristics	Materials	Study outcomes	Geographic location
Akinola & Mendes, (2012)	81 male police officers; 84% patrol officers, 7% sergeants, 9% investigators, 44 White, 25 Black, 10 Latino, 1 Asian	Stressful role play, saliva samples, videogame simulation	Neuroendocrine activity, decisions to shoot/not shoot, signal detection parameters	USA
James et al. (2013)	30 police officers, 100% White, 99% male, 1% female, age (M = 37, range 31–43 years)	High-definition simulators, shooting range, realistic weaponry	Reaction time to shoot (shooting unarmed suspect (error A), failing to shoot an armed suspect (error B)	USA
Peruche and Plant (2006)/ Plant and Peruche (2005)	50 police officers, 83% male, 84% White, 10% African American, 2% Native American, 4% Hispanic, age (M = 37, SD = 7.82), years of police experience (M = 11.13, SD = 5.94, range 2–32 years)	Computer simulation, laptop computer, questionnaire	Brigham (1993) ATB Scale, police experience on the job, the quality of police officer's contact with Black individuals both at work and in their personal lives	USA
Sim et al. (2013)	Experiment 1–45 White police officers (no demographic data reported); Experiment 2–22 special unit police officers, 1 female, 21 male, 12 White, 7 Black, 2 Latino/a, 1 Native American/Pacific Islander; age M = 36.8	Laptop computer, first-person-shooter task, button box, headphones, mock newspaper articles	Racial shooting bias, racial bias in shooting sensitivity	USA
Taylor (2011)	Study 1–47 police recruits, 35 male, 12 female, age M = 27.72, SD = 5.67; 49 police officers, 40 male, 9 female, age M = 38.63, SD = 6.42; Study 2–50 recruits, 40 male, 10 female, age M = 26.94, SD = 4.92; 30 police officers, 25 male, 5 female, age M = 39.90, SD = 6.37	Computer simulation, demographic questionnaire, stereotype measures	Reaction time, decisions to shoot/ not shoot, error rates, cognitive load ratings	Canada

respond (shoot/don't shoot) very quickly by pressing a button on the computer. Participants were awarded points for correctly shooting armed individuals and lost points for shooting an unarmed individual or not pressing the button within 850 ms after viewing an image of a Black or White male. Study findings show that higher cortisol levels among police officers resulted in fewer error decisions to shoot/not shoot. These results were more precise when the images depicted armed Black men than armed White men. Testosterone levels had no significant effect on racial bias shooting decisions.

James et al. (2013) developed scenarios based on actual events that resulted in the killing or assault of police officers. The scenarios were filmed and shown to participants in the experimental setting, which was a shooting range. Police officer participants used realistic weaponry. The filmed scenarios included African American, White, and Hispanic individuals, the majority of whom were male. Three experiments were conducted comprising police officers, military personnel, and civilian samples. Prior to participating in the experiment participants were instructed in the following: "The goal of a police officer in a deadly force encounter is to accurately identify a threat and neutralize it, while minimizing harm to bystanders, officers, and suspects" (p. 200). The authors found that among police, military, and civilian samples each sample took longer to make a decision to shoot African American suspects than White or Hispanic suspects and were less likely to shoot unarmed African American suspects then unarmed White or Hispanic suspects. These results contradict the initial findings reported by Plant and Peruche (2005).

The purpose of the study conducted by Plant and Peruche (2005) was to examine the effects of racial bias on police officer participants' decisions to shoot or not shoot. The authors hypothesized that the race of the individual shown in a picture would affect officers' decisions to shoot or not shoot, such that police officers' would be more likely to shoot unarmed Black males than unarmed

White males. All of the pictures that were shown depicted Black or White males who were either armed or unarmed and were shown on a laptop computer. Participants were told to press a computer key to shoot and a separate key to not shoot. Specifically the instructions to participants were the following:

> Today your task is to determine whether or not to shoot your gun. Pictures of people with objects will appear at various positions on the screen. … Some of the pictures will have a face of a person and a gun. These people are the criminals, and you are supposed to shoot at these people. Some of the pictures will have a face of a person and some other object (e.g., a wallet). These people are not the criminals and you should not shoot at them. Press the "A" key for "shoot" and press the "L" key on the keyboard for "don't shoot." (Plant & Peruche, 2005, p. 181)

Early in the experiment police officers shot unarmed Black males more frequently than White males who were not armed. However, as the experiment proceeded officers were no more likely to shoot Black males than White males. Thus, their shooting responses over the course of the experiment became more similar regarding their decisions to shoot or not shoot either Black or White males whether armed or unarmed.

In a later publication, Peruche & Plant, 2006 report the results of a questionnaire administered to police officers after they completed the computer-simulated experiment. The questionnaire assessed officers' attitudes toward African Americans, work experiences with African American and White suspects, and socialization with African Americans while not at work. Officers who reported more socialization with African Americans while not at work also reported favorable attitudes about African American suspects. When linking officers' attitudes toward African American suspects to their computer-simulated shooting responses, Peruche and Plant found that officers reporting more negative attitudes toward African American suspects were more likely to shoot African American males and less likely to shoot White males.

Sim et al. (2013) examined the effects of police training on racial shooter bias using a computerized first-person-shooter task (FPST). They conducted several experiments that comprised undergraduate students, police officers, and special unit police officers to investigate the effects that the latter experience in their work with violent individuals, particularly in Black and minority communities. After reading mock newspaper articles that reported Black or White male violent criminals, study participants were then asked to press a button on a laptop computer after viewing an image of a Black or White male who was armed or unarmed. Sim et al. found that police officers did not show racial bias in their decisions to shoot or not to shoot after reading the articles. Similarly, student participants who received practice with FPST also did not show racial bias. However, student participants who had no practice with the FPST showed racial bias toward Blacks males but not toward Whites males such that they were more likely to shoot images depicting Black males. The authors suggest that training may reduce shooter racial bias.

Finally, Taylor (2011) conducted several experiments that examined shooter racial bias among samples of Canadian police officers, recruits, and college students. The primary study aims were to examine the effects of years of police experience to shoot/not shoot in the computer-simulated tasks and to compare police officers responses with those of non–law enforcement. Taylor found that police officers with more years of police experience did not show less shooter racial bias or make fewer errors in their decisions to shoot. When compared with non–law enforcement study participants, police officers and recruits made fewer shooting errors. All study participants (police officers, recruits, and college students) exhibited a shooter bias toward Whites, such that participants were more likely to shoot White individuals than Blacks. In one experiment participants were instructed in advance that they would be making decisions to shoot/not shoot Black and White individuals, whereas in another experiment participants were not given such instructions prior to complete the computer-simulated task. This was done to examine whether the instructions resulted in participants masking racial bias. Taylor found that racial bias was "overcorrected" given that study participants were more likely to shoot White individuals than Blacks.

Discussion

Summarizing national data describing the occurrences of police shootings and homicides of unarmed African American males is extremely difficult because no national database exists to collect and summarize such data. Moreover, available data do not distinguish police shootings that result in injuries and shootings that result in homicides. In the absence of national data that can be used to identify how frequently these events occur, caution is needed when discussing the frequency of these high-profile events. As the results of this systematic review have shown, six studies were found that met the inclusion criteria of utilizing a sample of police officers or recruits, a comparison group and quantitative analysis. The review team ultimately made a substantive decision not to include these studies in a meta-analysis because of weak external validity and generalizaibility to real-world situations. The instructions given to study participants are also not consistent with the implicit intent of the systematic review, and it appears that scenarios consistent with *Tennessee v. Garner* were not used. The inclusion criteria were established in advance of the search, and consequently it was unknown that studies with such limited scenarios would be retrieved.

Because we wanted to be consistent in our search strategy we performed the same Boolean search in each database, even though not every database is equally capable of processing a search in an accurate and thorough manner. With that said, whenever a database yielded results for our search, the subsequent inclusion of the phrase "social work" usually eliminated or greatly curtailed the number of hits from that subset. The addition of terms to a Boolean search with the term "and" will necessarily reduce the results, so it was telling that out of hundreds of sources few included the term "social work." Of those sources that were located when including the term "social work" they were unrelated to the topic. It was also surprising that nothing on the topic of police shootings of unarmed African American males was found in *Social Work Abstracts* using standard Boolean search strategies given the profession's commitment to social justice causes.

Implications for social work practice

Importantly, the results of this systematic review have demonstrated why social workers require skills in research and understand research terminology. The situational factors involved in the police shooting of African American males are collected from documents and therefore subject to the limitations of secondary data analysis. Computer-simulated and high-fidelity deadly force simulators have been used in experimental studies to investigate the influence of racial bias among police officers regarding their decisions to shoot or not shoot unarmed African American males. These experiments are weak in external validity and generalizability. Social workers should be articulate in these concepts to understand the limitations of current knowledge on the topic of police shootings of unarmed African American males and when disseminating information on this topic as part of social justice efforts. How research informs knowledge in an area that is difficult to study is indeed important.

Secondary data describing the situational factors present in police shootings of African American males suggest that positive toxicology reports were found in the majority of shootings. Victims' behavior in the presence of the officer as well and the nature of the offense were also documented factors. Social workers as advocates should consider these individual factors cautiously because the role of these factors in decisions related to justifiable shootings or homicides or to indict police officers are not well understood. Similar caution is necessary when considering the role of the presence or absence of racial bias among police officers because the generalizability of the experimental studies is weak. Because of the effects that these high-profile shooting events have on communities it is imperative that social workers compile and disseminate accurate information.

Finally, regarding police departmental policies and practices greater transparency is needed, and departments should be encouraged to disseminate data on police shootings and the situational factors present in such shootings. These data should also differentiate whether shootings were justified or not justified. Such information can help reduce community residents' suspicions of police departmental policies and practices. Advocacy in this area also supports social workers with social justice efforts.

Social work practice implications resulting from computer-simulated experiments

The lack of data describing the frequency and situational factors present when a police officer shoots an unarmed African American male contributes to the difficulty associated with formulating implications for social work practice. The authors of the five computer-simulated experiments and one simulated shooting range experiment, while recognizing the limitations of their studies, provide study implications based on their findings that can be utilized as a basis for social work practice implications.

Extensive exposure to a computer-simulated program can reduce racial bias in decisions to shoot or not shoot unarmed African American males among a sample of police officers (Plant & Peruche, 2005). Because police officers are trained using simulated programs such as Firearms Training Systems (Plant & Peruche), it may be that extensive exposure to similar programs in real-world training settings can be beneficial.

In reality, police shootings of unarmed African American males are a complex issue. It is difficult to examine the underlying causes and consequently implement effective interventions. Current knowledge regarding police shootings of unarmed African American males is derived from laboratory experiments examining racial short bias. The social work profession could encourage police departments to test and evaluate these assumptions that are based on experimental studies. A specialty area of social work practice that can inform this issue is police social work. Patterson (2008) asserts that police social workers as employees of police departments provide services to individuals and families referred by police officers and provide training to police officers. This valuable experience contributes to an understanding of police culture and the nature of police work.

Police departments can promote police officer involvement in initiatives and programs in African American and predominately minority communities. Officer involvement should focus on increasing contact and communication between police officers and community residents. Such initiatives can improve police-community relations and have the potential to change the attitudes of both police officers and community residents. Examples include police officers volunteering in charitable organizations, community outreach programs, and local community projects (Peruche & Plant, 2006), which suggest another area where social work can have a significant role. Peaslee (2009) asserts that partnerships between police and social service organizations are a central component of community policing in which licensed clinical social workers can assist police and community residents.

Limitations and future directions

The review team did not hand search journals or books to locate studies relevant to the topic, scan reference lists and citations from retrieved studies, or contact authors as additional methods to locate studies. Only electronic databases were searched. Although time-consuming, future research should include these additional search methods. Future research should also examine taser use by police officers given the deaths that have occurred from these situations.

Acknowledgments

The authors would like to thank Dr. David B. Wilson for his helpful comments with revising this article and Jacob Gutter for preparing the PRISMA flow diagram.

References

Akinola, M., & Mendes, W. B. (2012). Stress-induced cortisol facilitates threat-related decision making among police officers. *Behavioral Neuroscience, 126*(1), 167–174. doi:10.1037/a0026657

Brigham, J. C. (1993). College students' racial attitudes. *Journal of Applied Social Psychology, 23*, 1933–1967.

Brown, J. M., & Langan, P. A. (2001). *Policing and homicide, 1976–98: Justifiable homicide by police, police officers murdered by felons.* Washington, DC: U.S. Department of Justice, Office of Justice Programs, Bureau of Justice Statistics.

Correll, J., Park, B., Judd, C. M., & Wittenbrink, B. (2002). The police officer's dilemma: Using ethnicity to disambiguate potentially threatening individuals. *Journal of Personality and Social Psychology, 83*(6), 1314–1329. doi:10.1037/0022-3514.83.6.1314

Correll, J., Park, B., Judd, C. M., & Wittenbrink, B. (2007). The influence of stereotypes on decisions to shoot. *European Journal of Social Psychology, 37*, 1102–1117. doi:10.1002/(ISSN)1099-0992

Correll, J., Urland, G. R., & Ito, T. A. (2006). Event-related potentials and the decision to shoot: The role of threat perception and cognitive control. *Journal of Experimental Social Psychology, 42*, 120–128. doi:10.1016/j.jesp.2005.02.006

Correll, J., Wittenbrink, B., Park, B., Judd, C. M., & Goyle, A. (2011). Dangerous enough: Moderating racial bias with contextual threat cues. *Journal of Experimental Social Psychology, 47*, 184–189. doi:10.1016/j.jesp.2010.08.017

Gill, J. R., & Pasquale-Styles, M. (2009). Firearm deaths by law enforcement. *Journal of Forensic Sciences, 54*(1), 185–188. doi:10.1111/jfo.2008.54.issue-1

Greenwald, A. G., Oakes, M. A., & Hoffman, H. G. (2003). Targets of discrimination: Effects of race on responses to weapons holders. *Journal of Experimental Social Psychology, 39*(4), 399–405. doi:10.1016/S0022-1031(03)00020-9

Harris, C. J. (2009). Police use of improper force: A systematic review of the evidence. *Victims & Offenders, 4*, 25–41. doi:10.1080/15564880701568470

James, L., Vila, B., & Daratha, K. (2013). Results for experimental trials testing participant responses to white, Hispanic and Black suspects in high-fidelity deadly force judgment and decision-making simulations. *Journal of Experimental Criminology, 9*, 189–212. doi:10.1007/s11292-012-9163-y

Karch, D. L., Dahlberg, L. L., & Patel, N. (2010). *Surveillance for violent deaths: National violent death reporting system, 16 states 2007.* Division of Violence Prevention, National Center for Injury Prevention and Control, Centers for Disease Control. Retrieved from http://www.cdc.gov/mmWR/preview/mmwrhtml/ss5904a1.htm

Kleider, H. M., & Parrott, D. J. (2009). Aggressive shooting behavior: How working memory and threat influence shoot decisions. *Journal of Research in Personality, 43*(3), 494–497. doi:10.1016/j.jrp.2008.12.007

Lipsey, M. W., & Wilson, D. B. (2001). *Practical meta-analysis* (Vol. 49). Thousand Oaks, CA: Sage.

Ma, D. S., & Correll, J. (2011). Target prototypicality moderates racial bias in the decision to shoot. *Journal of Experimental Social Psychology, 47*, 391–396. doi:10.1016/j.jesp.2010.11.002

Mekawi, Y., & Bresin, K. (2015). Is the evidence from racial bias shooting task studies a smoking gun? Results from a meta-analysis. *Journal of Experimental Social Psychology, 61*, 120–130. doi:10.1016/j.jesp.2015.08.002

Moher, D., Liberati, A., Tetzlaff, J., Altman, D. G., & PRISMA Group. (2009). *Reprint—preferred reporting items for systematic reviews and meta-analyses: The PRISMA statement. Physical therapy, 89*(9), 873–880.

National Association of Social Workers. (2008). *Code of ethics.* Retrieved from http://www.naswdc.org/pubs/code/code.asp

National Institute of Justice. (2015). *Police use of force.* Retrieved from http://www.nij.gov/topics/law-enforcement/officer-safety/use-of-force/pages/welcome.aspx

Park, S. H., & Kim, H. J. (2015). Assumed race moderates spontaneous racial bias in a computer-based police simulation. *Asian Journal of Social Psychology, 18*, 252–257. doi:10.1111/ajsp.2015.18.issue-3

Patterson, G. T. (2008). Police social work. In T. Mizrahi & L. Davis (Eds.), *Encyclopedia of social work* (Vol. 20, 20th ed., pp. 357–362). New York, NY: Oxford.

Peaslee, L. (2009). Community policing and social service partnerships: Lessons from New England. *Police Practice and Research, 10*(2), 115–131. doi:10.1080/15614260802264578

Peruche, B. M., & Plant, E. A. (2006). The correlates of law enforcement officers' automatic and controlled race-based responses to criminal suspects. *Basic and Applied Social Psychology, 28*(2), 193–199. doi:10.1207/s15324834basp2802_9

Plant, E. A., Goplen, J., & Kunstman, J. W. (2011). Selective responses to threat: The roles of race and gender in decisions to shoot. *Personality and Social Psychology Bulletin, 37*(9), 1274–1281. doi:10.1177/0146167211408617

Plant, E. A., & Peruche, B. M. (2005). The consequences of race for police officers' responses to criminal suspects. *Psychological Science, 16*(3), 180–183. doi:10.1111/psci.2005.16.issue-3

Plant, E. A., Peruche, B. M., & Butz, D. A. (2005). Eliminating automatic racial bias: Making race non-diagnostic for responses to criminal suspects. *Journal of Experimental Social Psychology, 41*(2), 141–156. doi:10.1016/j.jesp.2004.07.004

Refworks. (2009). *Refworks home page.* Retrieved from http://www.refworks.com/

Sadler, M. S., Correll, J., Park, B., & Judd, C. M. (2012). The world is not Black and White: Racial bias in the decision to shoot in a multiethnic context. *Journal of Social Issues, 68*(2), 286–313. doi:10.1111/j.1540-4560.2012.01749.x

Sim, J. J., Correll, J., & Sadler, M. S. (2013). Understanding police and expert performance: When training attenuates (vs. exacerbates) stereotypic bias in the decision to shoot. *Personality and Social Psychology Bulletin*, *39*(3), 291–304. doi:10.1177/0146167212473157

Taylor, A. (2011). *The influence of target race on split-second shooting decisions in simulated scenarios: A Canadian perspective* (Dissertation Abstracts International). Order No. AAINR83227.

Tennenbaum, A. N. (1994). The influence of the Garner decision on police use of deadly force. *Journal of Criminal Law & Criminology*, *85*(1), 241–260. doi:10.2307/1144118

Tennessee v. Garner 471 U.S. 1. (1985). Retrieved from https://supreme.justia.com/cases/federal/us/471/1/case.htmlJustia U.S. Supreme Court Center\

Tucker, E. (2015). *FBI to collect better data on police shootings, use of force*. Retrieved from http://www.pbs.org/newshour/rundown/fbi-collect-better-data-police-shootings-use-force/

Police killings of unarmed Black people: Centering race and racism in human behavior and the social environment content

Willie F. Tolliver[a], Bernadette R. Hadden[a], Fabienne Snowden[b], and Robyn Brown-Manning[a]

[a]Silberman School of Social Work at Hunter College, City University of New York, New York, New York, USA; [b]City University of New York Graduate Center, New York, New York, USA

ABSTRACT

The academic frames of diversity and, to a lesser extent, intersectionality mute the roles played by race and racism in the recent police killings of unarmed Black people in the United States. Most scholars agree that racism today is systemic, and the authors of this article assert that diversity content fails to prepare social workers to situate client issues in a social work practice that incorporates an understanding of the impact of racialization on Black people seeking social work services. Race and racism in the United States are creations of White supremacy and were initially crafted to justify the enslavement of Africans. The ideologies are a part of the founding principles of the U.S. democracy, and they are the genesis of White advantage in the United States achieved through law and social policy and still enacted daily in human interaction. In this article, the authors place police killings of unarmed Black people in a context that takes into consideration historical and contemporary evidence of the denigration of Black people in the United States. Then we specifically challenge the utility of diversity as a frame to prepare social work practitioners for practice with Blacks whose ancestral lineage traces back to people of African descent and whose lived experiences in the United States occurred during slavery and/or legally sanctioned apartheid (Jim Crow).

In 1983, Marable wrote, "Each member of the Black majority is a prisoner, and shares the marks of oppression upon his/her shoulders" (p. 28). Whether the Black person walks with a consciousness of this burden or not is a topic for future studies; however, what is clear is this, that notwithstanding "what we designate as progress wrought through struggle over many generations, [Blacks] remain what [they] were in the beginning: a dark and foreign presence, always designated other" (Bell, 1992, p. 10). The path to making sense of the killings of Michael Brown, Eric Garner, Tamir Rice, and all of the other unarmed Black people dead at the hands of police officers follows a pattern of denigration that is woven into the fabric of the United States of America.

In this article, the authors place police killings of unarmed Black people in a context that takes into consideration historical and contemporary evidence of the denigration of Black life in the United States. Next, we specifically challenge the utility of diversity as a frame to prepare social work practitioners for practice with Black people in the United States whose ancestral lineage traces back to persons of African descent whose lived experiences in the United States occurred during slavery and/or legally sanctioned apartheid (Jim Crow).

The authors use "Black" to encompass all people who identify as Black and/or African American. We made this choice because we are writing about police killings of unarmed Black people. In this usage, Black connotes race. We take this position because in the criminal justice literature, authors writing about police killings of Black people, and/or police interaction with Blacks in general, study the extent to which police engage in racial and/or ethnic profiling (Barnum & Perfetti, 2010; Novak & Chamlin, 2008; Tillyer & Engel, 2013; Warren & Tomaskovic-Devey, 2009). It is our view that police enact race in their dealings with Blacks. Ethnic profiling occurs in border states like Arizona where an immigration law was passed giving law enforcement officers authority to question people who they suspect are in the country without documents. In this instance, the people subjected to a higher scrutiny by law enforcement officers are non-White. In fact, Gilborn (2005) notes that there is no situation in the United States where a social policy has caused disparate outcomes for Whites and that policy was not changed. This is not the case for non-Whites and Blacks.

The authors also rely heavily on texts that fall outside of the 10-year rule for citations. In this instance the older text is required to build the historical narrative of the dehumanization of Black people in the United States.

Dehumanization of Blacks in the United States

With the development of slavery, according to Zinn (2001, p. 26), came "that special racial feeling—whether hatred, or contempt, or pity or patronization—that accompanied the inferior position of Blacks in America for the next 350 years." White supremacy is the ideology that gave birth to a racial hierarchy that resulted in the forced enslavement of Africans in the New World. Soon after the lie of a racial hierarchy created by White supremacy took hold in the United States, the creation process was obfuscated by the use of the term *racism*. So thorough is the alchemy of race that today, despite numerous protestations from the scientific community, the old lie of race as biology will not die (Smedley & Smedley, 2005).

White supremacy is a political system that is based on the exploitation of a group of human beings for the benefit of another group of human beings (Mills, 1998). This system of exploitation is justified by an ideology that a master White race and a subject Black race exist (Fanon, 1968; Mills, 1998). White supremacist ideology further posits that the hierarchical locations of both races are divinely ordained, and that it is the manifest destiny of the master race to subjugate the subject race (Fanon, 1968). Unlike other political systems based on exploitation, White supremacy racializes cultures, nations, communities, families, and individuals as being White, non-White, or Black (Mills, 1998).

Whiteness is normalized as having the privilege of full status as a person and worthy of respect. Non-Whites, especially Blacks, are consigned to subordinate moral status (Mills, 1998) and depicted by the master narrative as being culturally inferior (Fanon, 1968). Unlike Blacks, groups that are assigned to non-White status may at times be granted access to the privileges of full or fuller status as a person, being identified as salvageable, teachable, or redeemable, as it benefits the master race (Snowden, 2015). The parameters of a White supremacist political system are the normalizing of the routine restriction of full personhood to Whites and the stratification of non-Whites, especially Blacks, to the lower social and economic rungs of society, despite citizenship status (Mills, 1998). How a White supremacist political system maintains these norms is ever changing. However, racial projects enacted by social, political, and economic institutions adapt how White supremacist ideologies and ontologies are refined according to the changing needs of the master race (Mills, 1998; Omi & Winant, 1994). White supremacy is largely unacknowledged as the political and ideological system that produces social and economic inequities (Mills, 1998) and sanctions the killing of unarmed Black men by law enforcement agents.

The devaluation of Black lives in the United States accomplished through political systems of slavery and apartheid (Jim Crow) in the past continues today. That Black lives do not matter today is evidenced by the jarring data chronicling hyper-incarceration (Alexander, 2010; Bonilla-Silva, 2014), unemployment (Bonilla-Silva, 2014), restricted access to quality housing (Bonilla-Silva, 2014; Frey, 2015), the failure of public education in low-income communities (Bonilla-Silva, 2014; Editorial Board, 2015; Schott Foundation Report, 2015), and health disparities (White, 2011). In addition, the passage of laws like "stand your ground" joined with policing strategies such as "broken windows," "stop and frisk," and "predictive policing" (Eligon & Williams, 2015) results in Black and Brown people being exposed to surveillance by police, vigilantes, and the general public.

Of all the state-sanctioned violence against Black people to uphold the supremacy of Whites in the United States, one stands out as an act meant to strike terror into the hearts of free Black people; that tool was lynching. This system of control was necessary after slavery to keep newly freed Blacks in their place within the racial hierarchy (Marable, 1983). Blacks faced a virtual reign of terror (Berry & Blassingame, 1982). Lynching involved castration and mutilation, and in some instances, shots were fired into the dead bodies of Black people. Between the years 1882 and 1964, "the archives at Tuskegee University documented that at least 3,445 African Americans were brutally lynched in the United States. The lynchings in this statistic included men, women, and children" (King, 2014, para. 1). Lynching of unarmed Black people has much in common with police killings of unarmed Black people.

Police killings of unarmed Black people and social work responses

In 1892, the lynching of a friend of Ida B. Wells was the precursor for her chronicling the suffering of hundreds of Black people impacted by the violent tyranny of lynching in the United States (Scheter, 2001). Wells became the spokesperson against lynching of her day as she found words to narrate the horror of lynching in a country that depended on newspapers and word of mouth for information dissemination (Scheter, 2001).

The truth of her words was affirmed when family members of victims isolated and alienated by their pain, agony, and disenfranchised grief reconnected with their own humanity as the stories of their loved ones were told to sympathetic audiences. Because Ida B. Wells dared to speak of the horrors, citizens outraged by the stories embraced the victims' families whose lives had been ripped apart by racially charged hatred. Even citizens paralyzed by fear of reprisals joined the cause to outlaw lynching of Black people in the United States (Scheter, 2001). History is replete with story after story of ordinary people transformed by extraordinary events into activists and framers of solutions to achieve social justice. This was partially the case in the fall of 2014 as activism fueled by the Black Lives Matter movement showed up on campuses of social work education programs across the United States.

In response to the fatal shooting of an unarmed Black teenager on August 9, 2014, by a White police officer in Ferguson, MO, and the failure of a grand jury to indict the police officer, social work education programs across the United States issued statements on police violence against Black civilians. The statements called on schools to host dialogues on race, to give curricula attention to the history of race and racism in the United States, and to participate in policy conversations about police officers' use of deadly force against unarmed Black people (UC Berkeley School of Social Welfare, 2014; NYU Silver School of Social Work, 2014; Portland State University, 2014; Simmons School of Social Work, 2014; Smith College School for Social Work, 2014; The Social Work Leadership Forum, 2014).

Whether the social work program had issued a statement or not, the wake of the shootings gave rise to a social justice movement, and members of the social work community who joined the protest brought their concerns to classrooms and other social work education settings. Students, staff, administrators, and faculty held different and strong emotionally charged points of view on the shootings of unarmed Black people by police officers (Harmon, 2015; Wong, 2015). The presence of these points of view in classrooms generated conversations that challenged the resolve and skills of the most able educators and practitioners. The tone of the conversations coupled with strong emotions defied quick fixes, and the moments of discomfort for all involved were protracted and painful both to participate in and to witness.

The urgent need to protest the police shootings of unarmed Black men was emboldened in New York City after a Staten Island grand jury failed to indict police officers responsible for the death of

Eric Garner, an unarmed Black man. The loss of Mr. Garner's life was difficult to reconcile given what was seen in the video and what the media portrayed as the facts in the case. Here was an unarmed Black man dead at the hands of police officers sworn to protect and defend the public. The killing of Mr. Garner occurred in a city where West African immigrant Amadou Diallo was another unarmed Black man killed by police officers, who fired their guns 41 times. One of the officers reloaded his weapon during the assault. New York City was also home to Sean Bell, killed November 25, 2006, on the eve of his wedding by police officers who fired 50 times at the unarmed man (McFadden, 2006).

While the outpouring of statements from social work education programs encouraged the authors, at the same time we questioned the motivation. In our experience as social work educators, social work programs are woefully lacking in content on race and racism (NASW, 2007, 2013). Our own work in HIV research, racial disproportionality in child welfare, the struggles of low-income and middle-class Black mothers raising sons in the United States, and the African American church has informed us that structural barriers directly related to racism severely constrain Black people's access to food, health care, housing, safety, education, and employment (Bell, 2013; Brown-Manning, 2013; Snowden, 2015). We also know from multiple sources (Crenshaw, Ocen, & Nanda, 2015; Morris, 2014; Schott Foundation for Public Education, 2015) that the well-being of Black people in the United States is compromised in profound ways. In fact, the Civil Rights Project at UCLA released a report in March 2014 indicating that New York City's public schools are the most segregated in the United States (Kuscera, 2014).

The fact that Black people in the United States are disproportionately represented on the low end of every indicator of human well-being is not new. Where is the promise that an outpouring of statements of solidarity from social work programs portends anything more than business as usual?

On our campus, what was different this time was student reaction to the grand juries' failure to indict. The students expressed great anger in the face of legal systems that held Black unarmed men responsible for their own deaths. With the slogan Black Lives Matter, students joined protesters to focus a critical light on police profiling and what is not taught in schools of social work.

In addition, in the statements of solidarity issued by social work programs, the call for dialogue on race and racism was clear. This affirmed our belief that social work education's use of the term *diversity* is representative of yet another attempt to find a term that provides cover for thorny content on the oppression of human well-being—namely, racism. Diversity joins a list of words used over the years in social work education to hold, neglect, and/or avoid content on the isms, particularly racism. Intolerance, multiculturalism, and cultural competence are examples of terms used over the years. This subterfuge has moved the conversations to this point where both students and social work programs are calling for content on race and racism. Social work has the challenge of walking its 100 years of talk about a commitment to social justice. We believe that "walking the talk" requires a focus on White supremacy and its offspring, race and racism.

Race, racism, and the false promise of diversity

The origin of a focus on diversity in social work education can be traced back to the Civil Rights Movement (Banks & McGee-Banks, 2010). As the Civil Rights movement shifted the nation's agenda to equal rights for Blacks and integration, Black social workers and allies from other marginalized groups seized the moment to challenge social work leaders and educators to radicalize professional social work education by developing and adopting inclusive paradigms for social work practice and community empowerment (Reid-Merritt, 2010).

However, radicalization of social work education has been a long time coming. Social activism, as Phillips-Sullivan (1999) observes, moved from the streets, and for civil rights, the battles moved to the courtrooms. Social work educators began a path to develop frameworks to support teaching about the complexity of human diversity and barriers to human growth and development. That journey led the profession to diversity in the late 1980s, and by the late 1990s cultural competence was the preferred concept (Leigh, 1998). Today, diversity, cultural competence, cultural humility, and race equity are all listed in NASW publications (NASW, 2015). Each frame, with the exception of race equity, fails to provide the conceptual tools for understanding race and racism as ideologies and the cumulative impact of the ideologies on Blacks/African Americans and other people of color at the individual, family, community, and societal levels. All frames fail to consider how race and racism are maintained by White supremacy

According to Phillips-Sullivan (1999) the concept of diversity began appearing with increasing frequency during the late 1970s when popular opinion and federal courts were signaling hostility toward the equality claims put forth by the Civil Rights Movement on behalf of Blacks and African Americans. Dr. King and the stalwarts of the Civil Rights Movement had embraced a philosophy that was based on the false premise that there was a large residue of Christian love in White America to which Blacks could appeal (Berry & Blassingame, 1982). This was not the case, and with the election of Richard Nixon in 1968, the possibility for Black equality emanating from Washington was no more (Marable, 1983).

The term diversity has no ties to principles of equality and justice (Phillips-Sullivan, 1999). In fact, Berry and Blassingame (1982) noted that unequal employment, housing, and educational opportunities remained beyond legal and political solutions once the Civil Rights Movement achieved access to public accommodations and voting rights. Mainstream civil rights advocacy groups embraced the framing of diversity, and a phalanx of professionals spread out across the country to deliver diversity training (Blueprint 2000; MELDI, n.d.; Phillips-Sullivan, 1999; Thomas, 1996; www.humanfacets.com).

Diversity has a rich literature, and this literature has much to teach us about how difficult it is to teach White people about race and racism (DiAngelo, 2011; Goodman, 2012: Miller & Garran, 2007). Subsuming race and racism content under the heading diversity does not make the content any less onerous to deliver. Why not call a thing what a thing is, and at the very least we will not have to change the term used for oppression content every so many years because there is a new term that is more palatable.

The roles played by race and racism in the police killings of unarmed Black people cannot be understood in a diversity framework. Legislatures pass laws authorizing heightened scrutiny of people for whom police have reason to suspect criminal behavior. The historical legacy of White supremacy and the denigration of Blacks as well as cultural racism (Oliver, 2001) have resulted in a metanarrative of Black people as "less than."

In 2012, news stories broke about a program to screen travellers at the nations' airports to spot tell-tale mannerisms of potential terrorists. Boston's Logan Airport was chosen to pilot the program. More than 30 federal officers said the operation had become a magnet for racial profiling, targeting not only Middle Easterners but also Blacks, Hispanics, and other racial groups (Schmidt & Lichtblau, 2012). Why were Blacks and Hispanics targeted? The officers said, "managers' demands for high numbers of stops, searches and criminal referrals had led co-workers to target minorities in the belief that those stops were more likely to yield drugs, outstanding arrest warrants or immigration problems" (Schmidt & Lichtblau, 2012, para. 4).

We believe that the Logan Airport experience is an example of how a legacy of misinformation and denigration results in racial profiling that is sanctioned at an institutional/structural level. Omi and Winant (1994, p. 54) ask the question, "What is race?" To answer this question, the United States has tried many ways, from Supreme Court justices deciding whether or not a Japanese American was White, to justices asking people to roll up their sleeves to see the color of their skin (Rodeiger, 2005).

People determine the meaning of race each and every day in interactions with each other (Omi & Winant, 1994). Some of the interactions involve Black people in search of housing or employment (Wise, 2015). In other instances, race is determined (enacted) when a person visits a health care provider or a car dealership. Over and over, in ways too numerous to be conscious of, humans enact race.

Research shows that our enactment of race and other isms can be measured (Benaji & Greenwald, 2013). Under the best of circumstances, the research finds that people make choices that are consistent with their conscious beliefs about a just society. However, under stress, in life or death situations, or when people are exhausted, something else can happen. That something else could result in a tirade of expletives at a driver who cuts in front of a motorist, and it can also result in racial profiling as attested to by the federal officers at Logan Airport. Cognitive psychologists (Benaji & Greenwald, 2013) have covered a great deal of ground in the past 30 years studying how human beings are susceptible to unconscious bias. Given the history of this country's racial hierarchy that is still visible in statistics chronicling the well-being of Black and Brown people, it is fair to say that the United States still has racial inequities. One of those inequities is found in the police killings of unarmed Black people.

Racism has not remained the same over the past 400 years in terms of how it manifests at the personal level and is sanctioned at the structural and institutional levels (Omi & Winant, 1994). The virulent strain racism that came to the forefront after the first Reconstruction was the brainchild of populists who gained political power in the South (Berry & Blassingame, 1982). According to Vann Woodard (1974), federal protection was removed by northern elites because of their interests in pursuing their own subjugation of people of color in the Philippines. In this instance, Blacks were sacrificed to live in a system of racial apartheid from the end of the first Reconstruction until 1954.

The content on race and racism is essential for social work practice in the United States of America. It is especially essential at a time when in the time period from January to August 2015, 24 unarmed Black men have been killed by police officers in the United States (Somashekhar, Lowery, Alexander, Kindy, & Tate, 2015). At the very least, social workers need a way to find their own voices about what contributes to the alarming statistics of human suffering among Black people in the United States. There is no hierarchy of oppression, and the United States has a unique, horrific history of White supremacy that resulted in genocide for First Nations people and 350 years of slavery and apartheid for Black people. Social workers can and must understand race and racism, and social work education programs can and must teach this content.

Conclusion

The police killings of unarmed Black people in the United States has brought to the forefront the long simmering divide between two nations within this one nation—one Black and one White. This divide shows up in social work programs every day. Service users and agencies experience the divide also. Frontline workers and supervisors are mostly Black, African American, and/or people of color, while top executives are mostly White. These data are observed, and people make the data mean something.

The violence visited upon human beings by police, unproductive school settings, poor quality housing, unhealthy food, incarceration, intimate partner violence, domestic violence, mental illness, and immigration status exact a heavy toll on human functioning and well-being. There are rich traditions of resisting and organizing against oppression. This is why we included the brief story of Ida B. Wells in the article. Social workers need stories like Ida's and the stories of all of the other unsung champions of social justice who have faced oppression and transformed spaces of despair into bright possibilities for healthy growth and development.

References

Alexander, M. (2010). *The new Jim Crow: Mass incarceration in the age of colorblindness.* New York, NY: New Press.

Banks, J. A., & McGee-Banks, C. A. (Eds.) (2010). *Multicultural education: Issues and Perspectives.* Hoboken, NJ: John Wiley & Sons.

Barnum, C., & Perfetti, R. L. (2010). Race-sensitive choices by police officers in traffic encounters. *Police Quarterly, XX*(X), 1–30.

Bell, B. (2013). Uprooting racism in the food system: African Americans organize. *Huffington Post.* Retrieved from http://www.huffingtonpost.com/beverly-bell/uprooting-racism-in-the-f_b_2853804.html

Bell, D. (1992). *Faces at the bottom of the well: The permanence of racism.* New York, NY: Basic Books.

Benaji, M. R., & Greenwald, A. G. (2013). *Blind spot: Hidden biases of good people.* New York, NY: Delacorte Press.

Berry, M. F., & Blassingame, J. W. (1982). *Long memory: The Black experience in America.* New York, NY: Oxford University Press.

Bonilla-Silva, E. (2014). *Racism without racists.* Lanham, MD: Rowman & Littlefield.

Brown-Manning, R. (2013). *We don't give birth to thugs; we give birth to children: The emotional journeys of African-American mothers raising sons under American racism* (Unpublished doctoral dissertation). CUNY Graduate Center, New York, NY.

Crenshaw, K. W., Ocen, P., & Nanda, J. (2015). *Black girls matter: Pushed out, overpoliced and underprotected.* African American Policy Forum at the Center for Intersectionality and Social Policy Studies. Retrieved from http://www.law.columbia.edu/null/download?&exclusive=filemgr.download&file_id=613546

DiAngelo, R. (2011). *What does it mean to be White? Developing White racial literacy.* New York, NY: Peter Lang.

Editorial Board. (2015). *Racial isolation in public schools. New York Times,* January 9. Retrieved from http://www.nytimes.com/2015/01/10/opinion/racial-isolation-in-public-schools.html?_r=0

Eligon, J., & Williams, T. (2015). *Police program aims to pinpoint those most likely to commit crimes. New York Times,* September 24. Retrieved from http://www.nytimes.com/2015/01/10/opinion/racial-isolation-in-public-schools.html?_r=0

Fanon, F. (1968). *Wretched of the Earth.* New York, NY: Grove Press.

Frey, W. H. (2015). *Diversity explosion: How new racial demographics are remaking America.* Washington, DC: Brookings Institute Press.

Gilborn, D. (2005). Education policy as an act of White supremacy: Whiteness, critical race theory, and education reform. *Journal of Education Policy, 20*(4), 485–505. 10.1080/02680930500132346

Goodman, D. (2012). *Promoting diversity and social justice: Educating people from privileged groups* (2nd ed.). New York, NY: Routledge.

Harmon, D. K. (2015). Black Lives Matter: What a social work educator's students have to say. *The New Social Worker.* Retrieved from http://www.socialworker.com/extras/social-work-month-2015/black-lives-matter-what-social-work-educators-students-have-to-say/

King, S. (2014). *Five ugly and uncanny parallels between lynchings and police killings America. Daily Kos,* November 13. Retrieved from http://www.dailykos.com/story/2014/11/13/1344670/-5-ugly-and-uncanny-parallels-between-lynchings-and-police-killings-in-America

Kuscera, J. (2014). *New York state's extreme school segregation: Inequality, inaction and a damaged future.* The Civil Rights Project/Proyecto Derrechos Civile at University of California Los Angeles. Retrieved from http://civilrightsproject.ucla.edu/research/k-12-education/integration-and-diversity/ny-norflet-report-placeholder

Leign, J. W. (1998) *Communicating for cultural competence.* Boston, MA: Allyn & Bacon.

Marable, M. (1983). *How capitalism underdeveloped black America.* Boston, MA: South End Press.

McFadden, R. D. (2006). *Police kill man after a Queens bachelor party. New York Times,* November 26. Retrieved from http://www.nytimes.com/2006/11/26/nyregion/26cops.html?pagewanted=all&_r=0

MELDI. (n.d.) *Diversity and race relations consultants.* Retrieved from http://meldi.snre.umich.edu/diversityinitiative/Diversity+and+Race+Relations+Consultants?page=1

Miller, J., & Garran, A. M. (2007). *Racism in the United States: Implications for the helping professions.* Belmont, CA: Brooks/Cole.

Mills, C. W. (1998). *Blackness visible: Essays on philosophy and race.* Ithaca, NY: Cornell University Press.

Morris, M. W. (2014). *Black stats: African Americans by the numbers in the twenty-first century.* New York, NY: New Press.

NASW. (2007). *Racism the social work profession: A call to action.* NASW, The President's Initiative Weaving the Fabrics of Diversity. Retrieved from https://www.socialworkers.org/diversity/institutionalracism.pdf

NASW. (2013). *Achieving racial equity: Action Brief—Anti-Racist Alliance.* Retrieved from http://www.antiracistalliance.com/SWPIRacialEquityBrief.pdf

NASW. (2015). *New standards and indicators of cultural competence in social work practice.* Retrieved from www.nasw.org

New York University Silver School of Social Work. (2014). *Statement on Eric Garner and Michael Brown and systematic, structural injustice in American society.* Retrieved from http://socialwork.nyu.edu/news/2014/12/15/nyu-silver-statement-on-eric-garner-and-michael-brown-and-systematic-structural-injustice-in-american-society.html

Novak, K. J., & Chamlin, M. B. (2008). Racial threat, suspicion, and police behavior. *Crime & Delinquency, XX*(X), 1–25.

Oliver, W. (2001). Cultural racism and structural violence: Implications for African Americans. *Journal of Human Behavior in the Social Environment, 4*(2–3), 1–26. 10.1300/J137v04n02_01

Omi, M., & Winant, H. (1994). *Racial formation in the United States: From the 1960s to the 1990s*. New York, NY: Routledge.

Phillips-Sullivan, B. (1999). The gift of Hopwood: Diversity and the fife and drum march back to the nineteenth century. *Georgia Law Review, 31*, 291–334

Portland State University School of Social Work. (2014). *Ferguson: We stand with you*. http://www.cswe.org/File.aspx?id=78357

Reid-Merritt, P. (2010). *Righteous self determination: The Black social work movement in America*. Baltimore, MD: Imprint Editions.

Roediger, D. R. (2005). *Working toward whiteness: How America's immigrants became white*. New York, NY: Basic Books.

Scheter, P. A. (2001). *Ida B. Wells-Barnett & American reform 1880–1930*. Chapel Hill, NC: University of North Carolina Press.

Schmidt, M., & Lichtblau, E. (2012). *Racial profiling rife at airport, U. S. officers say. New York Times*, August 8. Retrieved from http://www.nytimes.com/2012/08/12/us/racial-profiling-at-boston-airport-officials-say.html

Schott Foundation for Public Education. (2015). *Black Lives Matter: The Schott 50 state report on public education and black males*. Retrieved from http://www.schottfoundation.org/publications-reports/

Simmons School of Social Work. (2014). *Ferguson: We stand with you.Our anti-racism commitment*. Retrieved from http://www.cswe.org/File.aspx?id=77861

Smedley, A., & Smedley, B. D. (2005). Race as biology is fiction, racism as a social problem is real: Anthropological and historical perspectives on the social construction of race. *American Psychologist, 60*(1), 16–26. 10.1037/0003-066X.60.1.16

Smith College School for Social Work. (2014). *Our anti-racism commitment: Understanding Ferguson, Missouri*. Retrieved from http://www.smith.edu/ssw/docs/fergusonstatement.pdf

Snowden, F. (2015). *What condoms can't cover: Do structural factors predispose Black, African Americans, and Latina/o adults in Harlem and the South Bronx to engaging in HIV sex risk behavior?* (Unpublished doctoral dissertation). City University Graduate Center, New York, NY.

Social Work Leadership Forum. (2014). *A message from the Social Work Leadership Forum*. Retrieved from http://secure.sswr.org/a-message-from-the-social-work-leadership-forum/

Somashekhar, S., Lowery, W., Alexander, K. L., Kindy, K., & Tate, J. (2015). *Black & Unarmed. Washington Post*, August 8. Retrieved from http://www.washingtonpost.com/sf/national/2015/08/08/black-and-unarmed/

Thomas, R. (1996). *Redefining diversity*. New York, NY: Amacom.

Tillyer, R., & Engel, R. S. (2013). The impact of drivers' race, gender, and age during traffic stops: Assessing interaction terms and the social conditioning model. *Crime & Delinquency, 59*(3), 369–395. 10.1177/0011128710389583

UC Berkeley School of Social Work. (2014). *Dean's message on police violence against Black citizens*. Retrieved from http://www.naddssw.org/pages/wp-content/uploads/2014/12/Berkeley-Social-Welfare-statement.pdf

Vann Woodard, C. (1974). *The strange career of Jim Crow* (3rd ed.). New York, NY: Oxford University Press.

Warren, P. Y., & Tomaskovic-Devey, D. (2009). Racial profiling and searches: Did the politics of racial profiling change police behavior? *Criminology & Public Policy, 8*(2), 343–369. 10.1111/cpp.2009.8.issue-2

White, A. A. (2011). *Seeing patients: Unconscious bias in health care*. Cambridge, MA: Harvard University Press.

Wise, T. (2015). *Under the affluence: Shaming the poor, praising the rich, and sacrificing the future of America*. San Francisco, CA: City Light Publishers.

Wong, J. C. (2015). Students at UC Berkeley turn the tables on a racist professor. *The Bold Italic*. Retrieved from http://www.thebolditalic.com/articles/6983-students-at-uc-berkeley-turn-the-tables-on-a-racist-professor

Zinn, H. (2001). *A people's history of the United States: 1492–present*. New York, NY: Harper Collins.

Parenting while powerless: Consequences of "the talk"

Tracy R. Whitaker and Cudore L. Snell

School of Social Work, Howard University, Washington, DC, USA

ABSTRACT

Historically, African American parents have struggled to negotiate the tensions related to raising their children in a hostile society. The recent and tragic events involving the murders of unarmed African American boys and men by police officers, enraged motorists, and vigilante neighbors have sparked a resurgence in discussion and activism related to these historic tensions. In addition to protests and a heightened level of public discourse, there is also new emphasis on African American parents having "the Talk" with their children, particularly their sons. "The Talk" represents the "surviving interactions with police or other members of authority" discussion and is largely considered an essential rite of passage in African American homes. And, although the pretext for "the Talk" is providing children with the rule book for survival from an authoritative source, the subtext for this conversation is the inherent powerlessness of African American parents and their *inability to protect* their children. Despite its necessity, "the Talk" has an ugly underside that also manifests in disruptions to child development, families, and the larger community. These disruptions are particularly critical in an allegedly postracial environment.

Historically, African American parents have struggled to negotiate the tensions related to raising their children in a racially hostile society. Generations of African American parents have consistently worked to make life better for subsequent generations. "Making life better" generally meant that each succeeding generation would experience less racial hostility, exclusion, and violence than the previous generation. African Americans have consistently pursued social, economic, and racial justice, from slavery through Jim Crow to the Civil Rights era. The Civil Rights era paved the road for racial integration in American and culminated in the election of the first African American president. The election of President Barack Obama seemed a fitting end to centuries of a racially divided country, and many Americans assumed that the United States was now in a postracial climate (Burnett, 2012; Fine & Johnson, 2013). However, within the past five years, and ironically, during President Obama's terms, the high-profile and tragic events involving the murders of unarmed African American boys and men by police officers, enraged motorists, and vigilante neighbors have sparked a resurgence in discussion and activism related to these historic tensions. *Florida, Ferguson, Staten Island, Cleveland,* and *Baltimore* have become one-word geographic codes for the unjustified murders of unarmed African American boys and men and the aftermath that has followed. In addition, the names Trayvon Martin, Michael Brown, Eric Garner, Tamir Rice, Jordan Dunn, and Freddie Gray are part of ever-growing list of African American men and boys whose lives seemingly had no value (Person, 2013).

The effects of racism on African American family structure have been debated for decades. What has been consistently true, particularly for African American parents, however, it that the same rules that apply to White children do not apply to their children (Burnett, 2012; Cooper, 2014; Fine &

Johnson, 2013; Jamieson, 2014). These different rules are often unspoken but largely understood in the African American community. The most obvious unstated concern is that African American children will have different consequences for the same behavior. However, the most painful, yet unstated fear, is that African American parents may not have the ability or the power to protect their children from these consequences (Amber, 2013).

Nonetheless, the task is left to African American parents to prepare their children to navigate an unfair and potentially deadly racial environment. This preparation, known as "racial socialization," is a combination of conversations and practices that parents hope will prepare their children to live in environments where they are not always welcomed and seldom cherished (Burt, Simons, & Gibbons, 2012; Peck, Brodish, Malanchuk, Banerjee, & Eccles, 2014; Thomas & Blackmon, 2015). Parental racial socialization can include hypervigilant parenting, excessive discipline and conversations both about racial pride and discrimination (Burt, Simons, & Gibbons, 2012; Grollman, 2012; Julian, McKenry, & McKelvey, 1994).

The combination of these recent events and a heightened sense of powerlessness in the African American community has sparked renewed discussion and emphasis on African American parents engaging in perhaps one of the most counterintuitive, painful, and heart-wrenching aspects of racial socialization, "the Talk" (Burnett, 2012; Hanley, 2012; Williams, 2014). This conversation has been described as "nausea-inducing," "shaming," and "universally uncomfortable" but is largely considered an essential rite of passage in African American homes and is a cultural legacy that has been practiced for generations (Burnett, 2012; Canedy, 2013; Thomas, 2013). "The Talk" is about preparing young African American children, particularly boys, to survive interactions with police or other members of authority. The content of this conversation is remarkably consistent and is passed down from generation to generation like a grandmother's recipe for cornbread (Burnett, 2012; Canedy, 2013; Murray, 2014; Person, 2013; Thomas, 2013; Williams, 2014). It is a discussion about where to put hands and eyes, how to manage the tenor of one's tone, what not to wear, and generally how to make sure that African American children do not frighten armed police officers into shooting and perhaps killing them (Burnett, 2012; Canedy, 2013; Murray, 2014; Person, 2013; Thomas, 2013; Williams, 2014). "The Talk" is about racial profiling and diffusing negative perceptions and stereotypes to avoid being hurt or killed by police during routine activities, such as driving or walking down the street (Fine & Johnson, 2013; Hanley, 2012).

Contrary to popular thought, "the Talk" is not about avoiding criminal behavior; rather, it is about avoiding the *perception* of criminal behavior. Unlike other important parent-child conversations, "the Talk" is not about helping the child take responsibility for the child's own actions; rather it is about preparing a child to take responsibility for the actions of the adults he may encounter (Burnett, 2012; O'Neal, 2015; Williams, 2014) It is the racial equivalent of a conversation in which young girls are told how to not to be victims of rape, as if the outcome of an encounter with a would-be rapist lies squarely in their female hands.

The time for "the Talk" generally occurs at the onset of adolescence, or in the space when Black boys morph into "being seen as suspect instead of sweet" (Canedy, 2013). And although many African American parents had hoped that in the new millennium this conversation would no longer be necessary (Thomas, 2013); in the jarring reality of the times in which we live, avoiding "the Talk" with African American children can be considered an abdication of parental responsibility and an act of negligence that leaves these children more vulnerable and subject to harm (Burt et al., 2012; O'Neal, 2015; Peck et al., 2014; Thomas & Blackmon, 2015; Williams, 2014).

Despite its necessity, this particular conversation is shaming for the parents and the child, because it solidifies the powerlessness of the parents and their inability to protect their child from forces over which neither have control (Amber, 2013). These parents swallow their pride in a way that "white fathers have never felt, because it has not occurred to them collectively that their sons could land in serious trouble for a look or a tone" (Burnett, 2012). Even the White mayor of New York City, Bill De Blasio, discussed the need to prepare his biracial son to handle encounters with the police, acknowledging, "it's different for a white child" (Jamieson, 2014). This conversation is rooted in a very deep and real parental fear that every time an African American boy leaves his home, he may not come home alive (Sultan, 2014). Every time this child leaves home, someone may see him as dangerous and interact with him in a way that treats his life as one without value (Person, 2013). And therein lies the most damning part of "The Talk." Parents cannot get through this conversation without acknowledging their own powerlessness and indicting their own impotence at creating a better, safer world for their children.

The roots of this conversation run deep, dating back to the Emancipation Proclamation, when newly freed slaves had to prepare for run-ins with former slave owners against whom they were completely powerless, despite their status as free persons (Burnett, 2012). Newly freed parents, like their enslaved counterparts, had no legal standing upon which they could challenge the mistreatment of their children. Therefore, they attempted to protect their children by making sure they did not come to the negative attention of those in power.

Even today, African American parents routinely attempt the nearly impossible task of raising empowered children with healthy self-esteem who are free to express themselves and explore the world around them, while simultaneously keeping a noose-like rein on their movements, attitudes, and behaviors. This impossible dance manifests most clearly in the differences between the disciplinary practices of African American and White parents (Cooper, 2014; Julian et al., 1994). These differences are rooted in hypervigilant protectionism on the part of African American parents (Grollman, 2012; Spano, Rivera, & Bolland, 2011). Their love for their children, while no less real or hearty than White parental love, is often shrouded in fear and powerlessness. Too many African American adults were raised with the thoughts of "I will kill you, before I let them hurt you" and continue these disciplinary patterns with their own children (Coates, 2015; Cooper, 2014; Patton, 2015).

This sentiment is reminiscent of Margaret Garner's protective love that is fictionalized in Toni Morrison's Pulitzer Prize–winning novel *Beloved* (1987). Margaret Garner chose to kill her children rather than permit them to grow up in slavery. Filicide is not usually considered an expression of love; however, in Ms. Garner's case, it was a demonstration of a love that was both fierce and powerful. But it was a distorted form of love, because she lacked the ability to choose from a range of good choices for her children. Ms. Garner did not have the option to choose a life of freedom or a life of slavery for her children; she had only the choice of a life in slavery or death. Both of these choices are painful, hard, and unfair gauges of love.

Yet, even into the second decade of the 21st century, African American adults may romanticize and fondly reminisce over harsh disciplinary practices they received as children, believing that these practices ultimately kept them from harm and bad decisions (Coates, 2015; Cooper, 2014; Patton, 2015). That these adults celebrate that they were beaten within the context of love, rather than hate—rather than celebrating that they were not beaten at all—is evidence of the ongoing legacy of slavery.

This tragic legacy revisits the African American community often, most recently in the celebration of a Baltimore mother who humiliated and beat her teenage son when she discovered him participating in the April 2015 uprising in that city (Patton, 2015). She beat him about his head and shoulders on a public street but was not accused of child abuse, but rather, hailed as "mother of the year" on top media outlets such as CNN (Graham, 2015). She was being celebrated for her fierce showing of "slave love" and unwittingly heralded for her powerlessness over a system that would harshly victimize her son (Patton, 2015).

The actions of this mother in Baltimore sparked a fierce debate in the African American community. However, in contrast, there was almost unanimous agreement about her motivations. Most people agreed that they witnessed a mother fueled by fear and love, attempting to save her son from more dire consequences than she could mete out. Whereas there was agreement on the display of love and strength, there was no clear agreement on the display of power. Some would argue that this mother showed power over her son. But an adult's ability to control a child is not true power. Rather, power is the ability to successfully challenge something potentially larger than oneself.

Unfortunately, this mother's videotaped reaction to her son is actually a testament to her powerlessness. Had she possessed the power to challenge or change a system that would criminalize her son based on his appearance, and not his behavior, she would not have needed to rescue her son in the midst of a riot (Patton, 2015). Had she had the power to beat back inequality and injustice, she would not have needed to beat her son, because he would have already been safe.

In general, although "the Talk" and other aspects of racial socialization are primarily viewed as protective factors within the African American community, there are downsides to these practices. Although strict disciplinary practices are often balanced with positive support and communication, racial socialization has also been linked to depression in African American young adults (Granberg et al., 2012; Julian et al., 1994). Like harsh disciplinary practices, 'the Talk" too, has consequences that are often unstated and undocumented. For most children, parents are their first and last line of defense. Parents tell a child who he is, demonstrate how he is to be treated, and affirm his worth and value in the family and ultimately the larger society. However, this discussion renders the parent as the agent of the oppressor (O'Neal, 2015). For, in this case, the parent tells the child that something is amiss with the child's role in society, that he is only not quite equal but inferior, and that he does not warrant the full protection of the law. The parent becomes the one who "must strip the innocence from my son forever" (O'Neal, 2015).

That "the Talk" occurs at the developmental state of adolescence also has ramifications for a child's development. Adolescence is a particularly turbulent time in the life cycle and racism exacerbates the turbulence. Erikson (1959) posited that the main quest in life is the development of individual identity. In his book *Identity: Youth and Crisis*, Erikson (1968) theorized that identity formation is the critical task of adolescence, which takes place "in the core of the individual and yet also in the core of his communal culture" (p. 22). In the context of responding to the question "Who am I?" the young person, in order to experience wholeness, must feel congruence between that which he perceives himself to be and that which he perceives others to see in him (Erikson, 1968). According to Erikson, during the fifth psychosocial crisis (adolescence, from about 13 or 14 to about 20) the child, now an adolescent, learns how to answer satisfactorily and happily the question of "Who am I?" But how does an African American child "happily" answer that question within the context of a society that vilifies his existence?

Erikson believes that during successful early adolescence, mature time perspective is developed; the young person acquires self-certainty as opposed to self-consciousness and self-doubt. He comes to experiment with different—usually constructive—roles rather than adopting a "negative identity" (such as delinquency). He actually anticipates achievement, and achieves, rather than being "paralyzed" by feelings of inferiority or by an inadequate time perspective. In later adolescence, clear sexual identity—manhood or womanhood—is established. The adolescent seeks leadership (someone to inspire him), and gradually develops a set of ideals (socially congruent and desirable, in the case of the successful adolescent). Erikson believes that, in our culture, adolescence affords a "psychosocial moratorium," particularly for middle- and upper-class American children. They do not yet have to "play for keeps," but can experiment, trying various roles, and thus hopefully find the one most suitable for them.

However, for too many African American males, adolescence is drastically truncated by racism (Schiele, 1998). In fact, the adolescent development "script" for young African American males is much different from those of their White counterparts as evidenced by not only the recent developments in our country but also the staggering statistics surrounding quality of life indicators for these young men. These categories include high rates of being victims and perpetrators of homicides (Fox & Swatt, 2008), declining rates for life expectancy (Anderson, 2006), and growing rates of suicide (Poussaint & Alexander, 2000). The rates of incarceration, conviction, and arrest are the highest for African American males compared to every other demographic group in the nation (Gilgoff, 2007). These young men are in fact "playing for keeps," without societal safety nets, just the attempts of their parents to keep them alive.

Recent studies of adolescent brain development raise more questions about the usefulness of "the Talk" (Blakemore & Choudhury, 2006; NIMH, 2011). Adolescents' brains are not as developed as those of adults, making adolescents more likely to engage in impulsive, risky behavior (Blakemore &

Choudhury, 2006; NIMH, 2011). African American parents having "the Talk" must put aside adolescent development issues and, instead, *insist* that their children are capable of level of control and rational decision making that may actual be beyond their developmental grasp. In the words of one parent,

> I don't have the words that will give him the judgment and restraint of a 40-year old man when he's in the seventh grade. Not even if his life depends on it. I don't have the words to quell his anger if he feels like he's being treated unfairly, and anger is called for. Most of us can even stop ourselves from getting mad when somebody cuts us off at the intersection. It is monstrous to expect preternatural calm from a teen in order that he not get shot. (O'Neal, 2015, p. C1)

This dialogue has other consequences as well. Most parents anticipate that their child's reaction to "the Talk" will be hurt (O'Neal, 2015: Simmons, 2014):

> One day I'll sit my beautiful brown babies down and tell them the awful, ugly truth about this land of the free and home of the brave. And I'll watch as tears well up in their eyes and listen as they fight to breathe. And then I'll have to kiss them up, dry their faces, and send them off into the same world I've warned them of. The same society that tells them in equal parts you can have anything your work for as long as you don't intimidate or threaten or scare anyone simply by being you. Simply by breathing. (Simmons, 2014)

Yet what is not anticipated is that deep anger may manifest instead of hurt. The predisposition to negatively judge African American children, not on their actions, but based on stereotyped perceptions of violence, reinforces the idea that these children do not belong, that they are neither welcomed, protected, nor inherently valuable in the country in which they are citizens (Amber, 2013; Fine & Johnson, 2013; O'Neal, 2015; Person, 2013). In addition to hurt and feelings of rejection, other reactions to "the Talk" may include a reluctance to participate in civil society or an apparent disinterest in and lack of investment in societal outcomes. These feelings may turn inward and then be expressed externally through protests, riots, violent confrontations and lack of political participation. Yet, whenever riots occur, the first question asked is, "why do they burn down their own neighborhoods?" Because the neighborhoods, the streets, the stores, are not their "own." If these children have been told that they do not have an equal right of protection in this country, is it unreasonable for them to believe they also do not equally share in the ownership of the communities in which they live? In fact, might not "the Talk" be the first step toward placing the hurled brick in a youngster's hand?

The current generation of African American children may be particularly disadvantaged because, for them, "the Talk" has lacked an ongoing context of racism. Rather than identifying and acknowledging racism throughout their lives, this generation and their parents have lived and believed in a postracial society. Simply put, unlike their grandparents and parents, young millennials and generation Xers do not have similar experiences with racism. The experiences of African American males especially contradict with those of their grandparents and parents. They have grown up in a more diverse society, one of integration and free movement, thus nullifying the progress and understanding of their parents' realities. They were prepared for neither the racially infused circumstances nor conversations that have become so prevalent (Sen, 2015; Toppo, 2014). However, unfortunately, this new generation of African American youth—the generation that has grown up largely ignoring color and with an African American president—must now confront the same realities of generations before them. They too must learn, with the complicity of African American parents, their precarious place in the larger society.

References

Amber, J. (2013, July 29). The talk: How parents raising black boys try to keep their sons safe. *Time*. Retrieved from http://content.time.com/time/magazine/article/0,9171,2147710,00.html

Anderson, J. L. (2006). An evaluation of African-American adolescent health status with gender comparison. *California Journal of Health Promotion*, *4*(2), 168–174.

Blakemore, S.-J., & Choudhury, S. (2006). Development of the adolescent brain: Implications for executive function and social cognition. *Journal of Child Psychology and Psychiatry*, *47*(3/4), 296–312. doi:10.1111/j.1469-7610.2006.01611.x

Burnett, J. (2012, April 7). After Travyon Martin, it's time for 'the talk'. *Boston.com*. Retrieved from http://www.boston.com/news/local/massachusetts/articles/2012/04/07/in_light_of_trayvon_martin_case_black_fathers_in_boston_are_scrambling_to_have_safety_talk_with_sons/

Burt, C. H., Simons, R. L., & Gibbons, F. X. (2012). Racial discrimination, ethnic-racial socialization and crime: A micro-sociological model of risk and resilience. *American Sociological Review*, *77*, 648–677. doi:10.1177/0003122412448648

Canedy, D. (2013, December 13). The talk: After Ferguson, a shaded conversation about race. *New York Times*. Retrieved from http://www.nytimes.com/2014/12/14/sunday-review/dana-canedy-the-talk-after-ferguson-a-shaded-conversation-about-race.html?_r=0

Coates, T. (2015, July 4). Letter to my son. *The Atlantic*. Retrieved from http://www.theatlantic.com/politics/archive/2015/07/tanehisi-coates-between-the-world-and-me/397619/

Cooper, B. (2014, September 16). The racial parenting divide: What Adrian Peterson reveals about black vs. white child-rearing. *Salon*. Retrieved from http://www.salon.com/2014/09/16/the_racial_parenting_divide_what_adrian_peterson_reveals_about_black_and_white_child_rearing/

Erikson, E. (1959). *Identity and the life cycle*. New York, NY: Norton.

Erikson, E. (1968). *Identity: Youth and crisis*. New York, NY: Norton.

Fine, M. G., & Johnson, F. L. (2013, December 10). When white parents have 'the talk' with black sons. *Huffington Post*. Retrieved from http://www.huffingtonpost.com/marlene-g-fine/when-white-parents-have-the-talk-with-black-sons_b_4386310.html

Fox, J., & Swatt, M. (2008). *The recent surge in homicides involving young Black males and guns: Time to reinvest in prevention and crime control*. Boston, MA: Northeastern University.

Gilgoff, J. (2007). *Boyz 2 Men: Responsible empowerment for inner-city adolescent males*. Retrieved from http://www.niost.org

Graham, T. (2015, April 29). 'Mother of the Year': Our kids don't need another label. *Anderson Cooper 360*. (A. Cooper, Interviewer) CNN.

Granberg, E. M., Edmond, E. B., Simons, R. L., Gibbons, F. X., & Man-Kit, L. (2012). The association between racial socialization and depression: Testing direct and buffering associations in a longitudinal cohort of African American young adults. *Society and Mental Health*, *2*, 207–225. doi:10.1177/2156869312451152

Grollman, E. A. (2012, March 15). Reflections on the murder of Trayvon Martin: Stereotypes, hypervigiliance & state-sponsored racism. *EGrollman*. Retrieved from http://egrollman.com/2012/03/15/trayvon-martin/

Hanley, D. (2012, May). Trayvon Martin and the 'The Talk' no American child should have to hear. *Washington Report on Middle East Affairs*. Retrieved from http://www.wrmea.org/2012-may/trayvon-martin-and-the-talk-no-american-child-should-have-to-hear.html

Jamieson, D. (2014, December 7). Bill de Blasio explains why his son needs to be careful around cops. *Huffington Post*. Retrieved from http://www.huffingtonpost.com/2014/12/07/bill-de-blasio-son_n_6283774.html

Julian, T. W., McKenry, P. C., & McKelvey, M. W. (1994). Cultural variations in parenting: Perceptions of Caucasian, African-American, Hispanic and Asian-American parents. *Family Relations*, *43*, 30–37. doi:10.2307/585139

Morrison, T. (1987). *Beloved*. New York, NY: Knopf.

Murray, R. (2014, December 8). The conversation black parents have with their kids about cops. *ABC News*. Retrieved from http://abcnews.go.com/US/conversation-black-parents-kids-cops/story?id=27446833

NIMH. (2011, January). *The teen brain: Still under construction*. Retrieved from http://www.nimh.nih.gov/health/publications/the-teen-brain-still-under-construction/index.shtml

O'Neal, L. (2015, January 15). On King holiday, second thoughts about 'The Talk'. *Washington Post*, p. C1.

Patton, S. (2015, April 29). Why is America celebrating the beating of a black child? *The Washington Post*. Retrieved from https://www.washingtonpost.com/posteverything/wp/2015/04/29/why-is-america-celebrating-the-beating-of-a-black-child/

Peck, S. C., Brodish, A. B., Malanchuk, O., Banerjee, M., & Eccles, J. S. (2014, July). Racial/ethnic socialization and identity development in black families: The role of parent and youth reports. *Developmental Psychology*, *50*, 1897–1909. doi:10.1037/a0036800

Person, D. (2013, July 14). Black parents fret over what to tell sons. *USA Today*. Retrieved from http://www.usatoday.com/story/opinion/2013/07/14/david-person-on-black-parents-and-sons/2516381/

Poussaint, A., & Alexander, A. (2000). *Lay my burden down: Unraveling suicide and the mental health crisis among African-Americans*. Boston, MA: Beacon.

Schiele, J. (1998). Cultural alignment, African American male youths, and violent crime. *Journal of Human Behavior in the Social Environment*, *1*(2–3), 165–181. doi:10.1300/J137v01n02_10

Sen, R. (2015, March 25). Millennials don't know how to talk about race, and that's a problem. *PBS*. Retrieved from http://www.pbs.org/newshour/updates/redefining-racism-systemic-unconscious-hidden/

Simmons, S. (2014, December 4). On being breathless. *Huffington Post*. Retrieved from http://www.huffingtonpost.com/safiya-jafari-simmons/on-being-breathless_b_6266256.html

Spano, R., Rivera, C., & Bolland, J. M. (2011, March). Does parenting shield youth from exposure to violence during adolescence? A 5-year longitudinal test in a high-poverty sample of minority youth. *Journal of Interpersonal Violence*, *26*, 930–949. doi:10.1177/0886260510365873

Sultan, A. (2014, September 29). Parents talk back: Black moms tell white moms about the race talk. *U Express*. Retrieved from http://www.uexpress.com/parents-talk-back/2014/9/29/black-moms-tell-white-moms-about

Thomas, A. J., & Blackmon, S. M. (2015, February). The influence of the Trayvon Martin shooting on racial socialization practices of African American parents. *Journal of Black Psychology*, *41*, 75–89. doi:10.1177/0095798414563610

Thomas, R. (2013, July 24). 'The Talk' has a double meaning for black people. *Huffington Post*. Retrieved from http://www.huffingtonpost.com/ron-thomas/the-talk-has-a-double-mea_b_3645809.html

Toppo, G. (2014, December 11). Growing up 'post-racial,' teens suddenly find a world that isn't. *USA Today*. Retrieved from http://www.usatoday.com/story/news/nation/2014/12/10/teen-attitudes-race-diversity-america/19749199/

Williams, I. (2014, August 20). For the children, bring back 'the talk'. *The Hill*. Retrieved from http://thehill.com/blogs/congress-blog/civil-rights/215547-for-the-children-bring-back-the-talk

The nation's unprotected children and the ghost of Mike Brown, or the impact of national police killings on the health and social development of African American boys

Raja Staggers-Hakim

Department of Health Science, College of Health Professions, Sacred Heart University, Fairfield, Connecticut, USA

ABSTRACT

The correlation of experienced violence and racism or the perceived threat of either on mental illness and overall health has been well documented in health disparities research. Racism, either experienced or perceived, is associated with adverse health outcomes, especially in racial ethnic minorities. The current study explores the impact of national police brutality cases and extrajudicial killings on the social development, mental health, and overall well-being of young African American males. Further, we explain the social epidemic of police killings on the emotional and psychological well-being of African American boys and young men. The needs of Black male youth, relative to police killings, are captured, and persistent racial stereotypes that are often used to justify the extrajudicial killings of unarmed African American boys and young men are challenged. The current research is a pilot study that explores how awareness of national police killings impacts the mental health and social development of young African American boys. The current study has implications for community and public health research on violence and racism and specifically the public health impact of police killings on African American boys and young men. Recommendations for social policies that address national policing reform are discussed.

Introduction

Public health statistics reveal that African American men have some of the poorest life expectancy and quality of life outcomes of any other racial or ethnic group. According to the Centers for Disease Control and Prevention (CDC), the age-adjusted death rates for Black non-Hispanic males is 1,052.8 out of 100,000 population compared to 639.8 in Hispanic males and 876 in White males (Heron, 2015). Throughout the life course, the death rates for Black males are higher than all combined racial/ethnic and gender groups. Black males less than 1 year of age had a death rate of 1,120.1 compared to 501.1 in Hispanic males and 571.5 in White males (Heron, 2015). The death rate of young African American males is 1.5 times the rate of their White and Hispanic counterparts (CDC/NCHS, 2015). As the overall death rate declines in all men between 25 and 29 years, rates increase among African American men (CDC/NCHS, 2015).

Although the leading causes of death in all males ages 15–29 are unintentional injury, suicide, and homicide; in African American men, homicide is the leading cause of death (Heron, 2015). In African American boys between the ages of 1 and 4, homicide is the second leading cause of death (Heron, 2015). According to the CDC, Vital Statistics Report, this becomes the first leading cause of death in boys ages 15–19 years, in young men 20–24 years, and in men through age 39 (Heron, 2015). Although environmental and neighborhood factors such as community violence pose a risk to young boys and men, police homicides are fast becoming recognized as a risk factor (Juzwiak & Chan, 2014).

Between 2005 and 2012 Black boys and men were brutally killed by police officers three times as often as Whites (Johnson, Hoyer, & Heath, 2014). Ambiguous data collection at the state and national levels has made it difficult to capture if there has been an increase in police killings over the last several years or if there is simply an increase in national awareness of police killings due to documented police abuse through technological advancements, video, and smart phones. Still, the sparse available data gathered through news reports and state police reports provided to the Department of Justice (DOJ) suggest that African Americans or Blacks have been killed by police on average two times per week (Johnson et al., 2014). Reports suggest that 18% of Blacks killed by police were under the age of 21 years compared to 8.7% of Whites. Overall, the data suggest that Blacks, consisting of 14% of the U.S. population, were three times more likely to be killed by police than any other racial and ethnic group (Johnson et al., 2014). According to 2015 estimates, 49.7% of people killed by law enforcement were White, 28.3% were Black, and 15.5% were Hispanic/Latino (Swaine, Laughland, & Lartey, 2015). More than one in five of those killed in 2015 were unarmed. However, Blacks killed by police were more likely to be unarmed (31.6%) than Whites (16.5%).

The killing of Black boys and men, often unarmed, has been met with apathy from the broader public and failure by the judicial system to hold perpetrators accountable (Ramsey, 2015). The slow government response and limited judicial action following national cases of police killings demonstrate the difference in how Black children and youth are protected under the law compared to Whites.

From the failure of national data collection monitoring systems to accurately capture the number of cases of extrajudicial killings by police, to the reluctance of the criminal justice system to appropriately indict police officers who intentionally profile and purposefully use deadly force, the United States faces a crisis in the policing system, and the most vulnerable victims are Black males. Extra-judicial killings in African American communities by police aggravate excess mortality rates and further advance dismal physical and psychological health outcomes as well as hopelessness (Gilbert, 2014). Provided the national exposure of police killings, it is assumed that Black boys will have concerns and fears related to this epidemic. Further, it is assumed that awareness of the national killings of Black boys and men may have a significant impact on their mental health, social development, and overall well-being.

Racism, violence, and health

Research on health disparities and equity suggest that communities of color, and African Americans in particular, are most vulnerable to the effects of social inequalities on overall health (LaVeist & Isaac, 2012). Higher rates of stress from racism and related social inequities including unemployment, poor quality housing, neighborhood and community underdevelopment, crowding, poverty, and violence all lead to the sequelae of disparate health outcomes in African Americans such as obesity, hypertension, physical inactivity, diabetes, heart disease, cancer, mental health outcomes, and overall premature mortality (LaVesit & Isaac, 2012). Within the last decade, a body of research emerged dedicated to the study of stress from interpersonal and institutional forms of discrimination on adverse health (Harrell, Hall, & Taliaferro, 2003; Jones, 2000). Harrell et al. (2003) noted adverse physical and psychological harm caused by racist insult. Through measuring perceived racism, internalized racism, and actual experiences of discrimination, heart disease, hypertension, depression, sleep disturbance, and more recently breast cancer have all been associated with frequency of discriminatory events in subjects (Paradies, 2006).

The health disparities literature has established an association between experienced or perceived discrimination and adverse mental health. The inherent discrimination and threat of violence from racial profiling impact the mental health of Africans and particularly African American boys and men (Gilbert, 2014). Accordingly, depression has been established as a direct effect of discrimination and as a mediator in the relationship between discrimination and physical health outcomes including cardiovascular disease, diabetes, and cancer (Borrell et al., 2007). According to the CDC (2012), African Americans are 20% more likely to experience serious psychological distress including sadness, hopelessness, and worthlessness than Whites. Further, more than Whites and Hispanics, African Americans were likely to report other debilitating signs of depression, noting difficulty completing everyday tasks (CDC, 2012). African American children continue to face growing emotional and psychological concerns. Heron (2015) reports that the U.S. Surgeon General found that from 1980 to 1995, the suicide rate among African American youth ages 10–14 increased 233% as compared to 120% in non-Hispanic Whites. According to the Federal Interagency Forum on Child and Family Statistics (2015), African American children demonstrated more minor to severe emotional and behavioral difficulties than Hispanic or White children.

The importance of coping factors on discrimination predicting depression has been emphasized. Jackson and Mustillo (2001) found that the relationship between discrimination and poor mental health was mediated through poor self-concept (self-esteem and self-efficacy). In a similar study Noh and Kaspar (2003) examined the effects of racial and ethnic discrimination on depression moderated by personal coping responses. Findings revealed the frequency of perceived discrimination and the emotional reaction effects were directly and significantly associated with depression. Finch et al. (2001) found depression to be a major mechanism through which discrimination may affect physical health. In Borrell et al. (2007) after adjusting for age, education, income, and skin color, the odds of poor physical and mental health were greater with experienced discrimination.

Similarly, there is a significant association between exposure to violence exposure feelings of safety and psychological and behavioral indicators (Schwab-Stone et al., 1995). This is particularly true in youth. In Lewis et al. (2011), regardless of agreement by parents about the trauma endured from violence, there was an association between youth-witnessed violence and mental health. According to Post et al. (2014) regardless of the proximity, community trauma, in the way of violence, may result in more hyperarousal symptoms among youth.

The current research is a pilot study to reveal the impact of national cases of police killings on the lives of African American boys between the ages of 14 and 18. It is assumed that witnessing violence toward other Black youth can be traumatizing for Black youth. Whether incidental or chronic, research demonstrates that stress from discrimination, such as the targeted killing of Blacks by police, and the violence exposure, seeing videos of police killings, can lead to mental health effects. We are most interested in understanding if the national cases of police brutality affect the emotional health of African American boys. Further, the pilot study purports to uncover any limitations to the social development, actions, and overall well-being of Black boys due to recent police killings. It is the intention of this study to elucidate the perspective of Black youth who are more directly affected by state-sanctioned violence and to capture anecdotal accounts of how social determinants such as discrimination and social inequality, through racial profiling, impact the health of African American boys. This may further extend current understanding of how social inequalities, such as race-based discrimination and violence, over the life course shape adverse health outcomes in African American men leading to premature death. This pilot may direct further research on the effects of state-sanctioned violence, such as police brutality, on public health and racial ethnic health disparities, in particular.

Methodology

Subjects

Three focus group sessions were conducted with African American/Black boys between the age of 14 and 18 years ($N = 16$). Two focus groups included five participants each, and one included six participants. All youth were high school students living in Connecticut urban centers of the greater Hartford and New Haven areas. Youth 14–18 were specifically asked to participate due to the increased desire, among this age group, to be more independent from their parents, to make their own decisions, and to accept more responsibility. Parents also begin to allow more independence to support the transition of their children into young adulthood. As well, youth become more aware of local and broader social issues through media exposure, at school, or at home. At this age, young Black boys may have participated in conversations about police brutality, police killings, or being safe in encounters with the police.

Measurement

The current research employed focus group methodology to encourage conversations between Black boys around police brutality and police killings and to observe the growth and development of their understanding, concerns, and needs for action. As a methodological approach, focus groups are useful to capture in-depth information about a specialized group that may not be gathered from surveys, questionnaires, or other quantitative assessments alone. Focus groups emphasize the group dynamic, as a source of data, differently than individual interviews, which focus on the development of an individual's thought process. Focus groups were also considered to offer a supportive circle for attendees and offer affirmation for youth participants who may not normally have a collective conversation on the topic of police violence, police killings, and the impact on African American youth. The group dynamic of focus groups offers empowerment opportunities for youth participants to direct future conversations and for advocacy and action efforts with youth as well as for policy recommendations.

Procedure

All participants were affiliated with youth-based programs through local churches or fraternities/ sororities in Connecticut. Prior approval was obtained from organizational leadership, and IRB approval was granted from Sacred Heart University to conduct research with human subjects. Two sessions were conducted as part of the normally scheduled youth activities with the sorority/fraternal organizations. One session was planned for the purpose of hosting a focus group with youth on the topic of police brutality. Each session lasted about an hour. The settings for the sessions varied and included community rooms at local libraries and a meeting room in a church. Each group was arranged in a small circle and facilitated by the same researcher for consistency of format. A semistructured protocol was developed to guide group discussions. The protocol included questions to gauge participant knowledge of national police killings and what the national cases mean to them as they grow and develop.

Analysis

The focus group recordings were transcribed and anonymized for thematic analysis using Dedoose software. Dedoose is a secure online application for coding and analyzing qualitative and or mixed-methods research and sorts coded information into themes by determining frequency of thematic content in data. Common themes that emerged using Dedoose were (1) Young Black Men Are Killed; (2) Black Males Seen as Threat (3) Fear of Police; (4) Black Boys Have to Be Careful; (5) Get Home Alive; (6) Police Killings Are Distant and Removed; and (7) Police Killings Could Happen Here.

Results

Theme 1: Young Black men are killed

Participants indicated having general knowledge and awareness around national cases of police brutality and extrajudicial killings. Participants had a broad understanding of the wave of violence targeting African American boys and men. Boys in all groups were able to recite locations for some of the cases. Certain names and cases were more familiar with the boys. Participants also discussed the racial and ethnic differences between the victims and the police officers involved. Information about national cases was received mostly from media outlets, including smart phone apps, and through conversations with friends and family and at school. Participants generally agreed that there was very little formal conversation around police brutality at school. However, the boys were aware of the events and were able to recount the stories of recent well-known cases. One participant noted, "I don't know if ironic or intentional, but it's been predominately Caucasian male police officers to African American males—especially young men." One participant described the Baltimore, Maryland, case involving 25-year-old Freddy Gray in which he described the cops "detaining a young black male—[the police] broke his back. [They] had a riot." Another participant stated that he was aware of the "Freddy Gray case … he was killed by an officer so I mean the officer was Caucasian." One participant described the Cleveland, Ohio, case involving 12-year-old Tamir Rice: "It was like a plastic gun. I remember watching the news and it had [the] police recording and it said [the suspect] is a young man with a plastic toy—and I remember the word 'toy'—and it said don't engage just watch. And I remember seeing the footage and seeing the cop cars drive up and shooting."

Another participant, referring to the killing of Eric Garner in Staten Island, New York, stated that "the guy telling them he couldn't breathe and the fact that [he] was already down and he was being put down [by] like five guys—[that] was crazy—[what did] he [the police officer] think he was going to get away now—you got him already." Another boy recalled the John Crawford case noting, "Or even, the guy in Walmart, he was waving a toy gun around and the cop came and shot him." One participant stated, "It goes back to Zimmerman—although not a police officer—still Caucasian and most of these officers are getting off the hook right away. And no indictment—nothing."

Theme 2: Black males seen as a threat

The groups noted that social perceptions and stereotypes held against Black boys and men were operating in the national police killings. The boys acknowledged that police officers assumed Black men were wrong, threatening, or in some cases not human. One participant described the string of cases of police brutality against Black boys and men more generally as "cops misjudging or assuming that guys are wrong and bad. And it ends up whoever they are stopping is not the guy—[not] the person they should be going for." Similarly another participant spoke of the larger issue with the police killings of young Black men illustrating the case in Ferguson, Missouri, of 18-year-old Michael "Mike" Brown. According to the participant, "they automatically see you as a threat cuz the Mike Brown police in the court hearing said 'it' approached me—it's like an n-word thing." The participant emphasized that "not seeing Black boys and men as people" is significant in the context in which the killings occur.

Another participant noted stereotypes of Black men relative to national cases of police killings. He indicated, "we are not stereotypes—not every Mexican is illegal—not every Latino steals cars—not every Black person robs stores. That is ignorant stereotyping, not one bad apple makes all rotten." Another participant indicated that "stereotypes aren't true." One participant commented that "every single Black guy doesn't sell drugs … isn't in a gang … [does] not do stereotypical things that media and society portrays us to be."

Theme 3: Fear of police

Participants noted a certain amount of fear of police and concern about the possibility of being racially profiled. Although some boys felt removed from the national cases, others identified with all or specific cases. One participant noted, "[I] am fearful for my life. If I walk by a policeman or someone with authority, being a Black man in this country in general is just a threat by itself." One participant indicated, "I fear it could be me. If I might be innocent or just down the street from an incident they assume I'm the guy—that's a fear—just the fact that I could be killed or beaten down." Another participant identified with the victims of the national cases; he stated, "It could be me. I feel scared when I walk by a policeman or woman. If I do something wrong." One participant also extended his fear to other young Black men; he noted, "I think I can be concerned for kids who might … dress a certain way and not cuz they want to but because they have to. It's just how they have to dress maybe because the environment they live in—they may have it a little harder than we have it because of where we are."

Theme 4: Black boys have to be careful

Groups discussed the impact of the national cases on their actions and behaviors. Largely the boys discussed being more aware of their actions and the need to change certain behaviors and dress. One participant noted that when "[I] walk outside of the house [I] have to take [my] hood down. I remember [my mother] always telling me like if I go into a store to take my hood down because when I walk in with a hood on I'm seen in a certain way, I gotta watch out." Many of the participants spoke broadly about distancing themselves from possible trouble to avoid police or police altercations. One participant noted that he is "mindful of who [I] hang out with. … Not everybody is your friend." One participant stated, "Anything bad going on, walk away [because] police might think you're involved." Another participant stated, "I watch who I hang around with. If they have trouble in the neighborhood, I try to avoid the trouble and avoid them." Another participant stated, "I was always taught if there is anything going on or anything … just like walk away." Another participant added, "Like if there is a fight … shooting or anything … robbery …. Something like that … just get away as soon as possible because [police] might think that you're involved."

In terms of feeling limited in actions and behaviors, one participant indicated that he "can't walk down the street at certain times—at night—also depends on where you are." Another participant spoke about the need to modify his behavior when he begins to drive. He noted,

> when I do drive, there is a thing when every single Black man at one point in his life will get pulled over by a cop, and I was always told like you tell the officer, "I'm going to go inside of my glove compartment to grab my license and registration" instead of actually doing it because you do it …. "oh, he is digging for a gun" so in that situation you always gotta be cautious and aware."

Theme 5: Get home alive

The participants, through conversations with parents and relatives, indicated that they discussed some strategies to help stay safe in encounters with the police. Across all focus groups, participants shared a knowledge of not inciting police and focused on the need to get home alive. All participants agreed with complying with police. One participant noted, "If it comes to police officers, if they ask you a question, just answer them honestly … to me do whatever you can to get home." Another participant indicated, "Whatever [he] tells you … do what the cop says—once it's all over, go to my parents and tell them what happened instead of having [a] conflict with the police." Others spoke about courtesy and respect. One participant was advised to "be careful" and "If police ask a question, answer respectfully." Another participant stated, "in terms of an encounter with a cop or authority just beat them … shock them with politeness. You know, be what they wouldn't expect you to be. [T]hey just assume you are [this] rude nasty person and … you know beat them with politeness." Another participant stated, "[my father] said always be respectful." One teenager indicated that, "for the most part, protect yourself, do right … for the most part just don't be in the situation and if [a cop] does come up to you, be respectful … get yourself home … be smart. Play it smart." One participant focused on avoiding police. He stated, "if possible, unless in dire circumstances, [I] stay away from a man in a badge, in general."

Theme 6: Police killings are distant and removed

Most notably the meaning of the national police cases to the boys varied by both location and how much each participant identified with the victims and understood that similar events might occur in their communities or to them. The focus group in Hartford County emphasized connectedness to national cases. Participants noted the importance of the issue of police brutality for them specifically as they were similar to the boys who were harmed in national cases. One participant stated that "a lot of these guys that are hurt are around my age." Another participant noted that the boys and young men being killed were "close in age, but [they were] also Black men [in general] and so it affects me in a certain type of way."

Others, mostly from the New Haven groups, indicated that the events were more or less "on the news and out there" but distant to them and their realities. One participant noted, "[T]o me personally, it's distant. To my grandmother it's personal." One participant stated that, "Baltimore it's like—there's people in Connecticut if their child was killed—it would be a similar outcome to the riots. I don't pay attention to stuff that's happening there." One participant suggested that current national cases of police brutality are still different today and unlike what happened to African Americans decades ago. He stated "to me it's different … [my] grandfather he told stories of one encounter … police stopped him … there were officers all around him and [they] said we will shoot you in the head—they threatened him."

Location was a factor in how participants reacted to or were affected by national police brutality cases. Violence exposure seemed to mediate the perspective of national cases with the police as perpetrators of violence. In New Haven, where two focus groups occurred, the prevalence of local violence and the proximity of cases involving community violence seemed to overshadow the national epidemic of police killings. New Haven participants focused more heavily on local violence, which they felt posed a greater threat to them than the idea of national police brutality and police killings. This was especially important as the participants in one group were directly affected by the recent loss of a classmate and neighbor. One participant noted, "When we lost one of our students that is when the awareness came about and we started to talk about gun violence." Regarding the murder of a classmate, one participant noted that "if that happened to him [his classmate who was murdered], what is the chance of that happening to me or one of my siblings."

Theme 7: It could happen here

Participants who indicated that national cases "[have] meaning" to them or "personal meaning" also felt that cases might occur in the town where they lived. There was an association between the level of connectedness to the national cases, and to the victims, direct exposure to aggressive policing, and the perspectives that participants held about whether or not aggressive police action might occur in one's town. One participant noted that what has happened nationally might also happen in his community. He stated "so we live here and it could easily happen here but I don't think we are aware that it can happen to anybody. … So I use here because it could happen anywhere and I've had an encounter with a cop that was just the same as the other guys. It can happen anywhere."

The participants who personally experienced unpleasant encounters with the police were more likely to be concerned about national police cases. One participant noted,

> There is a police officer in my school. [A] woman. She's Black. Not that she's a woman changes anything. To me, it's more like, she's part of the team now and I think if she felt like if she had to protect herself, like the other guys say they do, she would do the same thing. Probably get away with it. So it's like they are the police … they are a team.

Another participant indicated, "[when] I was little, I never saw cops as friendly. [In] a store one time and cop came over to me and asked me a bunch of questions and the entire time she had her hand on her gun and I was scared. Even now, I think [had I] done something wrong."

Implications and policy recommendations

Although the youth interviewed were able to clearly articulate their concerns, fear was a major factor for the boys. Aware of the national cases, the boys were concerned about being targeted by police. Although the youth indicated speaking to family about ways to be safe in encounters with police, including how they need to talk to police and interact with police, the boys continued to indicate that they were aware that police could easily assume that they were a suspect and attack them as they had other Black males in national cases. Further, the boys acknowledged that police might have the liberty to attack, even kill them, as so many officers have done and without consequence. The fear emphasized by participants suggests that exposure to violence in general traumatized boys. Although boys who were connected to local violence, unrelated to police, felt changed by violence in their immediate communities, the boys who were removed from community violence were especially traumatized by police violence and police killings. This was especially so for those who felt that were no different than the boys and young men who were killed by police in the national cases.

Although the participants spoke extensively about altering their behaviors to demonstrate that they were not doing anything wrong especially around police, and enacting the strategies as advised by their parents and family, participants did suggest that they still may be profiled and subjected to police harassment. Although the boys spoke extensively about staying away from trouble, being respectful, and hanging with the right crowd, they were concerned about mistaken identity and the need to avoid police altogether out of fear of being profiled and or pursued.

Although the boys spoke about being hyper-vigilant in their actions, aware of their surroundings, and mindful of the company they keep, across the regional groups, the youth, more broadly, focused on their actions and on their own accountability to prevent altercations with police and less on the limitations of the police officers who pursue African American boys and young men. In doing so, the boys seemed to acknowledge the way in which cases of police brutality, typically, unfold with the blame centered on the victims or the victims' families often with the first questions raised: "what was he doing to deserve being targeted or killed?" or "where were his parents?" Conversely, police officers are often eradicated from responsibility and unaccountable for their actions even in cases involving the murder of unarmed victims.

Youth clearly associated profiling by police with racial stereotypes and they spoke to the need to challenge those stereotypes of Black boys and men. Often due to the esteemed social status in which the United States regards police officers, there has been a failure to acknowledge racial profiling, racism among police officers, and systemic racism specifically that portrays Black boys and men as suspects, which is later used to justify their pursuit and murder.

Although the focus of the conversation was heavy at times, the boys did acknowledge that it was cathartic to talk about either community violence (in the case of the New Haven focus groups) and or the national police killings. This is indicative of the need to bring more youth into the national conversations around police brutality and police killings as well as the need to link conversations of community violence with that of police brutality and police killings. Further, in all groups, the youths indicated the desire to act and to continue such conversations in school and or in the community.

While the study revealed valuable information about the concerns of Black boys, the sample size was limited, and so the findings cannot be generalizable to all African American youth. Still this work has implications to advance further research on police brutality and state sanctioned violence on mental health, trauma, and health disparities in African Americans, and African American boys and men specifically. Further, this work may serve as a way to advance conversations with youth about the impact of police brutality. In addition there is opportunity to provide insight to policy makers and youth advocates on the impact of social policies, involving police violence, on youth development. This work merits further study to understand how Black boys and young men cope with the threat of violence broadly and state sanctioned violence specifically. Additionally, this work has implications for discussion of media portrayal of inflicted violence on trauma and the experience of chronic trauma or retraumatization through the threat of state-sanctioned violence on the health of racial and ethnic minorities.

Conclusion

It is important that the United States consider national policies that establish standards in policing practices that address racial bias and discrimination in the targeting and killing of unarmed Black boys and men. Unfortunately, state-level action does not accompany national oversight for training, best practice standards, and compliance concerning issues of racial discrimination in policing. Further, it is critical that the Justice Department lowers the bar and burden of proof in civil rights cases that may lead to the conviction of officers who are engaged in racial profiling, abuse of power, and reckless murder. Failure to hold police accountable sends the message to police that they are untouchable and to children and other vulnerable groups that they are unprotected from reckless actions and abuse of police officers or other authority figures. Further, lack of national action and failure to hold police accountable support the continuation of reckless killings of unarmed African Americans.

It is critical that parents, schools, and the nation acknowledge the trauma that Black youth and Black boys, in particular, experience in light of the national epidemic of police killings. This pilot demonstrates that Black boys have a great deal of fear due to the national cases of police brutality. Youth appreciate that making the slightest mistake or the possibility of their actions being taken out of context may serve as a death sentence. The focus groups suggest that the fear held by Black boys is not appropriately being addressed. Although it is protective for parents to talk to their children about racial profiling and police brutality to teach them to be safe in encounters with police, it is equally important to protect the mental health of African American boys and young men and to support them in feeling safe in their growth and development through discussing their fears. Also, it is necessary for parents and youth advocates to acknowledge police brutality and police killings as a child advocacy issue. Certainly this issue is larger than families and communities and requires national action. It is urgent that the nation protect Black children, as other children, from the psychological damage associated with the fear and real or perceived threat of premature death at the hands of police or from police-inflicted violence.

References

Arya, N., & Augarten, I. (2008). *Critical conditions: African American youth in the justice system*. Retrieved from https://ssrn.com/abstract=1892957

Borrell, L., Jacobs, D., Williams, D., Pletcher, M. J., Houston, T., & Kiefe, C. (2007). Self-reported racial discrimination and substance use in the coronary artery risk development in adults study. *American Journal of Epidemiology*, *166* (9), 1068–1079. doi:10.1093/aje/kwm180

Centers for Disease Control and Prevention (CDC). (2012). *Summary health statistics for U.S. adults: 2010. Table 14.* Retrieved from fromhttp://www.cdc.gov/data/series/sr_10/sr10_252.pdf

Centers for Disease Control and Prevention (CDC)/National Center for Health Statistics (NCHS). (2015). National Vital Statistics System. *National Vital Statistics Reports*, *64*(2). Hyattsville, MD: NCHS. Retrieved from http://www.cdc.gov/nchs/data/nvsr/nvsr64/nvsr64_02.pdf

Federal Interagency Forum on Child and Family Statistics. (2015). *America's children: Key national indicators of well-being*. Washington, DC: U.S. Government Printing Office.

Finch, B., Hummer, R. A., Kolody, B., & Vega, W. A. (2001). The role of discrimination and acculturative stress in the physical health of Mexican-origin adults. *Hispanic Journal of Behavioral Sciences*, *23*, 399–429. doi:10.1177/0739986301234004

Gilbert, K. (2014). *We see the dead and don't see the living: The realities of black men*. Retrieved from http://www.rwjf.org/en/culture-of-health/2014/08/we_see_the_dead_and.html

Harrell, J. P., Hall, S., & Taliaferro, J. (2003). Physiological responses to racism and discrimination: An assessment of the evidence. *American Journal of Public Health*, *93*, 243–248. doi:10.2105/AJPH.93.2.243

Heron, M. (2015). Deaths: Leading causes for 2011. *National Vital Statistics Reports*, *64*(7), Retrieved from http://www.cdc.gov/nchs/data/nvsr/nvsr64/nvsr64_07.pdf

Jackson, P.B., & Mustillo, S. (2001). I am woman: The impact of social identities on African American women's mental health. *Women and Health*, *32*(4), 33–59.

Johnson, K., Hoyer, M., & Heath, B. (2014, August 15). Local police involved in 400 killings per year. *USA Today News*. Retrieved from http://www.usatoday.com/story/news/nation/2014/08/14/police-killings-data/14060357/ http://www.usatoday.com/story/news/nation/2014/08/14/police-killings-data/14060357/

Jones, C. (2000). Levels of racism: A theoretical framework and a gardener's tale. *American Journal of Public Health*, *90* (8), 1212–1215. doi:10.2105/AJPH.90.8.1212

Juzwiak, R., & Chan, A. (2014, December 8). Unarmed people of color killed by police, 1999–2014. *Gawker*. Retrieved from http://gawker.com/unarmed-people-of-color-killed-by-police-1999-2014-1666672349

Laveist, T., & Issac, L. (2012). *Race, ethnicity and health: A public health reader* (2nd ed.). San Francisco, CA: Jossey-Bass.

Lewis, T., Thompson, R., & Dubowitz, H. (2011). Parent youth discordance about youth witnessed violence: Associations with trauma symptoms and service use in at-risk sample. *Child Abuse and Neglect*, *36*(11), 790–797. doi:10.1016/j.chiabu.2012.09.009

Noh, S., & Kaspar, V. (2003). Perceived discrimination and depression: Moderating effects of coping, acculturation, and ethnic support. *American Journal of Public Health*, *93*(2), 232–238.

Paradies, Y. (2006). A systematic review of empirical research on self-reported racism and health. *International Journal of Epidemiology*, *35*(4), 888–901. doi:10.1093/ije/dyl056

Post, M., Harten, G., Lu, X., Schmidt, A., Avci, G., Wilde, E., & McCauley, S. (2014). Dimensions of trauma and specific symptoms of complex post-traumatic stress disorder in inner city youth: A preliminary study. *Violence and Victims*, *29*(2), 262–279. doi:10.1891/0886-6708.VV-D-12-00097R1

Ramsey, D. (2015, April 4). White America's silence on police brutality is consent. *Gawker Justice*. Retrieved from http://justice.gawker.com/white-americas-silence-on-police-brutality-is-consent-1696780967

Schwab-Stone, M., Ayers, T.S., Kasprow, W., Voyce, C., Borone, C., Shriver, T., & Weissberg, R. (1995). No safe haven: A study of violence exposure in an urban community. *Journal of the American Academy Child and Adolescent Psychiatry*, *34*(10), 1343–52.

Swaine, J., Laughland, O., & Lartey, J. (2015, June 1). US policing the counted: Black Americans killed by police twice as likely to be unarmed as white people. *The Guardian*. Retrieved from http://www.theguardian.com/us-news/2015/jun/01/black-americans-killed-by-police-analysis

The death of Black males: The unmasking of cultural competence and oppressive practices in a micro-aggressive environment

Folusho Otuyelu, Warren Graham, and Shakira A. Kennedy

Graduate School of Social Work, Touro College, New York, New York, USA

ABSTRACT

This conceptual article critically examines the relationship between cultural competence, oppressive practices, and micro-aggression within the field of social work and the larger community. The Council on Social Work Education requires that topics of race, power, privilege, and cultural competence be included in the graduate schools of social work it endorses. However, the impact of race, culture, class, and privilege in society and the work environment in the form of micro-aggression remains ignored within the human service field. African American males are most often the beneficiaries of services that social workers offer. In addition, they are often the recipient of these embedded messages, which are often witnessed in the form of police brutality, aggressive policing practices, and disproportionate arrest rates. This article presents some of the barriers social workers must be familiar with when addressing micro-aggression, cultural competence, and the impact of micro-aggression on oppression. Finally, recommendations for addressing micro-aggressions within the workplace and the field of social work are discussed.

Introduction

There is a consensus amongst activist, research, and advocacy groups that substantial racial inconsistencies exist in the sentencing decisions of Black males in the U.S. Federal Court system (American Civil Liberties Union, 2014; National Research Council, 1983; Spohn, 2000; The Sentencing Project, 2000, 2014). These racial inconsistencies reflect that the sentencings imposed on Black males are approximately 20% longer than those of their White male counterparts convicted of similar crimes (American Civil Liberties Union, 2014; Spohn, 2000; The Sentencing Project, 2000, 2014).

According to the National Association for the Advancement of Colored People (2015) Criminal Justice Fact sheet, African Americans constitute nearly 1 million of the total 2.3 million incarcerated populations with an incarceration rate nearly six times the rate of Whites. Together, African American and Hispanics make up 58% of all prisoners in 2008, even though African Americans and Hispanics make up approximately one quarter of the U.S. population.

A larger discussion about race relations must be held to provide a social and cultural context to how these numbers are truly reflected in the policies that govern all members of society. Overt and subtle forms of racism have progressed in the United States; moreover, it has seeped into many of our structural institutions such as law enforcement and the justice system. The disparity between how Whites and Blacks view racism speaks to how unaware many Whites are of how bias and discrimination have taken on an invisible nature that protects them from realizing their own involvement in the continuation of unintended racism toward people of color (Dovidio, Gaertner, Kawakami, & Hodson, 2002; Constantine & Sue, 2007). However, Black Americans view this in a different way, as racism is a relentless reality that many naive Whites continue to respond with racial insensitivity, in the form of racial micro-aggressions (Sue et al., 2008). Link to reference needed The ignorance, whether intentional or not, is the underlying basis of power and privilege that manifests in an individual's ability to conceptualize race and race relations. The power differential that exists creates a barrier protecting Whites from having to understand or realize the reality of unequal systems that perpetuate bias and discrimination.

According to Swaine, Laughland, and Lartery (2015) Black Americans are more than twice as likely to be unarmed when killed during encounters with police. The authors found that 32% of Black people killed by police in 2015 were unarmed, as were 25% of Hispanic and Latino people, compared with 15% of White people killed. Black Americans make up 13% of the United States total population (United States Census Bureau, 2015); thus, these findings illustrate how disproportionately Black Americans are being killed by police.

These findings are in direct relationship with how the criminal justice system is viewed by many Black Americans when compared to their White counterparts. A study conducted by Newport (2014) for Gallup Review combined 2011–2014 data measuring Americans' confidence in law enforcement. Their results showed that 59% of Whites have a great deal or quite a lot of confidence in law enforcement, compared with 37% of Blacks. As it relates to race relations, the dichotomous relationship identified when engaging both Whites and Blacks continues to be problematic with the understanding that one group is privileged and the other attuned and hypersensitive to the racial landscape. As various communities across the country grapple with issues of police brutality, aggressive policing practices, disproportionate arrest rates, and rallies surrounding the aforementioned, this topic is of special importance for agents of change charged with advocating for social justice.

In "Can We Talk about Race?" Tatum (2007, p. 5) is quoted as saying, "the cultural images and messages that affirm the assumed superiority of whites and the assumed inferiority of people of color are like smog in the air. Sometimes it is so thick it is visible, other times, it is less apparent, but always, day in and day out, we are breathing it in." That specific quote is significant as it references the most powerful question in attempting to understand the complex dynamics of power, privilege, and oppression, whether we are socially allowed to discuss such a seemingly innocuous topic that has pervasively influenced race relations, self-esteem, and self-worth for millions of people. This lack of confidence and inability to discuss the dynamics of power, privilege, and oppression with law enforcement and the criminal justice system is also present in social services.

Social work and race relations

Critical thinking skills developed in graduate social work education, as it relates to cultural competence and anti-oppressive practices, often do not translate to professional practice in the field of social work. This can promulgate systems of power, privilege, and oppression that marginalize not only clients of color, but African American social workers as well. Social workers can be taught how to provide culturally competent services to marginalized populations and disenfranchised clients; however, often not conveyed in graduate school education is the perspective of the singular minority professional they may find sitting at a table among other social workers that do not look like them. More often, it is that person's perspective that is callously disregarded. The skill set necessary to tread those professional waters and boundaries is often ignored. We teach how to be culturally competent when we should be teaching how to sit with bias, while discussing its detrimental effect in practice. The African American social work experience can be best explained as being a convergence of professional values and ethics on a macro-level framed by the micro-aggressions on an individual level.

Micro-aggressions in social work practice

Racial micro-aggressions are defined as subtle insults directed toward people of color, often done unconsciously (Constantine & Sue, 2007; Solorzano, Ceja, & Yosso, 2000). Racial micro-aggression can take the form of micro-assaults, micro-insults, and micro-invalidations (DeAngelis, 2009). Micro-assaults are conscious and intentional actions or slurs, such as ignoring a person of color's request in a restaurant. Micro-insults are verbal and nonverbal communications that are insensitive and demeaning of a person's identity or racial heritage. Micro-invalidations are communications that subtly exclude, negate, or nullify the thoughts or experiential reality of a person of color (DeAngelis, 2009). Like a cancer undetected, racial micro-aggressions erode the relationship among us, often morphing into blatant racism that is normalized, perpetuated, and reinforced systematically in the work place, as well as in law enforcement and community relations.

The impact of racial micro-aggression in social work practice can be detrimental to service provision and staff development. While there are several studies (Constantine, 2007; Constantine & Sue, 2007; Hernandez, Carranza, & Almeida, 2010; Sue et al., 2008) in counseling and psychology that focus on racial micro-aggressions, there is a dearth of research in social work on this issue. Nevertheless, micro-aggressions are indicated in social work practice on the micro- and macro-levels. The sheer definition of racial micro-aggressions being unconscious speaks to the need for continuous and vigilant training and supervision around this issue in all areas of social work beyond the education arena.

Racial micro-aggressions have significant implication in social work practice, which was confirmed in a study by Constantine (2007). The findings showed that the perceived racial micro-aggressions were negatively associated with African American clients' perceptions of the therapeutic working alliance and White therapists' general and multicultural counseling competence. Also, when a White therapist unconsciously enacted a form of racial micro-aggression, it negatively impacted the client more than if a nonprofessional enacted a micro-aggression. This issue speaks to the impact that racial micro-aggressions have on the working alliance and treatment success. The weakening of the working alliance may occur when Black clients perceive White counselors as biased or prejudice, which may lead to premature termination of the counseling relationships by these Black clients (Constantine, 2007). Additionally, the study showed that it precipitated the termination of services by African American clients. An unintended impact that was not covered in the study was that pervasive racial micro-aggressions perpetuated on Black and other racial minority groups lead to the avoidance of needed services predominately provided by White providers. Examples of racial micro-aggressions can be seen in a practitioner's personal experience.

Personal experience #1

The realization of how other professionals "see" me came alive while employed by a State's Office of Court Administration. In 2008, when originally scheduled for a day off, I received a phone call advising me that there was a work-related emergency that needed attending to. Riding my motorcycle at the time, and in the interest of expediency, I decided to ride to the courthouse as opposed to going home to change into more appropriate business attire. Understanding that a lack of transparency in treatment court proceedings could erroneously lead to the beginning of a termination of parental rights filing, it was prudent for continued ethical program development and client relations to address an escalating or unresolved issue.

Upon arriving and speaking with the court officers, to which I showed my secure work identification, I boarded the elevator toward my third floor office. I was met by a Support Magistrate I had spoken to daily for years, in part due to a common refrigerator and water cooler located right behind my desk in a common area shared with other Court staff.

I greeted the magistrate and was immediately rebuffed as she mumbled a response, shifted toward the farthest corner of the elevator and clutched her pocketbook tighter after shifting it to the arm furthest away from me. At the time I didn't have a name for what I was feeling in response to this behavior, and it wasn't really apparent to me that there was anything wrong with it in that moment, irrespective of how I felt.

The next day, when in full business attire and costume, the magistrate greeted me as warmly as she always had and stopped for brief conversation as she retrieved her lunch. I asked her if she was feeling ok, considering I had seen her, greeted her, and she was out of sorts with her response. She admitted never seeing me. It was then that I recognized that in professional settings, the same level of intentional invisibility that affects homeless persons may marginalize people of color. She hadn't recognized me out of "uniform" and only saw racial category.

Racial micro-aggression in various settings

Sue, Lin, Torino, Capodilupo, and Rivera (2009) identify that micro-aggressions "assail the mental health of recipients, create hostile climates, perpetuate stereotype threat, and create physical health problems, and lower productivity and problem solving abilities" (p. 183). These are real and significant threats to professional personas accustomed to being caretakers, counselors, and clinicians.

Racial micro-aggressions are also applicable to the relationship between law enforcement and the Black community, particularly young Black men. The encounter that many young Black men have with law enforcement is laden with racial micro-aggressions and perceived as even overt racism, thus perpetuating a relationship with the law enforcement community tainted with mistrust and fear. The difference between this relationship and the counseling relationship is that in the counseling relationship the Black client can terminate services; however, Black men cannot terminate their interactions with law enforcement. In fact, the power in the relationship lies with law enforcement and in scenarios where racial micro-aggressions or blatant racism occur; there is limited recourse for the Black person, specifically Black men.

The need to address racial micro-aggressions is pertinent to social work practice as well. For example, in a study conducted by Sue et al. (2008), Black participants reported several racial micro-aggression themes on the job, such as assumptions of intellectual inferiority and assumed superiority of White cultural values/communication styles. Many of these themes are prevalent in social work practice. There have been occasions in the authors' experience where well-meaning White social workers have attributed Black clients' struggles as intellectual deficits and masked these racial micro-aggressions in assessment terms such as "at risk," "vulnerable," and "learning issues," to justify what was tantamount to an assumption of intellectual inferiority. When White social workers are questioned further about the basis of their assessment, it is often centered around "intuition" or "past experience" working with said population.

Sue et al. (2008) recognizes that racial micro-aggression themes around cultural values/communication style support the personal experience below.

Personal experience #2

According to a Black manager, a Black candidate for hire in a midsized social service agency came in for an interview for a direct practice position. The Black candidate was recommended for a second interview with a White senior-level manager. After the second interview, the Black candidate was deemed not a good fit for the organization and client population. After further exploration, it was discovered that the White senior-level manager disqualified the candidate due to the candidate's communication style not being professional and attire not being a good match for the program and its clients. The candidate's communication style was described by the Black manager as being normal with the exception of a cadence and pitch common among some Blacks. The candidate's attire exuded pride in her heritage but still met the qualification of being professional. In an effort not to appear racially biased, the White senior-level manager told the Black manager to keep the candidate's resume on file but to continue interviewing other candidates in the interim. This personal account shows diversity within any organization does not exempt it from practicing racial micro-aggressions.

Racial micro-aggression assumptions in the environment

The assumption that Black cultural values and communication style is inferior (Constantine, 2007) is also noted in law enforcement and community relations. For example, the reaction that police have when seeing a group of young Black men socializing often carries an assumption that there is either a crime or gang-related activity in progress. When young Black men are stopped and inquire about why they are being detained, the natural cadence, pitch, and tone of communication is assumed to be of aggression, whereas it may simply be one of frustration, fear, or concern about being questioned; but a lack of cultural awareness of Black cultural values and communication often leads to an escalation of an incident that is often based in unconscious racial micro-aggressions or even aversive racism. This inability to understand or pay attention to Black communication style is evident in the Eric Gardner case when he was saying, "I can't breathe." The blatant ignoring of his request shows law enforcement's focus on detaining him or simply thinking he is lying, which speaks to racial micro-aggression and a disregard for the person being interacted with.

Racial micro-aggressions are pervasive and need to be focused on in social work practice and police-community relations. The current mood of the country indicates a need for intervention services that are built on collaboration by everyone. Racial micro-aggressions are not specific to White people, as there are many people of color who also perpetuate micro-aggressions, thus making this relevant and appropriate for everyone to be aware of.

Below are recommendations for addressing racial micro-aggression in social work and in police-community relations.

Recommendations for addressing racial micro-aggression in social work practice

- Decision-making professionals must engage in frank conversations about what race and ethnicity mean to them.
- Supervision needs to include these dynamics and perspectives to either increase self-awareness to truly promote environments of cultural and racial acceptance.
- Consortiums, taskforces, committees, work groups, and group supervision must be formulated to the following: (1) acknowledging the difficulty discussing such topics and the potential vulnerability involved with admitting challenges and (2) routinely adding related topics and tangible examples of challenges for clients and workers as they relate to micro-aggressions, power, privilege, and oppression.
- Social Work School administrators must consider creating stand alone courses addressing issues of power, privilege, and oppression in addition to weaving the contents of the -isms throughout existing programs.
- Continuous training in racial micro-aggressions must be geared toward all practitioners, on all levels within human service organizations and the social work profession.
- Additional research within the social work arena must look at racial micro-aggression and other forms of racial micro-aggression in the work place to ascertain the prevalence rate and impact on Blacks and other minority groups.

Recommendations for addressing racial micro-aggression in law enforcement

- Law enforcement systems all over the country need to acknowledge that there is a significant pattern of racial micro-aggressions and possibly racism that is pervasive and detrimental in the policing of racial minority groups, particularly in the policing of Black men. This pattern of policing is divisive and does not ensure public safety but endangers the public as well as law enforcers.

- More emphasis must be placed on law enforcement representing and living in the community they serve. This will enhance community relations and change the negative perception of law enforcement in minority dominant communities.
- Law enforcement training needs to be ongoing and centered around cultural competence and being aware of racial micro-aggressions. There is a pattern of response/engagement with racial minority populations that involves aggressive and violent interaction that has led to numerous incidents involving the loss of Black lives.
- A national push for law enforcement personnel to wear body cameras must be in place, and all incidents should be reviewed for racial micro-aggressions on an ongoing basis.
- In the event where a law enforcement officer's interaction with any community is deemed or construed as displaying racial or any other form of micro-aggression, the law enforcement officer should receive additional training, supervision, and appropriate reprimand up to and including termination of employment. The law enforcement officer should also be monitored closely for a significant period after the additional training to verify change in attitude and behavior to prevent future incidents of racial micro-aggression.

As the social work profession continues to be the gatekeepers for social justice and community services, we have an ethical and social responsibility to the community at large to ensure social justice and equal access for all. Preparing social workers will undoubtedly alleviate racial tensions when communities are calling for leaders to bridge the gaps between racial divides, like those we are left with after the grand jury decisions of Eric Garner from Staten Island, New York, Mike Brown from Ferguson, Missouri, and Freddie Gray from Baltimore, Maryland.

References

American Civil Liberties Union. (2014). Racial disparities in sentencing. Hearing on reports of racism in the justice system of the United States. Submitted to the Inter-American Commission on Human Rights, 153rd session, pp. 225–258.

Constantine, M. G. (2007). Racial micro aggressions against African American clients in cross-racial counseling relationships. *Journal of Counseling Psychology*, *54*(1), 1–16. doi:10.1037/0022-0167.54.1.1

Constantine, M. G., & Sue, D. G. (2007). Perceptions of racial micro aggressions among black supervisees in cross racial dyads. *Journal of Counseling Psychology*, *54*(2), 142–153. doi:10.1037/0022-0167.54.2.142

DeAngelis, T. (2009). Unmasking racial micro aggressions. *Monitor on Psychology*, *40*(2), 42–25.

Dovidio, J. F., Gaertner, S. L., Kawakami, K., & Hodson, G. (2002). Why can't we all just get along? Interpersonal biases and interracial distrust. *Cultural Diversity and Ethnic Minority Psychology*, *8*, 88–102. doi:10.1037/1099-9809.8.2.88

Hernandez, P., Carranza, M., & Almeida, R. (2010). Mental health professionals' adaptive responses to racial micro aggressions: An exploratory study. *Professional Psychology, Research and Practice*, *41*(3), 202–209. doi:10.1037/a0018445

National Association for the Advancement of Colored People. (2015). *Criminal justice fact sheet*. Retrieved from http://www.naacp.org/pages/criminal-justice-fact-sheet

National Research Council. (1983). *Research on sentencing: The search for reform, Volume I*. Washington, DC: National Academies Press.

Newport, F. (2014, August 20). *Gallup Review: Black and White attitudes toward police*. Retrieved from http://www.gallup.com/poll/175088/gallup-review-black-white-attitudes-toward-police.aspx

Solorzano, M., Ceja, M., & Yosso, T. (2000). Critical race theory, racial micro aggressions, and campus racial climate: The experiences of African American college students. *Journal of Negro Education*, *69*(1/2), 60–73.

Spohn, C. C. (2000). Thirty years of sentencing reform: The quest for a racially neutral sentencing process. In J. Horney (Ed.), *Criminal justice 2000: Vol. 3. Policies, processes, and decisions of the criminal justice system* (pp. 427–501). Washington, DC: U.S. Department of Justice, National Institute of Justice.

Sue, D. W., Lin, A. I., Torino, G. C., Capodilupo, C. M., & Rivera, D. P. (2009). Racial micro aggression and difficult dialogues on race in the classroom. *Cultural Diversity and Ethnic Minority Psychology*, *15* (2), 183–190. doi:10.1037/a0014191

Sue, D. W., Nadal, K. I., Capodilupo, C. M., Lin, A. I., Torino, G. C., & Rivera, D. P. (2008). Racial micro aggressions against black Americans: Implications for counseling. *Journal of Counseling and Development*, *86*, 330–338. doi:10.1002/j.1556-6678.2008.tb00517.x

Swaine, J., Laughland, O., & Lartery, J. (2015). Black Americans killed by police twice as likely to be unarmed as White people. Retrieved from http://www.theguardian.com/us-news/2015/jun/01/black-americans-killed-by-police-analysis

Tatum, B. D. (2007). *Can we talk about race? And other conversations in an era of school desegregation.* Boston, MA: Beacon Press.

The Sentencing Project. (2000). *Reducing racial disparity in the criminal justice system: A manual for practitioners and policymakers.* Washington, DC: Author.

The Sentencing Project. (2014). *Disproportionate minority contact in the juvenile justice system.* Washington, DC: Author.

United States Census Bureau. (2015). *State and county quick facts.* Retrieved from http://quickfacts.census.gov

EVIP—Edutainment violence intervention/prevention model

Valerie Dorsey Allen[a] and Phyllis Solomon[b]

[a]African-American Resource Center, University of Pennsylvania, Philadelphia, Pennsylvania, USA; [b]School of Social Policy and Practice, University of Pennsylvania, Philadelphia, Pennsylvania, USA

ABSTRACT

The Edutainment Violence Intervention/Prevention Model (EVIP) is an exciting intervention to be used with Black adolescents who have been or will be exposed to the trauma of police brutality. Since such exposure to violence is associated with a diversity of negative consequences in developing adolescents, social workers need interventions to help Black adolescents acquire skills to navigate police interactions and to make sense of the brutality they witness. This article delineates the conceptual rationale, needed skills, and steps for implementing EVIP. EVIP incorporates the Centers for Disease Control's best practices for violence prevention programs and is congruent with Bandura's theory of self-efficacy. EVIP uses media, such as live theater, to give educational messages in an entertaining format. A pilot study has indicated that this intervention has promise. Furthermore, it is engaging and enables participants to explore multiple perspectives. This intervention can be seamlessly embedded by social workers in schools, churches, community centers, and other settings.

According to the Centers for Disease Control (CDC, 2015) Web-based Injury Statistics Query and Reporting System, deaths of Blacks in the United States by police continue to rise from 133 in 2011 to the most recent figures in the first nine months of 2015 of at least 242. News and social media outlets are regularly publicizing Blacks, and specifically Black males, being shot and/or killed by law enforcement officers as well as incidents of police brutality. Because of the access to video on phones and other handheld devices, people are more easily able to witness these occurrences. Consequently, these incidents impact not just the victims who are assaulted, but also the communities of people, including children and adolescents, who virtually witness this police violence. Police brutality and police violence are forms of community violence that cause trauma to both direct and indirect witnesses.

Because of the impact that exposure to violence, including police brutality, has on child and adolescent development, equipping current and future social workers with a model intervention to address the potential for such trauma is critical. Few empirically based treatments are available for youth exposed to violence. Those shown to be effective are long term, and most require significant time and monetary investments. Herein we present an intervention, the Edutainment (Educational Entertainment) Violence Intervention/Prevention Model (EVIP), which is short-term, cost-effective, accessible, and easily facilitated by social workers. EVIP has preliminary evidence that it can equip Black adolescents exposed to community violence with skills to navigate violent interactions and to make sense of the brutality they witness (Allen & Solomon, 2012). EVIP uses theater or other media to offer educational messages in an entertaining and engaging format and has a great appeal to target audiences such as youth in general and Black youth in particular (Ayala et al., 2015). This article will delineate the conceptual rationale, the needed skills, and the steps for implementing this exciting intervention.

Impact of witnessing violence

The impact of directly or indirectly witnessing police violence has great negative impacts because we teach children to trust police officers. Police officers, like health professionals, teachers, and clergy, carry a mantle of trust, and, therefore, if they are perceived as the perpetrators of violence, witnesses and victims feel that there is no safe place to turn (Rosetti, 1995). Although research on the effects of witnessing police violence is limited, the effects of witnessing violence by health care professionals, teachers, and clergy leave victims feeling fearful, distraught, and confused (Fogler, Shipherd, Clarke, Jensen, & Rowe, 2008; Lundgren, Needleman, & Wohlberg, 2004). Like community violence, it affects cognitive and psychological development (Fogler et al., 2008). Studies have linked exposure to violence, even as an observer, with heightened anxiety and depression (Acosta, Albus, Reynolds, Spriggs, & Weist, 2001; Busby, Lambert, & Ialongo, 2013), grief and loss reaction (Osofsky, Wewers, Hann, & Fick, 1993), PTSD symptomatology (Garbarino, Dubrow, Kostelny, & Pardo, 1992; Gellman & Delucia-Waack, 2006), sleep disturbances (Cooley-Quille & Lorion, 1999; Warner & Weist, 1996), and cognitive or academic delays (Sharkey, Tirado-Stayer, Papachristos, & Raver, 2012; Warner & Weist, 1996).

Besides the internalized symptoms, observing violence, such as police brutality, may be related to externalizing behaviors such as aggressive and delinquent behaviors (Attar, Guerra, & Tolan, 1994; Gorman-Smith & Tolan, 2003), increased recklessness in play (Gellman & Delucia-Waack, 2006; Schwab-Stone et al., 1999), and drinking alcohol, using drugs, carrying weapons, and fighting (Cooley-Quille, Boyd, Frantz, & Walsh, 2001). For youth, experimentation with drugs, alcohol, and sex is sometimes used as a coping mechanism for stressful environments caused by violence (Cooley-Quille, Turner, & Beidel, 1995).

Bronfenbrenner's ecological systems theory focuses on the quality and context of the child's environment (Paquette & Ryan, 2001). In the past 20 years, psychological development in adolescents has been conceptualized in more interdisciplinary and transactional models (Compas, Hinden, & Gerhardt, 1995). Models that explore the relationship between the developing child and his or her environment have acknowledged that humans develop in relation to their family, school, community, and society, not in isolation from these influences (Bronfenbrenner, 2004; Bronfenbrenner & Ceci, 1994). When there is conflict or violence in the child's social environment, it affects their development (Bronfenbrenner & Ceci, 1994). This theory supports and gives understanding for the impact of the increased stress and anxiety resulting from police violence on adolescent development. The environmental context including community, society, and family in which the adolescent is living will determine what kind of an emerging adult the young person will become.

Conceptual rationale for edutainment

One characteristic that mediates the impact of witnessing violence as well as the adolescent's ability to avoid and navigate violent situations is their level of self-efficacy. According to Bandura's self-efficacy theory (1994), one's confidence in his or her ability to be successful or to exercise control in a specific area affects whether he or she will perform effectively in that arena. Self-efficacy is seen as "the critical link between having knowledge or skills and engaging in relevant behaviour. … Thus if an adolescent has the knowledge to resolve social problems without the use of violence, … he or she is only likely to act accordingly if the confidence to do so exists" (Vera, Shin, Montgomery, Mildner, & Speight, 2004, p. 74).

Without a belief in the ability to exercise control, little incentive is at hand to act or to persevere in times of hardship or conflict (Bandura, 2001). Because, in the United States, homicide is the leading cause of death among African American adolescents (CDC, 2015), many adolescents believe

Table 1. Relationship between Bandura's theory, the CDC's best practices, and edutainment.

Bandura's self-efficacy theory: Areas of influence	CDC's best practices for violence prevention programs	Edutainment—Skill demonstrated through:
Mastery experiences	Role playing/ small group exercises	Discussion following presentation allows for role-play and the opportunity to demonstrate mastery of skills learned
Vicarious experiences	Active participation in story-based/narrative learning	Witnessing dramatic representation provides story-based/ vicarious experience
Social persuasion	Opportunity to practice and receive feedback	Receiving feedback from audience during discussion encourages positive choices
Increase positive mood	Increase knowledge and information	Positive feedback from adults and peer leaders is obtained during discussion
		Dramatic representation and discussion following presentation provides knowledge and information

they do not have any control, that they are not safe, and that the adults in their lives are not able to protect them from harm. If, as a result of witnessing police killings, young people think that there is a high likelihood of their early death and/or limited possibilities for success, thinking of consequences to negative behavior or poor decisions is of little importance (Caldwell, Wiebe, & Cleveland, 2006). Youth in violent communities are often unable to avoid witnessing violent situations. With advanced preparation, youth involved in programs that increase self-efficacy in managing violence are better able to navigate and avoid violence (Vera et al., 2004).

Bandura's theory states that people's belief about their efficacy can be developed by four sources of influence: (1) mastery experiences, (2) vicarious experiences, (3) social persuasion, and (4) increase in positive mood. These are relatively congruent with the CDC's best practices for violence prevention programs: (1) role-playing, (2) participation in story based learning, (3) an opportunity to practice and receive feedback, and (4) an increase in knowledge. Edutainment is an intervention that incorporates all of these practices (see Table 1).

Edutainment

Researchers have explored edutainment for varying issues, and all assert that drama can serve to educate and stimulate social and moral development (Belliveau, 2004, 2005; Bouchard, 2002; Edmiston, 2000). Viewing and discussing dramatic presentations can increase sensitivity toward issues and allow critical reflection on what individuals are witnessing or experiencing (Belliveau, 2005). Belliveau (2005) highlights the potential benefits of such interventions by stating that the process of drama permits participants to shift positions, observe multiple perspectives, and consider different points of view. The participants are in the position to observe what others have experienced.

The use of edutainment is one intervention in young people's lives that has been successful and is cost effective. The use of live theater or dramatic arts in particular has a long history as a means to educate the public, foster social change, and influence the knowledge and behaviors of target populations (Glik, Nowak, Valente, Sapsis, & Martin, 2002). Unlike pure entertainment, edutainment seeks to bring about "functional" learning, that is, learning that relates to a practical application to the audience members' lives (O'Dea, 1993). Edutainment is used to enable participants to safely explore emotions, to consider life choices, and to compare consequences of a variety of behaviors (Glik et al., 2002; Joronen, Konu, Rankin, & Åstedt-Kurki, 2012). Edutainment programs use performing and dramatic arts to capture the interest and curiosity of audience members. The entertainment mediums are diverse, including theater, radio, and television (Ayala et al., 2015).

This method of education and the consequent influence on behavior has been successful with the adolescent population generally and with minorities in particular. Allen and Solomon (2012) found edutainment to significantly increase violence avoidance self-efficacy, as well as a time effect with significant differences in pre- and postscores for anxiety, coping strategies, and self-efficacy for

African American adolescents exposed to or at risk of exposure to community violence. The participants in the pilot study were 9–15-year-old students in three community centers in the highest crime areas of Philadelphia. The study indicated limited but positive effects for edutainment (Allen & Solomon, 2012). The present article builds on the intervention from this pilot study to develop EVIP. (For more details on participants, measures, and outcomes of the pilot study, see Allen & Solomon, 2012).

Stephenson and Iannone (2006) used an interactive play to teach middle school students the dangers of using drugs and alcohol. Edutainment formats have also been a successful approach in enhancing social relationships and reducing school bullying behaviors in fourth- and fifth-grade students (Joronen et al., 2012) and effective in teaching HIV prevention skills to young people ages 14–24 (Glik et al., 2002). These researchers found the use of edutainment to be an effective method and an attractive alternative to traditional teaching of protective health behaviors.

Edutainment and group work

One common component of these prior edutainment programs was group discussions following the presentations. The discussion provides the audience participants with an opportunity to relate what they have observed in the presentation to what they have seen in their own lives, to discuss the feelings evoked by the presentation, to gain an awareness and an understanding of their feelings, and to practice skills that they observed others use effectively to avoid violence (Allen & Solomon, 2012).

This group discussion, following viewing of the edutainment medium, utilizes principles of social work group work. The purpose of group work is to develop the full capacity of the participant and to encourage a healthy relationship between the individual and his environment (Northen & Kurland, 2001). Like group work, the group discussion approach uses a multiperson process. Learning occurs in the interaction between members of the group as well as from the facilitators. The group functions as an instrument for strengthening the human capacity and for helping to facilitate the mastery of skills such as coping mechanisms among members to prepare them for encountering similar incidents in their daily lives. This occurs as participants identify with characters in the presentation and with each other, which enables them to share and support each other's understanding. Additionally, watching the presentation together provides participants with exposure to a common experience. This shared experience creates connections and fosters a desire to help each other master essential skills (Mitchell & Freitag, 2011).

Group work has been used with people who have been exposed to various types of violence with the potential for trauma. Studies have found that support from individuals who have had similar experiences is beneficial (Healy, 2012). According to Bandura's (1994) self-efficacy theory, one of the ways that efficacy can be developed is by vicariously experiencing a threatening situation and learning strategies that worked for others. This can occur by watching the edutainment presentation as well as from the group discussion that follows whereupon participants share their experiences.

In the group discussions following the edutainment presentation, the leader is responsible for (1) *processing* what has been witnessed, (2) *facilitating* the discussion, (3) *teaching* skills and giving information to expand the group's knowledge, (4) *mediating* any conflicts that occur among the group members, (5) *brokering* for services and resources that are identified by the group and, (6) *enabling* the group to identify strategies and find coping strengths to overcome community issues. Social workers are well equipped for leading this type of intervention because they receive training in these group work skills in most social work education programs. (See Table 2 for delineation of group leader functions.)

Edutainment violence intervention/prevention model (EVIP)

In response to the increase in homicides and the increase in publicity of homicides discussed at the beginning of this article, EVIP was developed and used to enhance coping strategies and decrease stress

Table 2. Group leader roles.

- Set the tone throughout the process
- Model communication and teach listening skills
- Teach skills for handling violence/potentially violent situations
- Create atmosphere of trust and support within the group
- Develop audience's/participants' self-confidence and mutual respect
- Ensure comfort level with sharing thoughts and feelings
- Encourage participation of all members
- Participate in role-plays
- Help connect what they have seen to their own experiences of violence
- Titrate to ensure the group is not overloaded

and anxiety among adolescents living in communities plagued by violence. The edutainment media employed during the pilot study was a play developed in collaboration with students, police officers, social workers, and community leaders. Engagement of community leaders was considered essential because they serve as the neighborhood gatekeepers. In communities with high crime rates, trust of strangers is minimal. The involvement of the community leaders helped ensure youth participation in the intervention. As a result of collaboration in developing the play, it presented current community issues and was written in language that was understood by the audience (Allen, 2010).

The community leaders utilized in the Allen and Solomon pilot study of EVIP came from community centers, which were one of the few places where these neighborhood children and teens could find recreation, companionship, and safety from their neighborhood streets plagued with violence. These centers had staff members trained in youth development and education. The centers also provided training for parents and youth leaders, after-school programs, summer camps, sports, performing arts, arts and crafts, homework assistance, tutoring, cultural trips, and computer labs. Bronfenbrenner's ecological theory indicates the importance of the quality and context of a child's environment and helps to identify factors that can influence the child's development (Paquette & Ryan, 2001). These centers embodied the factors of this theoretical framework. Interaction with these community centers impacted the participants' environment by providing communal values such as empathy, social responsibility, and prosocial interpersonal skills. Bonding and engagement with institutions like schools, churches, and community centers help buffer youth from negative influences and problem behaviors (Jagers, Sydnor, Mouttapa, & Flay, 2007). Involvement with community centers provides a protective factor against the environmental risks of violence in the community.

The media used in the pilot study was a play called "Journey of a Gun." "Journey of a Gun" was an original play by Gail Leslie (2002) that was performed at Freedom Theater in Philadelphia. The play tracked a gun through multiple hands, multiple crimes, and multiple arrests. The characters in the play were police officers, parents, neighborhood school children, young people who have died by violence, and youth who were living in the midst of violent situations. The focus of the play was on choices about violence, guns, and conflict resolution. Some cast members were in the same peer age group and attended the same schools and community centers as the audience members (Allen & Solomon, 2012).

The play ran for one hour and was followed by a 20–30 minute facilitated discussion between the audience members and the cast of the play. During the discussion, the audience and the cast role-played excuses the youth could give to escape potentially violent situations without looking afraid, as well as judicious ways to interact with police and to handle confrontations with violent situations. They were able to vicariously experience threatening acts and learn strategies that worked for others. The audience was presented with information about coping strategies and ways to stay safe, which was offered by peer leaders specifically trained for the role. The peer leaders were selected based on their awareness of issues effecting youth in their community and their ability to articulate these issues. As Bandura's self-efficacy theory suggests, the more individuals see and hear about success from others using these methods, the more the vicarious experience can subsequently influence the choices and behaviors they may make and exhibit when confronted with volatile events (Allen, 2010).

Another area that helped to influence the self-efficacy of adolescents that EVIP addressed was mastery experiences. The development of a sense of mastery when encountering difficult situations is essential for enhancing self-confidence in managing such encounters. As noted by Benight and Bandura (2004, p. 1142), "guided mastery instills both a resilient sense of coping efficacy and thought control efficacy. A strong sense of efficacy that one can cope with social threats make it easier to dismiss perturbing thoughts that intrude." During the discussion following the presentation, participants were able to role-play what may happen and experience success in navigating violent situations. This helped in increasing the youths' levels of confidence to handle such threats that may be encountered in the future. With this increased confidence, they have enhanced capability to control their thoughts about what can happen. This thought control increases their coping efficacy. To the extent that youth can exercise control over what they think, they can regulate how they feel and behave (Caprara, Regalia, & Bandura, 2002). Further elaborated by Benight and Bandura (2004, p. 1142), "perceived thought control efficacy and coping efficacy reduced perceived vulnerability, anxiety, arousal and avoidant patterns of behaviour."

A master's level social worker facilitated the discussion of topics raised immediately after the play and facilitated follow-up meetings at community centers near the audience members' homes occurring a few days later (Allen, 2010). These meetings also included role-playing by the participants. Before viewing the play, a facilitator guide was distributed and reviewed by social workers, community, and peer leaders, which consisted of general questions as well as questions specific to the play and opportunities for role-playing by the participants. The questions served as a guide for the discussion. One of the potential drawbacks of the use of edutainment was the possibility of the audience getting overly involved with the story and missing the pertinent message. One of the roles of the facilitator during the group discussion was to reduce the risk of this occurring by helping the audience to relate what they have seen to their own lives as well as to ask questions which served to keep them engaged in the lesson.

The inclusion of trained peers to lead, engage in group discussions, and give information was a significant component of EVIP. Having peers deliver positive messages has been shown to successfully influence positive choices (Crosnoe & McNeely, 2008). Peers were trained to deliver the material in a manner that was comfortable to adolescents without pressure, similar to delivering the information to a friend.

Although EVIP relies primarily on social workers, community centers, and peers for implementation, parents' and caregivers' involvement as observers was encouraged because it is recognized that they heavily influence the youths' development of coping strategies and self-efficacy. Unger (2004) found that teens' (age 13–17) interactions with parents and caregivers played a vital role in how they perceived their ability to overcome adversities and obstacles. Unger's research determined that youths' view of their caregivers' opinions and perspectives influenced how they perceived themselves. This supports the notion that parents who feel their children have greater self-efficacy in dealing with violence and conflict situations will have more productive ways of handling community violence and coping with negative police interactions (Unger, 2004).

During the previous pilot study, it was obvious that the audience knew the answers the parents, caregivers, and other adults wanted to hear and seemed to revel in the praise they received when giving those answers. However, upon further questioning by the group facilitator, it was apparent that there was often a difference between the initial answers given for adult approval and their reality. An example of this occurred following "Journey of a Gun" when one cast member told a story of a friend who was dating a drug dealer. Both her friend and her friend's boyfriend were killed in a deal gone wrong. She talked about how she was supposed to be with them the night they were killed, but when she realized where they were going and what was to transpire, she chose to go home instead. The initial response from the youth in the audience, which received applause from the adults, was that they would have gone home also. However, when probing further, we discovered that often they had been in places and situations where they knew they shouldn't have been but did not make the decision to leave. This allowed us to talk about how to escape from places you don't want to be without feeling embarrassed. Viewing the presentation with the youth gave the parents and caregivers in the audience a realistic glimpse of how their child responded in different situations (Allen, 2010). It also gave parents and caregivers information so they were better able to continue to have conversations at home about how to handle negative police interactions and what to do when faced with a violent situation.

Lessons learned for implementation

This intervention can be seamlessly integrated into youth programs at local community centers, churches, and schools and can be replicated in communities of youth across the nation. Below are some strategies for implementation.

When utilizing EVIP in a community in which you are not a member it is important to get buy-in from community leaders. Because of their relationships with the community, community leaders are able to engage and gain support from parents and guardians. Whenever possible, community leaders can be trained to cofacilitate the group discussions following the viewing of the media. Local youth programs often use a group format for giving information and for discussing issues that arise in the community. Although most social workers have received training in group work skills, the roles of the group leader are to model communication and listening skills, encourage participation of all members, and connect the media viewed to their own experience. These roles can be shared with community leaders. For delineation of group leaders' functions, see Table 2.

In addition to involving community leaders, it is beneficial to include peer leaders in engaging the group and giving information. Like community leaders, peer leaders support of EVIP makes it easier to get participation of the community youth. Using peer leaders has been found to be effective in communicating useful information likely to influence adolescent behavior (Crosnoe & McNeely, 2008). Peers used as leaders need to be respected and trusted by their peers as well as by the community leaders. See Table 4 for additional peer leader qualifications. In the pilot study, peer leaders were used for participant recruitment, group discussion facilitation, and follow-up with participants.

Peer leaders require training for EVIP by advanced viewing of the media to be used and by participating in a facilitated discussion. The viewing gives the peer leader the opportunity to see and participate in the process, which helps them understand what the media employed is about, what issues may be raised during the discussion, and how they can assist the group facilitator. The group facilitator role-plays how the peer leader is expected to participate in the discussion including how to ask open-ended questions, probe responses for more information, and recognize when the audience is saturated. Peers leaders must be given an opportunity to practice giving information to ensure that they present the information in a sincere manner, because adolescents will not find the information acceptable if they believe the peer is the voice box for well-meaning adults. Additional training components for peer leaders can be found in Table 6.

Although the attendance of parents and caregivers is encouraged, the facilitators need to make it clear at the beginning of the discussion that parents and other adults are there as observers. It is

Table 3. Criteria for selection of media.

- Be culturally, racially, and demographically relevant to the population
- Communicate information and desired message in an entertaining format that holds the attention of the audience
- Enable emotional identification and role modeling
- Promote empathy for one or more characters in the production
- Encourage personal growth of audience participants
- Present currently relevant/controversial issues regarding violence
- Critique current violent incidences and present alternatives for resolution
- Use language that is understandable by the audience
- When possible, engage the audience and local organizations in the creation or selection of the media employed (Singhal & Lacayo, 2008)

Table 4. Qualifications of peer leaders.

- Be respected and trusted by their peer group
- Have good peer relationships
- Have an ability to influence others
- Have prosocial skills
- Able to accept direction
- Be aware of issues effecting youth in their community
- Want to make a positive difference in their community
- Be trusted by community leaders
- Have good communication skills
- Have empathy for other's experiences

Source: http://mypeer.org.au/planning/what-are-peer-based-programs/program-types/peer-leadership/

necessary for the youth in attendance to see this as a chance for them to speak openly, honestly, and without being judged. Parental and caregiver opinions are important to youth, and they will likely answer questions in ways that will please the significant adults in their lives who are present (Unger, 2004). The facilitator must guard against this happening.

For the greatest impact, EVIP implementation requires the media to be culturally, racially, and demographically relevant to the population. It is essential that selected media present currently relevant/controversial issues and use language that is understandable by the audience. Although movies and television shows can be used as teachable tools, ensuring that what is used includes current violent incidences and alternative resolutions is vital. In the pilot study, community leaders and peer leaders assisted in the script development of the play used. Their inclusion ensured that the situations depicted in the play were realistic and the characters were representative of people the audience interacted with regularly. These factors served to promote empathy and identification with the characters and the incidences presented. Table 3 lists additional criteria for the types of media to select.

The edutainment presentations that have proven the most impactful have been followed by a facilitated group discussion. This discussion gives the audience the opportunity to relate what they have seen to their own lives. Suggested facilitation questions are presented in Table 5 as a starting point. The facilitator will likely need to make adjustments based on the responses to questions. Depending on time allotted for the group discussion, the facilitator may choose to ask fewer questions and to save the remaining questions for the follow-up groups at community centers. Although it is crucial that a group discussion be held immediately following the

Table 5. Facilitation questions.

- What happened?
- How was or was not the presentation realistic?
- What did you see that stood out for you?
- What did you see that could have been handled differently?
- What did you see that was handled well?
- How does this relate to the real world?
- Do any of the characters remind you of people you know?
- Did you feel any particular connection to a character and why?
- How do you feel after watching this presentation?
- Was there any scene that upset you?
- What would you do if you were in this situation? (Have participants role-play responses.)
- What advice would you to give to a friend in this situation?
- What should the characters do next?
- What are your concerns about violence in your community?
- How do you avoid violent situations?
- Who in your community/family/neighborhood can you talk to about violence in your community and why?
- What in your community would you like to change?
- Have you witnessed violence in your neighborhood? What happened?
- How was the situation managed? Would you do anything differently? If yes, what would you do differently? (Have participants role-play responses.)
- Would you recommend this presentation to your friends?

Table 6. Peer leader training.

- View media selected prior to presentation
- Participate in group discussion about the presentation
- Role play scenes from the media selected
- Review the facilitation questions
- Teach how to ask open-ended and follow-up questions
- Discuss the impact of violence
- Present information about media literacy and the violence indicators in their neighborhoods
- Explain the limits and responsibility of confidentiality

presentation, it is essential to have additional discussions with smaller groups a few days later. This component is based on the findings of the authors that participants in edutainment interventions increased coping strategies and levels of self-efficacy overtime (Allen & Solomon, 2012) Small groups of 10–15 participants enhance feedback and promote greater participation in the discussion. Those who may not have been comfortable speaking in a larger group can be more easily encouraged to participate and to speak in the smaller group. These group discussions are important in helping the audience to internalize the message of the presentation and relate it to their own lives. When asking questions, youth are more comfortable talking about their thoughts than their feelings; therefore it is important to ask questions in this order: What did they see, what do they think, what do they feel.

Conclusion

The exposure to violence and police brutality continues to be a trauma experienced by Black adolescents at an alarming rate. This exposure, even as a witness, has been linked to both internalized symptoms and externalized behaviors as well as symptomatology of posttraumatic stress syndrome (Cooley-Quille et al., 2001). EVIP is not designed to prevent episodes of police violence but can be beneficial in providing adolescents exposed to such violence with coping skills and strategies to avoid violent situations. EVIP is one intervention/prevention model easily accessible to social workers, which has been successful in educating and influencing the behavior of Black adolescents. EVIP has been shown in a pilot study to enhance violence avoidance self-efficacy and reduce stress related to witnessing violence by teaching prosocial skills and giving educational messages about violence prevention.

This novel approach, EVIP, can be seamlessly embedded by social workers in schools, churches, community centers, and other local settings. It could be used in any location where adolescents are exposed or have the potential to be exposed to community violence. This intervention is likely effective for adolescents because it captures their attention and enables the participants to explore multiple perspectives. The strategies, which can be integrated into practice with most vulnerable populations, are consistent with social work theories, values, and principles.

References

Acosta, O. M., Albus, K. E., Reynolds, M. W., Spriggs, D., & Weist, M. D. (2001). Assessing the status of research on violence-related problems among youth. *Journal of Clinical Child Psychology*, *30*, 152–160. doi:10.1207/S15374424JCCP3002_3

Allen, V. D. (2010). *Educational entertainment as an intervention with adolescents exposed to community violence* (Doctorate in Social Work Dissertation). Retrieved from http://repository.upenn.edu/edissertations_sp2/3

Allen, V. D., & Solomon, P. (2012). Educational-entertainment as an intervention with black adolescents exposed to community violence. *Journal of Prevention & Intervention in the Community*, *40*(4), 313–324. doi:10.1080/10852352.2012.707452

Attar, B. K., Guerra, N. G., & Tolan, P. H. (1994). Neighborhood disadvantage, stressful life events, and adjustment in urban elementary school children. *Journal of Clinical Child Psychology, 23*, 391–400. doi:10.1207/s15374424jccp2304_5

Ayala, G. X., Ibarra, L., Horton, L., Arredondo, E. M., Slymen, D. J., Engelberg, M., & Elder, J. P. (2015). Evidence supporting a promotora-delivered entertainment education intervention for improving mothers' dietary intake: The entre familia: Reflejos de salud study. *Journal of Health Communication, 20*(2), 165–176. doi:10.1080/10810730.2014.917747

Bandura, A. (1994). Self-efficacy. In V. S. Ramachaudran (Ed.), *Encyclopedia of human behavior* (Vol. 4, pp.71–81). New York, NY: Academic Press.

Bandura, A. (2001). Social cognitive theory: An agentic perspective. *Annual Review of Psychology, 52*, 1–26. doi:10.1146/annurev.psych.52.1.1

Belliveau, G. (2004). Pre-service teachers engage in collective drama. *English Quarterly, 35*(3), 1–6.

Belliveau, G. (2005). An arts-based approach to teach social justice: Drama as a way to address bullying in schools. *Journal of Arts Education, 3*(2), 136–165.

Benight, C. C., & Bandura, A. (2004). Social cognitive theory of posttraumatic recovery: The role of perceived self-efficacy. *Behaviour Research and Therapy, 42*, 1129–1148. doi:10.1016/j.brat.2003.08.008

Bouchard, N. (2002). A narrative approach to moral experience using dramatic play and writing. *Journal of Moral Education, 31*, 407–422. doi:10.1080/0305724022000029644

Bronfenbrenner, U. (Ed.). (2004). *Making human beings human: Bioecological perspectives on human development.* Thousand Oaks, CA: Sage.

Bronfenbrenner, U., & Ceci, S. (1994). Nature-nurture reconceptualized in developmental perspective: A bioecological model. *Psychological Review, 101*, 568–586. doi:10.1037/0033-295X.101.4.568

Busby, D. R., Lambert, S. F., & Ialongo, N. S. (2013). Psychological symptoms linking exposure to community violence and academic functioning in African American adolescents. *Journal of Youth and Adolescence, 42*(2), 250–262. doi:10.1007/s10964-012-9895-z

Caldwell, R. M., Wiebe, R. R., & Cleveland, H. H. (2006). The influence of future certainty and contextual factors on delinquent behavior and school adjustment among African American adolescents. *Journal of Youth and Adolescents, 35*, 587–598. doi:10.1007/s10964-006-9031-z

Caprara, G. V., Regalia, C., & Bandura, A. (2002). Longitudinal impact of perceived self-regulatory efficacy on violent conduct. *European Psychologist, 7*(1), 63–69. doi:10.1027//1016-9040.7.1.63

Centers for Disease Control and Prevention. (2015). *Fatal injury reports—WISQARS—Injury.* Atlanta, GA: Author. Retrieved from http://www.cdc.gov/injury/wisqars/fatal_injury_reports.html

Compas, B. E., Hinden, B. R., & Gerhardt, C. A. (1995). Adolescent development: Pathways and processes of risk and resilience. *Annual Review of Psychology, 46*, 265–293. doi:10.1146/annurev.ps.46.020195.001405

Cooley-Quille, M., Boyd, R. C., Frantz, E., & Walsh, J. (2001). Emotional and behavioral impact of exposure to community violence in inner-city adolescents. *Journal of Clinical Child Psychology, 30*, 199–206. doi:10.1207/S15374424JCCP3002_7

Cooley-Quille, M., & Lorion, R. (1999). Adolescents' exposure to community violence: Sleep and psychophysiological functioning. *Journal of Community Psychology, 27*, 367–375. doi:10.1002/(ISSN)1520-6629

Cooley-Quille, M. R., Turner, S. M., & Beidel, D. C. (1995). Assessing community violence: The Children's Report of Exposure to Violence (CREV). *Journal of the American Academy of Child & Adolescent Psychiatry, 34*, 201–208. doi:10.1097/00004583-199502000-00015

Crosnoe, R., & McNeely, C. (2008). Peer relations, adolescent behavior, and public health research and practice. *Family & Community Health, 31*, 571–580. doi:10.1097/01.FCH.0000304020.05632.e8

Edmiston, B. (2000). Drama as ethical education. *Research in Drama Education, 5*, 63–84. doi:10.1080/135697800114203

Fogler, J. M., Shipherd, J. C., Clarke, S., Jensen, J., & Rowe, E. (2008). The impact of clergy-perpetrated sexual abuse: The role of gender, development, and posttraumatic stress. *Journal of Child Sexual Abuse, 17*(3–4), 329–358. doi:10.1080/10538710802329940

Garbarino, J., Dubrow, N., Kostelny, K., & Pardo, C. (1992). *Children in danger: Coping with the consequences of community violence.* San Francisco, CA: Jossey-Bass.

Gellman, R. A., & Delucia-Waack, J. L. (2006). Predicting school violence: A comparison of violent and nonviolent male students on attitudes toward violence, exposure level to violence, and PTSD symptomatology. *Psychology in the Schools, 43*, 591–598. doi:10.1002/(ISSN)1520-6807

Glik, D., Nowak, G., Valente, T., Sapsis, K., & Martin, C. (2002). Youth performing arts entertainment-education for HIV/AIDS prevention and health promotion: Practice and research. *Journal of Health Communication, 7*(1), 39–57. doi:10.1080/10810730252801183

Gorman-Smith, D., & Tolan, P. H. (2003). Positive adaptation among youth exposed to community violence. In S. Luthar (Ed.), *Resilience and vulnerability: Adaptation in the context of childhood adversities* (pp. 392–413). New York, NY: Cambridge University Press.

Healy, K. (2012). *Social work methods and skills: The essential foundation of practice.* New York, NY: Palgrave Macmillan.

Jagers, R. J., Sydnor, K., Mouttapa, M., & Flay, B. R. (2007). Protective factors associated with preadolescent violence: Preliminary work on a cultural model. *American Journal of Community Psychology, 40,* 138–145. doi:10.1007/s10464-007-9121-4

Joronen, K., Konu, A., Rankin, S. H., & Åstedt-Kurki, P. (2012). An evaluation of a drama program to enhance social relationships and anti-bullying at elementary school: A controlled study. *Health Promotion International, 27*(1), 5–1. doi:10.1093/heapro/dar012

Leslie, G. (2002). *Journey of a gun.* Philadelphia, PA: New Freedom Theatre.

Lundgren, N., & Wohlberg, J. W. (2004). *Above all, do no harm: Abuse of power by health care professionals.* Retrieved from http://www.therapyabuse.org/p2-abuse-of-power.htm

Mitchell, K. S., & Freitag, J. L. (2011). Forum theatre for bystanders: A new model for gender violence prevention. *Violence against Women, 17*(8), 990–1013. doi:10.1177/1077801211417152

Northen, H., & Kurland, R. (2001). *Social work with groups.* New York, NY: Columbia University Press.

O'Dea, J. W. (1993). Teaching as entertainment: A comment on a 20th century phenomenon. *Education Canada, 37,* 24–29.

Osofsky, J. D., Wewers, S., Hann, D. M., & Fick, A. C. (1993). Chronic community violence: What is happening to our children? *Psychiatry: Interpersonal and Biological Processes Special Issue: Children and Violence, 56,* 36–45.

Paquette, D., & Ryan, J. (2001). *Bronfenbrenner's ecological systems theory.* Retrieved from http://pt3.nl.edu/paquetter yanwebquest.pdf

Rosetti, S. J. (1995). The impact of child sexual abuse on attitudes toward God and the Catholic Church. *Child Abuse & Neglect, 19*(12), 1469–1481. doi:10.1016/0145-2134(95)00100-1

Schwab-Stone, M. E., Chen, C., Greenberger, E., Silver, D., Lightman, J., & Voyce, C. (1999). No safe haven II: A study of violence exposure in an urban community. *Journal of American Child and Adolescent Psychiatry, 38,* 359–367. doi:10.1097/00004583-199904000-00007

Sharkey, P. T., Tirado-Strayer, N., Papachristos, A. V., & Raver, C. C. (2012). The effect of local violence on children's attention and impulse control. *American Journal of Public Health, 102*(12), 2287–2293. doi:10.2105/AJPH.2012.300789

Singhal, A., & Lacayo, V. (2008). *Engaging and mobilizing society through edutainment experience-sharing and cross-learning among four pioneering organizations.* Narrative report presentation to Oxfam-Novib/KIC, El Paso, TX.

Stephenson, S. D., & Iannone, R. (2006). A drug evaluation curriculum with drama as its base: The target project. *College Student Journal, 40*(3), 631–640.

Unger, M. (2004). The importance of parents and other caregivers to the resilience of high-risk adolescents. *Family Process, 43,* 23–41. doi:10.1111/j.1545-5300.2004.04301004.x

Vera, E. M., Shin, R. Q., Montgomery, G. P., Mildner, C., & Speight, S. L. (2004). Conflict resolution styles, self-efficacy, self-control, and future orientation of urban adolescents. *Professional School Counseling, 8,* 73–80.

Warner, B. S., & Weist, M. D. (1996). Urban youth as witnesses to violence: Beginning assessment and treatment efforts. *Journal of Youth and Adolescence, 25,* 361–377. doi:10.1007/BF01537390

"Hands up, don't shoot" or shut up and play ball? Fan-generated media views of the Ferguson Five

Emmett L. Gill, Jr.

Department of Social Work, College of Public Policy, University of Texas at San Antonio, San Antonio, Texas, USA

ABSTRACT

This article explores the intersection of sports and social activism in the wake of the police-involved death of Michael Brown. Traditionally, professional athletes have remained silent, or at the very best color-blind, regarding domestic social issues. It is customary for sports celebrities such as Michael Jordan to avoid compromising their status in the marketplace with politics, even when the social matter impacts males who look like them and unswervingly support their craft. Yet, in the wake of the death of Brown, several professional athletes, if only briefly, engaged in their own forms of activism. This article will implore a qualitative content analysis of mainstream media accounts and user-generated content to develop a case study on how Black professional athletes responded to police-involved deaths of Black men. In particular, the author will use the "data" to develop a case study on five St. Louis Rams athletes who staged a silent, pregame protest in the wake of the civil unrest in Ferguson, Missouri. The case study will include the response from the St. Louis police department and the National Football League. Fan-generated media content about the "Ferguson Five" will be used to analyze public perceptions of athlete activism. A grounded theory approach will be used to examine the immediate and intermediate prospect of civic involvement of professional athletes in social issues.

"The era of the activist athlete is dead." —Orin Starn (Clarke, 2009)

Professional athletes are human beings with opinions, causes, and issues they care about, but unlike many everyday people, their status and platform gives them incredible influence in American culture. A proportion of professional sports fans, media, and casual observers favor and encourage athlete involvement in charitable causes, even causes with robust political undertones. Another proportion believes that when it comes to athletes and activism that they should not use their platform, via their workplace, to share their beliefs and advance social causes. Professional athletes who engage in activism must worry about alienating their teammates, their organization, and any retaliation that might come with affecting the brand of an American sport organization. Take the case of Craig Hodges. Hodges, a three-pointer specialist, was instrumental in the initial (three-peat) championship run of the Bulls. When the Chicago Bulls visited the White House after winning the 1992 NBA championship, Hodges delivered a hand-written letter to then President George H. W. Bush. In the letter Hodges expressed his discontent with the administration's treatment of the poor and minorities (Bondy, 1996). The Bulls waived Hodges afterwards, and he never received an offer or even a tryout from another NBA team. Hodges misfortune exemplifies why no athletes' activism has approached the level of political and social involvement displayed by Jackie Robinson, Muhammad

Ali, Arthur Ashe, Bill Russell, Tommie Smith, and John Carlos. The stakes associated with athletes' civic involvement have far more zeros attached than in years past.

As opposed to speaking out on social issues, professional athletes preferred to use their influence to market products that enhanced their personal financial well-being. Athletes do not want to risk the employment status or opportunities to pursue endorsement revenue streams beyond their team contracts. Activism avoidance strategies were most vividly seen when Michael Jordan, arguably the greatest basketball player ever, reportedly explained his refusal to endorse a Democratic Senate candidate, Harvey Gant (against Jesse Helms), in his home state of North Carolina by saying, "Republicans buy shoes, too" (Clarke, 2009). Some of the most successful professional athletes, on the field, including Tiger Woods, have assumed a silent role and never taken a divisive stand because activism can influence endorsement income. "If you want to publicly support a controversial cause because it is truly important to you, good for you. Just know that many advertisers, many fans and many future employers don't look for trouble," said one unnamed agent (Thiel, 2014, para. 4). Even so, a set of issues has emerged, such as police brutality, that not only impact Black communities, but Black professional athletes as well.

Not only are athletes hesitant to engage in activism, but sports franchises have adopted a corporate mentality and do not want to get drawn into politicized issues. Sports franchises want to appeal to as many people as possible and are cognizant that fans spend money attending NFL games, on team merchandise, and in a myriad of other ways. Many hot button social issues cut across athlete and fan racial lines. In the case of the NFL fan base, 92% of fans attending NFL games are White (Domowitch, 1989) and 68% of NFL football employees are Black (Tapp, 2014). Professional athletes are a large component of a team that is the staple of a larger brand. "NFL teams are very much aware of brand awareness and they want to do everything in their power to make sure that as many people as possible will come watch football games," said Chris Kluwe (Waldron, 2014, para. 12). The Minnesota Vikings allegedly released Kluwe, who is White, because of his outspoken support for same-sex marriage (Waldron, 2014).[1] Donte Stallworth maintained, "I don't think the NFL itself has anything against guys speaking out" (Waldron, 2014, para 2). Stallworth played 10 NFL seasons and regularly talks publicly about political issues from the economy to the use of drones. "I think it's more so the structure of the team and not being in a position to be a distraction to the team. Conduct detrimental to the team is one of the biggest things guys can get in trouble for," said Stallworth (Waldron, 2014, para 6). The need for professional athletes to address the unrest in Ferguson, Missouri, dwarfed the notion of activism being a distraction.

During the first 6 months of 2015, there were 529 killings by law enforcement officers (*The Guardian*, 2015). A meaningful proportion of alleged police brutality and killings by law enforcement officers involve Black males. Abuse of police power and brutality present a different kind of social issue because some Black professional athletes can relate to the conundrum. On March 23, 2012, LeBron James and his Miami Heat teammates dressed in black hoodies and posed together for a team picture with their heads bowed and their hands in their pockets (Demby, 2012). The gesture was meant to show solidarity with Trayvon Martin, the black teenager shot and killed by George Zimmerman, a White/Hispanic man, while wearing a similar hooded sweatshirt (Blow, 2012). Juan Carlos, one of the Black athletes who led a protest at the 1968 Olympics by raising his fist, wearing a black glove, believed this was a watershed moment: "When the Heat stood up and made that statement, it was saying to everybody, 'Enough is enough.' Young people are losing their lives and feeling like there's no justice'" (Sheinin, 2014, para 15). Activism by professional athletes also has recognized larger movements exist to address the extrajudicial killings of Black males.

"Hands Up, Don't Shoot" is a mantra adopted by Black Lives Matter (BLM) protesters, which is a larger movement that started before the Michael Brown shooting. BLM began after the July 2013 acquittal of George Zimmerman in the Florida shooting death of Martin. BLM did receive fresh impetus from the Brown shooting (Demby, 2012).[2] The BLM movement is largely based on the protests of 19 deaths at the hands of law enforcement between 2009 and 2015.[3] Monifa Bandele says the mantra is about conveying a larger truth (Sexton, 2015). "'Hands up' is the ultimate truth, and the reason why 'hands up' has gone viral across the country is because it's a posture known to black people," said Bandele (Sexton, 2015, para 4). BLM organizers suggests that "Hands Up, Don't Shoot" has a symbolic meaning that is independent of whether Brown's hands were raised, and it serves as a means of expressing opposition to police violence. Speaking to the *Daily Mail*, Elizabeth Brondolo, a St. John's University professor, said, "The truth always really matters, but it's important to recognize that past experience to stereotypes also influences the perception of hands being raised (Evans, 2014).

Fans, media, and professional sport observers have suggested that professional athletes should be more civically engaged. Ferguson presented a social issue that hit close to home. This study explores the views of St. Louis Rams fans regarding activism by professional football athletes and ponders the future prospect for activism by athletes.

Conceptual framework

Under the umbrella of human behavior theories are conflict theories, which emphasize the social, political, or material inequality of a social group while critiquing broader sociopolitical systems (Wallace & Wolf, 1999). Conflict theories tend to contrast dominant ideologies and draw greater attention to race, gender, and sexual orientation power differentials. Sears (2008) suggests that disadvantaged people have structural interests that run counter to the current situation, but that once they become engaged they can help to lead social change. Conflict theory is most commonly associated with Marxism and positivist perspectives, but may also be associated with critical race theory (CRT). CRT is a tool through which scholars and researchers can outline, reveal, and tackle certain problems because it offers a way to understand how superficial race-neutral structures and processes are ways of forming the boundaries of racism (Ladson-Billings & Tate; 1995; Singer, 2005; Solorzano, Ceja, & Yosso, 2000). CRT suggests that power structures are based on White privilege and that certain freedoms Whites revel in can perpetuate the marginalization of people of color. CRT recognizes that racism is engrained in the fabric and system of the American society (UCLA School of Public Affairs, 2014). The CRT concepts directing this study are color-blindness (Bonilla-Silva, 2002, 2003), Black masculinity (Collins, 2004; Cooper, 2005; Ferber, 2007; Hooks, 1998; Leonard & King, 2010), bipolar depictions (Collins, 2004; Cooper, 2005; Ferber, 2007; Leonard & King, 2010), commodification (Andrews, King, & Leonard, 2011), and intersectionality (Leonard, 2004).

Color-blind racism is a common manifestation of the new racism (Bonilla-Silva, 2002, 2003; Buffington & Fraley, 2011; Teaching Tolerance, 2014; Williams, 2011). Color-blindness can be defined as "the mere recognition of someone's race as racism" (Cooper, 2005, p. 885). The purpose of color-blindness is to ignore racial differences in an effort to develop social homogeneity. In daily life, color-blindness asserts that everyone should behave according to hegemonic standards of conduct, or "white norms as the model for everyone's behavior" (Cooper, 2005, p. 885), regardless of racial difference. Color-blind discourses assert that we live in a postracial culture, thus everyone should receive equal treatment regardless of race. Further a color-blind line of reasoning argues that if a Black person is struggling with a social problem, then the problem was caused by individual choices and behaviors of that person or the culture in which the individual was raised and socialized. Race talk is a direct color-blind strategy. Race talk refers to public conversations generated around race and race-related issues that avoid direct references to race in favor of coded signals (Buffington & Fraley, 2011; Cole, 1996; Wheelock & Hartman, 2000). One of the distinctive threads of color-blind frames that are used to guide conversations about race is cultural racism (Bonilla-Silva, 2003) or the view there are cultural deficiencies within people of color (Leonard, 2004).

Another strategy to explore power relations, or conflict, among classes is via hegemonic masculinity. Hegemonic masculinity originates cultural hegemony theory and analyzes power relations or how a group claims and sustains a dominant position in society (Connell, 2005). Black masculinity intersects with CRT and allows for a more vigorous critical analysis of how the social constructs of gender, race, and sports influence power relations (Leonard, 2004; Ferber, 2007; Leonard & King,

2010, 2011). One White supremacist patriarchal (WSP) view of Black masculinity posits Black men as belonging to one of two categories: Good Black Men or Bad Black Men (Collins, 2004; Cooper, 2005; Ferber, 2007; Leonard, 2004; Leonard & King, 2010). Bipolar depictions of Black males serve the tenets of WSP by dictating acceptable ways for Black men to behave in a White society. Depictions of the Good Black Man encourage viewers to admire and be induced into purchasing products and depictions of the Bad Black Man serve to entertain, sell products, and create consumable news stories. Good Black Men succeeded because they submit to the social codes written by the patriarchy and assimilate into the passive, cautious mold that WSP dictates. Alternatively, Bad Black Men fail because they choose to not assimilate and perform loud, violent, and hypersexual behaviors, which are categorized by the media to fit hegemonic stereotypes about Black masculinity (Collins, 2004; Hooks, 2004a). Bad Black Men must be punished, in the public eye, via discourse about their corrupt culture.

The world of sports benefits from color-blind ideology; in fact, sports discourse is one of the primary "disseminators of colorblind ideology" (Leonard, 2004, p. 288). When race and gender are rendered invisible in media narratives about U.S. sports systems these systems maintain the WSP status quo by engaging in racist practices. By keeping Black men out of positions of influence, via commodification, sport organizations relegate Black males to the role of entertainer while maintaining the WSP and the social stratification of individuals (Collins, 2004; Hooks, 2004b). The commodification of Black bodies has a long history, beginning with slavery in the Americas in the 17th century, and is still in practice through constructing media depictions of Black athletes to be used for entertaining the WSP (Rhoden, 2006). Black males have been very successful in certain sports, but they are rarely found in positions of power and control. Color-blind ideologies ignore the intersections between race, class, and gender (Bonilla-Silva, 2003; Cooper, 2005). According to Ferber (2007, p. 20), "Success in the field of athletics does nothing to undermine the historical propensity to reduce Black men to their bodies." Color-blind ideologies focus on one aspect of a person's identity, primarily an individual's social class or status (Cooper, 2005). A singular focus hides how race, gender, and social status, such as an individual's status as a professional athlete, intersects with activism.

Methodology

This study engaged the critical case study approach as described by Flyvbjerg (2006), Yin (2010), and Hesse-Biber and Leavy (2011). Case study research is an in-depth exploration of a given issue, event, or system assessed from multiple perspectives. Critical case study research aims to capture a holistic understanding of a particular case and to have that understanding apply to similar cases (Flyvbjerg, 2006). The purpose of this case study is to understand fan-generated media written about the St. Louis Rams "Hands Up, Don't Shoot" (STRHUDS) controversy and the social construction of ideas about Black athlete activism.

The first step in the data collection was to construct a comprehensive timeline of events related to the STRHUDS. The author conducted a broad Internet search for news articles and fan-generated media content posted proceeding Internet news articles related to the STRHUDS. This search yielded 18 unique articles related to STRHUDS. The second step in the data collection was to determine any additional exclusion and inclusion criteria for article selection. The author decided that articles must include at least 50 fan-generated media comments. This process resulted in a cross section of 10 national, regional, positive, and negative articles produced by sports and nonsports journalists. By examining the sample data, the author was able to construct a timeline of events related to the case. This process also resulted in a sample of N = 1,266 fan-generated media comments for the content analysis.

Content analysis is a methodical, replicable procedure, which uses coding to establish the presence of words, ideas, and themes that exist in bodies of text (Krippendorff, 2012). The data analysis for this project occurred in three phases. For the first phase, the author conducted a preliminary search of conceptual literature related to Black athletes and activism. The second phase of analysis included reading the media articles and subsequent fan-generated media content at least three times (Hesse-Biber & Leavy, 2011). The comments were labeled and organized according to a priori categories. A priori codes included color-blindness, bipolar depictions (good Black and bad Black male athletes), commodification, and intersectionality. The third stage of data analysis involved pattern matching as described by Yin (2009) and content analysis as described by Krippendorff (2012). Pattern matching involves using an empirically established pattern to assess for the reemergence of the pattern while investigating case study content. As part of the pattern matching the author used themes that emerged from examining the conceptual literature to analyze how a priori codes, and their subthemes, were constructed by fan-generated media content of the STRHUDS controversy. The codes, and their intersections, were then applied in a deductive examination of the fan-generated media comments.

St. Louis Rams "hands up, don't shoot" (STRHUDS) case study

The STRHUDS controversy centers on the police shooting of Ferguson resident Michael Brown. The racial demography of Ferguson, Missouri, the Ferguson police department, and arrests the Ferguson police made are all meaningful in contextualizing the STRHUDS controversy. Ferguson, Missouri is 29.3% White and 67.4% Black (U.S. Census, 2015). Ferguson only has four nonwhite officers among the 54 officers on its police force (Chalabi, 2015). In Ferguson, Blacks accounted for 93% of arrests (Eligon, 2015).[4] The shooting of 18-year-old Michael Brown occurred between 12:01 and 12:03 p.m. on August 9, 2014. The fatal shooting, by then Police Officer Darren Wilson, touched off weeks of unrest (Ellis, Todd, & Karimi, 2014). The unrest continued after a St. Louis County grand jury voted on November 24, 2014, not to indict Wilson (Ellis et al., 2014). Edward Jones Dome, the Rams football stadium, is 12 miles west of Ferguson. (The team recently moved to Los Angeles.)

On August 20, 2014, the St. Louis Rams offered their practice fields to high school teams affected by the rioting (Wagoner, 2014). On August 19, 2014, the Rams donated over 200 tickets to their preseason game against the Green Bay Packers to three Ferguson-area high school football teams. Then on November 19, 2014, during the pregame of the Rams regular season game contest versus the Oakland Raiders, five Rams players—Jared Cook, Kenny Britt, Tavon Austin, Stedman Bailey, and Chris Givens—executed the "Hand Up, Don't Shoot" gesture. In addition to the pregame gesture, Rams running back Tre Mason and Britt held their hands up again after Mason's first quarter 35-yard touchdown reception.[5] Britt thought to act out the demonstration and organized the 'Hands Up, Don't Shoot' symbolism with his four fellow Rams (Associated Press, 2015). Fans, mostly White, also had signs stating "Rams fans know Black lives matter on and off the field" (Zirin, 2014). Britt also wrote on his wrist tape "MyKidsLivesMatter" and "Mike Brown" and published a photo of his wrists on his Twitter feed (Katz, 2014). On another occasion Britt had names of Michael Brown and Trayvon Martin written on his cleats (Katz, 2014).

"It's not one week we're thinking about it and the next week we've forgotten about it. This is going to be an ongoing thing to seek change.' We talked about the situation, what happened and what was going on around the country. We're in this, too. We're not just concentrating on football all day, every day. I don't want the people in the community to feel like we turned a blind eye to it" (Associated Press, 2014, para 7).Change query to ask which 2014: a, b, or c

On December 1, 2014, the St. Louis Police Officers Association Police (SLPOA) released the following statement:

> The St. Louis Police Officers Association is profoundly disappointed with the members of the St. Louis Rams football team who chose to ignore the mountains of evidence released from the St. Louis County Grand Jury this week and engage in a display that police officers around the nation found tasteless, offensive and inflammatory.

> Five members of the Rams entered the field today exhibiting the "hands-up-don't-shoot" pose that has been adopted by protestors who accused Ferguson Police Officer Darren Wilson of murdering Michael Brown. The gesture has become synonymous with assertions that Michael Brown was innocent of any wrongdoing and attempting to surrender peacefully when Wilson, according to some now-discredited witnesses, gunned him down in cold blood. (paras. 1 and 2 of the statement)[6]

> The SLPOA is calling for the players involved to be disciplined and for the Rams and the NFL to deliver a very public apology. I know that there are those that will say that these players are simply exercising their First Amendment rights. Well I've got news for people who think that way, cops have First Amendment rights too, and we plan to exercise ours. I'd remind the NFL and their players that it is not the violent thugs burning down buildings that buy their advertiser's products. It's cops and the good people of St. Louis and other NFL towns that do. Somebody needs to throw a flag on this play. If it's not the NFL and the Rams, then it'll be cops and their supporters. (SLPOA, 2014)

One website, suggesting a boycott of Rams games, collected 20,000 supporters, and another *Boycott the St. Louis Rams* Facebook page garnered 12,000 likes in less than 24 hours after the game (Hoft, 2014).

On December 1, 2014, the *St. Louis Post Dispatch* reported that St. Louis County Police Chief Jon Belmar sent an email to his staff saying the Rams' chief operating officer called him to apologize. "I received a very nice call this morning from Mr. Kevin Demoff of the St. Louis Rams who wanted to take the opportunity to apologize to our department on behalf of the Rams for the 'Hands Up' gesture that some players took the field with yesterday" (Yan, 2014).[7] The St. Louis Rams organization insisted that they did not issue an apology. "We did not apologize," said Rams spokesman Artis Twyman (Yan, 2014, para 7).

On December 1, 2014, NFL spokesman Brian McCarthy provided a one-sentence email response. "We respect and understand the concerns of all individuals who have expressed views on this tragic situation," McCarthy said (Farmer, 2014, para 2). The NFL did not discipline the Ferguson Five for their pregame "Hands Up" gesture.

Findings

The findings include the frequencies of themes related to the a priori codes. Themes were grouped if they appeared to be related. Preceding each set of themes are some representative qualitative samples of the fan-generated media. The themes were organized under the "Good" and "Bad" Black male themes because of the clear bipolar nature of comments.

Good Black male athletes

Themes related to "Good" Black male athletes refer to the idea of the Ferguson Five should follow the WSP status quo and not engage in activism. Four themes directly related to the notion of Good Black male athletes emerged including ignoring evidence contrary to the 'Hands Up, Don't Shoot' theory, dumb jocks, punishment for the Ferguson Five, and rebuffing freedom of speech for the Ferguson Five.[8] Forty-eight percent of fan-generated media content was directly and indirectly consistent with themes describing the Good Black male athlete relative to the SLRHUDS controversy:

> **Oldflyer**—The NFL like the NBA has a fairly high percentage of thugs so, as I do with the NBA, I guess the answer is to ignore all of them. Sooner or later they will kill the Golden Goose and have to go to work for a living—or go on welfare.

Twenty-two percent of fan-generated media content included expressions characterizing the Ferguson Five as dumb jocks, thugs, morons, dumb as a box of rocks, hoodlums, morons, woefully ignorant, African American jocks, ignorant fools, uneducated, ill-mannered thugs, and just sperm donors. Fifteen percent of the fan-generated media content was related to the fan's belief that the Ferguson Five were oblivious because they ignored evidence that indicated Michael Brown did not have his hands up and did not say "don't shoot" before he was fatally shot.

Color-blindness was evident in depictions of the Ferguson Five as Good Black male athletes in that race was not explicitly mentioned but repeatedly implied. Fewer than one tenth of the comments mentioned race, but more than one-half of the comments related to Bad Blacks mentioned race. Hip-hop football players, gold teeth and dreads, overpaid, beastly, and pimps were some additional expressions used to describe the Ferguson Five. Moreover, some posts even included references to the current president in attempt to underscore the race talk. Here the fan-generated media employed a new racist and color-blind technique referred to a race talk to characterize the Ferguson Five. Race talk embraces the language of class and geography as a way to signify race without explicitly saying it. In particular fan-generated media content included the frequent use of the word "thug." Thug is becoming used so frequently that some forget, or may not know, that the word means "a brutal assassin or gangster" (Merriam Webster, 2015). None of the Ferguson Five have been arrested for felonies such as murder or some form of organized crime, which are crimes consistent with the term thug:

> **WilyCoyoteSuperGenius**—Rams season ticket holders, most of whom are white, should demand these players be cut or refuse to renew their tickets.
>
> **Premier social critic**—The players have NO "free speech rights" with respect to the NFL. The first amendment says Congress may make no law abridging the right to free speech, but employers can and do punish employees for speech that brings disgrace onto the employers. Such punishment is legally upheld.
>
> **Eille**—When I go to a concert and spend my hard earned money to watch that group Rock and Roll my troubles away. I don't want to hear their rants on political views, I don't want to see their gestures. Even If I am on the same side of the fence as they are. I feel the same about a game. I am there to be entertained. They are paid to entertain.

Thirteen percent of fan-generated media content suggested that the Rams football employees should be punished. Firing, fining, and/or cutting the Ferguson Five were suggestions provided by fans. Four percent of fan-generated media content included narratives against athletes' freedom of speech during work hours and underscored the idea that the Ferguson Five should have chosen a more appropriate place or time for their activism. Three percent of fan-generated media content suggested that the Ferguson Five and/or the Rams organization should apologize to the St. Louis police officers.

Consistent with the idea of the Good Black male, fan-generated media included content that supported notions of commodification, containment, and criminalization. First, fans emphasized that they pay for an entertainment service, and by virtue of their investment athletes should not engage in activism during work hours. Second, fans speculated the Ferguson Five should be punished as if they committed a crime or that they should apologize as if there was some type of restorative justice that should result because of their gesture. Third, fans suggested players should not be involved in social issues on company time, which could be viewed as a containment strategy. However, the St. Louis Rams and its athletes participate in 19 charities and community programs (St. Louis Rams, 2015).[9] These charities are one form of advocacy for mainstream issues like gerontology, cancer, prenatal care, diversity and inclusion, education, and catastrophic disease. Another containment strategy was evident in that at least one member of the Ferguson Five received a death threat.

The quantitative results and qualitative samples suggest that when professional athletes engage in activism it is not well received by some fans. Some of the same fans that cheer for the St. Louis Rams football players frequently questioned their intelligence, wanted them fired from their jobs, and were generally unwilling to consider the athletes' race, gender, and personal experiences as each relates to the "Hands Up" movement. Black professional football employees are viewed differently when they become advocates against issues like excessive police force, as opposed to pursuing team charitable interests, while at work.

Bad Black male athletes

The themes for Bad Black male athletes included terms and expressions that supported of the Ferguson Five, professional athletes' activism, or ideas related to the Ferguson Five's counter-story. The fans who supported the Ferguson Five and themes related to Bad Black males grasped the impact of the intersectionality of professional athletes and activism and do not favor the status quo. Six themes directly related to the notion of "Bad" Black males emerged including support for the Ferguson Five's freedom of speech and gesture, recognition of the Black Lives Matter movement, detection of efforts to silence voices, some mention of police profiling/abuse of police power, furthering the football employees' activism, and past activism by Black athletes. Fifty-two percent of fan-generated media content was consistent with themes directly[10] supporting Bad Black male athletes:

> **NVGNVG**—Kudos to these players for finally being fully engaged in the world they live in. Today's generation of athletes are such minions of the NFL and their corporate masters. The police in Ferguson find this offensive? Really? Offensive is the continuous abuse of authority these Robocops have displayed in places like Ferguson.

> **DangerouslyCheesey**—I hope everyone on the team does this next week and both teams agree to have the first play of the game be a minute of silence as they stand around together in solidarity after snapping the ball. Now THAT would get some attention.

Eighteen percent of the fan-generated media content included expressions in favor of professional football employees' freedom of speech, and 4 percent of the fan-generated media content directly expressed favor of the Ferguson Five's gesture. An additional 4 percent of fan-generated media discussed silencing the voices both movements were intent on projecting. In particular this category of fan-generated media content suggested professional football employees should further their efforts to bring greater attention to extrajudicial killings of Blacks by the police. Another 8 percent of the fan-generated media content noted that other NFL, National Basketball Association (NBA) and Major League Baseball (MLB) teams should join in the activism surrounding police brutality.[11] One fan-generated media post alerted readers that SLPOA had a Black counterpart—the Ethical Society of Police (ESOP)[12]—and only one majority media outlet talked about the ESOP statement: "We think that their actions were commendable and that they should not be ridiculed, disciplined or punished for taking a stand on this very important issue which is of great concern around the world and especially in the community where these players work" (Molinet, 2014).

> **jnik23260**—I'm glad some pro athletes are taking up the mantle of tommie smith, Muhammad Ali and others in being politically involved, and not following the examples of Michael Jordan and Tiger Woods in being just about the money.

Direct fan-generated media contact explored systemic issues including past athlete activism, the BLM, and abusive policing practices. Relative to the history of activism among professional athletes, 2 percent of the fan-generated media content included references to earlier sports social activism including the 1968 protest in Mexico City and the draft entry protest of Muhammad Ali. Three percent of fan-generated media included content that served as a reminder that the "Hands Up, Don't Shoot" gesture was a component of the larger Black Lives Matter Movement. Six percent of fan-generated media content was related to fans expressions about police brutality and abusive policing practices, and another 5 percent of the fan-generated media content spoke to racial profiling:

> **native101**—It's not about false narratives or spin. It's about the Straw that Broke the Camel's Back. Have you thought about asking yourself where all this pent up rage and anger came from to begin with? Or do you think it just spontaneously erupted after one isolated event? Do you think any NFL players may have some experience or knowledge with any of the sentiments being expressed by protestors in St. Louis?

The quote above speaks to fan-generated media content that reflects support for the Ferguson Five because of an understanding of the influence in intersectionality and systemic issues on their activism. Above the fan alludes to the historical component of the counternarrative related to "Hands Up, Don't Shoot" gesture. Next, the fan sarcastically underscores that police brutality and abusive policing are social issues that are not unique to Ferguson. Foremost, the fan introduces the possibility that athletes, in part because of their race and gender, may have experienced situations that could have led to an extrajudicial homicide. Kenny Britt exemplifies this intersection. Kenny Britt, the Ferguson Five member who thought of and initiated the "Hand Up, Don't Shoot" demonstration, has a history with law enforcement. Britt experienced 17 traffic stops over a two-year period and expressed he is certain that some of his troubles are the result of being Black. "There's been times when I've been racially profiled and there's other times when they didn't (care) whether I was black, white or Spanish. (Fallstrom, 2014). Britt now uses a video recorder if he interfaces with law enforcement (Schrotenboer, 2013). Equally important, fan-generated media that supported Bad Black male athletes reflected an understanding of the role of systemic issues, such as extrajudicial killings, racial profiling, police brutality, and the demography of police departments and cities like Ferguson.

Implications for professional athletes and activism

> That act will continue to be labeled as a lot of things over the next few days. The most dominant one should be "courageous." (Strauss, 2014, para. 20)

While larger society wants professional athletes to display more civic involvement in social issues, the fundamentals of human behavior and conflict theory seriously prohibits their activism. Americans', in this case sports fans', attitudes, thoughts, and behaviors about national social issues do not sway because of their love for sports, sports teams, or professional athletes. Views about highly charged social issues, like extrajudicial killings, police brutality, or racial profiling, do not transcend sports. After the final whistle blows there are still "haves" who are trying to protect their interests from the "have-nots." Besides, professional athletes are well aware that the majority of their lifetime earnings originate, not from contracts with sports teams, but from endorsement deals and future coaching and front office positions. During professional athletes' playing days, franchises and corporate sponsors want them to keep their societal views, on the most controversial issues, to themselves. With that said, the prospect of professional athletes as advocates and activists is fairly weak, but this case study presents some positive feedback and lessons for Black male athletes with activist aspirations.

No professional football athlete has vigorously advocated for social issues while employed by the NFL. In order for professional athletes to safely engage in activism, while competing, further strategizing and organizing are necessary to provide opportunity, protection, and influence. First, athletes should be advised against engaging in activism during work hours and/or while in their sports uniform. There are no workspaces in America where overt activism is acceptable, especially when the employee works in front of millions of people. A prohibition on activism at work should apply to athlete's individual interests as well as the charities adopted by their respective NFL franchises. NFL teams, with their conservative causes, are unjust in requiring athletes to be organizational philanthropists. Second, professional athletes should avoid token activism, which might include an in-game gesture such as a name or slogan written on their uniform. Given the frequency, and apparent novelty, of token sports activism these gestures are likely to have a trivial impact at best. Professional athletes must strive to develop their identity as activist outside the workplace.

The Ferguson Five fan-generated media, inductively and deductively, engendered ideas about more secure modes for professional athletes to engage in activism. The STRHUDS controversy suggests that athletes who engage in activism in small groups may have a greater impact. Professional athletes might even consider developing a coalition where several athletes can engage in activism as a group. If there were a galvanized, maybe even nameless, effort, then there might be greater security, and thus participation by athletes across pro teams and sports. Second, education with insight as to how causes are socially constructed and how an issue relates to larger actions and agendas might help athletes develop an extended effort. A significant number of athletes understand the issues, because they have or they are living the issues under concern, but that does not inevitably translate into the skills to play a profound role in social change. Extrajudicial killings are a controversial and multilayered issue. During Tim Tebow's brief sojourn in the NFL he was able engage in activism around abortion, another controversial and multilayered issue. Black athlete activists might benefit from studying Tebow's methods and extrapolating any schooling from the experiences of a White professional athlete activist. Education also includes appraising the relationship between athletes' and team's social interests. Activism is a complicated social, organizational, racial, systemic, and political endeavor that requires strategies beyond gestures, Tweets, and tributes on shoes. Another strategy athletes might consider is to add monologues and dialogues before or after their demonstrations because the intersectional variables, unique to each participant, can add validity to his or her reasons for civic involvement. For example, for Jared Cook the Ferguson Five's activism was something for the people in Ferguson and around the world who were protesting peacefully:

> "Think about it; what real role models do we have nowadays? Young men are looking around for guidance and looking for people to look up to, and they have none. So why not be the voice and start here in the community when something so serious is going on 8 miles up the road?" (Wagoner, 2014, para. 9)

One thing is certain—professional athletes can have a demonstrable impact on critical social issues. The veracity with which SLPOA and fans responded to the Ferguson Five is one indicator. The visibility of the Ferguson Five was easily one of the top activism visuals surrounding the Michael Brown shooting. Not only did the majority of fan-generated media support their effort, but also a meaningful number of fans suggested the need for athletes to expand their efforts. Professional athletes have the capacity to reach millions, but in particular they can reach young people, at a time when their social values are taking shape. Athletes do not have to be role models to be activists, but true activism requires carving out an off-the-field identity and building on the lessons learned from the STRHUDS controversy.

Notes

1. Kluwe claims he was subjected to homophobic behavior by team officials and coaches. The team reached a settlement with Kluwe that included a donation to charities that support lesbian, gay, bisexual, and transgender causes.
2. There are 23 Black Lives Matter chapters in the United States, Canada, and Ghana (Segalov, 2015). As of March 2, 2015, at least 700 Black Lives Matter demonstrations had been held worldwide (Robinson, 2015).
3. Oscar Grant (2009) Aiyana Jones (2010), Kenneth Chamberlian (2011), Trayvon Martin, Rekia Boyd, Jordan Davis, Timothy Russell and Malissa Williams (2012), Renisha McBride (2013), Dontre Hamilton, Eric Garner, John Crawford III, Michael Brown, Ezell For, Akai Gurley, Tamir Rice (2014), Tony Robinson, Walter Scott, and Freddie Gray (2015).
4. Per State of Missouri records, in 2013, Ferguson police made 5,384 automobile stops. Of these, 686 were White; 4,632 were Black. Of 611 total vehicles searched, 47 were White: 562 were Black. Of 521 total arrests, 36 were White; 483 were Black. At least one University of Missouri professor/criminologist, Tim Maher (13-year police officer), believes the data should be explained to the public for racial profiling.
5. The Rams traded Mason after the team drafted Todd Gurley.
6. "Now that the evidence is in and Officer Wilson's account has been verified by physical and ballistic evidence as well as eye-witness testimony, which led the grand jury to conclude that no probable cause existed that Wilson engaged in any wrongdoing, it is unthinkable that hometown athletes would so publicly perpetuate a narrative that has been disproven over-and-over again. All week long, the Rams and the NFL were on the phone with the St. Louis Police Department asking for assurances that the players and the fans would be kept safe from the violent protesters who had rioted, looted, and burned buildings in Ferguson. Our officers have been working 12 hour shifts for over a week, they had days off including Thanksgiving cancelled so that they could defend this community from those on the streets that perpetuate this myth that Michael Brown was executed by a brother police officer and then, as the players and their fans sit safely in their dome under the watchful protection of hundreds of St. Louis's finest, they take to the turf to call a now-exonerated officer a murderer, that is way out-of-bounds, to put it in football parlance."
7. St. Louis County Police Chief Jon Belmar went on to say, "Mr. Demoff clearly regretted that any members of the Rams' organization would act in a way that minimized the outstanding work that police officers and departments carry out each and every day" (Brinson, 2014, para 3).

8. Three additional themes that were responses to the activism of the Ferguson Five emerged, including fans boycotting games, cops boycotting opportunities to work Rams games, and the St. Louis Rams moving back to Los Angeles (which indeed actually happened, but not for reasons directly connected to this controversy). Eleven percent of fan-generated media content endorsed St. Louis police officers boycotting security work for Rams games. Another 3 percent of the fan-generated media content expressed fan beliefs about the right of the St. Louis police officers' right to freedom of speech on their discontent about the Ferguson Five's pregame gesture.
9. The charities and community programs include the American Red Cross, Basket of Hope, Bikes for Kids, CHARACTERplus, Diversity Awareness Partnership, Everyday Heroes, Football Academy, Fuel Up to PLAY 60, Georgia Frontiere Community Quarterback Award, Heat Up St. Louis, Hometown Huddle, and Komen St. Louis Race for the Cure.
10. A meaningful percentage of the fan-generated media comments spoke to larger issues that possibly prompted the "Hands Up, Don't Shoot" gesture by the Ferguson Five. Relative to the St. Louis police, the grand jury process, and SLPOA, 4 percent of fan-generated media content spoke to conflicting evidence, the need to move beyond a grand jury, and the necessity of a trial.
11. One post noted that the Rams' opponent, the Oakland Raiders, should have joined in the demonstration. Another suggested NFL teams in other cities that had unjustified police shootings, such as the Cleveland Browns, New York Jets and Giants, Detroit Lions, and Cincinnati Bengals, should join in the activism surrounding police brutality. Two fan-generated media posts went one step further with suggestions for activism. One suggested that all the teams show some solidarity and protest the following week, and another indicated that they wanted to see it extended to National Basketball Association and Major League Baseball teams.
12. The ESP is a union of about 200 black police officers in St. Louis.

References

Andrews, D. L., King, C. R., & Leonard, D. J. (2011). America's son? Tiger Woods as commodification and criminalization. In D. J. Leonard and C. R. King (Eds.), *Commodified and Criminalized: New Racism and African Americans in Contemporary Sports* (pp. 249–253). Lanham, MD: Rowman and Littlefield.

Associated Press (2014, December 10). Kenny Britt emerging as a leader. Retrieved from http://www.ktrs.com/kenny-britt-emerging-as-a-leader/

Blow, C. M. (2012). The curious case of Trayvon Martin. *New York Times*. Retrieved from http://www.nytimes.com/2012/03/17/opinion/blow-the-curious-case-of-trayvon-martin.html?_r=0

Bondy, F. (1996, December 11) Hodges still fights system. *New York Daily News*. Retrieved from http://m.nydailynews.com/archives/sports/hodges-fights-system-article-1.746561

Bonilla-Silva, E. (2002). The linguistics of color blind racism: How to talk nasty about Blacks without sounding "racist." *Critical Sociology*, *28*(1–2), 41–64. doi:10.1177/08969205020280010501

Bonilla-Silva, E. (2003). *Racism without racists: Color-blind racism and the persistence of racial inequality in the United States*. Lanham, MD: Rowman & Littlefield.

Brinson, W. (2014, December 1). Rams deny apologizing to St Louis police for players' Ferguson tribute. Retrieved from http://www.cbssports.com/nfl/eye-on-football/24857481/rams-deny-apologizing-to-st-louis-police-for-players-ferguson-tribute

Buffington, D., & Fraley, T. (2011). Race talk and sport: The color consciousness of contemporary discourse on basketball. *Sociological Inquiry*, *81*(3), 333–352. doi:10.1111/soin.2011.81.issue-3

Chalabi, M. (2015, March 4). Are the racial disparities in Ferguson traffic stops unusual? Retrieved from http://fivethirtyeight.com/datalab/are-the-racial-disparities-in-fergusons-traffic-stops-unusual/

Clarke, L. (2009, June 27). Shut up and play? A dying tradition. Retrieved from http://www.dailytidings.com/article/20090627/SPORTS/306279977

Cole, C. L. (1996). P.L.A.Y., consensus, and punishment. *Sociology of Sport Journal*, *13*(4), 366–397.

Collins, P. H. (2004). *Black sexual politics: African Americans, gender, and the new racism*. New York, NY: Routledge.

Connell, R. W. (2005). *Masculinities* (2nd ed.). Berkeley, CA: University of California Press.

Cooper, F. R. (2005). Against bipolar black masculinity: Intersectionality, assimilation, identity performance, and hierarchy. *UC Davis Law Review*, *39*, 853.

Demby, G. (2012, May 23). LeBron James tweets picture of Miami Heat wearing hoodies in solidarity with family of Trayvon Martin. *Huffington Post*. Retrieved from http://www.huffingtonpost.com/2012/03/23/lebron-heat-trayvon-tweet_n_1375831.html

Domowitch, P. (1989, December 5). The seats blacks rarely sit in the problem is as puzzling as it is persistent: Blacks aren't going to professional sports events. *Philadelphia Inquirer*. Retrieved from http://articles.philly.com/1989-12-05/sports/26159992_1_blacks-sports-on-television-today-stadium-or-arena

Eligon, J. (2015, June 1). Missouri reports wide racial disparity in traffic stops. *New York Times*. Retrieved from http://www.nytimes.com/2015/06/02/us/big-disparity-for-blacks-pulled-over-in-missouri.html

Ellis, R., Todd, B., & Karimi, F. (2014, November 30). Citing security concerns, Darren Wilson resigns from Ferguson police force. *CNN*. Retrieved from http://www.cnn.com/2014/11/29/us/ferguson-protests/index.html?iid=article_sidebar

Evans, S. J. (2014, November 29). Did Michael Brown ever really say, Hands, Up, Don't Shoot? Ferguson protesters rallying cry may be based on a lie. Retrieved from http://www.dailymail.co.uk/news/article-2854388/Did-Michael-Brown-really-say-Hands-don-t-shoot-Ferguson-protesters-rallying-cry-based-lie.html

Fallstrom, R. B. (2014, December 10). Rams' 'Hands Up' protest was Britt's idea. Retrieved from http://sports.yahoo.com/news/rams-hands-protest-britts-idea-090142934–nfl.html

Farmer, S. (2014, December, 1). NFL will not fine Rams for hands-up gesture. *LA Times*. Retrieved from http://www.latimes.com/sports/sportsnow/la-sp-sn-rams-gesture-20141201-story.html

Ferber, A. L. (2007). The construction of black masculinity white supremacy now and then. *Journal of Sport & Social Issues, 31*(1), 11–24. doi:10.1177/0193723506296829

Flyvbjerg, B. (2006). Five misunderstandings about case-study research. *Qualitative Inquiry, 12*(2), 219–245. doi:10.1177/1077800405284363

Hartmann, D., & Wheelock, D. (2000, August). Midnight basketball and the 1994 federal crime bill debates: The symbolic politics of race, crime and public policy in the United States. Presented at the American Sociological Association annual meeting, Washington, DC.

Hesse-Biber, S. N., & Leavy, P. L. (2011). *The practice of qualitative research*. Thousand Oaks, CA: Sage.

Hoft, J. (2014, December 2). Update: 20,000 support Boycott Rams Page after 'Hands Up, Don't Shoot' stunt. Retrieved from http://www.thegatewaypundit.com/2014/12/hands-up-dont-go-to-rams-games-boycott-st-louis-rams-facebook-page-set-up/#ixzz3dpzkuJhn

Hooks, B. (1998). Representing whiteness in the black imagination. In D. Roediger (Ed.), *Black on white: Black writers on what it means to be white* (pp. 38–53). New York, NY: Schocken Books.

Hooks, B. (2004a). *The will to change: Men, masculinity, and love*. New York, NY: Atria Books.

Hooks, B. (2004b). *We real cool: Black men and masculinity*. New York, NY: Routledge.

Katz, M. (2014, December 1). Rams' Kenny Britt wears Mike Brown's name on field in Ferguson tribute. Retrieved from http://www.sbnation.com/lookit/2014/12/1/7313093/kenny-britt-rams-ferguson-tribute-mike-brown-hands-up-dont-shoot

Krippendorff, K. H. (2012). *Content analysis: An introduction to its methodology* (3rd ed.). Thousand Oaks, CA: Sage.

Ladson-Billings, G., & Tate, W., IV (1995). Toward a critical race theory of education. *Teachers College Record, 97*(1), 47–68.

Leonard, D. J. (2004). The next MJ or the next OJ? Kobe Bryant, race, and the absurdity of colorblind rhetoric. *Journal of Sport & Social Issues, 28*(3), 284–313.

Leonard, D. J., & King, C. R. (2010, April 16). White is right: Ben Roethlisberger and the power of privilege. [Weblog post]. Retrieved from http://newblackman.blogspot.com/2010/04/ben-roethlisbergerand-power-of.html

Molinet, J. (2014, December 2). Black cops blast St. Louis police organization, call 'hands up' gesture by Rams players 'commendable.' *New York Daily News* Retrieved from http://www.nydailynews.com/news/national/black-cops-call-hands-gesture-rams-commendable-article-1.2031197

Rhoden, W. C. (2006). *40 million slaves: The rise, fall, and redemption of the black athlete*. New York, NY: Crown Publishers.

Robinson, A. (2015, March 16). Black Lives Matter: The evolution of a movement. Retrieved from http://www.occupy.com/article/black-lives-matter-evolution-movement

Schrotenboer, B. (2013, November 29). Darnell Dockett, Kenny Britt among players using phones to record police. *USA* Today. Retrieved from http://www.usatoday.com/story/sports/nfl/2013/11/29/racial-profiling-nfl-players-video-phones/3779615/

Sears, A. (2008). *A good book, in theory: A guide to theoretical thinking* (pp. 34–36). North York, Ontario, Canada: Higher Education University of Toronto Press.

Segalov, M. (2015, February 2). We spoke to the activist behind #BlackLivesMatter about racism in Britain and America. Retrieved from http://www.vice.com/read/patrisse-cullors-interview-michael-segalov-188

Sexton, J. (2015, March 21). CNN misses: Hands up, don't shoot narrative suppressed the truth. Retrieved from http://www.breitbart.com/big-journalism/2015/03/21/cnn-misses-hands-up-dont-shoot-narrative-suppressed-the-truth

Singer, J. N. (2005). Addressing epistemological racism in sport management research. *Journal of Sport Management, 19*(4), 464–479.

Solorzano, D., Ceja, M., & Yosso, T. (2000). Critical race theory, racial microaggressions, and campus racial climate: The experiences of African American college students. *Journal of Negro Education, 1*, 60–73.

St. Louis Police Association. (2014, November 30). Police Officers Association letter about Rams. *STL Today*. Retrieved from http://m.stltoday.com/police-officers-association-letter-about-rams/pdf_e5c10bf2-53f9-5dee-8b6a-2c8789588181.html?mobile_touch=true

St. Louis Rams (2015). *Community outreach*. Retrieved from http://www.therams.com/ community/community-outreach.html

Strauss, C. (2014, December 1). Five St. Louis Rams players took a stand for something bigger than Ferguson. *USA Today*. Retrieved from http://ftw.usatoday.com/2014/12/st-louis-rams-ferguson-tavon-austin-hands-up-dont-shoot

Tapp, J. (2014, September 23). NFL census: Data on players' race, weight & height. Retrieved from http://heavy.com/sports/2014/09/what-percentage-of-nfl-players-are-black-white/

Teaching Tolerance. (2014, January 1). Colorblindness: The new racism? Retrieved from http://www.tolerance.org/magazine/number-36-fall-2009/feature/colorblindness-new-racism

The Guardian. (2015). [Ongoing database of individuals killed by law enforcement]. The counted: People killed by police in the US. Retrieved from http://www.theguardian.com/us-news/ng-interactive/2015/jun/01/the-counted-police-killings-us-database#

Thiel, A. (2014, December 13). Social activism is a tough call for Seahawks. Retrieved from http://sportspressnw.com/2194795/2014/thiel-social-activism-a-tough-call-for-seahawks

"Thug." (2015). In *Merriam-Webster.com*. Retrieved from http://www.merriam-webster.com/dictionary/thug

UCLA School of Public Affairs Critical Race Studies. (2014). What is critical race theory? [Weblog post]. Retrieved from http://spacrs.wordpress.com/what-is-critical-race-theory/

U.S. Census Bureau. (2015). State and county quick facts: Ferguson, MO. Retrieved from http://quickfacts.census.gov/qfd/states/29/2923986.html

Wagoner, N. (2014, August 20). Rams invite local teams to practice. *ESPN*. Retrieved from http://espn.go.com/nfl/story/_/id/11384930/st-louis-rams-invite-ferguson-area-high-school-football-teams-practice

Wagoner, N. (2014, December 3). Jared Cook: "Why not be the voice?" *ESPN*. Retrieved from http://espn.go.com/espn/print?id=11975145

Waldron, T. (2014, January 7). Where did all the activist athletes go? Retrieved from http://thinkprogress.org/sports/2014/01/07/3121151/did-activist-athletes/

Wallace, R. A., & Wolf, A. (1999). *Contemporary sociological theory: Expanding the classical tradition*. New York, NY: Pearson College Division.

Williams, T. C. (2011, September 20). Racism without racists. Retrieved from http://www.theatlantic.com/national/archive/2011/09/racism-without-racists/245361/

Yan, H. (2014, December 2). St. Louis County police, Rams spar over reported apology. CNN. Retrieved from http://www.cnn.com/2014/12/02/us/ferguson-nfl-st-louis-rams/

Yin, R. K. (2010). *Qualitative research from start to finish*. New York, NY: Guilford Press.

Zirin, D. (2014, December 2). St. Louis Rams players tell the world that #BlackLivesMatter. *The Nation*. Retrieved from http://www.thenation.com/blog/191697/st-louis-rams-players-tell-world-blacklivesmatter#

"Police took my homie I dedicate my life 2 his revenge": Twitter tensions between gang-involved youth and police in Chicago

Desmond Upton Patton[a], Patrick Leonard[a,b], Loren Cahill[c], Jamie Macbeth[d], Shantel Crosby[e], and Douglas-Wade Brunton[f]

[a]School of Social Work, Columbia University, New York, New York, USA; [b]SAFE Lab, Columbia University, New York, New York, USA; [c]School of Social Work, University of Michigan, Ann Arbor, Michigan, USA; [d]School of Engineering, Fairfield University, Fairfield, Connecticut, USA; [e]School of Social Work, Wayne State University, Detroit, Michigan, USA; [f]Department of Communication Studies, University of Michigan, Ann Arbor, Michigan, USA

ABSTRACT

The hostile and adversarial relationship between youth and police in urban settings has remained pervasive and persistent for centuries. This is a tension historically rooted in the miasma of lack of trust; racial, ethnic, and cultural differences; and fear, anger, and hostility from racialized surveillance and policing. Indeed, most Black youth have little contact with police unless it involves harsh profiling and/or criminalization. In this article, we leverage the policing literature to examine how the perpetual detestation between urban youth and police is expressed in physical and digital contexts (e.g., Twitter). We find that urban youth, particularly gang-involved youth, publicly articulate their disdain for law enforcement agents on Twitter. The young people in our study expressed chronic grief and anger after the fatal police shooting of a Southside Chicago gang member. Further, they expressed a strong desire to violently retaliate against the Chicago Police Department after their friend was killed. In fact, users on Twitter frequently posted the hash tag #CPDK—an acronym for Chicago Police Department Killer—shortly after this incident. We discuss the implications of using Twitter data to inform policing practices, as well as early intervention and prevention strategies for youth living in inner cities.

On August 9, 2014, Michael Brown, Jr., an 18-year-old Black male, was shot and killed by Darren Wilson, a White police officer who, at the time, was patrolling a predominantly Black neighborhood in Ferguson, Missouri (Coates, 2015; Roberts, 2015). As Brown's body laid unattended in the street for up to four hours, cell phone footage capturing critical moments following the police shooting was uploaded on Facebook, Twitter, Instagram, and other social network services (SNSs), eventually leading to a nationwide protest demanding justice for Brown and the hundreds of other youth who are victims of police brutality every day (Prusaczyk, Ravindranath, Davis, & Sewell, 2014).

The relative low cost of smartphones, emergence of social media and SNSs, and increased technological literacy has created new opportunities for everyday citizens to capture aggressive policing and other injustices that are borne disproportionately by people of color across the United States (Moule, Pyrooz, & Decker, 2013; Yar, 2012). Now, more than ever, community members are able to swiftly capture youth-police interactions on their mobile devices in real time and instantly upload and share content with others online. Concomitantly, social media sites have created a unique and safe space for diverse users to coalesce and engage in critical discourse regarding the tenuous and, in many cases, deadly interactions between young people of color and the police in their respective cities (Bora, Zaytsev, Chang, & Maheswaran, 2013; Hagan, Shedd, & Payne, 2005).

In this study we ask: How is disdain for police communicated on Twitter by urban, gang-involved youth following the police shooting of one of their fellow gang members? To further examine this question, we studied the Twitter communication of Gakirah Barnes, a recently deceased 17-year-old self-proclaimed gang member from Chicago, Illinois, as she publicly articulated her disdain for police following the fatal police shooting of her close friend Raason Shaw (Swaine, 2014). We use inductive textual analysis to analyze the communications of Gakirah and users with whom she frequently communicated on Twitter, which provides an in-depth and nuanced contextual and linguistic perspective of how urban youth respond to police in their neighborhood following this traumatic event.

Literature review

Prior research on youths' experience with police in urban neighborhoods suggests that aggressive policing of urban youth correlates with their having low trust in adults in authoritative roles, negative relationships with police, and feeling unwelcome in public spaces (Borrero, 2001; Brunson & Miller, 2006; Carr, Napolitano, & Keating, 2007; Fine et al., 2003). However, we argue that there is an important distinction between research that examines aggressive policing and our current challenges with police in urban communities intricately connected to ubiquitous social media consumption and use. Social media has changed the ways we access news and provides immediate notification of the social ills that plague marginalized communities—including aggressive policing. Social media also provides an outlet for individuals who live in marginalized urban communities to express the pain, frustrations, and contempt of negative relationships with police in their neighborhoods. Therefore, for youth who are born digital, the boundaries that theoretically exist between what happens online and in one's neighborhood are often nonexistent (Bora et al., 2013; Marwick & Boyd, 2011; Palfrey & Gasser, 2008).

Data show that youth, specifically Black youth and individuals who are gang involved, may live and narrate their lives on social media. In a study of outreach workers in five metropolitan areas, Decker and Pyrooz (2011) found that current and former gang members are highly active on the Internet and frequently navigate SNSs. Data from the Pew Research Center suggest that 73% of Black Internet users have some form of social media presence, and 96% of users 18–29 years of age are active on at least one social media platform. Twitter is a social media platform that is popular among Black youth and young adults. In fact, 22% of Black youth and young adults online use Twitter versus 16% of online Whites. Black youth and young adults between the ages of 18 and 29 are particularly active on Twitter with 40% using the site versus 28% of White users in the same age cohort (Smith, 2014).

Youths' anywhere-anytime engagement with social media suggests that youth who experience aggressive policing in their neighborhood may use social media platforms to talk about these experiences, as well as connect to a broader community who can share or sympathize with their lived experience. However, little to no empirical research has examined how urban youth respond on Twitter to perceived aggressive policing in their neighborhood.

Neighborhood relationships with the police

In the post–Civil Rights era, the hyper-policed ghetto and massive, ever expanding prison system have become increasingly indistinguishable, reinforcing in each other the marginalization and exclusion of Black men and women (Nuño, 2013; Rios, 2006; Wacquant, 2001). The resulting symbiosis between ghetto and prison creates a system of racial control that perpetuates socio-economic marginality. The result is punitive social and institutional structures replacing the social welfare treatment of poverty by penal management (Alexander, 2012; Ferguson, 2001; Rios, 2006; Wacquant, 2001)—a phenomenon often called the Prison Industrial Complex, school-to-prison pipeline, or cradle-to-prison pipeline. As a result of these oppressive social and institutional structures, youth of color living in disadvantaged communities often have few civil rights and are at high risk of experiencing direct or indirect contact with police because of the aggressive crime-control strategies to which they are exposed (Borrero, 2001; Brunson, 2007; Brunson & Miller, 2006; Carr et al., 2007; Rios, 2006), including being the routine subjects of police surveillance and harassment (Fine et al., 2003; Kerr & Stattin, 2000). In some instances, these investigatory stops can lead to violent and lethal police force. For example, the Centers for Disease Control and Prevention compiled data showing people of color are most likely to be killed by police overall (Patton et al., 2014), and a report issued by Malcolm X Grassroots movement found that a Black man was killed every 28 hours in 2012 (Akuno & Eisen, 2013).

Recent research on police surveillance of youth in public spaces suggests that urban youth, especially low-income youth of color, are being systematically surveilled and exposed to constant scrutiny and threat of criminalization (Kerr & Stattin, 2000; Leman-Langlois, 2008; Yar, 2012). Several researchers have found that violent, targeted enforcement in neighborhoods may diminish trust in police and lead to consistent negative appraisals of police (Brunson, 2007; Crank, 1990; Neely & Cleveland, 2011; Prenzler, Porter, & Alpert, 2013).

Adult attitudes and unwarranted aggressive neighborhood policing practices have made youth of color increasingly mistrustful and vulnerable as once safe schools, neighborhoods, and communities turn into hostile and threatening spaces. Through a street survey of 911 New York youths, Fine et al. (2003), found that Black and Latino males have the highest rates of adverse interactions and mistrust of the police and feel least safe in the city. The young people surveyed reported that the cumulative impact of adverse interactions with police, security guards, teachers, and store staff made them feel unwelcome in public spaces. Because of this developed mistrust, marginalized youth of color become increasingly unwilling to seek assistance from adults and can become further disconnected from positive networks of support (Brendtro and Brokenleg, 2002; Rios, 2011). Through these experiences, youth can feel disillusioned and resign to processing, grieving, and venting the associated trauma in their lives on SNSs (Christopherson, 2007; Martin, Coyier, VanSistine, & Schroeder, 2013).

Social media crime and violence

Youth of color use SNSs to express themselves, to socialize with their peers and to make sense of and help build the culture around them (Moreno and Whitehill, 2012; Moule et al., 2013). A major part of their daily lived experience is frequent police surveillance both on and offline (Borrero, 2001; Brunson and Miller, 2006; Myers & Thompson, 2000; Patton, Eschmann, & Butler, 2013; Trottier, 2012). Social media is particularly important because it allows youth to self-reflect and garner respect from a wider audience. The unique property of an invisible audience platform of their peers affects the ways in which youth interact (Boyd, 2007; Christopherson, 2007). More specifically, it gives them a public space to seek love and positive recognition, a reinforcement of self they receive in few other places where they are negatively surveilled and habitually suspected of wrongdoing by authority figures (Leary, 2001; Patton et al., 2013).

As public spaces become increasingly surveilled, gang-affiliated youth have moved their illicit activities to SNSs. They express this control by maintaining threatening public presences and by engaging in violent or criminal activity. Gang members often express themselves online by sharing provocative, threatening, and intimidating messages publicly on social media (Bora et al., 2013; Moule et al., 2013), a burgeoning phenomenon termed *Internet banging* (Patton et al., 2013). According to a survey, 74% of the gang members who participated identified themselves as frequent Internet users and had established an online presence to gain respect for their gang (King, Walpole, & Lamon, 2007). This high percentage of Internet use is surprising, given the illicit activity and negative connotations gangs are often affiliated with. Rather than finding public places where like-minded young gang members can congregate, they instead exhibit a preference for online public places (e.g., Twitter, Instagram, and YouTube) to express their affiliation, to sell drugs, and to publicize illegal activities (Ito et al., 2010). Several of them are completely unaware that police are observing their social media interactions at all (Chomos & Miller, 2015; Spizman & Miller, 2013), and police departments capitalize on these youths' naivety, spending thousands of dollars on unregulated, comprehensive social networking site data collection systems to monitor youth.

Police surveillance

Surveillance of youth, particularly youth of color, in schools and communities appears to be on the rise (Fine et al., 2003; Fuchs, 2015). More recently, police departments (PDs) are increasing their presence on SNSs to obtain more information on youth suspected of criminal involvement. Currently more than 75% of the 61 largest police departments in the United States have a presence on at least one of the three major SNSs, including Facebook, Twitter, and MySpace (Lieberman, Koetzle, & Sakiyama, 2013). Given the publicly available nature of this information, the police often do not even need a search warrant, subpoena, or court order to obtain social media evidence. In addition to searching for publicly available evidence, police evade the privacy settings of a person's social media account by creating fictitious online accounts and identities that grant them access to more personal and intimate information (Fontecilla, 2015; Lyon, 2002; Trottier, 2012).

Though gang involvement is not yet a crime, for decades, law enforcement has dedicated substantial resources to collecting personal information about youth suspected of such involvement (Wright, 2005). Surveillance of urban youth has been exacerbated with the advent of smartphones and the proliferation of social media platforms that allow them to express their authentic emotions as they navigate their communities. Now, highly advanced software platforms are able to aggregate and organize personal information such as a youth's name, address, typical dress, school location, behaviors, histories, friends, and locations typically frequented. This means that prior to a conviction, youth can be placed into databases and subject to high levels of surveillance, scrutiny, and frequent police encounters (Klein, 2009). Simply displaying a common hand symbol, favorite hip-hop artist, or colors tied to a gang faction can be evidence of gang involvement and warrant inclusion on gang databases (Jacobs, 2009).

Social networking site surveillance by police is extremely disconcerting, given that most youth are completely unaware that police and other governmental institutions have access to their accounts (Marwick, 2011; Raynes-Goldie, 2010) or that certain posts can lead to time being spent in prison. The process of compiling youth social networking data reveals the flawed usage of SNSs by police solely as mechanisms to find incriminating evidence. It begs the question why more literature is not being produced to inform and reform the practice of police using complied social networking site evidence as an entrance into the juvenile justice system (Lapp, 2015).

Gap in the literature

The literature tell us that aggressive policing is not a new phenomenon in urban neighborhoods and that youth, particularly youth of color, are disproportionately impacted by egregious forms of policing (Alexander, 2012; Borrero, 2001; Rios, 2006). Immediate access to technology makes it easier to identify and discuss forms and functions of aggressive policing, but our empirical work in this area has lagged behind our technology use (Moule et al., 2013; Prusaczyk et al., 2014; Yar, 2012). Absent in the literature and preventive practice is a thorough exploration and synthesis of how social media sites provide a different and new medium where youth can bare honest and transparent reactions to their interactions with police and the associated trauma surrounding those events.

Not only have researchers neglected to study social media communications, but there is an overall dearth of research exploring the narratives of residents themselves expressed on social media. Only recently have researchers attempted to document police legitimacy within minority communities or policing in general by collecting the narratives of minority residents themselves (Hinds & Murphy, 2007; Tyler, 2004). The police legitimacy literature infrequently acknowledges the countless experiences of inner-city individuals and neighborhoods that inform residents' conclusion that officers' authority should not be unquestionably accepted (Armaline, Sanchez, & Correia, 2014). In fact, recent research on police legitimacy has found that narratives from the residents themselves often conflict with romanticized expectations and descriptions of police legitimacy. These are the empirical and theoretical chasms that our research seeks to address, both in theory and in practice.

Methods

Studies that examine Twitter content typically examine millions of data points. However, to best examine how disdain for police is communicated on Twitter, we take an inductive qualitative approach, a textual analysis, to examine a relatively small subset of Twitter. We chose this method for several reasons. First, we are analyzing communications between urban gang involved youth who possess a unique style of communication that combines elements of Black vernacular English, language that is unique to their gang faction, and linguistic variation that is common on social media (e.g., shortened words, emojis). The language represented in these tweets exhibited significant sociolinguistic variation from "standard" English, the use of which represents a critical part of how urban youth construct their identity (Alim, 2004). Second, computational software often utilizes traditional keyword searches to analyze social media data, an approach that has been deemed inadequate by local law enforcement agencies studying the online communications of urban youth and gang members (Geofeedia, 2012).

To increase our chances of accurately deciphering the language, we engaged in a two-step process: (1) assembling a multidisciplinary team of researchers who have experience and expertise studying urban-based youth violence and cyber-bullying, and (2) interviewing gang-involved youth in the city of Chicago. Researchers designed a systematic process of team-based code development, textual analysis, and rigorous reconciliation that included weekly team consultations and ongoing collaboration until themes were clearly defined. To confirm the validity and reliability of these themes, we identified and trained two gang-involved youth from Chicago (one Black and one Latino), who are current participants in the Youth Violence and Prevention Program at the YMCA of Metro Chicago.

Twitter's personal-communication mechanisms

While Twitter is foremost a microblogging platform where users subscribe to messages by following other users, it does have mechanisms for targeted communications. Users can reply by starting a post with @ and the recipient's Twitter name or they can mention another user by placing that user's Twitter name (prepended with @) at another position in the post. Mentions are received by the sender's followers and viewed in the receiver's private "Mentions and Notifications Tab." Replies are received only by followers of both sender and receiver.

Twitter also allows users to *retweet*—to quote or repost another user's tweet. Typically a retweet begins with the characters *RT* and the handle of the user who made the original post. However, retweets are structured in many ways by third-party applications that use the Twitter Application Program Interface; recently Twitter has implemented *native retweeting*, a retweet that requires no special formatting. This diversity of retweet structure occasionally creates difficulty in distinguishing retweets from other kinds of posts.

Obtaining and coding @tyquanassassin Twitter posts

Tweets in this dataset use unique linguistic styles with distinct words, phrases, grammatical constructions, and slang references to neighborhood identities, rival gangs, and local music. Given linguistic variation by city regions and gang factions, these tweets would be difficult to decipher using automated scripts, network analysis tools, or crowdsourcing. This rich, complex communication required a robust case-study approach deeply examining conditions and factors that explicate how urban youth communicate on Twitter. The social scientists, with years of experience conducting qualitative research with youth of color in urban areas, debated whether to anonymize Twitter handles in academic research. We use real handles and names here, because Gakirah and her online presence has been covered extensively in mainstream news sources; we do, however, anonymize her followers' handles.

Tweets obtained using Radian6 lacked accurate representation of emoji used in original tweets. Often we retrieved original tweets with accurate emoji from the Twitter website by following links Radian6 provided for each tweet. Occasionally the original tweet had been removed from Twitter. In these latter cases, we present tweets without emoji.

Data collection

We collected a set of tweets that represented personal Twitter communications with "tyquanassassin": First, we used Radian6, a social-media tracking service, to obtain all tweets posted by @tyquanassassin or containing "tyquanassassin" in the tweet between March 29 and April 17, 2014. We chose this time period because it captured two critical trauma events and reactions: the death of Gakirah's friend Lil B (the individual allegedly killed by Chicago police) and the death of Gakirah. This was designed to capture all @tyquanassassin's tweets, all mentions and replies directed toward @tyquanassassin, and retweets of @tyquanassassin's tweets. Thus we collected data on how Gakirah and followers in her network responded to Lil B's death and how Gakirah's network responded to her death.

During this process we collected 408 tweets posted by Gakirah or tweets containing her @tyquanassassin Twitter handle. The content of those tweets ranged from acts of violence, direct threats, conversations around relationships, friends, the city of Chicago, and drug-related posts. Out of the 408 tweets identified during this time period, 27 tweets directly referenced the Chicago Police Department or law enforcement broadly. Because @tyquanassassin's tweets were retweeted by many users, and we did not consider retweets part of personal communication with @tyquanassassin, we filtered retweets from this set using common retweet formats (e.g., tweets beginning with RT), also removing advertisements or promotions for music albums and videos. For this study, we then reexamined the 408 tweets to identify communications that directly mention the police or use the hash tag #cpdk. During this process we identified 27 posts that we describe in the results section and Table 1.

Most frequent communicators identified

We also wanted to understand Gakirah's peer network and those with whom she communicated on Twitter. We identified Twitter handles communicating most frequently with the @tyquanassassin handle by first obtaining all tweets by all Twitter users from January 14 to April 17, 2014, containing the string "tyquanassassin." We excluded tweets sent by @tyquanassassin, and after retweets were filtered, this set captured all mentions and replies directed towards @tyquanassassin. Using number of replies to, and mentions of, as proxy measure of personal interaction and communication with @tyquanassassin, we identified her top five communicators during this period. We chose five communicators because we wanted to learn more about the individuals she was most communicative with on Twitter because we believe that insight from the top five communicators could provide a more in-depth understanding of Gakirah, her neighborhoods, her interactions, and her peer network. For each top communicator, we used the same procedure (obtain all tweets posted by the communicator's handle or containing the handle in the post) and filtered out retweets from this set to obtain all tweets for the period ranging from April 3–17, 2014, one week before Gakirah's death to one week after. We obtained 2,142 tweets, mentions, and replies for analysis.

Table 1. Examples of Twitter posts.

Type of tweet	Example of tweet
Grief	Police took folkz out dis shyt it's crazy man
	Police Dan took our boy man 10 year nigga dis shyt so Krazy man
	Da Police Took My mf nigga man
	Why da police have 2 kill my Broski
	DA POLICE TOOK MY BLOOD
	Da pain unbearable
Plans for retaliation	ain't no shootaz wit me I Keep killaz wit me cpdk rip blood
	Police took my homie I dedicate my life 2 his revenge
	DA Police I'd kill u Faster Dan niggaz on Da Corner Rip King Lil B CPDK
	I'm frm where if dey send shotz we send Em back we never gave af if it was da police
	@TyquanAssassin: How do we take dis do we drop a cop like he a opp c'mon y'all pay attention Lil b I'd do it for us
	@TyquanAssassin yall should just do a drill on 12 cpdk
	@TyquanAssassin y'all gone have the swat in the city if y'all go to war with CPD
Perception of police behavior	Da police think I run dis shyt dey say I'm da enforcer shyt dese goofys ain't runnin under me ´
	@bricksquadmain ima hyl police be watching my shyt delete dat killa
	@DutchieDntSHOOT u kno wen Mf pop out we show out jakes got Dis bitch on lock doe
	CPD all ova Me like Snoop u running Dis I'm like Ima Die a Real nigga
Questioning police legitimacy	Da police knew about bro dey wasn't comin 2 arrest dey came 2 kill cuzo ain't have dat robot dey did my nigga dirty cpdk call dis Shyt WAR
	Rip lil b this cracra cpdk they trying to take the rest of EBT thats left shit real time to turn up ten nouches
	Datz my blood left my nigga n cold blood
	@TyquanAssassin cpd gonna say he pointed a gun. hows that if he got shot in the back 7 times #cpdk
	It's bout 2 be a riot
	CPD killed my Broski raason treated Em like he wasn't
Enmity between youth and police	Cpdk middle fingerz 2 da law
	Lil B CPDK Middle Fingaz 2 da Law
	Pigs jst took lil b out dis shyt but its Gucci it only get worser now
	@freekyworld_hh: Fuck 12 always fuckin wit a niggaâ

Data analysis

In the first step of our analysis, the data scientists and qualitative researchers developed the coding scheme and coded the collected Twitter results, checking the accuracy of one another's coding (Ford, 2014). During this process we identified several preliminary codes including but not limited to grief, threat, police, drugs, and relationships. The qualitative researchers gained unique insights on the use of Twitter as an analytic tool for social work research. The data scientists developed and executed automated computer tools for gathering and filtering datasets from Twitter, analyzing communication patterns, and presenting the tweets in a suitable form for content analysis by the qualitative researchers. In addition, the data scientists benefited from more qualitative insights into the mechanisms of gang violence that may occur on Twitter.

We chose to have every tweet coded by three coders with diverse educational and cultural backgrounds and experiences. Three coders trained in qualitative methods utilized an inductive textual analysis to uncover the main content areas exhibited in this dataset, discussed codes iteratively to reconcile differences, and developed a codebook representing content areas. The coders used the codebook to independently code the tweets. We held reconciliation meetings where coders discussed and explained their codes and the meaning of each tweet when there were disagreements.

Next, we isolated the police code to further examine and identify any emergent themes that may explain how aggression is communicated on Twitter. The police code was defined as: descriptions of posts that include mentions of police or the hash tag #cpd (Chicago Police Department) or #cpdk (Chicago Police Department Killer). We identified 27 posts between Gakirah and her top correspondents that directly described how they felt about Chicago police directly following the alleged murder of Raason Shaw.

After identifying and analyzing the 27 Twitter posts, we connected with the YMCA Chicago Youth Violence Prevention Program in an effort to identify youth who would be willing to review our interpretations of the results. The YMCA identified two adolescent boys, one Black and the other Latino, who self-identified as gang involved, to review our interpretations of the Twitter posts. The youth were asked to first review our qualitative interpretations of the 27 posts and indicate whether they agreed with our interpretations by stating yes or no. In cases where our interpretations may not have been accurate, we asked the youth to describe their interpretation of the Twitter post. We had 93% agreement on the Twitter posts across both youth.

Results

We found that Gakirah and users in her Twitter network communicated feelings of disdain for police in three ways following the police shooting of Raason Shaw: (1) grief, anger, and plans for retaliation; (2) negative perceptions of police behavior and legitimacy; and (3) distrust and antipathy toward police. See Table 1 for a complete list of these tweets.

Grief, anger, and plans for retaliation

On Friday, April 3, 2014, at 2:10 A.M. Gakirah tweeted "Da Police I'd kill u Faster Dan niggaz on Da Corner Rip King Lil B CPDK." In this post, Gakirah threatens the police by expressing her ability to effortlessly harm police officers "faster" than rival gang members "on Da Corner." The tweet ends with "RIP King Lil B," to memorialize and apprise her audience of her respect for Raason (also known as "Lil B"). Her reference to CPDK, meaning Chicago Police Department Killer, is a popular acronym among gang-involved youth living in Chicago who have been exposed to routine police violence and often view authorities as the "opps," or opposition, another violent, threatening force to their individual and/or group survival. Interestingly, similar language is used when gang members refer to rival factions (i.e., BDK: Black Disciple Killer). See Figure 1.

On Friday, April 3, at 3:41 A.M., an hour after her retaliatory message directed at police, Gakirah tweeted a message describing her emotional experience coping with the unanticipated loss of Raason: "Da pain unbearable." And a day later, she searches for meaning: "Why da police have 2 kill my Broski [?]"

These posts visibly expressed her sad emotional state through the use of frowning emoji, indicating that Gakirah was mourning the loss of Raason—whom she affectionately called her "Broski" or brother—as she continued to yearn for answers and accept a new social reality. The tweets were also posted in the late evening or early morning, suggesting that Gakirah was frequently experiencing intense emotions and turning to Twitter as an outlet to express these feelings at all hours. See Figure 2.

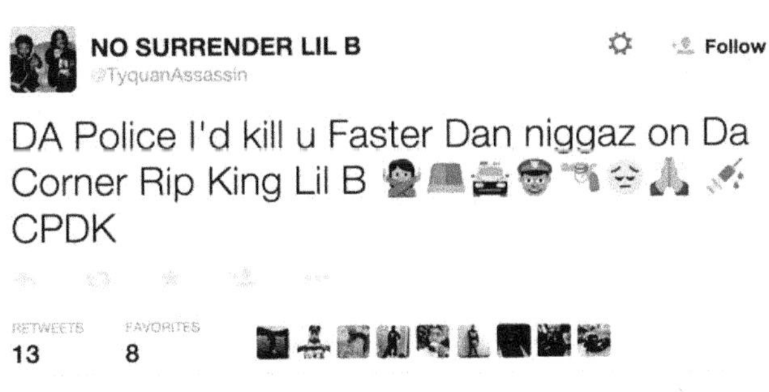

Figure 1. Example 1.

Figure 2. Example 2.

Figure 3. Example 3.

Posts that described how one should react when threatened, challenged, and/or experiencing an injustice often followed direct threats. Gakirah wrote "I'm frm where if dey send shotz we send Em back we never gave af if it was da police." This implies an eye-for-an-eye mentality, or that individuals who harm or threaten others should be penalized to a similar degree. In this case, victims of violence have an obligation to confront perpetrators and seek revenge through similar violent means, even if this means harming authorities. To that end, Gakirah's most retweeted post among the tweets analyzed in this study described her loyalty to Raason and firm commitment to seeking justice for his death. Just a day before Gakirah was fatally shot she tweeted: "Police took my homie I dedicate my life 2 his revenge." This was retweeted to more than 53 Twitter users, and 25 users marked it as one of their "favorites" on Twitter. From our conversations with gang-involved youth in Chicago, we learned that Gakirah was seeking to avenge the death of Raason by targeting police involved in the shooting. See Figure 3.

Negative perceptions of police behavior and legitimacy

Gakirah questioned the motive behind the police shooting of Raason, writing "Da police knew about bro dey wasn't comin 2 arrest dey came 2 kill cuzo ain't have dat robot dey did my nigga dirty cpdk call dis Shyt WAR." In this post, Gakirah suggests that the police knew of Raason and came with the intent to kill him. Gakirah uses CPDK as an expression of violence against the police and declares "war" to correct what she perceives as an unjust killing of her friend. Gakirah's Twitter followers supported her claims and also questioned the intent of police. A Twitter user used @ to mention Gakirah in a post saying "cpd gonna say he pointed a gun. hows that if he got shot in the back 7 times." See Figure 4.

Gakirah also expressed a keen awareness of police behavior and questioned the legitimacy of police officers and their authority in the neighborhood. On April 6, 2014, Gakirah responded to a friend's message saying "hyl [help you later] police be watching my shyt delete dat killa." Gakirah believed that police were lurking on her Twitter account and that some level of

Figure 4. Example 4.

censorship was needed to limit information made available to police. Gakirah was also aware of police surveillance in her community. During a Twitter conversation with one of her friends, she said "u kno wen Mf pop out we show out jakes got Dis bitch on lock doe." In this post, "jakes got Dis bitch on lock" refers to police having a presence in the community, which may have shifted or altered gang activity and how Gakirah and her peers navigated both physical and digital spaces.

Distrust and antipathy toward police

Gakirah's posts indicate that there was strong distrust and hostility between her and law enforcement. See Figure 5. She directly expressed her animosity toward the Chicago Police Department by posting "CPDK middle fingerz 2 da law" and days later, retweeted a message from a Twitter user she was following that read: "Fuck 12 always fuckin wit a nigga." Exacerbating this tension was Gakirah's belief that the fatal shooting of Raason was a deliberate attack against the EBT gang and its affiliates. She writes, "Rip lil b this cracra cpdk they trying to take the rest of EBT thats left shit real time to turn up ten nouches." In this post, Gakirah believes the Chicago Police Department was trying to disband her gang and in response felt that her crew should "turn up ten nouches." Therefore, she felt it was important for the gang to come together to confront the Chicago Police Department and even hinted of impending conflict by saying "Pigs [police] jst took lil b out dis shyt but its Gucci it only gets worser now." It is evident that the police shooting of Raason altered Gakirah's perception of safety, protection, and the role of law enforcement in her community. This sentiment led to a vicious and pervasive cycle that preserved hostility between Gakirah's Twitter network and law enforcement throughout the study.

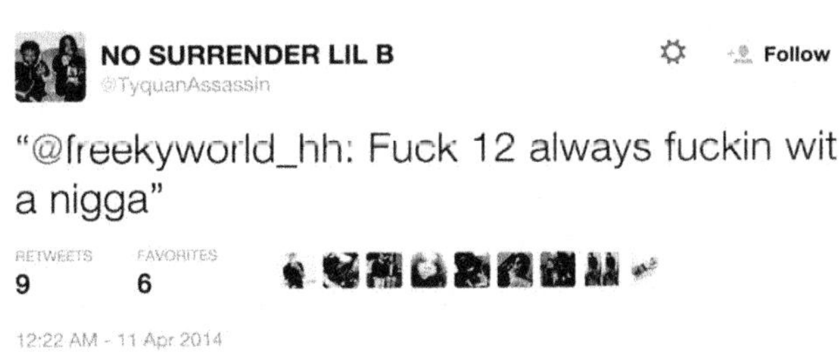

Figure 5. Example 5.

Discussion

The aim of this study was to examine how disdain for police was communicated on Twitter by urban, gang-involved youth. Our results indicate three prevalent themes among the analyzed online postings, which included (1) grief, anger, and plans for retaliation, (2) negative perceptions of police behavior and legitimacy, and (3) distrust and antipathy toward police. These findings are consistent with recent literature on urban policing, which suggests that urban youth of color are surveilled and policed more aggressively than those in other communities (Kerr & Stattin, 2000; Leman-Langlois, 2008; Yar, 2012), leading these youths to develop more negative perceptions of, and relationships with, law enforcement officials (Fine et al., 2003). Additionally, these youths often have greater contact with police and experience higher levels of police crime-control tactics (Brunson, 2007), which also impacts their perception. Several studies support the notion that negative police-related perceptions and feelings (i.e., anger, animosity) are not at all arbitrary, but are rather the result of the severe and violent policing that regularly occurs in urban communities of color across the United States (Brunson, 2007; Crank, 1990; Neely & Cleveland, 2011; Prenzler et al., 2013). In the context of this study, such policing allegedly resulted in the death of one young person of color, Raason, similar to the many other people of color who have been killed by police across the United States. Our results support the literature, illustrating how these experiences impact not only the emotional well-being of youth, but also their perception of and general disposition toward law enforcement.

Similar to the findings of Fine et al. (2003), our results also demonstrate that these youth feel unsafe, lacking in overall trust and belief in the integrity of police officials. Twitter posts highlighted youth suspicions about being surveilled and even intentionally killed by police officers. This, as Fine et al. (2003) suggest, along with negative interactions with authority figures in other contexts (e.g., school, neighborhood store), can greatly impair youths' ability to feel safe and welcomed in their own community. For example, schools often become another hostile environment for youth in urban neighborhoods, where similar aggressive behavioral interventions are used to keep students safe (Miller, 2014; Wacquant, 2001) but are instead perceived as threatening. Without robust supports to help youth navigate these ubiquitous threats, they may continue to feel distrust toward their environment and resent the authority figures (i.e., police officers) that support the maintenance of these punitive systems.

Our results also show that gang-involved youth who experience perceived aggressive policing in their neighborhoods are not only willing to publicly talk about their feelings toward police and their own emotional state following the death of friend but may also make direct threats toward the very police they feel are responsible for the death. The "Plans for Retaliation" theme displays this desire for retribution by youths for the perceived injustices taking place at the hands of police. This is not completely unexpected, given the aforementioned findings on negative youth emotions and perceptions of law enforcement. Such strong feelings of anger and vengeance demonstrate their desire for justice and retribution, even through aggressive means, and may be indicative of possible imminent violence or other risk-taking behaviors. However, this may also be a form of harmless expression to cope with the overwhelming emotional strain and trauma resulting from feelings of grief, discrimination, and oppression. Regardless, this theme demonstrates the widening chasm between law enforcement officials and the individuals that they are charged with protecting in urban neighborhoods.

Furthermore, the varied ways in which the gang-involved youth in this study communicate on Twitter is in need of further inquiry to explore why youth are willing to discuss deeply personal emotions and make incriminating remarks that can be seen by multiple audiences. Perhaps a relevant concept in addressing this inquiry is what Marwick and Boyd (2011) call the *audience invoked* or rather the idea that Twitter users have a particular audience in mind when writing a post. Our results show that gang-involved urban youth are speaking directly to police and to each other. In this way, youth in our study negotiated how to effectively communicate between multiple audiences, expressing their disdain to police while also rallying support from their peers. Understanding the powerful vehicles for expression that SNSs have become and the unique insights that they can provide, future research might explore the ways social media can be used to enhance and further develop culturally attuned, community-based policing in a digital age.

Implications

These themes urgently highlight a need among youth in this population, which social work professionals are uniquely equipped to meet. For social workers in practice and policy, this may mean becoming more aware of SNSs, how they are utilized by youth, and how they can be leveraged as a tool for advocating for disadvantaged populations. SNSs provide an ever-growing forum for youth expression and our findings clearly illustrate how youth are utilizing social media to provide commentary that may even be deemed as socially adversarial. Literature has discussed how youth of color often use SNSs to express their emotions and to make sense of their environmental and cultural context (Moreno & Whitehill, 2012), and our results also display the possibility of using SNS data to inform our knowledge of youth feelings and perceptions related to policing practices. Therefore, emerging forms of effective social work practice to address issues of oppression, marginalization, and trauma may benefit from some level of SNS usage.

Social work professionals can utilize social media outlets as both a prevention and intervention tool as they attempt to engage youth. This is especially important for practitioners working with youth of color, who may be reticent to share their thoughts with authority figures and whose voices are so often ignored in the mainstream narrative. Prevention and intervention practice strategies might include clinical or school social workers inviting youth to share and process their SNS posts during therapy or counseling sessions. It might also be useful for practitioners, especially those in child-serving systems (e.g., schools, community agencies) to explore the use of SNSs as an organized forum for youth to share their perspectives, comment on and process difficult social and community-related problems, and receive positive guidance in dealing with such issues. This may serve to prevent youth from employing maladaptive responses to community problems, while also providing methods for coping and socioemotional support for youth currently engaged in negative coping behaviors.

Social work professionals engaged in policy work can utilize SNSs to work toward improving relationships between law enforcement and communities of color. They can use SNSs to publicly advocate for reforming police policy and practice, as well as alternatives to discriminatory surveillance and other policing practices that exacerbate youths' perceptions of police. Utilizing social media as a platform for such advocacy provides social workers with a more youth-friendly medium for garnering youth voice, support, and investment. It also provides a wider audience, quicker dissemination of information, and greater opportunities to organize around issues relevant to improving the experiences of youth in these communities.

Strengths and limitations

As a major strength, this study is among the first to use Twitter data to capture the police-related perceptions of youth of color. However, this study is not without limitations. Our data come from a self-identified female gang member and a few of her most frequent communicators on Twitter. As such, our results cannot be generalized outside of our data set. Although intentional, our analysis focused on posts following a traumatic experience, the loss of a loved one. As such, studying Twitter data during ordinary everyday interactions may not necessarily yield the same results. Third, our sample is small, and data are cross-sectional and may be given to human error in interpretation of the Twitter posts. However, we believe that focusing on a small subset of Twitter posts from a small group of people allowed us to take a more robust and in-depth approach that would be necessary when analyzing complex and nuanced language on Twitter. Future studies should explore SNS postings from non-gang-affiliated youth of color, youth SNS postings over time, and across other forms of social media to gather a wider range of youth perspectives. Research should also investigate ways to effectively utilize SNSs to strengthen social work practice.

Conclusion

The strongest statement that can be made is the statement of self; the *I am*. Our research demonstrates that for urban youth of color, these statements tend to be reactive, predicated responses to external punitive actions, traumatic experiences, and assumptions that challenge and call into question their very right to be. Intimidated and surveilled out of their physical spaces, urban youth of color have taken this performance of self online in an attempt to assert their identities and reclaim their agency. That these performances, on the surface, tend to be emotional and anti-establishment is what Rios (2011) refers to as *deviant politics*—a resistant, often deviant performance of self in response to the ubiquitous persecution and surveillance that dominates their existence. The challenge now is to redetermine the boundaries between surveillance and intelligence, between self-expression and intent, and between the punitive and the rehabilitative.

Acknowledgment

We acknowledge the Social Media Listening Center at Clemson University for access to the Radian6 social-media tracking platform.

References

Akuno, K., & Eisen, A. (2013). *Operation Ghetto Storm: 2012 annual report on the extrajudicial killings of 313 black people by police, security guards, and vigilantes*. Retrieved from https://mxgm.org/wp-content/uploads/2013/04/operation_ghetto_storm_updated_2013.pdf

Alexander, M. (2012). *The new Jim Crow: Mass incarceration in the age of colorblindness*. New York, NY: New Press.

Alim, H. S. (2004). Hip hop nation language. In E. Finegan & J. Rickford (Eds.), *Language in the USA: Themes for the 21st century*. Cambridge, UK: Cambridge University Press.

Armaline, W. T., Sanchez, V. C., & Correia, M. (2014). The biggest gang in Oakland: Rethinking police legitimacy. *Contemporary Justice Review*, *17*3–4, 375–399.

Bora, N., Zaytsev, V., Chang, Y. H., & Maheswaran, R. (2013, September). Gang networks, neighborhoods and holidays: Spatiotemporal patterns in social media. In *2013 International Conference on Social Computing (SocialCom)* (pp. 93–101). IEEE.

Borrero, M. (2001). The widening mistrust between youth and police. Families in society. *Journal of Contemporary Social Services*, *82*(4), 399–408. doi:10.1606/1044-3894.180

Boyd, D. (2007). Why youth (heart) social network sites: The role of networked publics in teenage social life. In D. Buckingham (Ed.), *Youth, identity, and digital media* (pp. 119–142). Cambridge, MA: MIT Press. Macarthur Foundation Series on Digital Learning.

Brendtro, L., & Brokenleg, M. (2002). *Reclaiming youth at risk: Our hope for the future*. Bloomington, IN: Solution Tree Press.

Brunson, R. K. (2007). Police don't like black people: African-American young men's accumulated police experiences. *Criminology & Public Policy*, *6*(1), 71–101. doi:10.1111/cpp.2007.6.issue-1

Brunson, R. K., & Miller, J. (2006). Young black men and urban policing in the United States. *British Journal of Criminology*, *46*(4), 613–640. doi:10.1093/bjc/azi093

Carr, P. J., Napolitano, L., & Keating, J. (2007). We never call the cops and here is why: A qualitative examination of legal cynicism in three Philadelphia neighborhoods. *Criminology*, *45*(2), 445–480. doi:10.1111/crim.2007.45.issue-2

Chomos, J. C., & Miller, M. K. (2015). Understanding how individual differences are related to community sentiment toward safe haven laws using a student sample. In *Handbook of Community Sentiment* (pp. 83–97). New York, NY: Springer.

Christopherson, K. M. (2007). The positive and negative implications of anonymity in Internet social interactions: "On the internet, nobody knows you're a dog." *Computers in Human Behavior*, *23*(6), 3038–3056. doi:10.1016/j.chb.2006.09.001

Coates, T. (2015, March 5). The gangsters of Ferguson. *The Atlantic*.

Crank, J. P. (1990). The influence of environmental and organizational factors on police style in urban and rural environments. *Journal of Research in Crime and Delinquency*, *27*(2), 166–189. doi:10.1177/0022427890027002004

Decker, S., & Pyrooz, D. (2011). *Leaving the gang: Logging off and moving on*. Retrieved from http://i.cfr.org/content/publications/attachments/SAVE_paper_Decker_Pyrooz.pdf

Ferguson, A. A. (2001). *Bad boys: Public schools in the making of Black masculinity*. Ann Arbor, MI: University of Michigan Press.

Fine, M., Freudenberg, N., Payne, Y., Perkins, T., Smith, K., & Wanzer, K. (2003). Anything can happen with police around: Urban youth evaluate strategies of surveillance in public places. *Journal of Social Issues, 59*, 141–158. doi:10.1111/1540-4560.t01-1-00009

Fontecilla, A. (2015). The ascendance of social media as evidence. *Criminal Justice, 2013*(Spring), 55.

Ford, H. (2014). Big data and small: Collaborations between ethnographers and data scientists. *Big Data & Society, 1* (2). doi:10.1177/2053951714544337

Fuchs, C. (2015). Social media surveillance. In *Handbook of digital politics* (chapter 22). Northhampton, MA: Edward Elgar.

Geofeedia (2012). *Detroit crime commission: Securing the 2012 world series through real-time location based social media monitoring*. Case Study. Chicago, IL: Author.

Hagan, J., Shedd, C., & Payne, M. R. (2005). Race, ethnicity, and youth perceptions of criminal injustice. *American Sociological Review, 70*(3), 381–407. doi:10.1177/000312240507000302

Hinds, L., & Murphy, K. (2007). Public satisfaction with police: Using procedural justice to improve police legitimacy. *Australian & New Zealand Journal of Criminology, 40*(1), 27–42. doi:10.1375/acri.40.1.27

Ito, M., Baumer, S., Bittanti, M., Cody, R., Herr-Stephenson, B., Horst, H. A., & Pascoe, C. et al. (2010) Hanging out, messing around, and geeking out. *Digital Media*.

Jacobs, J. B. (2009). Gang databases. *Criminology & Public Policy, 8*(4), 705–709. doi:10.1111/cpp.2009.8.issue-4

Kerr, M., & Stattin, H. (2000). What parents know, how they know it, and several forms of adolescent adjustment: Further support for a reinterpretation of monitoring. *Developmental Psychology, 36*(3), 366–380. doi:10.1037/0012-1649.36.3.366

King, J. E., Walpole, C. E., & Lamon, K. (2007). Surf and turf wars online growing implications of internet gang violence. *Journal of Adolescent Health, 41*(6), S66–S68. doi:10.1016/j.jadohealth.2007.09.001

Klein, M. W. (2009). Street gang databases. *Criminology & Public Policy, 8*(4), 717–721. doi:10.1111/cpp.2009.8.issue-4

Lapp, K. (2015). Databasing delinquency. *Hastings Law Journal, 676*, 195.

Leary, J. D. (2001). *Trying to kill the part of you that isn't loved*. (Ph.D. dissertation). Portland State University, Portland, OR.

Leman-Langlois, S. (2008). The local impact of police videosurveillance on the social construction of security. In S. Leman-Langlois (Ed.), *Technocrime: Technology, crime, and social control* (pp. 27–45). New York, NY: Routledge.

Lieberman, J. D., Koetzle, D., & Sakiyama, M. (2013). Police departments' use of Facebook: Patterns and policy issues. *Police Quarterly, 16*(4), 438–462. doi:10.1177/1098611113495049

Lyon, D. (2002). Surveillance studies: Understanding visibility, mobility and the phenetic fix. *Surveillance & Society, 1*(1), 1–7.

Martin, R. C., Coyier, K. R., VanSistine, L. M., & Schroeder, K. L. (2013). Anger on the Internet: The perceived value of rant sites. *Cyberpsychology, Behavior, and Social Networking, 16*(2), 119–122. doi:10.1089/cyber.2012.0130

Marwick, A., & Boyd, D. (2011 September). I tweet honestly, I tweet passionately: Twitter users, context collapse and the imagined audience. *New Media & Society, 13*(1), 114–133. doi:10.1177/1461444810365313

Marwick, A. E. (2011). Social privacy in networked publics: Teens' attitudes, practices, and strategies. In *Proceedings of the A Decade in Internet Time: OII Symposium On the Dynamics Of the Internet and Society*. Oxford, United Kingdom: University of Oxford.

McArdle, A., & Erzen, T. (Eds.). (2001). *Zero tolerance: Quality of life and the new police brutality in New York City*. New York, NY: NYU Press.

Miller, R. (2014). Devolving the carceral state: Race, prisoner reentry and the micro-politics of urban poverty management. *Punishment & Society, 16*(3), 305–335. doi:10.1177/1462474514527487

Moreno, M. A., & Whitehill, J. M. (2012). New media, old risks: Toward an understanding of the relationships between online and offline health behavior. *Archives of Pediatrics and Adolescent Medicine, 166*(9), 868–869. doi:10.1001/archpediatrics.2012.1320

Moule, R. K., Pyrooz, D. C., & Decker, S. H. (2013). From 'What the F#@% is a Facebook?' to 'Who Doesn't Use Facebook?': The role of criminal lifestyles in the adoption and use of the Internet. *Social Science Research, 42*(6), 1411–1421. doi:10.1016/j.ssresearch.2013.06.008

Myers, M. A., & Thompson, V. L. S. (2000). The impact of violence exposure on African American youth in context. *Youth & Society, 32*(2), 253–267. doi:10.1177/0044118X00032002006

Neely, P., & Cleveland, C. S. (2011). The impact of job-related stressors on incidents of excessive force by police officers. *American Journal of Health Sciences, 3*(1), 63–74.

Nuño, L. F. (2013). Police, public safety, and race neutral discourse. *Sociology Compass, 7*(6), 471–486. doi:10.1111/soco.2013.7.issue-6

Palfrey, J., & Gasser, U. (2008). *Born digital: Understanding the first generation of digital natives*. New York, NY: Basic Books.

Patton, D. U., Eschmann, R. D., & Butler, D. A. (2013). Internet banging: New trends in social media, gang violence, masculinity and hip hop. *Computers in Human Behavior, 29*(5), A54–A59. doi:10.1016/j.chb.2012.12.035

Patton, D. U., Hong, J. S., Ranney, M., Patel, S., Kelley, C., Eschmann, R., & Washington, T. (2014). Social media as a vector for youth violence: A review of the literature. *Computers in Human Behavior, 35*, 548–553. doi:10.1016/j.chb.2014.02.043

Prenzler, T., Porter, L., & Alpert, G. P. (2013). Reducing police use of force: Case studies and prospects. *Aggression and Violent Behavior, 18*(2), 343–356. doi:10.1016/j.avb.2012.12.004

Prusaczyk, B., Ravindranath, D., Davis, M., & Sewell, W. (2014). The Ferguson verdict. *Economic and Political Weekly, 49*(4), 22.

Raynes-Goldie, K. (2010). Aliases, creeping, and wall cleaning: Understanding privacy in the age of Facebook. *First Monday, 15*(1). doi:10.5210/fm.v15i1.2775

Rios, V. M. (2006). The hyper-criminalization of Black and Latino male youth in the era of mass incarceration. *Souls, 8* (2), 40–54. doi:10.1080/10999940600680457

Rios, V. M. (2011). *Punished: Policing the lives of Black and Latino boys*. New York, NY: NYU Press.

Roberts, D. J. (2015). The killing of Mike Brown: Ferguson, Missouri and color blindness in the contemporary United States. *Dialogues in Human Geography, 5*(2), 249–252. doi:10.1177/2043820615574443

Smith, A. (2014). *African American and technology use: A demographic report*. Pew Research Center, Internet, Science and Tech. Retrieved December 1, 2014.

Spizman, R. J., & Miller, M. K. (2013). Plugged-in policing: Student perceptions of law enforcement's use of social media. *Applied Psychology in Criminal Justice, 9*(2), 100–123.

Swaine, J. (2014). Chicago gang shootings go on as Mayor Emanuel boasts crime at record low. *The Guardian*. Retrieved December 1, 2014.

Taylor, J. (2013). We are all Oscar Grant: Police brutality, death, and the work of mourning. *Transforming Anthropology, 21*(2), 187–197. doi:10.1111/traa.2013.21.issue-2

Trottier, D. (2012). Policing social media. *Canadian Review of Sociology/Revue Canadienne de Sociologie, 49*(4), 411–425. doi:10.1111/cars.2012.49.issue-4

Tyler, T. R. (2004). Enhancing police legitimacy. *Annals of the American Academy of Political and Social Science, 593* (1), 84–99. doi:10.1177/0002716203262627

Wacquant, L. (2001). Deadly symbiosis: When ghetto and prison meet and mesh. *Punishment & Society, 3*(1), 95–133. doi:10.1177/14624740122228276

Wright, J. D. (2005). The constitutional failure of gang databases. *Columbia Journal of Gender & Law, 2*, 115.

Yar, M. (2012). E-crime 2.0: The criminological landscape of new social media. *Information & Communications Technology Law, 21*(3), 207–219. doi:10.1080/13600834.2012.744224

Law enforcement perceptions of their relationship with community: Law enforcement surveys and community focus groups

Juan J. Barthelemy[a], Cassandra Chaney[b], Elaine M. Maccio[c], and Wesley T. Church, II[a]

[a]School of Social Work, Louisiana State University, Baton Rouge, Louisiana, USA; [b]Department of Child and Family Studies, Louisiana State University, Baton Rouge, Louisiana, USA; [c]School of Social Work and Women's and Gender Studies, Louisiana State University, Baton Rouge, Louisiana, USA

ABSTRACT

The Baton Rouge Area Violence Elimination (BRAVE) Project is a group violence reduction strategy based on the Boston Gun Project's Operation Ceasefire. This violence reduction model is predicated on the idea that violence can be dramatically reduced when community members and law enforcement join together to directly engage with criminal groups. In Baton Rouge, selected law enforcement officers have received specialized training regarding the implementation of the BRAVE Project and additional training with regard to working with residents in the community. To that end, surveys and focus groups were administered to residents in the intervention target area to identify their perceptions of crime, law enforcement, and leaders in their community. In addition, law enforcement officers completed surveys that focused on their perceptions of crime and other problems in the target area and their thoughts about whether this intervention could be successful. Results suggest that law enforcement and community members agree on what the problems are but disagree on who is responsible for them and how to solve them. Follow-up surveys and focus groups have been administered to determine whether residents in the target area have changed their perceptions of law enforcement. This article discusses the results of those surveys, the implications of such a violence reduction model, and recommendations for similar models in other cities.

According to *USA Today* (Johnson, Hoyer, & Heath, 2014), an African American male is killed by police almost twice a week. In addition, police officers are involved in as many as 400 killings a year. In a related story, reported by Juzwiak and Chan (2014), the NAACP Legal Defense and Educational Fund listed 76 men and women of color who were killed by police between 1999 and 2014. In the majority of cases, the officers were determined to be justified in their killings. However, some of the deaths resulted in civil judgments against the police departments involved, but this was rarely the case. Such statistics highlight the disconnect between law enforcement officials and the communities they are sworn to serve and protect.

This study examined survey and focus group results provided by members of law enforcement and the community regarding the Baton Rouge Area Violence Elimination (BRAVE) Project, a group violence reduction strategy based on the Boston Gun Project's Operation Ceasefire (Kennedy, Braga, Piehl, & Waring, 2001). This topic is important for three reasons. First, since neighborhood residence is highly correlated with increased gang activity, violence, and crime (Dottolo & Stewart, 2008; Moore, 1990; Sampson, Raudenbush, & Earls, 1997; White, Yehle, Serrano, Oliveira, &

Menezes, 2014), it is important that community policing strategies consider how police and community residents view crime in their community. Since police and community residents may hold very different perceptions of crime (Stein & Griffith, 2015), an evaluation of community perceptions of crime activity *before and after* the implementation of the BRAVE Project can pinpoint to what extent, if any, this crime intervention strategy has been effective.

Second, in light of the increased distrust of law enforcement (Boyer, 2001; Chaney & Robertson, 2013; Chronopoulos, 2015; Hassell & Archbold, 2010; Jefferis, Butcher, & Hanley, 2011; Savali, 2012), it is important to examine how community members perceive police. Since perceptions of police are directly related to the confidence that community members have in law enforcement (Bjornstrom, 2015; Elicker, 2008; Nix, Wolfe, Rojek, & Kaminski, 2015; Walker, 2011), this study sought to determine whether a relationship exists between law enforcement's involvement with the BRAVE Project and community members' willingness to call police during times of need. On the other hand, since police are more likely to form alliances with individuals who share their view of crime (Hughey, 2015; Jackson & Wade, 2005), this study also highlights the characteristics that make individuals in low-income communities more or less likely to work with police.

Finally, since community policing interventions have been found to be effective (Star et al., 2014; White, 2014), positive effects of the BRAVE Project may reduce many of the punitive crime policies that incarcerate a substantial number of African Americans[1] (Hetey & Eberhardt, 2014; Smith & Hattery, 2010). While several community policing interventions have produced mixed results (Braga, Papachristos, & Hureau, 2014; Lum & Koper, 2014; Weisburd & Telep, 2014), it is important to pinpoint the strengths and limitations of the BRAVE Project. Although we live in what many consider to be a postracial society (Gonzalez-Sobrino & Hughey, 2015; Howard & Flennaugh, 2011), different racial experiences invariably determine the extent to which community members and police work together to reduce violent crime. Ultimately, this study provides specific recommendations that can help police and community members simultaneously reduce violent crime and build stronger and more productive relationships with one another.

Review of literature

As a societal problem, criminal activity threatens the physical safety and emotional well-being of individuals, families, and communities. Although anyone in society can be a victim of crime, some areas possess contextual factors that bolster antisocial activity. Specifically, poor neighborhoods frequently have higher levels of unemployment, single parenthood, juvenile delinquency, and criminal activity (Boxer, 2014; Clinard & Meier, 2016; Engel, Smith, & Cullen, 2012; Erickson & Erickson, 2014; Henrich, 2015; Krivo & Peterson, 1996; Moore, 1990; Papachristos, 2014; Sampson et al., 1997). Therefore, economic deprivation, residential instability, and high rates of homicide are strongly linked to gangs, drug activity, and violent crime (Krivo & Peterson, 1996; Morenoff & Sampson, 1997; Peterson, Krivo, & Harris, 2000; Sampson et al., 1997). Since offenders typically commit crimes in areas with which they are familiar (e.g., close to home; White et al., 2014), individuals who live in low-income communities are more likely to be victims of violent crime than individuals who live in more financially affluent neighborhoods (Hur & Nasar, 2014; Leventhal & Brooks-Gunn, 2000; Stein & Griffith, 2015; Wilson, 2013). Thus, when compared to individuals who reside in neighborhoods with a lower rate of crime, individuals who reside in a low-income community generally have higher communal fear of crime (Brunton-Smith & Sturgis, 2011).

Race is highly correlated with poverty and low-income-neighborhood residence (Darrah & DeLuca, 2014; Massoglia, Firebaugh, & Warner, 2013; Sharkey, 2013; Small & Newman, 2001). Since the poverty rate is substantially higher for Blacks than Whites (Brunn-Bevel, 2015; Gurin, Sorensen, Lopez, & Nagda, 2015), members of the former group are more likely to reside in low-income communities and reenter these neighborhoods after exiting them (Quillian, 2003). In other words, even when Blacks have an opportunity to leave poor neighborhoods, there is a high likelihood that social and financial setbacks will cause them to return to these communities. Thus, African American males from poor, urban neighborhoods are markedly more likely than men of other races to be convicted of crimes related to gangs, drugs, and violence (Cush, 2013; Greene & Gabbidon, 2011; Pettus, 2013). In addition, the incarceration of Black men significantly weakens the financial, human, social, and political strength of the communities from which they come (Smith & Hattery, 2010).

To reduce the adverse consequences of violent crime, several recommendations have been offered. While some scholars advocate that schools become more proactive in minimizing gang activity (Estrada, Gilreath, Astor, & Benbenishty, 2014; Higginson et al., 2014), others consider law enforcement as imperative to maintain social order (Rossmo, 2014; Worden, Bynum, & Frank, 1994). Since recidivist offenders usually perform large numbers of crimes and/or commit the most dangerous crimes in society (rape, murder, arson, and armed robbery), many believe a community policing approach can protect communities by reducing the number of "career criminals," or professional criminals motivated by material gain (Edelstein, 2015, p. 2). While a community policing philosophy emphasizes close involvement between police and community residents to reduce crime (Greene & Decker, 1989), incidents of police misconduct may make effective collaborations between these entities extremely difficult.

Scholars have identified several correlates that lead some members of law enforcement to engage in and/or be terminated for misconduct (Fyfe & Kane, 2006; Kane & White, 2009; Savali, 2012). One quantitative study found that officers whose personal histories included arrest, traffic violations, and failure in other jobs were more likely than other officers to be terminated from their jobs because of misconduct (Fyfe & Kane, 2006). In addition, officers who held associate or higher degrees were less likely than those without them to be dismissed for misconduct, and those who did well in the academy's recruit training program were also less likely than marginal recruits to be terminated for misconduct (Fyfe & Kane, 2006). Since the actions of some members of law enforcement may threaten the safety of marginalized communities of color (Joh, 2015; Smith & Holmes, 2014), it is imperative to examine how the police and low-income communities generally perceive each other.

Police perceptions of the community

Police perceptions of the communities they serve directly influence their level of interaction with the individuals within those communities. While existing scholarship has explored how police feel about domestic violence (Homant & Kennedy, 1985), strategies for interviewing children with intellectual disabilities (Aarons, Powell, & Browne, 2004), as well as how to defuse community conflict (Drury, Stott, & Farsides, 2003), few recent studies have specifically examined how members of law enforcement generally perceive the communities they serve. Although dated, one study is especially noteworthy. In their qualitative study of how 522 policemen that worked in Black ghettos perceived those communities, Groves and Rossi (1970) asserted White policemen's perceptions of Black hostility were a projection of their own fears and prejudices, and not a legitimate reaction to actual hostility.

Police perceptions of community policing programs are linked to whether these efforts can reduce crime in low-income areas. For example, how members of law enforcement perceived the Chicago Alternative Policing Strategy (CAPS), a well-known community policing program in Chicago, is informative. In this pre- and posttest examination (e.g., officers were surveyed about their job satisfaction, their supervisors, and their opinions regarding community policing), the officers were supportive of some CAPS-related activities (e.g., solving noncrime problems) but not others (e.g., foot patrol) and had doubts about the program's effects on crime and neighborhood relations (Lurigio & Skogan, 1994). On the other hand, a community response to crime may actually enhance how that community is perceived by law enforcement. To support this, Stein and Griffith (2015) found police had more positive perceptions of White communities that had an active crime prevention program. Thus, it appears that what is on the surface is directly related to how police conscientiously interact with individuals within a community.

Community perceptions of the police

Over the past few decades, the media have been extremely instrumental in featuring reports on "bad cops." For example, the Rampart Scandal revealed that bogus arrests, perjured testimony, and planting "drop guns" on unarmed civilians were common practices in the Los Angeles Police Department during the 1990s (Boyer, 2001). Furthermore, the documented murders of many unarmed African Americans by police between 1999 and 2014 (Juzwiak & Chan, 2014), as well as the negative treatment their families received from police (Erfani-Ghettani, 2015), have led many to openly question whether law enforcement is truly committed "To Serve and Protect" African Americans in society (Chaney & Robertson, 2013). Added to this, the Department of Justice's discovery of "implicit and explicit racial bias" by the Ferguson, Missouri, Police Department against African American residents further crystallized the lack of trust that many Blacks have for members of law enforcement (Berman & Lowery, 2015</link>). Sadly, mistrust in law enforcement greatly undermines community confidence in police and makes it substantially more difficult to create effective collaborations with this segment of the criminal justice system.

Community perceptions of police can be influenced by a multitude of factors. Some of these factors include, but are not limited to, law enforcement's use of excessive force (Chaney & Robertson, 2013; Jefferis et al., 2011; Joh, 2015; Skolnick & Fyfe, 1994), the criminal activity of police (Stinson, Todak, & Dodge, 2015), and the increased militarization of law enforcement (Mead, 2015). In addition, community perceptions of police are shaped by race-ethnicity, personal experiences, and neighborhood characteristics (Bjornstrom, 2015; Callanan & Rosenberger, 2011; Chaney & Robertson, 2014; Frank, Smith, & Novak, 2005; Schafer, Heubner, & Bynum, 2003; Weitzer & Tuch, 2004). For example, perceived unjust policing (Corsaro, Frank, & Ozer, 2015), being more fearful of crime (Haberman, Groff, Ratcliffe, & Sorg, 2013), and wanton gang-labeling, which substantially contributes to the over-policing of Black and Latino men (Williams, 2015), all contribute to lower satisfaction with and trust of police.

Community residence directly impacts how the police are perceived. Nearly four decades ago, Thomas and Hyman (1977) found that perceptions among those who were less affluent and lived in inner-city areas were less favorable than among respondents who resided in suburban areas. In addition, Blacks and younger people have less favorable attitudes of police than affluent and more educated Whites (Thomas & Hyman, 1977). Other studies support the salience of race and police perceptions. In their examination of how Whites, African Americans, and Hispanics view four types of police misconduct (e.g., verbal abuse, excessive force, unwarranted stops, and corruption), Weitzer and Tuch (2004) found Blacks and Hispanics were more likely than Whites to report having negative interactions with police, to be exposed to media reports of police misconduct, and to live in high-crime neighborhoods where policing was contentious. Recent findings support the increased number of racial majority and minority members who do not trust police (Van Craen, 2013).

In addition to race, personal experiences with members of law enforcement also affect how the police are generally perceived. Usually, when individuals are asked how they feel about police overall, they base their answers on specific incidents (Chaney & Robertson, 2013; Erfani-Ghettani, 2015; Frank et al., 2005). Moreover, when they were asked to reflect on incidents of police arrest or questioning that they personally experienced and deemed unfair, these individuals demonstrated a high level of rational thought and expression (Pollock & Menard, 2014).

Other studies have examined how race-ethnicity, nativity, and community characteristics are associated with reports of unfair treatment by police. Through her use of the Los Angeles Family and Neighborhood Survey, Bjornstrom (2015) revealed foreign-born Latinos were less likely than African Americans and U.S.-born Whites to report unfair treatment. Furthermore, in regard to resident context, U.S.-born Latinos who resided in more affluent neighborhoods were less likely to report unfair treatment than African Americans (Bjornstrom, 2015). Thus, the findings of this study suggest that the characteristics of a neighborhood may be directly related to how the police are perceived by community members.

Race and ethnicity greatly influence judgments and behaviors in the criminal justice and legal contexts. Since police officers are more likely to stop, search, arrest, and shoot Blacks, members of this group (along with Latinos) are substantially more likely to be murdered by police (Cush, 2013; Erfani-Ghettani, 2015; Plant & Peruche, 2005; Thomas & Sha'Kema, 2015; White, 2014). In addition, Black and Latino defendants are more likely to receive sentences involving incarceration, and the death penalty is most likely to be imposed in cases in which Black defendants are convicted of killing White victims. Consequently, Blacks and Latinos have more negative views of police and the justice system (Chaney & Robertson, 2013, 2014; Hunt, 2015; Peck, 2015).

Even victims whose assailants had been arrested under the provisions of the New York Family Protection and Domestic Violence Intervention Act noted how the demeanor of police officers (e.g., dismissive, invalidating, callous, arrogant, etc.) was directly related to the victims' level of trust in law enforcement (Stephens & Sinden, 2000). More recent studies have revealed the negative perceptions that many have of the police. In their examination of the comments provided on the Cato Institute's National Police Misconduct Statistics and Reporting Project (NPMSRP) website, Chaney and Robertson (2013) found that while some individuals respected members of law enforcement, the majority of commenters had contempt for law enforcement, were suspicious of law enforcement, and perceived members of law enforcement as agents of brutality. Given the high level of societal cynicism for police, it is imperative that members of law enforcement recognize their ability to change many of the negative perceptions of them held by many communities and the individuals within them (Thomas & Hyman, 1977).

Reducing violent crime in inner-city communities

Scholars have examined several ways to reduce violent crime in inner-city communities. One way may be to develop a larger base of certain types of local institutions (e.g., recreation centers, coffee shops, and cafes) and prevent the invasion of others (i.e., bars and liquor stores; Peterson et al., 2000; Wo, 2014). Although increased street-drug policing could lead to the arrests of individuals engaged in this form of criminal activity (Cordner, 2014; Hibdon & Groff, 2014; Linton, Jennings, Latkin, Kirk, & Mehta, 2014), specific efforts such as "War on Drugs policing" typically increase police brutality in Black communities and do little to reduce street-level drug activity (Cooper, 2015). While increasing the intensity of random patrol activity may not necessarily decrease crime (Nagin, Solow, & Lum, 2015), positive perceptions of community policing may lead to less fear of crime (Scheider, Rowell, & Bezdikian, 2003) and an increased desire for neighborhood residents to conscientiously work with police to reduce crime (Reisig & Giacomazzi, 1998).

Methodology

The research design in this study is a secondary data analysis of a law enforcement survey and data from community focus groups. The Law Enforcement Survey is comprised of 66 items with Likert-type scale responses. Additionally the survey included demographic information, which included race, gender, education level, years in law enforcement, and marital status.

The Law Enforcement Survey comprises sections that ask questions regarding the following topics: (1) perceptions of neighborhood safety and possible contributors to crime, (2) perceptions of neighborhood crime activity and behaviors, (3) perceptions of people's attitudes toward police, and (4) collective efficacy. In addition, law enforcement officers were asked about what they thought neighbors could do and what law enforcement could do to improve the relationship between the community and law enforcement.

The BRAVE Research Team conducted 12 focus groups during August 2012. The focus groups were conducted at local social service providers that were central to the target area of the intervention. The focus groups averaged about 10 participants in each group. Four follow-up focus groups were conducted in the same locations in June and July 2014. These focus groups also averaged about 10 people in each group.

The focus groups asked the participants the following questions.

Community

(1) Who are the community leaders (formal and informal) to get involved?
(2) How do both types of community leaders feel about there being a "gang or violence problem?" Are they prepared to respond?
(3) Are there any specific feelings parents in the community might feel about their children's risk for involvement?

Offenders

(1) Which of the well-known offenders would be most likely to join the fight?
(2) What are the needs of the youth or community members affiliated with gang activity/violent crime?
(3) What would persuade gang members to leave the gang or youth to stop offending?

Violent/gang activity

(1) What issues are contributing to the area's, gang and violence problems?
(2) Who is involved in gang and violent activity, and why did they join/become involved?
(3) What types of gang/violent crime are being committed? How much of it is by youth?

Law enforcement

(1) What past efforts have worked to reduce crime or violence? How were they implemented?
(2) What are the community members' feelings toward law enforcement? What influences these feelings?
(3) How have community members been treated by law enforcement in the past?
(4) Are community members confident that law enforcement will resolve problems when called?

Descriptive statistics were used to analyze the demographic data in the survey. These analyses primarily involved tabulating frequencies and percentages for the respondents on those items. The open-ended Law Enforcement Survey questions and the Community Focus Group questions were analyzed using a content analysis to identify the themes that were present in the responses. In addition to identifying themes, some direct quotes were provided when they were deemed to provide more context to the respective questions.

Results

Law enforcement responses

Two local law enforcement agencies were asked to complete surveys about the communities where they work and their perceptions of the problems within those communities. Of the 82 surveys returned, five had to be discarded due to the amount of missing data, leaving 77 usable surveys. The sample was primarily White (48%), male (81%), and married (62%), with an Associate's degree or higher (35%), and up to 10 years' employment in law enforcement (80%). (See Table 1 for complete sample demographics.)

Table 1. Sample characteristics (*N* = 77)

Characteristic	*n* (%)
Race (*n* = 76)	
Black/African American	16 (21%)
White	39 (48.0%)
Other	8 (15.0%)
No answer	13 (16.0%)
Sex (*n* = 68)	
Male	55 (81.0%)
Female	6 (9.0%)
No answer	7 (10.0%)
Length of law enforcement employment	
9 months to 10 years	65 (80.0%)
10+ years	16 (20.0%)
Education (*n* = 71)	
High school	13 (18.3%)
Some college	25 (35.2%)
Associate's degree	4 (5.6%)
Vocational school	2 (2.8%)
Bachelor's degree	18 (25.3%)
Postundergraduate	3 (4.2%)
Relationship status (*n* = 73)	
Single/not partnered	10 (13.7%)
Married	45 (61.6%)
Partnered	4 (5.5%)
Divorced/no longer partnered	2 (2.7%)
Separated	1 (1.3%)
No answer	11 (15.0%)

Note. Percentages may not total 100 due to rounding.

Law enforcement officers were asked how much they agreed or disagreed with statements related to crime reduction. Nearly three quarters or more agreed or strongly agreed that "early prevention programs will help to reduce crime," officers should build relationships with young males in the community, "building strong relationships in communities can provide law enforcement with community cooperation and support," "overlooking family violence is only likely to lead to additional violence," "policing should take different approaches to suit different communities," "working with partners such as schools, social services agencies, and recreation groups is an important practice for law enforcement, and "it is important for law enforcement to get out of the squad car and interact with neighbors to build relationships." There was less agreement among respondents on risk factors. Approximately 42% of respondents strongly agreed or agreed with the statement "law enforcement should avoid making risk factors worse, for example, by arresting a parent in front of children," while 37% strongly disagreed or disagreed, and 21% had no opinion. (See Table 2 for complete survey responses.)

Law enforcement officers provided the following responses to questions about their perceptions about the communities where they work and the problems in those communities.

What do you consider to be the most serious problem in the neighborhood?

Drug using and drug selling was the most frequently reported problem in neighbors reported by law enforcement officers. Of the 71 responses to this question, drug use and selling accounted for 24% of the responses. This was followed by armed robbery of persons and stores, battery, burglary, and theft, which accounted for 17% of the responses. Lack of morals/lack of personal responsibility and poor parenting each accounted for about 10% of the responses. Other responses included guns/violence with weapons (7%), lack of education (6%), a culture of tolerating criminality and accepting it as being normal/"rapper thug life glorification" (4%), domestic abuse (3%), current attitudes toward police, poverty, racism, and "No Snitching" (1% each).

Table 2. Survey item responses (*N* = 77)

Item	*n* (%)
"Early prevention programs will help to reduce crime."	
Strongly agree	18 (23.4%)
Agree	40 (51.9%)
No opinion	8 (10.4%)
Disagree	8 (10.4%)
Strongly disagree	3 (3.9%)
"Officers should build relationships with young males in the community."	
Strongly agree	28 (35.9%)
Agree	32 (41.0%)
No opinion	11 (14.1%)
Disagree	6 (7.7%)
Strongly disagree	1 (1.3%)
"Building strong relationships in communities can provide law enforcement with community cooperation and support."	
Strongly agree	30 (38.5%)
Agree	34 (43.6%)
No opinion	8 (10.3%)
Disagree	5 (6.4%)
Strongly disagree	1 (1.3)
"Overlooking family violence is only likely to lead to additional violence."	
Strongly agree	43 (55.1%)
Agree	26 (33.3%)
No opinion	8 (10.3%)
Disagree	0 (0.0%)
Strongly disagree	1 (1.3%)
"Policing should take different approaches to suit different communities."	
Strongly agree	33 (42.3%)
Agree	24 (30.8%)
No opinion	5 (6.4%)
Disagree	10 (12.8%)
Strongly disagree	6 (7.7%)
"Working with partners such as schools, social services agencies, and recreation groups is an important practice for law enforcement."	
Strongly agree	26 (33.3%)
Agree	34 (43.6%)
No opinion	9 (11.5%)
Disagree	6 (7.7%)
Strongly disagree	3 (3.8%)
"Law enforcement should avoid making risk factors worse, for example, by arresting a parent in front of children."	
Strongly agree	9 (11.0%)
Agree	24 (29.3%)
No opinion	16 (19.5%)
Disagree	22 (26.8%)
Strongly disagree	7 (8.5%)
"It is important for law enforcement to get out of the squad car and interact with neighbors to build relationships."	
Strongly agree	28 (35.9%)
Agree	39 (50.0%)
No opinion	6 (7.7%)
Disagree	2 (2.6%)
Strongly disagree	3 (3.8%)

Note. Percentages may not total 100 due to rounding.

What is needed to improve this problem?

Approximately 17% of the responses were coded as parental accountability/teaching kids morals. Another 12% indicated that judicial improvements/court system/stronger sentencing would help to improve the crime problem. About 9% of the respondents suggested that a higher number of patrol officers/increased police visibility was needed. Another 9% responded that community involvement was necessary to improve problems in the communities. Arrests/law enforcement interaction/more enforcement accounted for 9% of the responses. Other responses included "don't know" (7%), city needs to fix abandoned and vacant houses (5%), counseling/family mentors/off duty mentor programs (5%), education (3%), people need to be held accountable for their actions (3%), and spiritual leadership/strong leadership (3%).

In order to improve relationships, what can neighbors do?

Law enforcement officers overwhelmingly responded that communication was imperative. Approximately 26% of the 72 respondents to this question indicated that neighbors could help by sharing information and cooperating with investigators. Another 22% indicated that communication with law enforcement would help to improve relationships. About 15% of law enforcement officers also indicated that neighbors' accountability to their own families and children was important. Other themes included more community involvement (11%), trust police more (8%), stop labeling police as crooked or racist every time an arrest is made (6%), show children how to respect everyone including the police (6%), and approach officers without being frightened or in fear of being arrested (6%).

When talking about what neighbors can do, one officer provided the following response: "Look at the men and women in uniform as people. Law enforcement for the most part are just normal people who are out there doing a job to better the lives of citizens they serve." Another officer stated, "Speak to law enforcement, not yell, curse, and accuse."

In order to improve relationships, what can law enforcement do?

Of the 66 respondents to the question what can law enforcement do, 39% indicated that more frequent face-to-face contact/more dialogue/be more visible would help to improve the relationship between law enforcement and communities in the target areas. About 15% of the respondents stated that law enforcement officers need to have compassion for the victims of crime/care about people and treat all residents with respect. Approximately 9% of the respondents stated that they need to improve communication skills. Other responses included approach your neighborhood with an open mind/be approachable (8%), increase number of officers (8%), accountability (3%), be more passionate about the job we attempt to do every day/be professional (3%), and invite the public to attend events at the police department to get more involved and encourage young people to get involved in law enforcement (3%).

When responding to the question about what law enforcement officers can do to improve relationships, one officer stated, "I get out and visit people and listen to their concerns. Treat all complaints as a serious issue. Most people only interact with police a few times in their life. What is trivial to the officer is serious to the complainant. Show them you are concerned and are going to handle the call to their satisfaction."

Similarly, another officer stated, "Get out of their units in the community and treat the citizens that they contact in the same manner that they would like their own family treated by police officers." Another officer stated, "Interaction with residents. Change our mind-set that not all Blacks are bad people and treat them with dignity. Encourage positive interaction." Last, "Law enforcement can do better by talking to neighbors. Not because we have to or at an 'organized event' put on by the community or the Police Department, but during foot patrols or neighborhood patrols contact people randomly in the community and get a feel of what's going on in the neighborhood."

Some law enforcement officers gave responses that provided different viewpoints; for example, one officer stated, "The problem is larger than just law enforcement. The first thing that needs to happen, when law enforcement has a good case on a suspect, attorneys need to fight to keep them in jail instead of settling the case. Start to fight for the community where it will make a difference."

Another respondent stated, "Unfortunately it does not appear we can do much. Children in these areas are raised from a young age to fear and hate us in large." Despite law enforcement's efforts to gain the communities trust, the public continues to pull away and grasp at every reason to dislike law enforcement.

Community responses

Community leaders

The majority of the focus groups yielded similar results with regard to community leaders. The most commonly reported names were the mayor and their local councilperson. In addition, responses ranged from local pastors, not always mentioned by name, to the local "Dope Boys." The participants typically expressed negative sentiments with regard to political leaders. The overwhelming response was that they heard from local leaders only during election time. Furthermore, they commonly expressed a thought that local leaders tend to ignore problems in their community.

While the majority of the participants in the focus groups shared negative feelings with regard to the local leaders, they did express that there are people in the community who try to reach out and talk to the youth. Moreover, some participants expressed the following: "They may not be official leaders, but our community members try to do the job of policing things and each other." Additional sentiments revolved around the desire for business owners to do their parts. For instance, some participants stated, "Business owners in the community should be more responsible and close earlier than 2 a.m., when people are to go and hang by the store and start problems." Another telling response was the following: "People don't even view the pastors as leaders anymore because we can't trust them." The lack of trust appeared to be a prevailing theme, as others stated, "They didn't trust leaders because they felt like leaders often said one thing and did something different."

Parenting

Focus group participants also discussed their concerns as parents. They expressed concerns about cars speeding through the neighborhood and the fact that it is dangerous for children to walk to school. Participants also expressed concerns that some parents may be doing the best they can, but it is still not enough sometimes. Conversely, others expressed that they didn't feel like all parents are responsible parents. A common perception was that some parents let their children do whatever they want to do and there needs to be more parental supervision. In addition, the lack of involvement by fathers was expressed as a problem. Additionally, while participants expressed it multiple different ways, the common theme was that many children are ungovernable and parents need to learn how to parent better. Some participants expressed that neighbors don't support one another anymore with regard to looking out for each other's children, and they also stated that parents don't take their children to church anymore. Hence, the feeling of community is not there. Moreover, participants suggested that they would like to see more positive outlets for children in the community, as well as parenting education to teach parents how to effectively parent their children.

Offenders

Participants frequently indicated that they were aware of the major offenders in their communities, but they also were not willing to share this information because they did not feel safe and they feared retaliation. Some participants suggested that the police already knew who these people were, but they would not do anything about it.

With regard to offender characteristics, they were generally described as truant, bold, young, and unemployed. Some participants suggested that offenders were most often males with no fathers involved in their lives. Furthermore, it was suggested that they get turned away from programs that they qualify for. One participant stated, "They have experienced so much negativity that they gave up." Another participant stated, "They may have a desire to change but when they get out of jail, they don't know other ways to live." Drugs and easy access to guns were also believed to contribute to the problem.

Unmet needs

Participants indicated that unmet needs consisted of parental guidance, employment, structure, routine, and positive role models. Other reported needs included substance abuse education and rehab, help from police and leaders before being punished, as well as legal advice. Some participants suggested that young offenders could also benefit from engagement and something to boost self-esteem, love and support, constructive outlets, family programs, and early childhood interventions.

Violent crimes

Participants were also candid about the types of crimes that take place in the community. They stated that violent crimes occur during broad daylight, and it happens because they don't have jobs. One participant stated, "Fights, sexual offenses, drug transactions, crimes over drug issues, theft, turf wars over drugs, retaliation crimes—if you speak out against them, they will get you or have their families do something to you." Some participants expressed that most gang crimes are drug related, yet another participant stated, "There may be more gang activity than even we know about."

Law enforcement

The vast majority of participants stated that they could not think of anything that has worked with law enforcement. The majority of them indicated that they do not think that law enforcement cares about them. Another major theme was the lack of trust between this community and law enforcement. They felt like they were negatively prejudged by law enforcement and that law enforcement did not listen to them.

Focus group participants were asked about how they were treated by law enforcement. Some participants reported negative perspectives related to their experiences with law enforcement. Negative responses included, "They stop us for nothing and meanwhile all the real crime is not even noticed," "Kick in doors for no reason," "Don't do their job, police are just as involved in drug activity as gang members," "They stereotype us by our looks," "They park and hide behind buildings instead of patrolling," "I've asked them not to approach my door if I call in a crime and they do it anyway," and "I don't feel protected enough by the police to speak out against offenders."

Some focus group participants reported positive interactions with law enforcement. Some examples included, "Some community members put out negativity and bring negative involvement with cops on themselves," "Police doing a beautiful job," "Cops have always treated me well," "Cops are human too, when they pass I wave," and "The community should work with cops to end crime, not against them."

When asked about confidence in law enforcement's ability to resolve issues, responses included the following: "They don't come for hours and hours; I mean, I just saw a murder," "When the cops don't respect confidentiality of identities, I get amnesia," "They don't like us and we don't like them," "They try to help but they are limited without community support," "Sending our kids away to jail with these cops will just make them worse," "There is no confidence, we have to be careful of what we say or we'll get shot," "There needs to be special assignments for officers so we can get comfortable with dealing with the same ones because they will know us," "The cops should work with us to develop a neighborhood watch with meetings so we can stop being so scared of the cops," "They seem like they are bothered when you call them," "It seems like the cops drive criminals around the block and then release them," "The cops are involved in more crime than we are" (in reference to police allegedly raping a neighborhood prostitute), "I'll call the cops and tell on anyone," "These criminals aren't going to run me off," "I've called them before and I'm the one who ended up in jail," "Most people won't call the cops because they have warrants or pending charges and they don't want to go to jail," "I'm very confident that the cops will come and help," and "If you call and leave the scene then nothing gets solved; but if you call and stay on the scene to give info they usually handle it well."

Post-implementation focus group

Community leaders

Participants identified different religious leaders and law enforcement leaders as community leaders. Some participants felt like leaders are trying to address crime, whereas others typically reported that they didn't feel like leaders were getting involved in the gang or violence problem. Similar to pre-implementation focus groups, many participants felt like leaders come around only during election time.

Parenting

Participants indicated that problems with children include peer pressure, sagging pants, drug involvement, shootings and robberies, sex abuse, need more activities for kids, and lack of respect for elders. Some participants also indicated that neighborhoods are segregated by race in Baton Rouge.

Offenders

Participants identified several needs of the youth or community members affiliated with gang activity/violent crime. These needs included summer jobs, sports activities, and boys and girls clubs. They also identified parks and recreation summer programs, parent classes, community policing, and work programs.

Violent/gang activity

Participants suggested the following factors as contributing to violent and/or gang activity: video games that desensitize youth to violence, lack of respect, most children not knowing the Bible or prayer, lack of discipline from parents, teen pregnancy, rap videos, skimpy clothing (including sagging pants, which some suggested needed to be criminalized), and abandoned houses.

Law enforcement

When asked about their feelings toward law enforcement, many participants expressed negative feelings. They indicated that many of them are afraid of law enforcement, because they feel like law enforcement are prejudiced against them. They indicated that many are scared to sit in their front yards for fear of harassment. Other participants indicated that they do not trust law enforcement, and some see their children being harassed by the police. Moreover, one participant stated that she saw law enforcement pull guns on her two male children.

Not all residents felt negatively toward law enforcement. For example, one participant expressed confidence in law enforcement's willingness to respond, but that the individual would "live a life so I don't need them." However, another participant stated that her nephew busted her windows in her house and although she gave a report with witnesses about 3 months ago, no arrest was ever made. Her identity was stolen.

Perceptions about BRAVE

Although the BRAVE Project has been in the community for 2 years, most of the participants indicated that they were not familiar with BRAVE, and they had no knowledge of the community events. However, some of the participants acknowledged that they heard about BRAVE through their church. In addition, some participants stated that they were only aware of the law enforcement side of BRAVE.

The participants who were aware of BRAVE reported mixed feelings. Senior citizens stated that they like the idea that BRAVE was started, and others stated that it is working to provide a needed service. They also stated that they see the BRAVE signs. However, not all participants had positive perceptions of BRAVE. Some participants stated that they don't associate with BRAVE because it is law enforcement and they will be labeled a snitch. Moreover, others stated that they associate BRAVE with kicking in doors. Yet another participant stated that some people are scared to come out, so they stay in the house.

BRAVE changes

Participants stated that they have noticed a change in community safety, but not all were ready to state that it is because of BRAVE. Yet they reported that people are not hanging on the corners like they used to selling drugs, and they reported an increased police presence. Moreover, it was also stated, "Think BRAVE is doing a good job." Another participant stated, "Law enforcement is doing a very good job since BRAVE started." Conversely, some participants stated that there have been more killings since implementation, and others stated that BRAVE is not effective. (It should be noted that this is statistically incorrect.) In addition to changes in safety, one participant stated that he noticed a change in people picking up trash around his apartment complex.

Community suggestions for change

Participants stated that they want to see police come through neighborhoods and get out of cars and talk to people. In addition, they would like to see more night patrols, because that is when they hear gunshots. Furthermore, it was suggested that law enforcement knock door to door between 9 p.m. and 12 a.m. to see if children are at home, because it is up to everyone to work with our children. Participants also stated that they need BRAVE team community meetings to help change attitudes about BRAVE, while others stated, "Council meeting should be held in neighborhoods, and churches should just help and not recruit membership." It was also suggested that BRAVE have more programs with music and food to meet young people where they are.

Discussion

Many of the problems identified by law enforcement were also identified as problems by the community members who participated in the community focus groups. However, there is a disconnect between law enforcement and the community with regard to how each side views the other with regard to addressing mutually agreed upon problems. For example, both law enforcement and community members acknowledge parenting to be a major point of emphasis with regard to youth who are responsible for much of the crime in the target areas. Yet it appears that more energy has been spent on blaming one another than trying to work together. Law enforcement officers and community members have also acknowledged that there is a contemptuous relationship between them, but there is less agreement about how to improve the relationship. For example, there is a small segment of the community who would like law enforcement officers to turn a blind eye to crime, but the vast majority of community members are in favor of law enforcement doing their jobs. As previously mentioned, law enforcement is necessary to maintain social order (Rossmo, 2014; Worden et al., 1994). Conversely, several law enforcement officers acknowledged that there is room for improvement with regard to how they approach and talk to some community residents. Law enforcement officers also suggested that residents have a responsibility to engage law enforcement officers in a respectful manner as well.

While many residents and law enforcement officers have expressed skepticism about seeing improvements in the community in the near future, it should be noted that violent crime has decreased and some respondents have shared stories of feeling safer in their neighborhoods.

Suggestions for ways to improve the relationship between law enforcement and the community included building relationships with young males in the community. This could be done through off-duty mentoring programs. Off-duty mentoring is currently facilitated through one of the local social service partners who is responsible for recruiting, screening, and pairing mentors with young men who have been referred to the program.

Law enforcement officers indicated that building strong relationships in communities can provide law enforcement with community cooperation and support. In addition, some officers also suggested having community events at the local police departments to educate citizens on some of the different aspects of law enforcement. Many respondents suggested that an increase in law enforcement personnel would make it easier to increase face-to-face visits and engage the public more. As law enforcement officers recognize the importance of increasing opportunities to improve communication with the public, they also acknowledged that there was room for improvement on the part of officers as well.

One example of how the BRAVE Project is addressing this recommendation is through the Cops and Clergy program. This program was adapted from a similar program in Memphis, Tennessee. The Cops and Clergy program is a 6-week program that invites local clergy members to come to the local police training academy where they are educated on the different aspects of police work. This training is based on the notion that the clergy members will serve as a liaison between their congregations and law enforcement. Moreover, clergy members will help to educate their congregations on the arrest process and the importance of sharing information with law enforcement with regard to criminal activities in their neighborhoods. These partnerships will also work to help law enforcement to become more compassionate to the plight of the residents in the communities through open dialogue with clergy leaders.

Directions for future research

Several articles have suggested that social work should play a role in the mediation in the relationship between law enforcement and the Black community. As law enforcement agencies across the country seek to move toward increased police legitimacy, there appears to be an opportunity for social workers to develop partnerships to aid in this training. Moreover, community triaging should also be an integral part of any movement, as the tension between law enforcement and the Black community is not a one-sided affair. As law enforcement officers have pointed out, there also needs to be some accountability on the side of law enforcement.

Note

1. The terms “African American” and “Black” will be used interchangeably in this article.

References

Aarons, N. M., Powell, M. B., & Browne, J. (2004). Police perceptions of interviews involving children with intellectual disabilities: A qualitative inquiry. *Policing and Society*, *14*(3), 269–278. doi:10.1080/1043946042000241848

Berman, M., & Lowery, W. (2015, March 4). The 12 key highlights from the DOJ’s scathing Ferguson report. *Washington Post*. Retrieved from http://www.washingtonpost.com/news/post-nation/wp/2015/03/04/the-12-key-highlights-from-the-dojs-scathing-ferguson-report/

Bjornstrom, E. E. (2015). Race-ethnicity, nativity, neighbourhood context and reports of unfair treatment by police. *Ethnic and Racial Studies*, *38*(12), 2019–2036. doi:10.1080/01419870.2015.1023821

Boxer, P. (2014). Youth gangs and adolescent development: New findings, new challenges, and new directions: Introduction to the special section. *Journal of Research on Adolescence*, *24*(2), 201–203. doi:10.1111/jora.2014.24.issue-2

Boyer, P. J. (2001, May 21). Bad cops. *The New Yorker*. Retrieved from http://www.newyorker.com/archive/2001/05/21/010521fa_FACT

Braga, A. A., Papachristos, A. V., & Hureau, D. M. (2014). The effects of hot spots policing on crime: An updated systematic review and meta-analysis. *Justice Quarterly*, *31*(4), 633–663. doi:10.1080/07418825.2012.673632

Brunn-Bevel, R. J. (2015). Black asset poverty and the enduring racial divide. *Ethnic and Racial Studies*, *38*(3), 473–475. doi:10.1080/01419870.2014.943785

Brunton-Smith, I., & Sturgis, P. (2011). Do neighborhoods generate fear of crime? An empirical test using the British Crime Survey. *Criminology*, *49*(2), 331–369. doi:10.1111/j.1745-9125.2011.00228.x

Callanan, V. J., & Rosenberger, J. S. (2011). Media and public perceptions of the police: Examining the impact of race and personal experience. *Policing & Society*, *21*(2), 167–189. doi:10.1080/10439463.2010.540655

Chaney, C., & Robertson, R. (2013). Racism and police brutality in America. *Journal of African American Studies*, *17*(4), 480–505. doi:10.1007/s12111-013-9246-5

Chaney, C., & Robertson, R. (2014). “Can we all get along?” Blacks’ historical and contemporary (in) justice with law enforcement. *Western Journal of Black Studies*, *38*(2), 108–122.

Chronopoulos, T. (2015). Police misconduct, community opposition, and urban governance in New York City, 1945–1965. *Journal of Urban History*. doi:10.1177/0096144215574695

Clinard, M., & Meier, R. (2016). *Sociology of deviant behavior* (15th ed.). Boston, MA: Cengage Learning.

Cooper, H. L. (2015). War on drugs policing and police brutality. *Substance Use & Misuse, 50*(8–9), 1188–1194. doi:10.3109/10826084.2015.1007669

Cordner, G. (2014). Community policing. In M. D. Reisig & R. J. Kane (Eds.), *The Oxford handbook of police and policing* (pp. 148–171). New York, NY: Oxford University Press.

Corsaro, N., Frank, J., & Ozer, M. (2015). Perceptions of police practice, cynicism of police performance, and persistent neighborhood violence: An intersecting relationship. *Journal of Criminal Justice, 43*(1), 1-11. doi:10.1016/j.jcrimjus.2014.10.003

Cush, I. (2013). Still not easy being an African-American. *New African, 47*(534), 72–74.

Darrah, J., & DeLuca, S. (2014). "Living here has changed my whole perspective": How escaping inner-city poverty shapes neighborhood and housing choice. *Journal of Policy Analysis and Management, 33*(2), 350–384. doi:10.1002/pam.21758

Dottolo, A., & Stewart, A. (2008). "Don't ever forget now, you're a Black man in America": Intersections of race, class and gender in encounters with the police. *Sex Roles, 59*(5–6), 350–364. doi:10.1007/s11199-007-9387-x

Drury, J., Stott, C., & Farsides, T. (2003). The role of police perceptions and practices in the development of "public disorder." *Journal of Applied Social Psychology, 33*(7), 1480–1500. doi:10.1111/jasp.2003.33.issue-7

Edelstein, A. (2015). Rethinking conceptual definitions of the criminal career and serial criminality. *Trauma, Violence, & Abuse*. doi:10.1177/1524838014566694

Elicker, M. K. (2008). Unlawful justice: An opinion study on police use of force and how views change based on race and occupation. *Sociological Viewpoints, 24*, 2433–2449.

Engel, R. S., Smith, M. R., & Cullen, F. T. (2012). Race, place, and drug enforcement. *Criminology & Public Policy, 11* (4), 603–635. doi:10.1111/j.1745-9133.2012.00841.x

Erfani-Ghettani, R. (2015). The defamation of Joy Gardner: Press, police and Black deaths in custody. *Race & Class, 56* (3), 102–112. doi:10.1177/0306396814556228

Erickson, R. J., & Erickson, S. J. (2014). Target selection by criminal groups and gangs. In S. J. Morewitz & M. L. Goldstein (Eds.), *Handbook of forensic sociology and psychology* (pp. 87–102). New York, NY: Springer.

Estrada, J. N., Gilreath, T. D., Astor, R. A., & Benbenishty, R. (2014). A statewide study of gang membership in California secondary schools. *Youth & Society*. doi:10.1177/0044118X14528957

Frank, J., Smith, B. W., & Novak, K. J. (2005). Exploring the basis of citizens' attitudes toward the police. *Police Quarterly, 8*(2), 206-228. doi:10.1177/1098611103258955

Fyfe, J. J., & Kane, R. (2006). *Bad cops: A study of career-ending misconduct among New York City police officers* (NCJ Report No. 215795). Retrieved from National Criminal Justice Reference Service website: https://www.ncjrs.gov/pdffiles1/nij/grants/215795.pdf

Gonzalez-Sobrino, B., & Hughey, M. W. (2015). White race discourse: Preserving racial privilege in a post-racial society. *Ethnic and Racial Studies, 38*(3), 493–495. doi:10.1080/01419870.2014.928341

Greene, H. T., & Gabbidon, S. (2011). *Race and crime: A text/reader*. Thousand Oaks, CA: Sage.

Greene, J. R., & Decker, S. H. (1989). Police and community perceptions of the community role in policing: The Philadelphia experience. *Howard Journal of Criminal Justice, 28*(2), 105–123. doi:10.1111/hojo.1989.28.issue-2

Groves, W. E., & Rossi, P. H. (1970). Police perceptions of a hostile ghetto: Realism or projection. *American Behavioral Scientist, 13*(5–6), 727–743. doi:10.1177/000276427001300507

Gurin, P., Sorensen, N., Lopez, G. E., & Nagda, B. R. A. (2015). Intergroup dialogue: Race still matters. In R. Bangs & L. E. Davis (Eds.), *Race and Social Problems* (pp. 39–60). New York, NY: Springer.

Haberman, C. P., Groff, E. R., Ratcliffe, J. H., & Sorg, E. T. (2013). Satisfaction with police in violent crime hot spots: Using community surveys as a guide for selecting hot spots policing tactics. *Crime & Delinquency*. Retrieved from http://www.researchgate.net/publication/262636382_Satisfaction_with_police_in_violent_crime_hot_spots_Using_community_surveys_as_a_guide_for_selecting_hot_spots_policing_tactics

Hassell, K. D., & Archbold, C. A. (2010). Widening the scope on complaints of police misconduct. *Policing, 33*(3), 473–489. doi:10.1108/13639511011066863

Henrich, J. (2015). Culture and social behavior. *Current Opinion in Behavioral Sciences, 3*, 84–89. doi:10.1016/j.cobeha.2015.02.001

Hetey, R. C., & Eberhardt, J. L. (2014). Racial disparities in incarceration increase acceptance of punitive policies. *Psychological Science, 25*(10), 1949–1954. doi:10.1177/0956797614540307

Hibdon, J., & Groff, E. R. (2014). What you find depends on where you look: Using emergency medical services call data to target illicit drug use hot spots. *Journal of Contemporary Criminal Justice*. doi:10.1177/1043986214525077

Higginson, A., Benier, K., Shenderovich, Y., Bedford, L., Mazerolle, L., & Murray, J. (2014). *Preventive interventions to reduce youth involvement in gangs and gang crime in low and middle-income countries: A systematic review*. Retrieved from www.campbellcollaboration.org/lib/project/297/

Homant, R. J., & Kennedy, D. B. (1985). Police perceptions of spouse abuse: A comparison of male and female officers. *Journal of Criminal Justice, 13*(1), 29–47. doi:10.1016/0047-2352(85)90024-8

Howard, T. C., & Flennaugh, T. (2011). Research concerns, cautions and considerations on Black males in a 'post-racial' society. *Race Ethnicity and Education, 14*(1), 105–120. doi:10.1080/13613324.2011.531983

Hughey, M. W. (2015). The Five I's of five-o: Racial ideologies, institutions, interests, identities, and interactions of police violence. *Critical Sociology, 41*(6), 857–871. doi:10.1177/0896920515589724

Hunt, J. S. (2015). Race in the justice system. In B. L. Cutler & P. A. Zapf (Series Eds.), *APA handbook of forensic psychology: Vol. 2. Criminal investigation, adjudication, and sentencing outcomes* (pp. 125–161). Washington, DC: American Psychological Association.

Hur, M., & Nasar, J. L. (2014). Physical upkeep, perceived upkeep, fear of crime and neighborhood satisfaction. *Journal of Environmental Psychology, 38,* 186–194. doi:10.1016/j.jenvp.2014.02.001

Jackson, A. L., & Wade, J. E. (2005). Police perceptions of social capital and sense of responsibility: An explanation of proactive policing. *Policing, 28*(1), 49–68. doi:10.1108/13639510510580977

Jefferis, E., Butcher, F., & Hanley, D. (2011). Measuring perceptions of police use of force. *Police Practice and Research, 12*(1), 81–96. doi:10.1080/15614263.2010.497656

Joh, E. (2015). Robert J Kane and Michael D White, *Jammed up: Bad cops, police misconduct, and the New York City Police Department. Punishment & Society, 17*(2), 262–264. doi:10.1177/1462474514538019

Johnson, K., Hoyer, M., & Heath, B. (2014, August 15). Local police involved in 400 killings per year. *USA Today.* Retrieved from http://www.usatoday.com/story/news/nation/2014/08/14/police-killings-data/14060357/

Juzwiak, R., & Chan, A. (2014). *Unarmed people killed by police 1999–2014.* Retrieved from http://gawker.com/unarmed-people-of-color-killed-by-police-1999-2014-1666672349

Kane, R. J., & White, M. D. (2009). Bad cops. *Criminology & Public Policy, 8*(4), 737–769. doi:10.1111/j.1745-9133.2009.00591.x

Kennedy, D. M., Braga, A. A., Piehl, A. M., & Waring, E. J. (2001). *Reducing gun violence: The Boston gun project's operation ceasefire.* Retrieved from https://www.ncjrs.gov/pdffiles1/nij/188741.pdf

Krivo, L. J., & Peterson, R. D. (1996). Extremely disadvantaged neighborhoods and urban crime. *Social Forces, 75*(2), 619–648. doi:10.1093/sf/75.2.619

Leventhal, T., & Brooks-Gunn, J. (2000). The neighborhoods they live in: The effects of neighborhood residence on child and adolescent outcomes. *Psychological Bulletin, 126*(2), 309–337. doi:10.1037/0033-2909.126.2.309

Linton, S. L., Jennings, J. M., Latkin, C. A., Kirk, G. D., & Mehta, S. H. (2014). The association between neighborhood residential rehabilitation and injection drug use in Baltimore, Maryland, 2000–2011. *Health & Place, 28,* 142–149. doi:10.1016/j.healthplace.2014.04.005

Lum, C., & Koper, C. S. (2014). Evidence-based policing. In G. Bruinsma & D. Weisburd (Eds.), *Encyclopedia of criminology and criminal justice* (pp. 1426–1437). New York, NY: Springer.

Lurigio, A. J., & Skogan, W. G. (1994). Winning the hearts and minds of police officers: An assessment of staff perceptions of community policing in Chicago. *Crime & Delinquency, 40*(3), 315–330. doi:10.1177/0011128794040003002

Massoglia, M., Firebaugh, G., & Warner, C. (2013). Racial variation in the effect of incarceration on neighborhood attainment. *American Sociological Review, 78*(1), 142–165. doi:10.1177/0003122412471669

Mead, M. (2015, February). The war against ourselves: Heien v. North Carolina, the war on drugs, and police militarization. *University of Miami Law Review.* Retrieved from http://ssrn.com/abstract=2588859/

Moore, J. W. (1990). Gangs, drugs, and violence. *Drugs and Violence: Causes, Correlates, and Consequences, 103,* 160–175.

Morenoff, J. D., & Sampson, R. J. (1997). Violent crime and the spatial dynamics of neighborhood transition: Chicago, 1970–1990. *Social Forces, 76*(1), 31–64. doi:10.1093/sf/76.1.31

Nagin, D. S., Solow, R. M., & Lum, C. (2015). Deterrence, criminal opportunities, and police. *Criminology, 53*(1), 74–100. doi:10.1111/crim.2015.53.issue-1

Nix, J., Wolfe, S. E., Rojek, J., & Kaminski, R. J. (2015). Trust in the police: The influence of procedural justice and perceived collective efficacy. *Crime & Delinquency, 61*(4), 610–640. doi:10.1177/0011128714530548

Papachristos, A. V. (2014). The network structure of crime. *Sociology Compass, 8*(4), 347–357. doi:10.1111/soc4.v8.4

Peck, J. H. (2015). Minority perceptions of the police: A state-of-the-art review. *Policing, 38*(1), 173–203. doi:10.1108/PIJPSM-01-2015-0001

Peterson, R. D., Krivo, L. J., & Harris, M. A. (2000). Disadvantage and neighborhood violent crime: Do local institutions matter? *Journal of Research in Crime and Delinquency, 37*(1), 31–63. doi:10.1177/0022427800037001002

Pettus, K. I. (2013). *Felony disenfranchisement in America: Historical origins, institutional racism, and modern consequences* (2nd ed.). Albany, NY: State University of New York Press.

Plant, E. A., & Peruche, B. M. (2005). The consequences of race for police officers' responses to criminal suspects. *Psychological Science, 16*(3), 180–183. doi:10.1111/psci.2005.16.issue-3

Pollock, W., & Menard, S. (2014). Perceptions of unfairness in police questioning and arrest incidents: Race, gender, age, and actual guilt. *Journal of Ethnicity in Criminal Justice, 13*(3), 237–253. doi:10.1080/15377938.2015.1015197

Quillian, L. (2003). How long are exposures to poor neighborhoods? The long-term dynamics of entry and exit from poor neighborhoods. *Population Research and Policy Review, 22*(3), 221–249. doi:10.1023/A:1026077008571

Reisig, M. D., & Giacomazzi, A. L. (1998). Citizen perceptions of community policing: Are attitudes toward police important? *Policing, 21*(3), 547–561. doi:10.1108/13639519810228822

Rossmo, D. K. (2014). Geographic profiling. In G. Bruinsma & D. Weisburd (Eds.), *Encyclopedia of criminology and criminal justice* (pp. 1934–1942). New York, NY: Springer.

Sampson, R. J., Raudenbush, S. W., & Earls, F. (1997). Neighborhoods and violent crime: A multilevel study of collective efficacy. *Science, 277*(5328), 918–924. doi:10.1126/science.277.5328.918

Savali, K. W. (2012, July 12). Criminal attorney on police brutality: 'Many officers are thugs with badges.' Retrieved from http://newsone.com/2024867/police-brutality-against-blacks-eric-guster

Schafer, J. A., Huebner, B. M., & Bynum, T. S. (2003). Citizen perceptions of police services: Race, neighborhood context, and community policing. *Police Quarterly, 6*(4), 440–468. doi:10.1177/1098611102250459

Scheider, M. C., Rowell, T., & Bezdikian, V. (2003). The impact of citizen perceptions of community policing on fear of crime: Findings from twelve cities. *Police Quarterly, 6*(4), 363–386. doi:10.1177/1098611102250697

Sharkey, P. (2013). *Stuck in place: Urban neighborhoods and the end of progress toward racial equality.* Chicago, IL: University of Chicago Press.

Skolnick, J. H., & Fyfe, J. J. (1994). *Above the law police and the excessive use of force.* New York, NY: Free Press.

Small, M. L., & Newman, K. (2001). Urban poverty after the truly disadvantaged: The rediscovery of the family, the neighborhood, and culture. *Annual Review of Sociology, 27*, 23–45. doi:10.1146/annurev.soc.27.1.23

Smith, B. W., & Holmes, M. D. (2014). Police use of excessive force in minority communities: A test of the minority threat, place, and community accountability hypotheses. *Social Problems, 61*(1), 83–104. doi:10.1525/sp.2013.12056

Smith, E., & Hattery, A. (2010). African American men and the prison industrial complex. *Western Journal of Black Studies, 34*(4), 387–398.

Star, C., Heath, M., Anderson, K., Hayes, A., Reynolds, L., Stephenson, H., & Voss, D. (2014). Good CoP or Bad CoP? What makes a community of practice successful: Learning from experience at Flinders University. *Ergo, 3*(1), 23–28. Retrieved from http://www.ojs.unisa.edu.au/index.php/ergo/article/view/940/672

Stein, R. E., & Griffith, C. (2015, March 17). Community policing strategies need to take into account police and residents' different perceptions of neighborhood crime. Retrieved from http://blogs.lse.ac.uk/usappblog/2015/03/17/community-policing-strategies-need-to-take-into-account-police-and-residents-different-perceptions-of-neighborhood-crime/

Stephens, B. J., & Sinden, P. G. (2000). Victims' voices: Domestic assault victims' perceptions of police demeanor. *Journal of Interpersonal Violence, 15*(5), 534–547. doi:10.1177/088626000015005006

Stinson, P. M., Todak, N. E., & Dodge, M. (2015). An exploration of crime by policewomen. *Police Practice and Research, 16*(1), 79–93. doi:10.1080/15614263.2013.846222

Thomas, A. J., & Sha'Kema, M. B. (2015). The influence of the Trayvon Martin shooting on racial socialization practices of African American parents. *Journal of Black Psychology, 41*(1), 75–89. doi:10.1177/0095798414563610

Thomas, C. W., & Hyman, J. M. (1977). Perceptions of crime, fear of victimization, and public perceptions of police performance. *Journal of Police Science and Administration, 5*(3), 305–317.

Van Craen, M. (2013). Explaining majority and minority trust in the police. *Justice Quarterly, 30*(6), 1042–1067. doi:10.1080/07418825.2011.649295

Walker, A. (2011). Racial profiling separate and unequal keeping the minorities in line-the role of law enforcement in America. *St. Thomas Law Review, 23*, 576–619.

Weisburd, D., & Telep, C. W. (2014). Hot spots policing: What we know and what we need to know. *Journal of Contemporary Criminal Justice, 30*(2), 200–220. doi:10.1177/1043986214525083

Weitzer, R., & Tuch, S. A. (2004). Race and perceptions of police misconduct. *Social Problems, 51*(3), 305–325. doi:10.1525/sp.2004.51.3.305

White, M. D. (2014). The New York City Police Department, its crime control strategies and organizational changes, 1970–2009. *Justice Quarterly, 31*(1), 74–95. doi:10.1080/07418825.2012.723032

White, S., Yehle, T., Serrano, H., Oliveira, M., & Menezes, R. (2014). The spatial structure of crime in urban environments. In L. M. Aiello & D. McFarland (Eds.), *Social informatics* (pp. 102–111). Retrieved from http://link.springer.com/book/10.1007%2F978-3-319-15168-7

Williams, P. (2015). Criminalising the other: Challenging the race-gang nexus. *Race & Class, 56*(3), 18–35. doi:10.1177/0306396814556221

Wilson, J. (2013). *Thinking about crime* (revised ed.). New York, NY: Basic Books.

Wo, J. (2014, August 22). Neighborhood institutions like coffee shops and bars can have a significant positive or negative impact on local crime rates. Retrieved from http://blogs.lse.ac.uk/usappblog/2014/08/22/neighborhood-institutions-like-coffee-shops-and-bars-can-have-a-significant-positive-or-negative-impact-on-local-crime-rates/

Worden, R. E., Bynum, T. S., & Frank, J. (1994). Police crackdowns on drug abuse and trafficking. In D. L. MacKenzie & C. D. Uchida (Eds.), *Drugs and crime: Evaluating public policy initiatives* (pp. 95–113). Thousand Oaks, CA: Sage.

An authentic discourse: Recentering race and racism as factors that contribute to police violence against unarmed Black or African American men

Bernadette R. Hadden[a], Willie Tolliver[a], Fabienne Snowden[b], and Robyn Brown-Manning[a]

[a]Silberman School of Social Work, Hunter College, City University of New York, New York, New York, USA; [b]CUNY Graduate Center, City University of New York, New York, New York, USA

ABSTRACT

This study explores the relationship between race, racism, and attitudes toward police violence against adult males. Study participants comprised a national sample (N = 1,974) of adult males and females (M = 48 years) who completed the 2012 General Social Survey (GSS). Secondary data analysis of surveys administered in-person or on the telephone by trained GSS interviewers indicated that race is a key predictor of police violence against adult males [χ^2 (7) = 85.710, p < .0001], even after controlling for sex, education, income, and age. Study findings also revealed that attitudes supportive of police violence are associated with negative cultural images of Blacks or African Americans. Participants who approved of police violence against males attributed disparities in employment, income, and housing between Blacks or African Americans and Whites to a lack of motivation and ability to learn, rather than to racial discrimination and lack of education incurred through poverty. These findings challenge us as social work educators and practitioners to further explore the association between racism and police violence and to unmask the debilitating consequences of the presumed limitations of Blacks or African Americans.

Police shootings of unarmed Black or African American men are occurring at alarming rates (Wihbey, 2014) and are indicative of a national trend of excessive force used by law enforcement agents on the bodies of people of color (American Civil Liberties Union [ACLU], 2014). These incidents are happening inside and outside of Black and Hispanic neighborhoods (Carroll & Gonzalez, 2014), to low-income and middle-class Blacks or African Americans (Jones-Brown, 2009), and are frequently the result of routine encounters (ACLU, 2014). One of several challenges in obtaining an accurate count of the number of the police shootings of unarmed Black or African American men in the United States is that there are no nationally consistent measures of collecting these data (Department of Justice, 2015).

This lack of standardized reporting, accompanied by public outrage, civil unrest, and community activism, calls for investigations into, and law enforcement reporting of, fatal police shootings of unarmed Black or African American men. Suggestions of racial profiling in police shootings have been presented as an explanation of the phenomenon of the disproportionate shooting of unarmed Black or African American men by law enforcement agents (Amajor, Sandars, & Pitts, 1999). In 2007 researchers found that in 10 of the United States's largest cities, Blacks or African Americans were overly represented among victims of police shootings (Lowerstein, 2007). These findings were most visible in New York City, Las Vegas, and San Diego (Lowerstein, 2007).

Supplementary files are available for this article at http://dx.doi.org/10.1080/10911359.2015.1129252.

At a 2010 hearing calling for the investigation of police-involved shootings in Oakland, California, the National Association for the Advancement of Colored People (NAACP) reported that from 2004 and 2008, 37 of the 45 police shootings in that city were at Black or African American suspects (Bulwa, 2010). A report from the New York City Police Department (NYCPD) illustrates that between 2000 and 2013, 97 Blacks or African Americans, 41 Hispanics, and 21 Whites were killed by NYPD police officers (NYCPD, 2014). In other words, from 2000 to 2013, more Blacks or African Americans were killed by NYCPD weapon discharges than Latinos and Whites combined. These reports identify and document the phenomenon of Black or African American men being shot and/or killed by police officers, despite the limitations in data tracking police shootings (Graham, 2015). However, they do not inform us of the incidence or prevalence of this phenomenon.

Gabrielson, Jones, and Sagora (2014) used police reported accounts of homicides in an FBI report to identify a prevalence rate or the proportion of the population that is shot by law enforcement agents during a specified period. These authors found that between 2010 and 2012, Black or African American males ages 15–19 were 21 times more likely than Whites to be shot by the police (Gabrielson, Jones, & Sagora, 2014). Harris-Perry (2014) reported an incidence rate or a measure of the frequency with which new shootings of Black or African Americans occurred from 2006 to 2012. Within this period, the killing of a Black or African American person occurred on an average of twice a week (Harris-Perry, 2014).

Social work as a profession has a long tradition of studying the effects of, and providing services to, survivors of interpersonal violence, domestic violence, intimate partner violence, and more recently structural violence. The study of police violence as structural violence (Oliver, 2001), and the literature on the provision of social work services to individuals, families, groups, and communities affected by police violence, is, however, an emerging area in social work education and research. Few studies in social work have specifically looked at the extent to which structural violence manifested as cultural racism may contribute to police violence against Blacks and African Americans. The vivid media exposure of the police shooting of Michael Brown in August 2014, and the nation's reaction to that, as well as subsequent shootings of unarmed Black or African American men have renewed efforts among scholars to bring conceptual clarity to a phenomenon that has far-reaching consequences.

Theoretical background

Intersectionality theory has provided a useful framework for social workers to understand the interconnectedness of institutionalized oppressions based on race, class, and gender (Cho, Crenshaw, & McCall, 2013; Crenshaw, 1991) and the production and maintenance of these groupings by forces of history, political economy, and power (Schulz & Mullings, 2006). Concepts such as race, gender, and class are fluid and change over time (Kinloch, 1974; Lind, 1969), and scholars agree that when these concepts are studied individually and/or separately, they do not adequately capture how they shift as a function of, and in relation to, each other (Combahee River Collective, 2009), thereby producing varied outcomes among and within different groups (Schulz & Mullings, 2006). Interpreting the different forms of oppression as independent of each other essentially minimizes complex relationships to power into a single category. However, refraining from centering race as an independent and key predictor in an exploration of the attitudes that approve of police violence against Black or African American men supports the prevailing metanarrative of a postracial society. Metanarratives are overarching paradigms or beliefs that serve the power interests of the group or groups that constructed them (Drake & Jonson-Reid, 2008), and this metanarrative needs to be deconstructed.

Intersectionality theory is limited in its assertion that race cannot be meaningfully examined separately from the other oppressive institutions. Furthermore, we submit that intersectionality theory, itself, serves as an oppressive force. By diluting or minimizing the deeper discourse on race, it colludes in ignoring the subjugated knowledge of Blacks or African Americans. It either marginalizes or invalidates the lived experiences of those who are most negatively impacted by policing policies and tactics. Such invisibility over extended periods helps to form a "psychological death," which is a key outcome of any type of oppression.

Critical race theory (CRT), on the other hand, posits the centrality of race in U.S. policy and the law (Delgado & Stefancic, 2001) and simultaneously acknowledges the interconnectedness of race, gender, and class oppression. It links race to racism and power, challenges the social construction of race, and shows how the racialization of constructed race groups may be used at different times to serve different policy and legal needs. Furthermore, CRT examines the ways in which racism is normalized and made invisible, thereby making it difficult to address any but the most blatant forms of discrimination. Critical race theory proposes a "voice-of-color thesis" (Delgado & Stefancic, 2001, p. 9.) whereby scholars of color write about their unique perspective of race and racism, thereby changing the dominant narrative about race and racism. Finally, CRT offers an examination of race separately from gender, education, and income and then in relation to these other oppressions for the following reasons: (1) race is predictive and has a key influence on public opinion, which in turn, shapes public policy, and (2) it has a unique history in the United States as a tool of racial oppression, which when joined to other oppressive systems places people at even greater risk for harm.

Contrary to intersectionality theory and a diversity approach, which infer that all oppressions are equal, they are not. Critical race theory informs our proposition that race should be recentered in the discourse on the police shootings of unarmed Black or African American men. We present race as a perspective that Whites have of Blacks or African Americans, a perspective that in turn informs interactions between Whites, and Blacks or African Americans, including interactions with law enforcement agents.

We propose an application of the group-position model of race relations (Blumer, 1958) and social identity theory (Hogg, 2006; Hogg & Vaughan, 2002; Tajfel & Turner, 1986) to inform an understanding of the police shootings of unarmed Black or African American men. Social identity theory examines the cognitive processes influencing social categorization, social identification, and social comparison associated with prejudice and discrimination related to perceived group membership. Perceived membership in a group that is evaluated or treated more favorably (i.e., the dominant group) is seen to enhance social identity with that group. Being evaluated and/or treated less favorably factors into identifying with a negative social identity—informed by race prejudice and discrimination. The initial approach to social identity theory was on the positive aspects of group identity, even for the group targeted for prejudice and discrimination by the dominant group, in that the former would have access to their identified group to collectively work on enhancing their group position. Social identity theory has been extended to the group-position model of race relations, which is a "variant of conflict theory" (Weitzer & Tuch, 2004a, p. 306).

The group-position model of race relations (Blumer, 1958) posits that group interest in maintaining a dominant position is the driving force that underlies contentious intergroup racial relations. Weitzer and Tuch (2004a, 2004b) used the group-position model to analyze group relations within social institutions, with policing being "one such institution" (p. 306). Their findings indicated that Blacks or African Americans and Latinos were more likely than Whites to report having negative interactions with police, and different perceptions of police misconduct existed among Blacks or African Americans, Hispanics, and Whites, with the latter having less negative perceptions.

We offer a postconflict pedagogy (Jansen, 2008) as a practical application of critical race theory, social identity theory, and the group-position model of race relations in recentering race in our discourse on the police shootings of unarmed Blacks or African Americans. A postconflict pedagogy has the potential to create an arena in which police officers and Black or African American men cross Jansen's "allegorical bridge" (p. 14) to discuss race, police violence and reconciliation. In his account of post-Apartheid violence against Blacks by White youth, Jansen outlined three core messages of what he termed "troubled knowledge" (p. 13) transmission that have remained intact for many of these young White men: "The first message is about racial exclusivity (we belong by ourselves); the second is about racial supremacy (we are better than them); and the third is about racial victimization (we are being targeted by them)" (p. 13). In beginning to redress this problem of racially transmitted troubled knowledge and its sequelae, Jansen challenges the post-Apartheid South African national policies' neglect in "disrupting the bitter knowledge" transfer (p. 14). He suggests pedagogical reciprocity in which both sides are prepared to make the move toward each other.

We wondered to what extent attitudes and opinions, and a perceived threat to power, influenced interactions between Whites, Blacks or African Americans, and law enforcement agents. We asked the following research questions: Are there differences in race with regard to support for police violence? Does prejudice regarding reasons for socioeconomic disparities between Blacks or African Americans and Whites inform supportive attitudes of police violence? Does cultural racism inform the perceptions that Blacks or African Americans and Whites have of the lived experiences of each other and their support for police aggression? We hypothesized the following: (1) that race predicts support for police violence; (2) that racial prejudice is manifested in opinions regarding the reasons for income, housing, and employment disparities between Blacks or African Americans and Whites; and (3) and that cultural racism is associated with support for police violence.

Definitions of concepts

Discussions about race and its effects are often diluted and rendered unsound by criticisms about the way in which the terms are used and the attributions assigned to them. We use Van den Berghe's (1967) and Kinloch's (1974) definitions of race, purposefully reaching beyond the 10-year "rule" in our citations, to situate the historicity of race in this discourse—understanding that although the definitions are not static, the basic premise remains. Race is not a biological construct (Gravelee, 2009; Zubaran, 2009) but a social one, with perceived physical differences between racial groups informing the way we think, behave, and react toward each other.

The term "race" has been identified with physical phenomena and with related terms such as "physical subpopulation, ethnicity, and human species" (Kinloch, 1974, p. 51). It is also defined by a perception of the existence of "innate and immutable physical characteristics," which are "believed to be intrinsically related to moral, intellectual, and other nonphysical attributes or abilities" (Van den Berghe, 1967, p. 9). Banton (1967) saw race as a "role sign" (pp. 57–62), and Kinloch (1974) added that "perceived physical differences are used on the basis of assigning people to particular roles or tasks in the social order" (p. 52). Hall's (1997) reference to race as a "signifier" points out how skin color in addition to physical characteristics becomes a signifier of race. Within this frame, actions and responses, including those of law enforcement agents, are informed by the concomitant stereotypes that are attributed to different races or persons whose skin color implies a particular race.

Race continues to exist as a biologic construct for many, despite evidence to the contrary, and for most, it exists as a social construct imbued with all of the properties that proponents of the biologic validity of differences in race held (Smedley & Smedley, 2005). In addition, as Kinloch (1974) indicates, race is "viewed as a reciprocal social definition based upon the perception of physical differences as significant" (p. 51). These perceptions continue to inform the way we think about each other, and the way we make sense and meaning of people's behaviors, which in turn inform the way in which we think those behaviors ought to be dealt with.

The concepts of racism, prejudice, and discrimination are often used indiscriminately and interchangeably. We conceptualize racism as the "uncritical acceptance of a negative social definition of a group as a race on perceived physical grounds along with the legitimacy of the discriminatory treatment accompanying that definition" (Kinloch, 1974, p. 54). This discriminatory treatment systematically deprives individuals of equal access to opportunity (Oliver, 2001). Our data analysis explored the acceptance of negative social definitions of Blacks or African Americans and the ways in which Americans think about racial equity and reasons for socioeconomic disparities between Whites and Blacks or African Americans. In addition, we use the term *cultural racism*, which Oliver (2001) defines as "the systematic manner in which the White majority has established its primary cultural institutions to elevate and glorify European physical characteristics, character and achievement, and to denigrate the physical characteristics, character and achievement of nonwhite people" (p. 5). Frederickson (2003) traces the roots of cultural racism to historical attitudes that perceived racial differences to be immutable.

Prejudice is defined as the "acceptance of negative social definitions without consideration of their validity in reference to ethnic as well as race groups (Kinloch, 1974, p. 54). Prejudice is an attitude (Brown, 2004; Kinloch, 1974), and Blumer (1958) identified race-based prejudice as a "sense of group position" (pp. 1–4). He described four basic types of feeling representing race prejudice in the dominant group: "(1) a feeling of superiority, (2) a feeling that the subordinate race is intrinsically different and alien, (3) a feeling of proprietary claim to certain areas of privilege and advantage, and (4) a fear and suspicion that the subordinate race harbors designs on the prerogatives of the dominant race." Kinloch (1974) added that "prejudice is based on a perceived group threat" (p. 52) to the dominant group's position. He defined discrimination as "applied prejudice in which negative social definitions are translated into action and political policy through the subordination of minorities and deprivation of their political, social, and economic rights" (pp. 53–54). Kinloch (1974) conceptualized discrimination as "the institutional expression of these attitudes in the social control of minorities, i.e., institutionalized racism" (pp. 53–54).

We differentiate between ethnicity and race, because the former is often used as a euphemism for race (Zubaran, 2009). Kinloch (1974) indicates that ethnicity is based "on perceived cultural differences, such as religion, dress, and nationality" (p. 53). Race and ethnicity are social constructs, with physical characteristics attributed to both. Kinloch (1974) adds that "it is important to distinguish analytically between the two concepts" with race being regarded as the broader concept with "race groups internally differentiated by ethnicity" (p. 53). In addition, he indicates that "a high level of intraracial ethnic differentiation contributes to the heterogeneity of the general social situation, making racial problems more complex" (p. 53). The gravity of this complexity underscored our approach to an authentic discourse on race and its possible implications in the killing of unarmed African American and Black men in the United States.

Method

Participants

The National Opinion Research Center (NORC) at the University of Chicago, as part of the National Data Program for the Social Sciences, has been collecting data since 1972 on the opinions, attitudes, and behaviors of American adults aged 18 and older, living in noninstitutional settings in the United States (Smith, Marsden, Hout, & Kim, 2014). The data collected through the use of a standard questionnaire (the General Social Survey [GSS]) also serve the purpose of monitoring social change in America.

Initially, GSS data were collected only from English-speaking Americans, but since 2006, data have been collected from both English- and Spanish-speaking Americans. The GSS is administered by trained interviewers in the respondent's home or on the telephone and provides information on a nationally representative sample obtained through multistage probability sampling. Since its inception in 1972 through to 2014, NORC has administered 30 cross-sectional surveys, which were initially conducted annually but since 1994 have been administered biannually. GSS respondents are asked a core set of permanent questions at each administration, which include demographic questions in addition to questions that relate to topical modules to assess participants' viewpoints on specific subject areas (Smith, Marsden, Hout, & Kim, 2014).

GSS interviews are conducted in February, March, and April. At the time of submission of our abstract for publication in this journal, we accessed the 2012 GSS data (the most recent at the time) to examine a host of variables related to race, racism, critical race theory, social identity theory, and the group-position model of race relations. These variables include race, prejudice, discrimination, racism, beliefs about socioeconomic inequities, and attitudes toward police violence.

Operational definitions of study variables

Race

We used the Office of Management and Budget (Federal Register Notice, October, 1997) guidelines and the U.S. Census (2010) to define and operationalize the concept race. The Office of Management and Budget (OMB), in its acceptance of the recommendations of the Interagency Committee for the Review of Racial and Ethnic Standards, stipulated the use of the following five minimum categories for data on race: American Indian or Alaska Native; Asian; Black or African American; Native Hawaiian or Other Pacific Islander; and White. These revisions were the outcome of a comprehensive review process, and comments were supportive of the Interagency Committee's recommendation to change the use of the term "Black" to "Black or African American."

We use the term "Black or African American" throughout our study in keeping with the OMB's decision to use this term. In addition, the OMB accepted the Interagency's recommendation for the definition of "Black or African American" as "a person having origins in any of the black racial groups of Africa" (OMB, 1997, p. 9). The OMB also accepted the additional use of terms such as "Haitian" or "Negro" to designate Blacks or African Americans. The GSS uses the terms Black/ African American as well as "Negro."

We use the term White as defined and operationalized by the OMB as well. The race category White is defined as "A person having origins in any of the original peoples of Europe, the Middle East, or North Africa" (OMB, 1997, p. 12). The 2010 Census Briefs, a document published by the U.S. Census Bureau (U.S. Department of Commerce, Economics and Statistics Administration, U.S. Census Bureau, 2011), included in this definition of White persons who identify as Caucasian, have Middle Eastern entries such as Arab, Lebanese, and Palestinian, and North African entries such as Algerian, Moroccan, and Egyptian. We aggregated these data in the GSS study and use the term White in keeping with the OMB federal standards (OMB, 1997).

In its decision to accept recommendations made by the Interagency Committee recommendations for collecting data on race and ethnicity, the OMB made two distinctions clear. The one was that the OMB decisions do not identify or designate certain groups as "minority groups" (OMB, 1997, p. 6). We also do not use this term because it has negative and pejorative connotations.

The OMB also made clear that the term "nonwhite" is not acceptable for use in the presentation of any federal government data and is not to be used in any publications or in the text of any report (OMB, 1997, p. 14). We also do not use the term, but it informs the profiling of the unarmed men of color shot by the police. Zubaran notes that "swarthiness of complexion, facial features, hair texture and assumptions about inferior intelligence" (2009, p. 48) serve as race markers and these markers often are framed in "nonwhite" profiles.

We use the terms Black or African American to represent those who identify racially as Black and who trace their ancestry to the African continent. We also use both terms as an acknowledgment of the ability of those within the African diaspora to both utilize and respond to multiple labels, depending on the context (Census, financial aid, friendship, etc.). Labels have constantly changed throughout history (colored, Negro, Black, Afro-American, African-American, African-Caribbean, etc.), but the oppression has remained the same regardless of which one was used. Knowledge of this reality has enabled a level of comfort with the fluidity and interchangeability of terminologies.

The GSS, since 2000, has operationalized the variable "race" in keeping with the U.S. Census approach toward race classification (U.S. Census, 2010). Respondents may select more than one race, and these data are tabulated based on first, second, and third race mentioned. Since 2002, the race variable has been imputed based on a computation that includes the first, second, and third race mentioned, the question on ethnicity that identifies participants' first, second, and third country of origin, as well as whether they identify as Spanish, Hispanic, or Latino/a (Smith, Marsden, Hout, & Kim, 2014, p. 172). This computation results in the GSS "race" variable comprising three categories: White, Black, and "Other."

Ethnicity

The OMB standards indicate that two categories should be used for data on ethnicity: "Hispanic or Latino" and "Not Hispanic or Latino" (OMB, 1997, p. 12). The OMB accepted the Interagency Committee's definition of the term Hispanic or Latino as "A person of Cuban, Mexican, Puerto Rican, South or Central American or other Spanish culture or origin, regardless of race" (OMB, 1997, p. 12). The Committee suggested the use of the term "Spanish-origin" in addition to Hispanic or Latino.

The ethnicity variable in the GSS includes three questions: two are on "Hispanic-ethnic heritage" (Smith, Marsden, Hout, & Kim, 2014, appendix D, p. 41), which were asked before the race questions. The first question asked is: Are you Spanish, Hispanic or Latino/a? If a respondent says yes, they are asked if they are (1) Mexican, Mexican American, Chicano/Chicana; (2) Puerto Rican; (3) Cuban; (4) Other Hispanic. The GSS mnemonic for this variable is "Hispanic." Next, respondents are asked about the country of family origin. The GSS uses the mnemonic "ethnic" for this question. Respondents are asked: From what countries or part of the world did your ancestors come? If more than one country is named, a follow-up question is asked: Which one of these countries do you feel closer to? We have disaggregated the GSS data on ethnicity to distinguish between Spanish, Hispanic, or Latino/as who identify as White and those who identify as Black or African American and "Other." This latter category is for those participants who identified as neither Black or African American nor White.

We report on the study's descriptive findings first, followed by bivariate analysis of race and other critical variables. Four mnemonics—racdifl, racdif2, racdif3, and racdif4, which tapped into opinions regarding the reasons for differences in income, employment, and housing between Blacks or African Americans and Whites (see Appendix, available online)—reflect racial inequity (Kirwan Institute for Study of Race and Ethnicity, 2013). Data for this variable were collected by reading the following statement: On the average (Blacks/African Americans) have worse jobs, income, and housing than White people. This statement was followed with the question: Do you think these differences are: (1) Mainly due to discrimination? (2) Because most (Blacks/African Americans) just don't have the motivation or will power to pull themselves up out of poverty? (3) Because most (Blacks/African Americans) don't have the chance for education that it takes to rise out of poverty? (4) Because most (Blacks/African Americans) have less in-born ability to learn?

Last, but not least, we conducted a forward logistic regression analysis to determine which independent variables are predictors of approval of police violence (the dependent variable). This variable was derived from a combination of five questions that were transformed into one dichotomous variable. The questions included the following: (1) Are there any situations you can imagine in which you would approve of a policeman striking an adult male citizen (yes/no)? (2) Would you approve of a policeman striking a citizen who was attempting to escape from custody? (3) Would you approve of a policeman striking a citizen who was being questioned as a suspect in a murder case? (4) Would you approve of a policeman striking a citizen who said vulgar and obscene things to the policeman? (5) Would you approve of a policeman striking a citizen who was attacking the policeman with fists?

The following independent variables were fitted into the regression model with the dependent variable: (1) race; (2) opinions regarding employment, income, and housing differences between Blacks or African Americans and Whites represented by the four indicators (discrimination, lack of an in-born ability to learn, education, and lack of motivation or will power); (3) attitude toward a close relative marrying a Black or African American; (4) confidence in Congress; (5) and courts dealing with criminals. We included gender, income, education, and age as control variables.

Results

The sample of 1,974 participants (Table 1), was predominantly White (74.9%, n = 1,477) and non-Latino (86.3%, n = 1,701). Among Whites reporting a country of origin (n = 1,203), the largest ancestral group was German (19.5%), followed by Irish (16.2%) and English and Welsh (13.2%). The largest ancestral group among Blacks (n = 233) was African (69.1%) followed by "American Only" (14.2%). For respondents identifying as "Other" (n = 188), the largest ancestral group was Mexican,

Table 1. Demographics of GSS respondents (*N* = 1,974).

	White *n* (%)	Black *n* (%)	Other *n* (%)	Total *N* (%)
Race	1477 (74.8)	301 (15.2)	196 (9.9)	1,974 (100)
Ethnicity				
Not Hispanic or Latino	1309 (88.8)	293 (97.7)	99 (50.5)	1,701 (86.3)
Hispanic or Latino	168 (11.4)	8 (2.7)	97 (49.5)	273 (13.8)
Sex				
Female	804 (54.4)	186 (61.8)	98 (50.0)	1088 (55.1)
Male	673 (45.6)	115 (38.2)	98 (50.0)	886 (44.9)
Marital status				
Married	719 (48.7)	85 (28.2)	96 (49.0)	900 (45.6)
Widowed	133 (9.0)	24 (8.0)	6 (3.1)	163 (8.3)
Divorced	245 (16.6)	59 (19.6)	13 (6.6)	317 (16.6)
Separated	44 (3.0)	13 (4.3)	11 (5.6)	68 (3.4)
Never married	336 (22.7)	120 (39.9)	70 (35.7)	526 (26.6)
Work status				
Full-time	679 (46.0)	131 (43.5)	102 (52)	912 (46.2)
Unemployed/laid off	69 (4.7)	23 (7.6)	12 (6.1)	104 (5.3)
Religion: Protestant	670 (45.5)	205 (68.3)	41 (21.0)	916 (46.6)
Political party affiliation: Democrat	598 (40,5)	243 (80.7)	93 (47.4)	934 (35.7)

Note. Due to rounding, percentages may not add to 100. Only select work statuses, religion, and political party affiliations are included.

Mexican American(s), and Chicano/a (24.5%), followed by American Indian (12.8%) and "Other Spanish" (12.2%). Mexicans, Mexican American, and Chicano/as also represented the largest subgroup among those who identify as Spanish, Hispanic, or Latino/a, followed by Puerto Rican. Of the 269 participants identifying as Spanish, Hispanic, or Latino/a, 61.3% identified themselves as White, 2.6% identified themselves as Black or African American, and 36.1% identified as "Other."

More than half the respondents (55.1%) were female, with an average age of 48 years, and an average education of 14 years that included two years of college. Fifty-eight percent were working either full-time or part-time, most had been married at some point (73.4%), with 45.6% being currently married and 26.6% being never married. Sixty-two percent ($n = 1{,}214$) reported a family income of $250,000 or more in the last year. The average household size was two, and the average number of children was two as well, with more than a quarter of the sample (27.2%) having no children. Almost half of the respondents were Protestant (46.6%), and 35.7% identified themselves as Democrat.

Chi-square was used to determine the bivariate relationship between race and approval of police violence. As indicated in Tables 2, 3, and 4, Whites consistently approved of a police officer striking a citizen, at higher rates than did Blacks or African Americans and those who identified as "Other."

Table 2. Ever approve of police striking citizen and race of respondent.

			Race of respondent		
			White	Black	Other
Ever approve of police striking citizen	Yes	Count	717	104	59
		% within race of respondent	74.7%	55.0%	45.4%
	No	Count	243	85	71
		% within race of respondent	25.3%	45.0%	54.6%
Total		Count	960	189	130
		% within race of respondent	100.0%	100.0%	100.0%

Table 3. Approval of police violence when citizen attempting to escape custody.

			Race of respondent		
			White	Black	Other
Citizen attempting to escape custody	Yes	Count	752	114	81
		% within race of respondent	79.0%	59.4%	61.4%
	No	Count	200	78	51
		% within race of respondent	21.0%	40.6%	38.6%
Total		Count	952	192	132
		% within race of respondent	100.0%	100.0%	100.0%

Table 4. Approval of police violence when citizen attacking policeman with fists.

			Race of respondent		
			White	Black	Other
Citizen attacking policeman with fists	Yes	Count	903	153	101
		% within race of respondent	92.1%	77.3%	74.3%
	No	Count	77	45	35
		% within race of respondent	7.9%	22.7%	25.7%
Total		Count	980	198	136
		% within race of respondent	100.0%	100.0%	100.0%

The association between race and approval of police violence was statistically significant for responses to "ever" striking an adult male ($\chi^2 = 65.415$, $df = 2$, $p <.0001$), striking a citizen attempting to escape custody ($\chi^2 = 44.840$, $df = 2$, $p < .0001$), and striking a citizen who was attacking a policeman with fists ($\chi^2 = 62.029$, $df = 2$, $p < .0001$).

Findings on the question which examined beliefs about the reasons for differences in employment, income, and housing between Blacks or African Americans and Whites are reported in Table 5. All but one (education) of the findings was statistically significant. Fifty-percent ($n = 619$) of respondents believed the reasons for these socioeconomic differences are due to lack of motivation or will power ($\chi^2 = 7.722$, $df = 2$, $p = .021$). Thirty-six percent ($n = 445$) believed the inequities are due to discrimination ($\chi^2 = 25.603$, $df = 2$, $p < .001$), and 9.8% ($n = 125$) believed the inequities exist because most Blacks or African Americans have less in-born ability to learn ($\chi^2 = 21.028$, $df = 2$, $p < .001$).

Finally, logistic regression results indicated (Table 6) that an overall model with five predictors was statistically reliable in distinguishing between participants who approved of police violence and those

Table 5. Socioeconomic disparities between Blacks or African Americans and Whites.

On the average (Blacks/African Americans) have worse jobs, income, and housing than White people. Do you think these differences are ...

	Whites (%)	African Americans/Black (%)	Other (%)	Total sample size
Because most (Blacks/African Americans) just don't have the motivation or will power to pull themselves up out of poverty?				
Yes	48.5	50	62.3*	619
No	51.5*	50	37.7	619
N (sample size)	928	196	114	1,238
Because most (Blacks/African Americans) don't have the chance for education that it takes to rise out of poverty?				
Yes	43.1	45.9*	44.8*	552
No	56.9*	54.1	55.2	711
N	953	194	116	1,263
Mainly due to discrimination?				
Yes	32.1	51.0*	38.3*	445
No	67.9*	49.0	61.7	803
N	937	196	115	1,248
Because most (Blacks/African Americans) have less in-born ability to learn?				
Yes	7.8	13.8*	19.8*	125
No	92.2*	86.2	80.2	1,146
N	960	195	116	1,271

*Observed residuals larger than expected.

Table 6. Regression coefficients predictive of police violence approval.

	B	Wald	*df*	*p*	Odds ratio
Race (Whites)	1.647	24.211	1	<.000	5.190
Race (Blacks or African Americans)	.923	5.549	1	.018	2.516
Racdif1 (Discrimination)	−.419	4.075	1	.044	.658
Racdif2 (Less inborn ability to learn)	.727	4.476	1	.034	2.070
Education	.144	16.015	1	<.000	1.155
Income	.088	3.900	1	.048	1.092
Sex (Male)	.471	5.363	1	.021	1.601
Constant	−4.279	33.145	1	.000	

who did not [−2 log likelihood = 605.809, χ^2 (7) = 85.710, $p < .0001$]. Race was the strongest predictor, with odds ratios for Whites [Exp(B) = 5.190] indicating the largest change in the likelihood of approval of police violence. Blacks approved of violence against adult males by a factor of 2.516. In addition, participants were twice as likely to attribute disparities in income, housing, and employment to Blacks or African Americans having less in-born ability to learn rather than to discrimination and/or lack of education incurred by poverty. The model correctly classified 71.2% of the cases.

Discussion

In summary, most GSS participants were White, with Germany being the primary country of origin. Among Blacks or African Americans, the primary country of origin was Africa, and among those identified as "Other," their primary country of origin was Mexico. Slightly more than two-thirds of those reporting as Hispanic or Latino ethnic heritage identified as Mexican, Mexican American, and Chicano/a. Our demographics reflect statistics provided by the *Business Insider* (O'Connor, Lubin, & Spector, 2013), which indicates that Germans make up the largest ancestral group in the United States.

The bivariate analyses indicate that Americans differ along racial lines in their perceptions of the reasons for socioeconomic differences in income, employment, and housing between Blacks or African Americans and Whites. The latter did not see these differences as being primarily related to discrimination, yet the former were more likely to locate the reasons for their income, employment, and housing disparities in discrimination. Education is a marker of the extent to which a nation is fulfilling its promise of being a true democracy. Although the differences in perceptions between Blacks or African Americans and Whites are not statistically significant on education, this finding indicates that Whites did not regard education or the lack thereof as being a factor related to the enduring socioeconomic differences between them and Blacks or African Americans.

The constructions of race, class, and gender are not stagnant, but instead are reified in macro-, mezzo-, and micro-level relationships (Schulz & Mullings, 2006). Mullings (1997) and Collins (2000) add that these classifications are themselves raced, gendered, and classed in their production and maintenance. The concept of race has changed over time, but the meanings associated with race have not changed. Difficulty in measuring the unique and specific contribution of race did not render the endeavor to isolate race and its unique contribution to explaining attitudes toward Blacks or African Americans impossible. This study successfully measured race as a single variable in public opinion. Research findings present race as a perspective that Whites have of Blacks or African Americans, which in turn is manifested in macrolevel institutions, such as law enforcement. Study findings illustrate Whites are significantly ($p < .001$) more likely than Blacks or African Americans to approve of police aggression whether or not the citizen tried to escape arrest or attacked the policemen.

Multivariate analyses also showed that even after controlling for age, gender, income, and education, race was still a primary factor influencing approval of police violence against adult males. Combining class, race, and gender without assessing the influence of race as a key predictor variable mutes how race continues to be used to inform the contexts of these interlocking oppressions. The contexts of race and these interlocking oppressions are products of how the United States has navigated, problematized, and maintained a status quo of diversity in relationship to "belonging" (Hooks, 2009, p. 3). The trajectory of Black citizenship in the United States exemplifies these contexts and how they have been maintained (Snowden, 2015). Blacks or African Americans were granted citizenship in 1866 through the 14th Amendment (Lee, 2010). However, they continue to be barred from the necessities and entitlements that citizenship status provides (Snowden, 2015), including unbiased treatment from law enforcement agents (Weitzer & Tuch, 2004). Thus, the attitude held by Whites, that of being in greater support of police aggression than Blacks or African Americans, is the judicial and legislative footprint of historic and contemporary inequities among Black or African American communities in the United States.

These inequities also translate into health (Gravelee, 2009), and incarceration (NAACP, 2013) disparities for Black or African American communities. Blacks or African Americans make up 13%

of the United States population (U.S. Census Bureau, 2015), yet they are disproportionately represented among HIV/AIDS and incarcerated populations. Blacks or African Americans accounted for 44% of all new HIV infections in 2010 (CDC, 2014) and in 2011, 49% or almost half of all new AIDS diagnoses (Kaiser Family Foundation, 2013). In addition, Blacks or African Americans account for 1 million of the 2.3 million people incarcerated in the United States (NAACP, 2013). Inherent in these data are indicators of a serious burden being shouldered by Blacks or African Americans in a country with a long history of apportioning resources based on the constructions of gender and class norms that are exacerbated by raced ideologies.

The statistics regarding the negative toll of the myriad macrolevel arrangements on the life experiences of Blacks or African Americans are telling. Black or African American men lead all other race and gender groups in incarceration rates, HIV infection, homicide rates, poverty levels, and diagnosed learning disorders (Noguera, 2003; Tucker & Dixon, 2009). The data from the first decade of this millennium are disheartening, and the troubling trajectory begins at a very young age. Studies from a variety of disciplines consistently suggest that racism is a key contributing factor and a common denominator in explaining the disproportionate manner in which Black or African American males are impacted by these systems (Bent-Goodley, 2003; Gabbidon & Peterson, 2006; Leary, 2005; Tucker & Dixon, 2009).

Conclusion

The recent developments in Charleston, South Carolina, where nine African American churchgoers were murdered by a 21-year-old White male underscore the critical need to recenter race in discussion of social justice. According to a survivor of this massacre, alleged perpetrator, Dylann Roof, justified the killings because Black or African American people are "raping our women and taking over our country" (Corasaniti, Perez-Pena & Alvarez, 2015, p. 18). This line of thinking connects with Jansen's (2008) model of transmission of "troubled knowledge" and broadens its understanding from a South African context to a United States context as well.

The common historical and contemporary denominator for these two countries is the issue of race, giving further credence to the legitimacy of bringing this racialization to the forefront. Although there was no overt interaction with law enforcement agents in the Charleston situation, we wonder to what extent the social environment that enables such an occurrence in an Emanuel AME Church is the same as the social environment that permitted a White police officer, in McKinney, Texas, to slam a 14-year-old Black or African American teenaged girl into the ground and to draw his gun on her friends who came to her defense. We wonder how the police killings of Eric Garner, John Crawford, Michael Brown, Ezell Ford, Levar Jones, Akai Gurley, and 12-year-old Tamir Rice, within a four-month period, are being made sense of in a country with a history of racial antipathy. Social media and smart phones have given birth to a new generation of civil rights activists who are not dependent on mass meetings to collectively analyze the events occurring daily. Modern-day activists take to Twitter and Facebook, supplanting titillating headline news, providing a substantive and meaningful inquiry and discourse on race and law enforcement. As a result of a long history of Blacks or African Americans being in close proximity to societal dis-ease, there exists within these communities, a collective gnawing "knowing" that the next incident is right around the corner.

Lawrence et al. (2009) suggest that race equity may be one of the ways to remedy race-based injustice. They regard racial equity as being the substantive alternative to structural racism, a social outcomes "picture" in which race is not consistently associated with privilege and disadvantage. From their perspective, the goal of racial equity is to produce fairness and social justice—race would no longer be a factor in the assessment of merit or in the distribution of opportunity. Systems of dominance, however, uphold structural racism, and more is required than declaring racial equity and have it replace structural racism to bring about equity. Our experience of oppression makes us think there is a whole lot more involved. We envisage a society where race is not a factor in the distribution of opportunity or resources or in the assessment of merit and character. When Dr.

King proclaimed a similar vision for the United States, what followed was an era of color-blind racism. At this juncture we will pursue additional opportunities to develop and name an approach that combines critical race theory, social identity theory, and the group position model and go beyond what the three so far have had to offer.

References

American Civil Liberties Union (ACLU). (2014). *Comment on Ferguson Grand Jury decision.* Retrieved from https://www.aclu.org/news/aclu-comment-ferguson-grand-jury-decision

Amajor, C., Sandars, M., & Pitts, D. (1999, June). *How racism in American institutions results in harsher treatment in law enforcement for minorities. Edge: Ethics of development in a global environment.* Conference paper presented at Stanford University, Stanford, CA. Retrieved from https://web.stanford.edu/class/e297c/poverty_prejudice/mediarace/howracism.htm

Banton, M. (1967). *Race relations.* New York, NY: Basic Books.

Bent-Goodley, T. B. (2003). Policy implications of the criminal justice system for African- American families and communities. In T. B. Bent-Goodley (Ed.), *African-American social workers and social policy* (pp. 137–161). Binghamton, NY: Haworth Press.

Blumer, H. (1958). Race prejudice as a sense of group position. *Pacific Sociological Review, 1*(1), 3–7. doi:10.2307/1388607

Brown, R. (2004). *Prejudice: Its social psychology.* Malden, MA: Blackwell.

Bulwa, S. (2010, December 17). The NAACP focuses on officer involved shootings. *San Francisco Gate.* Retrieved from http://www.sfgate.com/

Carroll, L., & Gonzalez, M. L. (2014). Out of place: Racial stereotypes and the ecology of frisks and searches following traffic stops. *Journal of Research in Crime and Delinquency, 51*(5), 559–584. doi:10.1177/0022427814523788

Centers for Disease Control (CDC). (2014). *CDC fact sheet. HIV and AIDS among African Americans.* Retrieved from http://www.cdc.gov/nchhstp/newsroom/factsheets.html

Cho, S., Crenshaw, K. W., & McCall, L. (2013). Toward a field of intersectionality studies: Theory, applications, and praxis. *Signs, 38*(4), 785–81. doi:10.1086/669608

Collins, P. H. (2000). *Black feminist thought.* New York, NY: Routledge.

Combahee River Collective. (2009). A Black feminist statement—The Combahee River Collective 1978. In S. M. James, F. S. Foster, & B. Guy-Sheftall (Eds.), *Still brave: The evolution of Black women's studies* (pp. 3–11). New York, NY: Feminist Press.

Corasaniti, N., Perez-Pena, R., & Alvarez, L. (2015, June 18). Church massacre suspect held as Charleston Grieves. *The New York Times.* Retrieved from http://www.nytimes.com/2015/06/19/us/charleston-church-shooting.html?_r=0

Crenshaw, K. (1991). Mapping the margins: Intersectionality, identity politics, and violence against women of color. *Stanford Law Review, 43*(6), 1241–129. doi:10.2307/1229039

Delgado, R., & Stefancic, J. (2001). *Critical race theory: An introduction.* New York, NY: NYC Press.

Department of Justice. (2015). *Attorney General Lynch: Use-of-force data is vital for transparency and accountability.* Retrieved from http://www.justice.gov/opa/pr/attorney-general-lynchuse-force-data-vital-transparency-and-accountability

Drake, B., & Jonson-Reid, M. (2008). *Social work research methods: From conceptualization to dissemination.* Boston, MA: Pearson.

Fredrickson, G. M. (2003). The historical origins and development of racism. *PBS.* Retrieved from http://www.pbs.org/race/000_About/002_04-background-02-01.htm

Gabbidon, S. L., & Peterson, S. A. (2006). Living while Black: A state-level analysis of the influence of select social stressors on the quality of life among Black Americans. *Journal of Black Studies, 37*(1), 83–102. doi:10.1177/0021934705277475

Gabrielson, R., Jones, R. G., & Sangara, E. (2014, October 10). Deadly force, in Black and White. *ProPublica.* Retrieved from http://www.propublica.org/article/deadly-force-in-black-and-white

Graham, D. A. (2015). Why is it so hard to track police-shootings? *The Atlantic.* Retrieved from http://www.theatlantic.com/politics/archive/2015/06/why-is-it-so-hard-to-track-police-killings/394772/

Gravelee, C. C. (2009). How race becomes biology: Embodiment of social inequality. *American Journal of Physical Anthropology, 139*(1), 47–57. doi:10.1002/ajpa.20983

Hall, S. (1997). The work of representation. In S. Hall (Ed.), *Representation: Cultural representations and signifying practices* (pp. 13–69). London, UK: Sage.

Harris-Perry, M. (2014, August 16). *The deaths of Black men in America* [video file]. Retrieved from http://www.msnbc.com/melissa-harris-perry/watch/the-deaths-of-black-men-in-america-318795331819

Hogg, M. A. (2006). Social identity theory. In P. J. Burke (Ed.), *Contemporary social psychological theories* (pp. 112–136). Stanford, CA: Stanford University Press.

Hogg, M. A., & Vaughan, G. M. (2002). *Social psychology* (3rd ed.). London, UK: Prentice Hall.

Hooks, B. (2009). *Belonging: A culture of place*. New York, NY: Routledge.

Jansen, J. (2008). *Bearing whiteness: A pedagogy of compassion in a time of troubles*. Bishop Hans Memorial Lecture Catholic Institute of Education. Retrieved from https://ujdigispace.uj.ac.za/handle/10210/1263

Jones-Brown, D. (2009). The right to life? Policing, race, and criminal injustice. *Human Rights Magazine, 36*(2), 1–7.

Kaiser Family Foundation (2013). *Black Americans and HIV/AIDS fact sheet*. Retrieved from www.kff.org

Kinloch, G. C. (1974). *The dynamics of race relations: A sociological analysis*. New York, NY: McGraw-Hill.

Kirwan Institute. (2013). *Structural racialization: A systems approach to understanding the causes and consequences of racial inequity*. Retrieved from http://kirwaninstitute.osu.edu/brochure-structural-racialization-a-systems-approach-to-understanding-the-causes-and-consequences-of-racial-inequity/

Lawrence, K., Anderson, A. A., Susi, G., Sutton, S., Kubisch, A. C., & Codrington, R. (2009). *Constructing a racial equity theory of change: A practical guide for designing strategies to close chronic racial outcome gaps*. Aspen Institute Roundtable on Community Change. Retrieved from http://www.aspeninstitute.org/sites/default/files/content/images/Roundtable%20on%20Community%20Change%20RETOC.pdf

Leary, J. D. (2005). *Post traumatic slave syndrome: America's legacy of enduring injury and healing*. Milwaukee, WI: Uptone Press.

Lee, M. M. (2010). *Birthright citizenship under the 14th Amendment of persons born in the United States to alien parents* (CRS Report for Congress No. 7–5700). Washington, DC: Congressional Research Service.

Lind, A. W. (1969). *Hawaii: The last of the magic isles*. London, UK: Oxford University Press.

Lowerstein, J. K. (2007, November 4). Killed by the cops. Retrieved from http://www.colorlines.com/articles/killed-cops

Mullings, L. (1997). *On our own terms: Race, class and gender in the lives of African American women*. New York, NY: Routledge.

National Association for the Advancement of Colored People (NAACP). (2013). *Criminal justice fact sheet*. Retrieved from http://www.naacp.org/pages/criminal-justice-fact-sheet

New York City Police Department (NYCPD). (2014). *2013 New York City Police Department annual firearms discharge report*. Retrieved from http://www.nyc.gov/html/nypd/downloads/pdf/analysis_and_planning/nypd_annual_firearms_discharge_report_2013.pdf

Noguera, P. (2003). The trouble with Black boys: The role and influence of environmental and cultural factors on the academic performance of African-American males. *Urban Education, 38*(4), 431–459. doi:10.1177/0042085903038004005

O'Connor, L., Lubin, G., & Spector, D. (2013, August 13). The largest ancestry groups in the United States. *Business Insider*. Retrieved from http://www.businessinsider.com/largest-ethnic-groups-in-america-2013-8

Office of Management and Budget (OMB) (1997, October 30). *Revisions to the standards for the classification of federal data on race and ethnicity* (Federal Register notice). Retrieved from https://www.whitehouse.gov/omb/fedreg_1997standards

Oliver, W. (2001). Section I: A new look at cultural violence. Cultural racism and structural violence: Implications for African Americans. *Journal of Human Behavior in the Social Environment, 4*(2/3), 1–26.

Schulz, A. J., & Mullings, L. (2006). *Gender, race, class, and health: Intersectional approaches*. San Francisco, CA: Jossey-Bass.

Smedley, A., & Smedley, B. D. (2005). Race as biology is fiction, racism as a social problem is real: Anthropological and historical perspectives on the social construction of race. *American Psychologist, 60*(1), 16–26. doi:10.1037/0003-066X.60.1.16

Smith, T. W., Marsden, P., Hout, M., & Kim, J. (2014). General social surveys, 1972–2014 [machine-readable data file]. Chicago, IL: National Opinion Research Center, University of Chicago.

Snowden, F. (2015). What condoms can't cover: Do structural factors predispose Black, African American, and Latina/o adults in Harlem and the South Bronx to engaging in HIV sex risk behavior? (unpublished dissertation). City University Graduate Center, New York, NY.

Tajfel, H., & Turner, J. C. (1986). The social identity theory of inter-group behavior. In S. Worchel & L. W. Austin (Eds.), *Psychology of intergroup relations*. Chicago, IL: Nelson-Hall.

Tucker, C., & Dixon, A. L. (2009). Low-income African American male youth with ADHD symptoms in the United States: Recommendations for clinical mental health counselors. *Journal of Mental Health Counseling, 31*(4), 309–322. doi:10.17744/mehc.31.4.j451mx7135887238

U.S. Census. (2010). *Overview of race and Hispanic origin*. Retrieved from www.census.gov/prod/cen2010/briefs/c2010br-02.pdf

U.S. Census Bureau. (2015). *State and county quickfacts. Data derived from population estimates, American community survey, census of population and housing, state and county housing unit estimates, county business patterns, non-employer statistics, economic census, survey of business owners, building permits*. Retrieved from http://quickfacts.census.gov/qfd/states/00000.html

U.S. Department of Commerce, Economics and Statistics Administration, U.S. Census Bureau. (2011). *The White population: 2010*. 2010 Census Briefs. Retrieved from http://www.census.gov/content/dam/Census/library/publications/2011/dec/c2010br-05.pdf

Van den Berghe, P. L. (1967). *Race and racism: A comparative perspective.* New York, NY: Wiley.

Weitzer, R., & Tuch, S. A. (2004a). Race and perceptions of police misconduct. *Social Problems, 51*(3), 305–325. doi:10.1525/sp.2004.51.3.305

Weitzer, R., & Tuch, S. A. (2004b). Reforming the police: Racial differences in public support for change. *Criminology, 42*(2), 391–416. doi:10.1111/crim.2004.42.issue-2

Wihbey, J. (2014). *Excessive or reasonable force by police? Research on law enforcement and racial conflict in the wake of Ferguson.* Journalist's Resource at the Harvard Kennedy School Shorenstein Center Retrieved from http://journalistsresource.org/studies/government/criminal-justice/police-reasonable-force-brutality-race-research-review-statistics

Zubaran, C. (2009). Human nomenclature: From race to racism. *World Health & Population, 11*(2), 43–52.

Vile vigilance: An integrated theoretical framework for understanding the state of Black surveillance

Whitney Sewell[a], Christina E. Horsford[b], Kanisha Coleman[b], and Charity S. Watkins[b]

[a]George Warren Brown School of Social Work, Washington University in St. Louis, St. Louis, Missouri, USA; [b]School of Social Work, University of North Carolina at Chapel Hill, Chapel Hill, North Carolina, USA

ABSTRACT

The family is the principal source of socialization and protection against racism for many Blacks. Transmitting values, norms, morals, and beliefs (i.e., racial socialization) to successive generations is done to promote racial awareness and to prepare an individual to survive in racist environments. Further, developing a sense of security, resiliency, and cultural pride provides psychological protection against racial prejudice and discrimination. Protective socialization is even more critical when it becomes the difference between life and death at the hands of law enforcement—a fate faced by too many Black males as a result of racist policing practices, including the over-patrolling of Black communities. Because discriminatory surveillance and over-patrolling can incite a number of social, physical, and mental health issues, a holistic approach to understanding the interaction between Blacks and law enforcement is critical. This article reviews the Mundane Extreme Environmental Stress (MEES) model, racial socialization theory, and Family Stress Model in the development of a theoretical framework for understanding the patterns of interactions between Blacks and law enforcement, the immediate and long-term effects of unjustified shootings on Black families and communities, and the response of sociopolitical systems. The new theoretical framework will be used to inform the work of human service providers and practitioners by identifying targets for interventions to improve relations and trust between Black communities and law enforcement institutions.

On March 4, 2015, the U.S. Department of Justice released its findings from an investigation of the Ferguson, Missouri, police department following the shooting of an unarmed Black teenager by a White police officer in Ferguson on August 9, 2014. The report revealed years of discriminatory conduct and violations of citizens' constitutional rights by the police and municipal courts. According to the report, "the harms of Ferguson's police and court practices are borne disproportionately by African Americans, and there is evidence that this is due in part to intentional discrimination on the basis of race" (DOJ, 2015, p. 4). Ferguson is now one of many cities publically fighting to eliminate discriminatory policing practices to repair trust between minority communities and police departments across the nation. Although the events in Ferguson have produced greater visibility of the issues related to the discriminatory policing of people of color, Blacks in America have long suffered from overt and covert forms of surveillance and over-patrolling. These forms of hyper-surveillance perpetuate strained and contentious relationships between law enforcement and the Black communities. Black males, as a result of hyper-surveillance and discrimination, suffer social, physical, and mental health challenges. Chronic environmental stressors have detrimental effects on the individual, family, and community. To gain a greater understanding of the myriad impacts that result from over-patrolling, this article explores the historical and contemporary issues related to Blacks' law-enforcement interactions. An overview of hyper-surveillance in the Black community will analyze how the phenomenon contributes to the criminalization of an entire ethnic population. An overview of the Mundane Extreme Environmental Stress (MEES) model, racial socialization theory, and Family Stress Model are provided to inform a new theoretical framework. This innovative framework seeks to advance our understanding of the effects of interactions between Blacks and law enforcement on individuals, families, and communities. The proposed integrated theoretical framework aims to (1) explain the impact of negative police interactions and recognize the effects of the interactions extend past the individual, affecting families and communities, (2) describe how negative police interactions are stressors that cause psychological and physical challenges, and (3) describe the types of coping mechanisms that Black families employ as a result of negative police interactions. Providing greater insight regarding how police hyper-surveillance impacts the well-being of Black families and communities, the integrated theoretical framework has the potential to influence how human services professionals intervene to assist individuals and families within communities, and has implications for future research and practice.

A brief history of surveillance and the over-patrolling of Blacks

The relationship between Blacks and law enforcement has been contentious throughout America's history. Dating back to slavery, law enforcement has kept Blacks subdued and subjugated by both formal and informal means of surveillance and criminalization (Jeffries, 2001; Murphy & Wood, 1984). Following Blacks' emancipation from slavery in 1865, the role of the police in many states did not differ from the plantation overseer. Physical abuse as a means of oppression by police was not uncommon.

Blacks during the early- to mid-1900s were kept "in their place" through the enforcement of Jim Crow laws (Jeffries, 2001). Jim Crow used police and civilians to enforce coercive methods to maintain social segregation and racial hierarchies and promote White supremacy. For example, between 1920 and 1932 police were responsible for more than 50% of the deaths of Blacks, and White police were often present at their lynchings (Jeffries, 2001). Law enforcement deputized White citizens and asked that they monitor Blacks to enforce the Jim Crow laws (Packard, 2003).

The racist, terrorist, and White supremacist hate group the Ku Klux Klan (KKK) was founded in 1865 and served as an extension of law enforcement in many communities (Waldrep, 2008). The KKK beat, lynched, and tortured Black Americans from 1865 to the mid-1900s. At the height of its power, the KKK was responsible for the murder and assault of hundreds of Blacks, civil rights supporters, and those persons merely suspected of not supporting their cause (McVeigh & Cunningham, 2012). The KKK is still active, although widely regarded as a fringe group, with concentrations of members across the United States (Chalmers, 2015).

The contentious relationship between law enforcement and Blacks reached a crisis point at the height of the Civil Rights Era (1954–1968); federal policies to monitor the activity of social activists contributed to the hyper-surveillance of Black communities. J. Edgar Hoover, the first head of the Federal Bureau of Investigation (FBI), targeted Black Power leaders and their followers. Operating under the guise of counterterrorism efforts (Greenberg, 2011), Hoover's COunter INTelligence PROgram (COINTELPRO) was designed to monitor Black nationalists' operations. FBI transcripts of COINTELPRO revealed that many Blacks, not only those in power movements, were targets of surveillance based on the criteria of race alone (Day & Whitehorn, 2001). FBI memos report that the purpose of COINTELPRO–Black Nationalist program was to use aggressive surveillance tactics to repress, dismantle, and discredit the Black Power movement's Black leaders and to universally subjugate Black Americans (Day & Whitehorn, 2001). Hoover's COINTELPRO anti–Black Nationalism program was a calculated effort to halt and reverse the economic, political, and social progress of millions of Black Americans (Cunningham, 2003; Day & Whitehorn, 2001).

Declared by President Richard Nixon in 1971, the "war on drugs" continued the use of federally supported law enforcement action against Black communities. More than a decade later, President Ronald Reagan passed the Anti-Drug Abuse Act in 1986. Direct and immediate effects of the act were mass arrest and incarceration of Black men (Nunn, 2002). The act also harshly criminalized the possession, sale, and use of controlled substances. Under both the Reagan and Bush administrations, the Anti-Drug Abuse Act cultivated federal and state laws reminiscent of Jim Crow because the laws strategically targeted low-income communities of color. Police officers had federal permission to "search and destroy" Black men (Jeffries, 2001; Nunn, 2002). The new federal policies sanctioned and encouraged police officers to over-patrol Black communities. Black men were disproportionately targeted for drug arrests, and the results of mass incarceration have had a devastating impact on Black communities (Goode, 2002).

Black men remain targets of draconian laws, whether they are guilty or not of committing any crime. "Stop and frisk" practices and arrests for nonviolent crimes, such as loitering, target Black men. Overwhelmingly, it is the myth of the deviant Black male that perpetuates the need for these laws. For example, U.S. Congressman Ron Paul stated, "I think we can safely assume that 95% of the Black males [in Washington, DC] are semi-criminal or entirely criminal" (Legum, 2011). This sentiment reflects the historical and contemporary beliefs about Blacks, in general, that fuel hyper-surveillance activities.

The prevalence of police hyper-surveillance and misconduct

National police misconduct data are often dependent upon *voluntary* state and local reporting. The data highlight significant differences in the treatment of Blacks while in police custody by law enforcement, as compared to persons of other racial and ethnic groups. The exact number of police assault and murder incidents involving Black victims is unknown, and this is due to the lack of any comprehensive federal program to track this information. At a local level, organizational culture, including professional integrity and attitudes about peer reporting, in addition to the circumstances of specific incidents, affects whether police will report police misconduct (Long, Cross, Shelley, Ivkovic, 2013). For example, in 2013 the FBI received 461 "justifiable homicide" reports deemed excusable by police officers nationwide. However, online crowdsourced campaigns revealed more than 300 additional police-involved fatalities (*The Guardian*, 2015). Significant discrepancies exist in the number of reported homicides by law enforcement to the government and larger population.

Missing and inaccurate information about police assault and homicide rates is common, and, due to this fact, independent organizations have begun tracking trends. Mapping Police Violence (MPV), a research collaborative, determined there were 1,149 known police killings (including 1,045 arrest-related deaths) in 2014 (Mapping Police Violence, 2015). MPV contends their database has accurately tracked the homicides of 88–96% of all Americans by culling information from three of the largest online crowdsourcing sites (Mapping Police Violence, 2015). A second organization using crowdsourcing information is named The Counted, developed by the Pulitzer Prize–winning media outlet *The Guardian*. The Counted claims that more than 500 people have been killed by law enforcement in the United States by mid-2015 (*The Guardian*, 2015).

Recent protests against police brutality and the murders of Blacks are the products of increased activism efforts, especially digital (online) activism. The protests bring attention to the frequency of homicides of unarmed Black men and women by police (Bonilla & Rosa, 2015) and highlight the lack of any comprehensive and systematic method of recording and analyzing law enforcement-caused injuries and deaths.

Black males are *21 times more likely* to be fatally shot by police (Gabrielson, Jones, & Sagara, 2014). From 2010 to 2012, more Black males ages 15 to 19 were killed by police as compared to White males of the same age (31.17 versus 1.47 per million; Gabrielson et al., 2014). In cases where the cause of death by the police officer was "undetermined," 77% of victims were Black (Gabrielson et al., 2014). In diverse cities such as Champaign, Illinois, where Blacks are a minority, discrimination by police still exists. For example, Blacks constituted 16% of the city's population from 2007 to 2011 but accounted for 40% of all arrests (Cha-Jua, 2014). Similarly, in 2011 744 people were arrested for jaywalking, a nonviolent offense, in Champaign, and 88% of those arrested for jaywalking were Black (Cha-Jua, 2014). Oppressive, parasitic, and punitive social control generates revenue for the city; the jaywalking fine is $120 in Champaign (Cha-Jua, 2014). In New York City, where Blacks were 23% of the city's population from 2008 to 2013, Blacks filed 55% of alleged police misconduct cases. During the same time period Whites, 34% of the city's population, constituted only 9% of alleged police misconduct cases (CCRB, 2014).

Politicians and legislators decry police violence against all unarmed citizens, and many support increased law enforcement training and improving the problem of low reporting of police misconduct. U.S. Senators Barbara Boxer (D-California) and Cory Booker (D-New Jersey) proposed the *Police Reporting of Information, Data and Evidence Act* (PRIDE; S. 1476, 2015) in 2015. PRIDE would mandate that states report to the U.S. Department of Justice (DOJ) when law enforcement-involved injuries or deaths occur. Law enforcement would be required to record and report the age, race and ethnicity, number of victims, number of police, and armed/unarmed status of the victim to the DOJ.

Social effects of hyper-surveillance

The racial disparity in rates of arrest and police-involved homicide of Blacks negatively affects individuals and Black communities. The higher number of arrests and deaths by law enforcement are a direct consequence of the hyper-surveillance of Blacks in communities and more frequent rates of police interaction when compared to individuals of other ethnic groups. The Broken Windows theory, a framework for policing first explored by Kelling and Wilson (1982), assumes that "if a window is broken and is left unrepaired, all the rest of the windows will soon be broken" (Kelling & Wilson, 1982, p. 6). The analogy is meant to compare broken windows to minor criminal offenses, which, if left unrepaired or corrected, later contribute to the prevalence of more serious property and personal crimes. Broken Windows theory suggests, for example, that if police do not address minor offenses such as noise, open alcohol containers, and loitering, then more serious crimes such as burglary, assault, and murder are more likely to occur. However, researchers have disproven the Broken Windows theory in several longitudinal studies. In a study of 196 Chicago neighborhoods, Sampson and Raudenbush (1999) found that examples of community disorder (e.g., loitering, panhandling, prostitution, vandalism) were *indirectly* related to more serious property and personal crimes (e.g., burglary, robbery, and homicide). Community disorder, the analogous broken window, was *not* predictive of more serious crime.

Disorder does cause families to move out of neighborhoods and business investments to be directed to other areas. When families leave and community investments are diverted to other areas, these two actions destabilize neighborhoods and lead to an increase in the frequency and severity of crime (Sampson & Raudenbush, 1999). Similar to the study conducted in Chicago, Harcourt and Ludwig (2006) found policing practices in New York City that focused on reducing community disorder to reduce future crime were not an effective or efficient use of scarce government resources. New York City neighborhoods monitored in the study were those communities most affected by the 1980s crack epidemic, which caused an increase in the number of misdemeanor and felony crimes during the same period. Researchers argued that the nationwide drug epidemic was responsible for increases in serious crimes, not only unchecked minor crimes. Following the end of the nationwide epidemic, declines in serious crimes occurred, which further questioned the validity of the Broken Windows theory.

Over-policing practices are ineffective and inconsistent deterrents to crime. The social well-being of Black communities is greatly impacted by systematic mass arrest and incarceration. Blacks made up 12.5% of the total U.S. population in 2009 but accounted for 30% of all arrests (U.S. Census Bureau, 2010, 2012). Once arrested, Blacks are more likely to be charged and convicted of a felony offense, which results in jail or prison confinement. Access to public housing, food stamps, federal education grants and loans, employment, and the right to vote are placed in jeopardy or lost altogether (National Inventory of Collateral Consequences of Conviction, 2013). Penalties for incarceration extend to the families of the individuals who become involved in the criminal justice system.

More than 3 million Black adults are arrested each year (U.S. Census Bureau, 2012). Blacks who go to jail and prison face longer sentences, stripping Black communities of human and financial capital—human capital that is responsible for combating poverty. When hundreds of individuals from a community are imprisoned, social networks that function as sources of emotional, financial, and social support are grossly impaired, or eliminated altogether. As a result socioeconomically disadvantaged families, in particular, face simultaneous losses of income, child care, and relationships (Roberts, 2004). Family members of incarcerated individuals must find money and allocate resources to pay for additional and unexpected costs, further straining families. Lawyer fees, court costs, collect calls, and funding commissary accounts place added financial burdens on the family of an incarcerated individual while trying to offset the loss of income in the household (Roberts, 2004). Hyper-surveillance with frequent arrest disrupts any community's capacity to build wealth and develop human capital, and perpetuates generational poverty.

Disenfranchisement of Blacks in the criminal justice system has also had significant social and political effects. In her critically acclaimed book *The New Jim Crow* (2011)—a work that has been widely cited for bringing the issue of racial disparities in the criminal justice system to the forefront of current policy reform—Michelle Alexander writes that in the 2004 presidential election more than 600,000 individuals were excluded from the voting polls in Florida alone. If individuals in this single state could have voted, the 2004 presidential election may have ended very differently, sharply changing the course of history.

Similar to the rates of arrest among adults, repeat arrests of Black adolescents and young adults is largely due to police hyper-surveillance. The racialization of crime yields considerable societal costs: Black youth account for more than *10 times* the costs imposed by White offenders on the public taxpayer (Cohen, Piquero, & Jennings, 2010). Black youth interact with police at a higher rate than Whites, and the costs of these interactions is high due to the frequency of arrests of Black youths.

In Philadelphia, Blacks from birth to age 26 on average had 18 law enforcement contacts before the age of 18; by age 24, these same young adults had nearly *nine times* the number of encounters with law enforcement and the criminal justice system as their White counterparts (Cohen et al., 2010). Criminal penalties result in higher court costs and room and board expenses and necessitate that local and state taxes are used to employ higher numbers of law enforcement and criminal justice employees (Cohen et al., 2010). In the Philadelphia study, Black youth with "low" police contact (i.e., low frequency of contacts over time) cost taxpayers $413,000 each, totaling $777 million for all participants by young adulthood (Cohen et al., 2010). Costs to the public were even more staggering for Black youth with "high" police contact: $1.6 million per Black youth before the age of 27 (Cohen et al., 2010).

Microlevel effects of hyper-surveillance

Blacks who experience interpersonal racism, including negative interactions with police officers, have generally lower levels of psychological and physical health (Clark, Anderson, Clark, & Williams, 1999; Harrell, 2000; Landrine & Klonoff, 1996; Utsey & Payne, 2000; Utsey, 1999). There is a relationship between self-reported exposure to interpersonal racism and poor mental health (Brondolo, Ver Halen, Pencille, Beatty, & Contrada, 2009); anxiety disorders, clinical depression, personality disorders, and post-traumatic stress disorder (PTSD) result from race-based discrimination (Carter, 2007). Anxiety and worry, in particular, are frequently occurring reactions to racism that prompt individuals to rehearse aggressive and defensive responses as a way to cope and adapt to these incidents (Carter, 2007; Harrell, Hall, & Taliaferro, 2003).

Environmental stressors change physiological functioning (Grzywacz & Fuqua, 2000) and interpersonal racism (Carter, 2007; Harrell et al., 2003) can increase the risk of developing diseases such as hypertension (HTN) and coronary artery disease (CAD; Brondolo et al., 2009). Measures of cardiovascular reactivity (CVR) may act as markers for processes that lead to the development of HTN and CAD (Brondolo et al., 2009). Racial identity is positively correlated with systolic blood pressure (SBP) reactivity to race and non-race-related stressors (Brondolo et al., 2009; Torres & Bowens, 2000); however, the effects of racial identity on psychological and physical health are complex, and this identity alone will not buffer the effects of racism on depressive symptoms or hypertension (Brondolo et al., 2009) for most Blacks.

Mesolevel effects of surveillance

Despite the cultural differences among different Black ethnic groups (e.g., African Americans, West Indians, European Blacks, Africans) within the Black diaspora structural racism has a cumulative effect in many Black communities, particularly in low-income neighborhoods where reduced employment opportunities, low wages, and inconsistent funding of public education exist. Neighborhood effects due to segregation (Sampson, Sharkey, & Raudenbush, 2008) impede navigation in the larger society, despite the fact that many Americans think causes of poverty lie mostly with the individual and their culture (Wilson, 2010).

Frequent discriminatory acts experienced by Blacks that are systemic over time, such as "stop and frisk" by police, can generate common psychological states and behavior patterns (Wilson, 2010). Parents living in segregated communities, for example, teach children a set of beliefs about what to expect and how to respond when police stop them on the street. This may lead to an interpretation of how to navigate the world and the belief that they are treated differently because they are Black; the beliefs become crystallized in cultural practices (Wilson, 2010).

The psychological effects of stress are persistent and cumulative (Carter, 2007). Black people fare poorly when faced with stress regardless of economic resources (Smedley, Stith, & Nelson, 2003). Blacks constitute 12.8% of individuals who meet criteria for any current depression, *the highest rates for depression when compared to Whites, Latinos, and other groups* (DHHS, 2010). Historical marginalization may account for psychological functioning in ways not well captured by individual-level measures (Norris, Friedman, & Watson, 2002).

Stress due to racism is a likely factor in higher rates of PTSD and reactions to stress; people of color experience PTSD after exposure to traumatic events at higher rates than the rest of the population (20–40% versus 5–10%; Carter, 2007). Being stopped by the police because of race produces traumatic reactions, and it is also a form of harassment. Racial harassment is a type or class of experiences characterized by hostile racism that involves feelings, thoughts, actions, strategies, behaviors, or policies that are intended to communicate the target's subordinate or inferior status because of his or her membership in a nondominant racial group (Carter, 2007). This type of harassment perpetuates institutional racist practices and forces targets to "fall into line" as a condition of continued social participation; individuals may fear repercussions for reporting acts of racism (Carter, 2007).

Overview of an integrated theoretical framework

The economic, psychological, and social effects of discriminatory police practices call for closer examinations of the ways Blacks can avoid, adapt, and manage the deleterious effects of hypersurveillance, an environmental stressor that increases the likelihood of interactions between Blacks and police, when compared to other racial and ethnic groups. The innovative framework presented in this article incorporates aspects of the Mundane Extreme Environmental Stress (MEES) model, racial socialization theory, and Family Stress Model to explain how racial socialization, a parenting practice that promotes racial and ethnic pride, helps Black youth develop effective coping

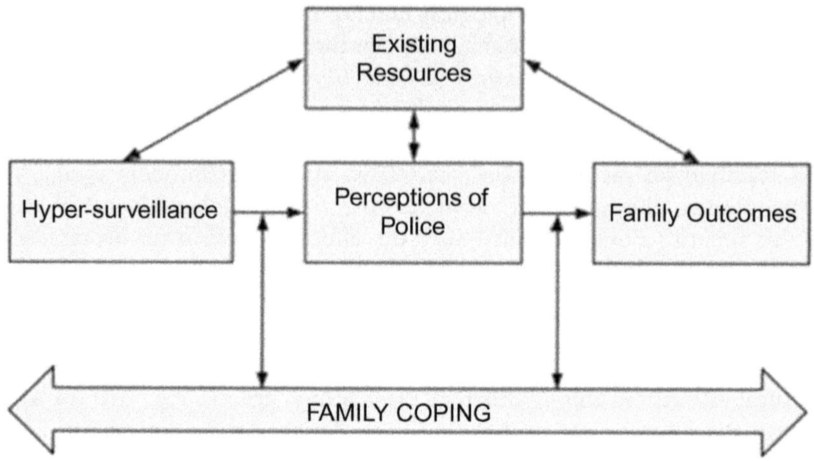

Figure 1. An integrated theoretical model of the effects of discriminatory policing practices on Black families.

mechanisms for dealing with hyper-surveillance. We assume that, through racial socialization, Blacks become aware of the historical and current treatment of their racial group by law enforcement and other groups, and adopt feelings of fear and mistrust toward law enforcement. However, because Blacks are also taught how to identify and prepare for racial bias, racial socialization may help to mitigate the harmful consequences of hyper-surveillance. The integrated theoretical framework (Figure 1) can offer contributions to the literature on reducing the effects of hyper-surveillance through adaptive parenting practices. It can also be used to explore relationships among hyper-surveillance and well-being outcomes of members of racial and ethnic minority groups, while considering mediating influences. Mediators include available resources, perceptions of law enforcement, degree of racial and ethnic identity, and preparation for racial bias and may act to support or change the direction of these relationships.

Environmental stressor: Hyper-surveillance of Black communities by law enforcement

Peters and Massey's (1983) Mundane Extreme Environmental Stress (MEES) model posits that Black families are encumbered by the constant threat and occurrences of intimidation, discrimination, and denial because of race. Factors of American life are particularly stressful to Black Americans due, in large part, to race. Higher than average unemployment and unequal educational opportunities, for example, causes Blacks to need to adapt to manifestations of racism (Peters & Massey, 1983) in everyday life. The MEES model includes two additional stress factors for Black families, as compared to a traditional stress and coping framework: extreme but mundane stress of omnipresent racism, and chronic and unpredictable racially caused stressful events throughout the life cycle (Peters & Massey, 1983).

Black families can attenuate or exacerbate frustration and tension experienced outside of the family. Attitudes, behavior patterns, and practices help these families to maintain family life and survive the American "system" of racism and racial discrimination (Peters & Massey, 1983). The MEES model employs an A-B-C-D-X-Y formula, where A (the event(s)), B (crisis-meeting resources; each family member's ability and interaction effects), C (definition of the event by each individual), D (mundane extreme environmental stress), X (the product of the crisis), and Y (the action-no action response to the crisis) explain how experiences with real or perceived racism can facilitate the analysis of stress or crisis within Black families (Peters & Massey, 1983).

The MEES model can offer a unique framework for understanding the relationship between Blacks and police at both individual and family levels. While many studies of resisting racism among Blacks focus on individual coping responses and internal resources (Szymanski, 2012), experiences of real and perceived racial discrimination require that group-level interactions may serve as a better resource for coping with racism (Szymanski, 2012); validation by the group, counteracting devaluation, contextualizing versus internalizing oppression, developing resources to help with racialized stressors, and achieving ethnic group survival (Mattis et al., 2004) are components of pro-social, group-level coping strategies within the Black family.

A unique application of the MEES model in the integrated theoretical framework acknowledges that racial bias, or the beliefs in negative stereotypes about Blacks (Black males in particular), and acts of discriminatory policing practices by police officers act as contributing factors to the hyper-surveillance of Black communities. Individuals within Black families learn how to cope with racist police policies and practices based on cumulative event experiences, family members' ability to manage the crisis individually and as a group, individual definitions of the event, perceived degree of racism experienced in the environment, the result(s) of the police activity, and the action of the person(s) involved in the event.

The influence of racial socialization on perceptions of law enforcement

Microlevel approaches for understanding race-specific interactions with law enforcement can shed light on the protective and adaptive practices Black families use to navigate an oppressive society. Through the process of racial socialization, Black children are taught the values and rules of society, and what to expect when rules are adhered to or violated. Thornton, Chatters, Taylor, and Allen (1990), states that individuals are taught different roles, statuses, and behaviors to learn how to "locate themselves" and others in the social structure. Thus, minority families use racial socialization to promote minority children's self-esteem, ethnic identity, and cultural and racial pride and teach skills to cope with racial discrimination (Neblett et al., 2008). Black youth receive positive messages about their heritage and culture, history, important Black historical figures, and culturally relevant books, music, and holidays. Racial socialization is positively correlated with higher self-esteem (Stevenson, Reed, Bodison, & Bishop, 1997), academic achievement (Anglin & Wade, 2007; Smith, Walker, Fields, Brookins, & Seay, 1999), and fewer externalizing and internalizing problems (Bynum, Burton, & Best, 2007; Caughy, O'Campo, Randolph, & Nickerson, 2002).

The frequency and content of racial socialization may vary depending on parents' racial socialization and experiences with racial discrimination. Therefore, Black youth have different beliefs about their culture and society (Hughes et al., 2006) and different coping styles when faced with racial discrimination. According to Burt and colleagues (2012), preparing children for explicit racial bias and discrimination necessitates that Black parents translate direct and indirect social experiences for their children to increase the capacity to appraise and cope with racism. Racial discrimination is consistently linked to poor psychological functioning in Blacks (Berger & Sarnyai, 2015; Broman, Mavaddat, & Hsu, 2000; Sellers & Shelton, 2003; Sellers, Copeland-Linder, Martin, & Lewis, 2006). However, preparation for future racial bias and fostering positive beliefs about one's racial group can serve as a buffer against the harmful psychological effects of racial discrimination. Research on racial socialization suggests that Black children who report receiving early messages about other groups' racial biases toward Blacks tend to have more positive psychological (e.g., Fischer & Shaw, 1999; Neblett, Banks, Cooper, & Smalls-Glover, 2013; Sellers et al., 2006) and physiological outcomes (Neblett & Carter, 2012) and fewer negative behavioral responses (Burt et al., 2012; Neblett, Terzian, Harriott, 2010).

Racial socialization theory offers a lens to examine how Blacks and police interact. To further explain the macrolevel structural processes that lead to the disproportionate number of Black Americans who experience racial profiling, police brutality, arrests, and sentencing, racial socialization theory posits that, at the microlevel (interpersonally), Blacks receive messages about police officers and the legal system. These messages shape their perceptions of and behaviors toward police. For example, Black youth at an early age learn that people believe that they are criminals and expect negative police treatment (Brunson & Miller, 2006; Carr, Napolitano, & Keating, 2007; Fine et al.,

2003; Hinds, 2007). Different racial and ethnic groups vary on their perceptions of law enforcement (Huebner, Schafer, & Bynum, 2004). Blacks view police more negatively when compared to other groups (Reitzel & Piquero, 2006; Weitzer & Tuch, 2004). For example, after controlling for demographic, neighborhood, and policing variables, Weitzer and Tuch (2004) found that Blacks and Latinos were significantly more likely to believe police engage in misconduct. Lee and colleagues (2011) found that those who were more likely to identify with their ethnic or racial group had more positive perceptions of the role law enforcement plays in society. Complex views about law enforcement suggests that, on one hand Blacks realize police are necessary for controlling and reducing crime, and on the other hand, they are simultaneously distrustful of police because of previous misconduct and murder.

Racial socialization and prior experiences with police determine how individuals act toward police, either passively or aggressively. Even if fully cooperative, Black Americans are more likely to become the victims of police misconduct. Police officers' fears, biases, or discriminatory practices are often directed at Blacks with or without any criminal history. Future research should consider how racial socialization impacts Blacks' perceptions of and interactions with law enforcement, and additional studies should assess individuals' levels of racial and ethnic pride, racial identity, and beliefs about police treatment toward members of particular ethnic or racial groups.

Existing resources and strategies for coping with the stress of police hyper-surveillance

American families in recent years have navigated turbulent economic, political, and social landscapes. Economically, stagnant or lower net income, high rates of unemployment, costs of living, and fewer social welfare programs pervade the economic landscape. Formerly middle-class families experience difficulty "making ends meet," while low-income families have suffered the most, falling deeper into poverty (Conger, Conger, & Martin, 2010). Simultaneously, families contend with mental health challenges, domestic violence, poor physical health, and general family instability (Donnellan, Martin, Conger, & Conger, 2013). The economic and social effects of the recessions have had a profound effect on Black communities. These communities, in particular, face higher levels of socioeconomic disadvantage, which was the case prior to economic recessions (Pfeffer, Danziger, & Schoeni, 2013), and this disadvantage has worsened over time.

Black households, generally, earn lower annual incomes, have higher rates of unemployment, and are more likely to lose their homes in the housing crisis (Pfeffer et al., 2013). For each dollar of wealth of White families, Black families, in comparison, have only eight cents (Pfeffer et al., 2013). Without employment opportunities to generate income, Black male youths, in particular, are at significantly greater risk of engaging in criminal activity (Cox, 2010). The confluence of the lack of employment, criminal activity, and hyper-surveillance increases the risk of being arrested, placing immense stress on families (Cox, 2010; Roberts, 2004).

The Family Stress Model, developed by Conger and colleagues (2010), allows us to explore how families' experiences of economic distress contribute to coping strategies among and within family members (see Figure 2).

The main assumption of the Family Stress Model is that economic hardships are the predominant influencing factor of children's development through the lives of parents (Conger et al., 2010). As depicted in Figure 2, family economic hardships contribute to family economic pressure and define the "psychological meaning of the economic hardship for families" (Donnellan et al., 2013, p. 343). Parents' economic pressures lead to emotional and behavioral problems, such as poor parenting styles, which may be the direct or indirect spillover of interparental conflict, which contributes to disrupted parent-child interactions. Children in poor parenting households, characterized by harsh punishments, inconsistent discipline, and lower levels of responsiveness, are at greater risk for the development of emotional and behavioral problems and compromised cognitive development (Conger et al., 2010; Donnellan et al., 2013).

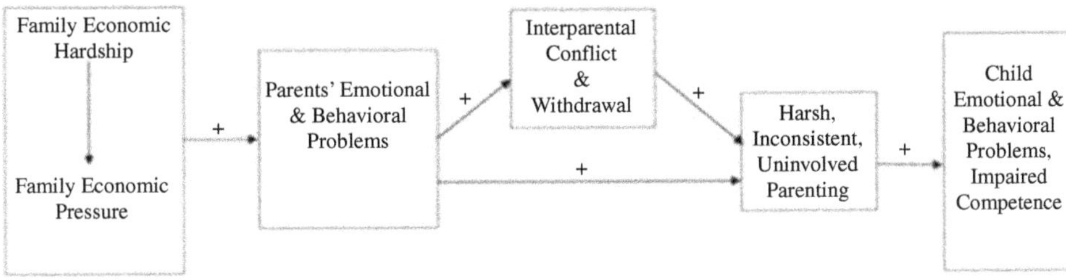

Figure 2. Family stress model (Conger et al., 2010).

Although the Family Stress Model has been primarily employed to examine the influence of socioeconomic disadvantage on family dynamics (Conger et al., 2010; Donnellan et al., 2013), the model can also be used to explore how other stressors, such as police hyper-surveillance, may influence family functioning and coping. Discriminatory policing practices impact family social pressure, or the beliefs, attitudes, and perceptions families hold about how one functions and interacts with the social environment. In turn, families seek to reduce perceived police suspicion to avoid criminal justice (Brayne, 2014) involvement. Overall, social pressures affect how parents socialize and parent their children. For example, after the shooting death of 17-year-old Trayvon Martin in 2013, many Black parents increased protection of their children by instilling racial pride and educated their children on how to be observant, vigilant, and cautious of people and their environment. These parents taught their children how to adapt their behavior to increase the likelihood they could survive dangerous situations and as a way to cope with racial profiling (Thomas & Blackmon, 2015).

The Family Stress model contributes to a new integrative theoretical framework because it illustrates how resources, or the lack thereof, influence how police hyper-surveillance affects Blacks' perceptions of the police. Family outcomes and racial socialization strategies of Black parents can mitigate the effects of surveillance and teach family members how to cope. Future research is needed to explore how the types of existing resources (e.g., legal, neighborhood, and social), combined with racial socialization strategies, may vary based on the degree of surveillance. For example, families who live in neighborhoods with a high police presence may incorporate more "strict" racial socialization strategies into their parenting practices due to a greater threat of police interaction and poorer perceptions of police. The frequency and depth of parents' racial socialization messages to children may also depend on families' history of interactions with the criminal justice system.

Discussion and conclusions

Patterns of interaction between Blacks and law enforcement are volatile. This is due to many factors: individual perceptions of police, discriminatory policing practices, and long-term structural inequalities. Blacks have had to contend with unequal treatment for generations. The intersection of lack of access to quality education, and the hallmarks of middle-class status such as regular employment and standard housing, leads to generational poverty. In low-income neighborhoods, residents are disproportionately targeted for illegal activity by law enforcement. Surveillance, search, seizure, and arrest, whether it is warranted or not, are frequent occurrences.

Hyper-surveillance directly impacts how Black individuals perceive law enforcement and influences the coping behaviors of Black families. The threat of arrest and actual incarceration have immediate and long-term effects on individuals and their families and perpetuates the breakdown of social cohesion and trust between law enforcement and the citizens they serve.

Resources and coping strategies (i.e., social support, racial socialization, degree of identity, social position, socioeconomic status, and physical health) impact how law enforcement is perceived by

Blacks—either as a threat, ally, or combination of both. Resources also affect the ability of the family to maintain homeostasis; family outcomes are dependent on the family's ability to interact with law enforcement and deal with the subsequent results of the interaction. Coping is complex and dynamic; the success of navigating stressful events depends on the adaptation of coping strategies, such as racial socialization, that will help alleviate psychological and physical distress, or avoidance of the stressor altogether.

Hyper-surveillance is an environmental stressor, and it has an effect on the psychological and physical health of Blacks. Race-based discriminatory practices lead to higher rates of anxiety, depression, and stress, in addition to higher rates of hypertension and heart disease in the population (Brondolo, Love, Pencille, Schoenthaler, & Ogedegbe, 2011; Brondolo et al., 2009; Williams & Mohammed, 2009). Aggressive policing creates feelings of "hopelessness" and being "dehumanized" (Brunson & Weitzer, 2009). Blacks who report more police contact tend to show higher levels of anxiety and PTSD symptoms associated with their experiences (Geller, Fagan, Tyler, & Link, 2014). Because costs outweigh benefits, hyper-surveillance is a public health concern for individuals and communities targeted by police.

Racial socialization is known to promote a range of positive outcomes and protect Blacks from the harmful effects of racial discrimination (Anglin & Wade, 2007; Burt et al., 2012; Caughy et al., 2002). However, less known about the nature of the adaptive parenting practice commonly used in Black families to cope with the consequences of hyper-surveillance. Using the integrated conceptual framework presented in this article, future research should examine what types and frequency of messages Blacks receive to avoid involuntary contact with police, such as the specific mannerisms they should have, styles of dress, and places and people to avoid. For example, parents may refrain their children from wearing hooded sweatshirts ("hoodies"), a type of clothing often deemed emblematic of criminal behavior and deviance (Bonilla & Rosa, 2015). Additionally, future studies should explore how these messages may vary by different racial and ethnic groups, gender, age, peer group, neighborhood context, and socioeconomic status (Hughes & Chen, 1999). In addition, with the growing use of digital activism and social media campaigns to display and protest instances of police misconduct, investigations should take into account other nonfamilial sources that shape how Blacks perceive or interact with law enforcement.

Regardless of income or neighborhood, Blacks are the frequent targets of surveillance and distrust by law enforcement. Implicit bias is evident when Blacks are assumed to be "guilty" of an offense, even when none has been committed. Erasing the pall of the supposition of guilt is rooted in eradicating individual bias and racism. This can be achieved only through increased familiarity and positive experiences with "the other," continued earnest conversations about the roles that racial profiling and racialization of crime play in law enforcement, changes in policing practices that limit the undue burden on communities of color from the threats associated with police surveillance, and limiting the frequency of opportunistic and punitive sanctions for minor offenses, particularly among persons living in low-income communities. Social justice necessitates that each and every person deserves equal economic, political, and social rights and opportunities.

Limitations

The new integrated theoretical framework is a starting point for understanding how Black families cope with disproportionate rates of surveillance and interactions with law enforcement. Because the impact of hyper-surveillance on the psychological well-being and coping behaviors of Black families is understudied, there are some limitations to the framework. These limitations include uncertainty about which family outcomes are most likely to be affected, paucity of mediators to explain the relationship between increased police contact and negative family outcomes, and characteristics of the family (e.g., family composition, resources, socioeconomic status) and their environment (e.g., neighborhood crime, community support) that may affect the strength and direction of the relationship. Well-established theories that have not been applied to this topic were used to construct the framework. Thus, constructs from theories, existing in the gray or unpublished literature, could further develop the integrated framework. Despite these limitations, the integrated theoretical framework is a foundation for exploring the underlying mechanisms affecting how Blacks perceive and cope with the hyper-surveillance of their communities by law enforcement and illuminates how these phenomena impact Blacks at the individual, family, and community levels.

Implications for human service professionals

To improve relations and trust between Blacks and law enforcement at the interpersonal level, human service providers play an important role. At the microlevel, targets for intervention include increased training and education of police officers in the areas of bias and cultural sensitivity. By becoming more aware of the role that race, racialization of crime, and supposition of guilt play in hyper-surveillance, law enforcement professionals have an opportunity to change policy and practices that perpetuate these activities. Reducing instances of unjust surveillance in "hot spots," and improved communication with individuals living in the communities they serve will help to attenuate the negative effects of the long-term patterns of unequal treatment between Blacks and law enforcement.

Additionally, human service professionals must continue to provide consultation and training in the identification of psychiatric disorders to law enforcement professionals. Approaching and detaining persons with serious mental illnesses is not consistent within departments, across precincts, and nationwide. Persons living with mental illness are more likely to be assaulted or killed than those not living with mental illness when approached by police. This is unnecessary; by employing trained mental health professionals to work with members of law enforcement, the number and frequency of encounters resulting in serious injury or death can be reduced.

Human service professionals should be aware of the role that environmental stress plays on the psychological and physical well-being of all people. However, culturally relevant practice includes knowing that Blacks may present psychological distress differently from the majority population; depression, as an example, may present as increased hostility, agitation, or anger as opposed to sadness, hypersomnia (excessive sleepiness), or changes in appetite (Wohl, Lesser, & Smith, 1997). Awareness of these signs allows human service professionals to screen for depression, provide appropriate referrals, or offer treatment.

On the macrolevel, working toward more equitable treatment of Blacks by law enforcement necessitates that human service professionals recommend policies and practices that serve all people fairly. Advocating for just treatment of persons who are under threat of detention or incarceration is necessary; when Black men are largely targeted for arrest, it becomes less of an individual issue and more of a systemic miscarriage of justice. By acknowledging the inequity of the criminal justice system, human service professionals must work to advocate changes to policies that determine who is incarcerated and for what length of time. To do this, collaboration with community leaders, advocacy groups, policymakers, lawyers, and law enforcement are necessary.

Proponents of improving relationships between Blacks and law enforcement argue that it is necessary to increase the number of Black police officers and change the racial and ethnic composition of law enforcement (Brunson & Gau, 2015). The challenge of this, however, is that Blacks with a criminal history may become ineligible to serve due to the nature of their convictions. Second, in areas where the predominance of law enforcement is Black—like Washington, DC—the rate of arrest and conviction is comparable, or greater, than in areas where the police force is majority non-Black. Thus, the racial or ethnic composition of law enforcement does not guarantee less surveillance, arrest, and detention.

Instead of only arguing that Blacks need more roles within law enforcement, human service professionals should advocate that a less adversarial and more collaborative relationship be achieved. This can be done successfully in the form of more citizen-led neighborhood watches, increasing the number of referrals to social services versus arrest, and offering opportunities for civic engagement through liaison building between community leaders and law enforcement personnel. Earnest evaluation of hyper-surveillance and mistreatment of Blacks by law enforcement over time shows the detrimental effects of these practices. Improving trust and relations between these groups requires the promotion of interventions to correct and repair damage caused by harassment and disenfranchisement over multiple generations.

References

Alexander, M. (2011). *The new Jim Crow: Mass incarceration in the age of colorblindness.* New York, NY: New Press.

Anglin, D. M., & Wade, J. C. (2007). Racial socialization, racial identity, and Black students' adjustment to college. *Cultural Diversity and Ethnic Minority Psychology, 13*(3), 207–215. doi:10.1037/1099-9809.13.3.207

Berger, M., & Sarnyai, Z. (2015). "More than skin deep": Stress neurobiology and mental health consequences of racial discrimination. *Stress, 18*(1), 1–10. doi:10.3109/10253890.2014.989204

Bonilla, Y., & Rosa, J. (2015). #Ferguson: Digital protest, hashtag ethnography, and the racial politics of social media in the United States. *American Ethnologist, 42*(1), 4–17. doi:10.1111/amet.12112

Brayne, S. (2014). Surveillance and system avoidance: Criminal justice contact and institutional attachment. *American Sociological Review, 79*(3), 367–391. doi:10.1177/0003122414530398

Broman, C. L., Mavaddat, R., & Hsu, S. Y. (2000). The experience and consequences of perceived racial discrimination: A study of African Americans. *Journal of Black Psychology, 26*(2), 165–180. doi:10.1177/0095798400026002003

Brondolo, E., Love, E. E., Pencille, M., Schoenthaler, A., & Ogedegbe, G. (2011). Racism and hypertension: A review of the empirical evidence and implications for clinical practice. *American Journal of Hypertension, 24*(5), 518–529. doi:10.1038/ajh.2011.9

Brondolo, E., ver Halen, N. B., Pencille, M., Beatty, D., & Contrada, R. J. (2009). Coping with racism: A selective review of the literature and a theoretical and methodological critique. *Journal of Behavioral Medicine, 32*(1), 64–88. doi:10.1007/s10865-008-9193-0

Brunson, R. K., & Gau, J. M. (2015). Officer race versus macro-level context: A test of competing hypotheses about black citizens' experiences with and perceptions of black police officers. *Crime & Delinquency, 61*(2), 213–242. doi:10.1177/0011128711398027

Brunson, R. K., & Miller, J. (2006). Young black men and urban policing in the United States. *British Journal of Criminology, 46*(4), 613–640. doi:10.1093/bjc/azi093

Brunson, R. K., & Weitzer, R. (2009). Police relations with black and white youths in different urban neighborhoods. *Urban Affairs Review, 44*(8), 858–885. doi:10.1177/1078087408326973

Burt, C. H., Simons, R. L., & Gibbons, F. X. (2012). Racial discrimination, ethnic-racial socialization, and crime: A micro-sociological model of risk and resilience. *American Sociological Review, 77*(4), 648–677. doi:10.1177/0003122412448648

Bynum, M. S., Burton, E. T., & Best, C. (2007). Racism experiences and psychological functioning in African American college freshmen: Is racial socialization a buffer? *Cultural Diversity and Ethnic Minority Psychology, 13*(1), 64–71. doi:10.1037/1099-9809.13.1.64

Carr, P. J., Napolitano, L., & Keating, J. (2007). We never call the cops and here is why: A qualitative examination of legal cynicism in three Philadelphia neighborhoods. *Criminology, 45*(2), 445–480. doi:10.1111/j.1745-9125.2007.00084.x

Carter, R. T. (2007). Racism and psychological and emotional injury: Recognizing and assessing race-based traumatic stress. *Counseling Psychologist, 35*(1), 13–105. doi:10.1177/0011000006292033

Caughy, M. O. B., O'Campo, P. J., Randolph, S. M., & Nickerson, K. (2002). The influence of racial socialization practices on the cognitive and behavioral competence of African American preschoolers. *Child Development, 73*(5), 1611–1625. doi:10.1111/1467-8624.00493

Cha-Jua, S. K. (2014). "We believe it was murder:" Mobilizing black resistance to police brutality in Champaign, Illinois. *Black Scholar, 44*(1), 58–85. doi:10.1080/00064246.2014.11641212

Chalmers, D. (2015). *Essay: The Ku Klux Klan.* Retrieved from http://www.splcenter.org/get-informed/intelligence-files /ideology/ku-klux-klan/the-ku-klux-klan-0

Clark, R., Anderson, N. B., Clark, V. R., & Williams, D. R. (1999). Racism as a stressor for African Americans: A biopsychosocial model. *American Psychologist, 54*(10), 805–816. doi:10.1037/0003-066X.54.10.805

Cohen, M. A., Piquero, A. R., & Jennings, W. G. (2010). Monetary costs of gender and ethnicity disaggregated group-based offending. *American Journal of Criminal Justice, 35*(3), 159–172. doi:10.1007/s12103-010-9071-5

Conger, K. J., Conger, R. D., & Martin, M. J. (2010). Socioeconomic status, family processes, and individual development. *Journal of Marriage and Family, 72*(3), 685–704. doi:10.1111/j.1741-3737.2010.00725.x

Cox, R. (2010). Crime, incarceration, and employment in light of the great recession. *Review of Black Political Economy, 37*(3), 283–294. doi:10.1007/s12114-010-9079-6

Cunningham, D. (2003). The patterning of repression: FBI counterintelligence and the New Left. *Social Forces, 82*(1), 209–240. doi:10.1353/sof.2003.0079

Day, S., & Whitehorn, L. (2001). Human rights in the United States: The unfinished story of political prisoners and COINTELPRO. *New Political Science, 23*(2), 285–297. doi:10.1080/07393140120056009

Department of Health and Human Services (DHHS). (2010). Current depression among adults—United States, 2006 and 2008. *Centers for Disease Control of Prevention Morbidity and Mortality Weekly Report, 59*(38), 1229–1234. Retrieved from http://www.cdc.gov/mmwr/preview/mmwrhtml/mm5938a2.htm?s_cid=mm5938a2_w

Department of Justice Civil Rights Division (DOJ). (2015). *Investigation of the Ferguson police department.* Retrieved from http://www.justice.gov/sites/default/files/opa/press-releases/attachments/2015/03/04/ferguson_police_department_report_1.pdf

Donnellan, M. B., Martin, M. J., Conger, K. J., & Conger, R. D. (2013). Economic distress and poverty in families. In M. A. Fine & F. D. Fincham (Eds.), *Handbook of family theories: A content based approach* (pp. 338–355). New York, NY: Routledge (Taylor & Francis).

Fine, M., Freudenberg, N., Payne, Y., Perkins, T., Smith, K., & Wanzer, K. (2003). "Anything can happen with police around": Urban youth evaluate strategies of surveillance in public places. *Journal of Social Issues, 59*(1), 141–158. doi:10.1111/1540-4560.t01-1-00009

Fischer, A. R., & Shaw, C. M. (1999). African Americans' mental health and perceptions of racist discrimination: The moderating effects of racial socialization experiences and self-esteem. *Journal of Counseling Psychology, 46*(3), 395–407. doi:10.1037/0022-0167.46.3.395

Gabrielson, R., Jones, R. G., & Sagara, E. (2014). Deadly force, in black and white. *Propublica.* Retrieved from http://www.propublica.org/article/deadly-force-in-black-and-white

Geller, A., Fagan, J., Tyler, T., & Link, B. G. (2014). Aggressive policing and the mental health of young urban men. *American Journal of Public Health, 104*(12), 2321–2327. doi:10.2105/AJPH.2014.302046

Goode, E. (2002). Drug arrests at the millennium. *Society, 39*(5), 41–45. doi:10.1007/BF02717543

Greenberg, I. (2011). The FBI and the making of the terrorist threat. *Radical History Review, 2011*(111), 35–50. doi:10.1215/01636545-1268686

Grzywacz, J. G., & Fuqua, J. (2000). The social ecology of health: Leverage points and linkages. *Behavioral Medicine, 26*(3), 101–115. doi:10.1080/08964280009595758

Harcourt, B. E., & Ludwig, J. (2006). Broken windows: New evidence from New York City and a five-city social experiment. *University of Chicago Law Review, 73*(1), 271–320.

Harrell, J. P., Hall, S., & Taliaferro, J. (2003). Physiological responses to racism and discrimination: An assessment of the evidence. *American Journal of Public Health, 93*(2), 243–248. doi:10.2105/AJPH.93.2.243

Harrell, S. P. (2000). A multidimensional conceptualization of racism-related stress: Implications for the well-being of people of color. *American Journal of Orthopsychiatry, 70*(1), 42–57. doi:10.1037/h0087722

Hinds, L. (2007). Building police-youth relationships: The importance of procedural justice. *Youth Justice, 7*(3), 195–209. doi:10.1177/1473225407082510

Huebner, B. M., Schafer, J. A., & Bynum, T. S. (2004). African American and White perceptions of police services: Within- and between-group variation. *Journal of Criminal Justice, 32*(2), 123–135. doi:10.1016/j.jcrimjus.2003.12.003

Hughes, D., & Chen, L. (1999). The nature of parents' race-related communications to children: A developmental perspective. In L. Balter & C. S. Tamis-LeMonda (Eds.), *Child psychology: A handbook of contemporary issues* (pp. 467–490). Philadelphia, PA: Psychology Press.

Hughes, D., Rodriguez, J., Smith, E. P., Johnson, D. J., Stevenson, H. C., & Spicer, P. (2006). Parents' ethnic-racial socialization practices: A review of research and directions for future study. *Developmental Psychology, 42*(5), 747–770. doi:10.1037/0012-1649.42.5.747

Jeffries, J. L. (2001). Police brutality of black men and the destruction of the African-American community. *Negro Educational Review, 52*(4), 115–130.

Kelling, G. L., & Wilson, J. Q. (1982). Broken windows: The police and neighborhood safety. *The Atlantic, 29*(38), Retrieved from http://www.theatlantic.com/magazine/archive/1982/03/broken-windows/304465/

Landrine, H., & Klonoff, E. A. (1996). The schedule of racist events: A measure of racial discrimination and a study of its negative physical and mental health consequences. *Journal of Black Psychology, 22*(2), 144–168. doi:10.1177/00957984960222002

Lee, J. M., Steinberg, L., Piquero, A. R., & Knight, G. P. (2011). Identity-linked perceptions of the police among African American juvenile offenders: A developmental perspective. *Journal of Youth and Adolescence, 40*(1), 23–37. doi:10.1007/s10964-010-9553-2

Legum, J. (2011). *Fact check: Ron Paul personally defended racist newsletters.* Retrieved from http://thinkprogress.org/politics/2011/12/27/395391/fact-check-ron-paul-personally-defended-racist-newsletters/

Long, M. A., Cross, J. E., Shelley, T. O. C., & Ivković, S. K. (2013). The normative order of reporting police misconduct examining the roles of offense seriousness, legitimacy, and fairness. *Social Psychology Quarterly, 76*(3), 242–267. doi:10.1177/0190272513493094

Mattis, J. S., Beckham, W. P., Saunders, B. A., Williams, J. E., Myers, V., Knight, D., … Dixon, C. (2004). Who will volunteer? Religiosity, everyday racism, and social participation among African American men. *Journal of Adult Development, 11*(4), 261–272.

Mapping police violence. (2015). *2015 Police violence report.* Retrieved from http://mappingpoliceviolence.org

McVeigh, R., & Cunningham, D. (2012). Enduring consequences of right-wing extremism: Klan mobilization and homicides in southern counties. *Social Forces, 90*(3), 843–862. doi:10.1093/sf/sor007

Murphy, W., & Wood, B. (1984). *Slavery in colonial Georgia.* Athens, GA: University of Georgia Press.

National Inventory of Collateral Consequences of Conviction. (2013). *Federal.* Retrieved from http://www.abacollateralconsequences.org/search/?jurisdiction=1000

Neblett Jr, E. W., Banks, K. H., Cooper, S. M., & Smalls-Glover, C. (2013). Racial identity mediates the association between ethnic-racial socialization and depressive symptoms. *Cultural Diversity and Ethnic Minority Psychology, 19* (2), 200–207. doi:10.1037/a0032205

Neblett Jr, E. W., & Carter, S. E. (2012). The protective role of racial identity and Africentric worldview in the association between racial discrimination and blood pressure. *Psychosomatic Medicine, 74*(5), 509–516. doi:10.1097/PSY.0b013e3182583a50

Neblett, E. W., White, R. L., Ford, K. R., Philip, C. L., Nguyên, H. X., & Sellers, R. M. (2008). Patterns of racial socialization and psychological adjustment: Can parental communications about race reduce the impact of racial discrimination? *Journal of Research on Adolescence, 18*(3), 477–515. doi:10.1111/j.1532-7795.2008.00568.x

Neblett Jr, E. W., Terzian, M., & Harriott, V. (2010). From racial discrimination to substance use: The buffering effects of racial socialization. *Child Development Perspectives, 4*(2), 131–137. doi:10.1111/j.1750-8606.2010.00131.x

New York City Civilian Complaint Review Board (CCRB). (2014). *2013 report.* Retrieved from www.nyc.gov/ccrb

Norris, F. H., Friedman, M. J., & Watson, P. J. (2002). 60,000 disaster victims speak: Part II. Summary and implications of the disaster mental health research. *Psychiatry, 65*(3), 240–260. doi:10.1521/psyc.65.3.240.20169

Nunn, K. B. (2002). Race, crime and the pool of surplus criminality: Or why the war on drugs was a war on blacks. *Journal of Gender, Race, and Justice, 6*(2), 381–445.

Packard, J. M. (2003). *American nightmare: The history of Jim Crow.* New York, NY: Macmillan.

Peters, M. F., & Massey, G. (1983). Mundane extreme environmental stress in family stress theories: The case of Black families in White America. *Social Stress and the Family, 6*(1), 193–218. doi:10.1300/J002v06n01_10

Pfeffer, F. T., Danziger, S., & Schoeni, R. F. (2013). Wealth disparities before and after the Great Recession. *Annals of the American Academy of Political and Social Science, 650*(1), 98–123. doi:10.1177/0002716213497452

Police Reporting Information, Data, and Evidence Act (PRIDE) of 2015, S. 1476, 114th Cong. (2015). Retrieved from https://www.govtrack.us/congress/bills/114/s1476/text

Reitzel, J., & Piquero, A. R. (2006). Does it exist? Studying citizens' attitudes of racial profiling. *Police Quarterly, 9*(2), 161–183. doi:10.1177/1098611104264743

Roberts, D. E. (2004). The social and moral cost of mass incarceration in African American communities. *Stanford Law Review, 56*(5), 1271–1305.

Sampson, R. J., & Raudenbush, S. W. (1999). Systematic social observation of public spaces: A new look at disorder in urban neighborhoods. *American Journal of Sociology, 105*(3), 603–651. doi:10.1086/210356

Sampson, R. J., Sharkey, P., & Raudenbush, S. W. (2008). Durable effects of concentrated disadvantage on verbal ability among African-American children. *Proceedings of the National Academy of Sciences, 105*(3), 845–852. doi:10.1073/pnas.0710189104

Sellers, R. M., Copeland-Linder, N., Martin, P. P., & Lewis, R. H. (2006). Racial identity matters: The relationship between racial discrimination and psychological functioning in African American adolescents. *Journal of Research on Adolescence, 16*(2), 187–216. doi:10.1111/j.1532-7795.2006.00128.x

Sellers, R. M., & Shelton, J. N. (2003). The role of racial identity in perceived racial discrimination. *Journal of Personality and Social Psychology, 84*(5), 1079–1092. doi:10.1037/0022-3514.84.5.1079

Smedley, B. D., Stith, A. Y., & Nelson, A. R. (Eds.). (2003). *Unequal treatment: Confronting racial and ethnic disparities in health care.* Washington, DC: National Academies Press.

Smith, E. P., Walker, K., Fields, L., Brookins, C. C., & Seay, R. C. (1999). Ethnic identity and its relationship to self-esteem, perceived efficacy and prosocial attitudes in early adolescence. *Journal of Adolescence, 22*(6), 867–880. doi:10.1006/jado.1999.0281

Stevenson, H. C., Reed, J., Bodison, P., & Bishop, A. (1997). Racism stress management racial socialization beliefs and the experience of depression and anger in African American youth. *Youth & Society, 29*(2), 197–222. doi:10.1177/0044118X97029002003

Szymanski, D. M. (2012). Racist events and individual coping styles as predictors of African American activism. *Journal of Black Psychology, 38*(3), 342–367. doi:10.1177/0095798411424744

The Guardian. (2015). *The counted: People killed by police in the US.* Retrieved from http://www.theguardian.com/us-news/ng-interactive/2015/jun/01/the-counted-police-killings-us-database

Thomas, A. J., & Blackmon, S. M. (2015). The influence of the Trayvon Martin shooting on racial socialization practices of African American parents. *Journal of Black Psychology, 41*(1), 75–89. doi:10.1177/0095798414563610

Thornton, M. C., Chatters, L. M., Taylor, R. J., & Allen, W. R. (1990). Sociodemographic and environmental correlates of racial socialization by Black parents. *Child Development, 61*(2), 401–409. doi:10.2307/1131101

Torres, A., & Bowens, L. (2000). Correlation between the internalization theme of Racial Identity Attitude Survey-B and systolic blood pressure. *Ethnicity & Disease, 10*(3), 375–383.

U.S. Census Bureau. (2010). *American Community Survey (ACS) demographic and housing estimates*. Retrieved from http://factfinder.census.gov/faces/tableservices/jsf/pages/productview.xhtml?src=bkmk

U.S. Census Bureau. (2012). Table 325. *Arrests by race: 2009*. Retrieved from http://www.census.gov/compendia/statab/2012/tables/12s0325.pdf

Utsey, S. O. (1999). Development and validation of a short form of the index of race-related stress (IRRS)—brief version. *Measurement and Evaluation in Counseling and Development, 32*(3), 149–167.

Utsey, S. O., & Payne, Y. (2000). Psychological impacts of racism in a clinical versus normal sample of African American men. *Journal of African American Men, 5*(3), 57–72. doi:10.1007/s12111-000-1004-9

Waldrep, C. (2008). National policing, lynching, and constitutional change. *Journal of Southern History, 74*(3), 589–626. doi:10.2307/27650230

Weitzer, R., & Tuch, S. A. (2004). Race and perceptions of police misconduct. *Social Problems, 51*(3), 305–325. doi:10.1525/sp.2004.51.3.305

Williams, D. R., & Mohammed, S. A. (2009). Discrimination and racial disparities in health: Evidence and needed research. *Journal of Behavioral Medicine, 32*(1), 20–47. doi:10.1007/s10865-008-9185-0

Wilson, W. J. (2010). Why both social structure and culture matter in a holistic analysis of inner-city poverty. *Annals of the American Academy of Political and Social Science, 629*(1), 200–219. doi:10.1177/0002716209357403

Wohl, M., Lesser, I., & Smith, M. (1997). Clinical presentations of depression in African American and White outpatients. *Cultural Diversity and Mental Health, 3*(4), 279–284. doi:10.1037/1099-9809.3.4.279

Police-involved homicide of unarmed Black males: Observations by Black scholars in the midst of the April 2015 Baltimore uprising

Natasha C. Pratt-Harris[a], Michael M. Sinclair[a], Cynthia Barbara Bragg[a], Nicole R. Williams[b], Kalfani Nyerere Ture[c], Belinda Davis Smith[c], Isiah Marshall Jr.[d], and Lawrence Brown[c]

[a]Department of Sociology, Anthropology, and Criminal Justice, Morgan State University, Baltimore, Maryland, USA; [b]Department of Human Services, Anne Arundel Community College, Hanover, Maryland, USA; [c]Morgan State University, Baltimore, Maryland, USA; [d]Department of Sociology and Social Work, Daemen College, Amherst, New York, USA

ABSTRACT

Black scholars who reside in the United States balance their teaching, research responsibility, and lived experience with the urgent need to address the racial inequality and violence that has characterized Black life. The authors of this article explore police-involved homicides of unarmed Black males through the unique lens of Black scholars. Embedded in an ecological perspective, the authors address three critical questions: (1) From the viewpoint of the Black scholar, what was the impact of the recent events? (2) To what extent have the recent events influenced pedagogical and community work by Black scholars? and (3) In light of the recent events, what can be done to improve policies and strengthen your academic discipline? The insights offered by eight multidisciplinary authors offer promising alternatives to current public policy, training, and general community practice.

Background

Victimization of Black males by police extends beyond the scope of scholarly discourse; it is a personal reality for Black scholars. Black scholars do not exist in a vacuum. The accounts of unarmed Black males killed by the police are part of their lived reality. Black scholars, such as the authors, often serve as experts when addressing race, violence, and homicide. In doing so, they exist in a dual reality: one that empirically and objectively addresses homicide of unarmed Black victims as a social problem, and one that recognizes their own victimization, especially the victimization of their students and children. Although their professorial achievements might be measured as a form of success, the potential for police-led victimization, coupled with a social justice orientation, pedagogy, and research on the Black experience, warrants personal reflection and examination of police-involved deaths of unarmed Black males.

On April 27, 2015, the city of Baltimore, Maryland, experienced serious unrest after Freddie Gray's funeral. Gray, a 25-year-old Black male, suffered a spinal cord injury and crushed voice box while in Baltimore city police custody on April 12; he died on April 19. Gray's death capped more than 3 years of national and international attention turned to homicides of unarmed Black males in the United States: Trayvon Martin (a 17-year-old shot and killed in Sanford, Florida, by a neighborhood self-appointed watchman in February 2012), Eric Garner (a 43-year-old who died in July 2014 due to a choke hold by a Staten Island New York City police officer), Michael Brown (an 18-year-old who was shot and killed by a Ferguson, Missouri, police officer in August 2014), Tamir Rice (a 12-

year-old who was shot and killed seconds after a Cleveland, Ohio, police officer approached him in November 2014), and Walter Scott (a 50-year-old who was fatally shot in the back as he ran from a North Charleston, South Carolina, police officer on April 4, 2015), and others.

Historically, there has been an intersection between Black faculty, the institutions where they teach, and their felt need to address issues that affect the Black community. For example, Carlton-LaNey (1999), a Black scholar who has been on the forefront of examining Black social welfare pioneers' commitment to the Black community, asserted that Black pioneers were expected to extend moral, financial, and service support to uplift the Black race. Black faculty members function similarly, as they often assume prominent roles in advising and mentoring students, developing a research agenda to advance the body of knowledge to focus on issues that affect the Black community and are actively involved in service to the community through membership organizations such as sororities, fraternities, and other academic, civic, and social groups. Furthermore, a unifying connection exists among Black faculty members, regardless of their academic discipline, based on racial identity that heightens their awareness of the gravity of police brutality and homicide against Black males. For these reasons, the authors of this article, who represent the disciplines of Anthropology, Criminology/Criminal Justice, Public Health, Psychology, Social Work, Sociology, and Theology, feel responsible to share their perceptions and experiences.

To examine this problem through an interdisciplinary lens, we organized our perspectives in three critical areas. Using Urie Bronfenbrenner's ecological perspective as a framework, we responded to questions regarding the impact of the recent events in Baltimore, the influence of these events on our pedagogical and community work, and our suggestions regarding public policy and our professional discipline's response to the events. The goal of this article is to demonstrate that Black scholars are committed to teaching, by way of educating an emerging cadre of sociopolitical activists, to improve our communities. We maintain that the voice of the Black scholar is important to lead the charge against continuing social injustice within the wider epistemological frameworks that seek to explain police brutality, racial profiling, and Black victimization (Gabbidon & Greene, 2012).

Literature review

We examined literature focused on the historical trends of police brutality, race-based policies, stereotypical perceptions, White privilege/superiority, and media coverage of Black males. For the most part, the literature amplifies the targeted mistreatment of Black males in every segment of their social existence. The literature review affirms inherent bias against Black males perpetuated by the dominant class and exercised through social control by police.

Police brutality

Racial profiling and police brutality against Blacks in America are neither emergent social phenomena nor uncommon practice. However, increased access to video of such incidents, social networking, and various forms of media outlets have magnified police victimization of Black males. For example, it has been well noted in the literature and public discourse that Blacks in America are at greater risk of experiencing police brutality and are more likely to be stopped by police while driving than people of other races (Dottolo & Stewart, 2008; Elicker, 2008; Gabbidon & Greene, 2012).

American policing, from its onset, targeted Blacks, via slave patrols that captured runaway Black slaves. Police have always relied on violence, but a "shoot-to-kill" trend began during the Progressive Era of law enforcement in the United States (Adler, 2007; Alexander, 2010). Black males are consistently disproportionate victims of racial profiling and police brutality (Binder & Fridell, 1984).

Historical and cultural epithets related to police-involved homicides of unarmed Black males were examined. Social work scholar Schiele's (2007) citations of Franklin's (1989) assertions were examined. State and federal policies were described as having a longstanding history of disparate treatment of and violence against Blacks. Since Blacks were forcibly brought to the United States, they have been victimized by racist and discriminatory practices that include attacks and assaults (Chaney & Robertson, 2013). Enslaved people were viewed as property, so violence was a common mechanism utilized by slave owners to manage their property (Moss & Franklin, 2000; Schiele, 2007; Stampp, 1956).

Instructive here is the late jurist A. Leon Higginbotham, who examined appellate cases of crimes charged against Black American slaves compared to Whites from 1630 to 1865. Out of this examination, Higginbotham (1996) developed his frequently cited "Ten Precepts of American Slavery Jurisprudence" that concluded that Black Americans were to be maintained in inferior conditions through generous application of violence.

W. E. B. Du Bois wrote in *Black Reconstruction in America* (1935) that, by 1860, poor White Southerners outnumbered the enslaved population, 5 million to 4 million. Unlike the West Indies, where enslaved Africans and their descendants outnumbered the planter class of Whites and effectuated successful revolutions, Southern Whites in the United States prevented successful revolts by enslaved Africans and their descendants. This class of 5 million poor Whites, who did not own slaves, were employed by White Southern planters as overseers, slave drivers, and members of slave patrols. According to Du Bois,

> The system of slavery demanded a special police force and such for was made possible and unusually effective by the presence of the poor whites. ... Gradually the whole white South became an armed and commissioned camp to keep Negroes in slavery and to kill the black rebel. ... (p. 12) They constituted the police patrol who could ride with the planters and now and then exercise unlimited force upon recalcitrant or runaway slaves. (p. 27)

From the period of enslavement down to the purported postracial and digital age, the use of police and extrajudicial violence has continued to be a significant feature in the lived experiences of Black Americans, particularly males. Jones (2006) contended that police departments in metropolitan cities have historically been detached and nonresponsive to poor communities in responding to calls for help. The police have historically been indifferent to serving and protecting residents of color who live in poor communities (Jones, 2006). Despite this indifference, there has been disproportionate level of contact between police and Black males, with those who reside in underserved urban communities receiving the highest rate of involuntary contact with the police (Brunson & Miller, 2006).

The 1991 beating of Rodney King by Los Angeles, California, police officers set the stage for contemporary assessments of police brutality. The actions of the police in the brutalization of King and their affirmative defense suggest that a "racially saturated field of visibility" operated within the criminal justice system of Los Angeles such that the Black male was perceived to be a perpetual threat that must be incapacitated through the most brutal use of force (Butler, 1993). More than two decades since the King beating, the exponential police-involved homicides of unarmed Black males suggest that what might have been considered a regionally specific racist orientation is a far more putative, conventional, and ritualistic performance across the United States.

White privilege and superiority

An examination of the National Police Misconduct Statistics and Reporting Project reflects citizens' perceptions of the police. This examination identifies the concept of White supremacy as a major factor contributing to brutality against and homicide of unarmed Black males (Chaney & Robertson, 2013).

The concept of White superiority teaches White dominance and Black inferiority; it guides daily life in America, and it breeds racism and discrimination. Chaney and Robertson (2013) cited Marger's earlier definition of *racism and discrimination*: "Racism is an ideology, or belief system designed to justify and rationalize racial and ethnic inequality" (p. 25) and "discrimination, most basically, is behavior aimed at denying members of particular ethnic groups equal access to societal rewards" (p. 57).

Inherent in this structure is a strategic means to make Blacks appear deviant. Various scientific theories and reasoning have historically been used to describe Blacks as "lazy," "unintelligent," "animal-like," and "uncivilized." This perception of the malevolent Black male is based on myths, half-truths, and lies (Gottdiener & Hutchison, 1994). The image was created during the European conquest of Africa, nurtured during slavery and reinforced during the Jim Crow years of Southern segregation. In 2015 the media has played a significant role in perpetuating the myth that Black males are criminogenic, sociopathic, incorrigible, academically incompetent, barbaric, and menaces to society. The stereotypic imagery of Black males as prone to violence, which moved inexorably across the nation in the antebellum era, serves as the basis for contemporary policing.

White supremacy guides perceptions of Blacks in general and Black males specifically. It encourages Whites to hate Blacks and Blacks to hate Blacks. While the infamous Willie Lynch letter written to slave owners describing how slaves can be controlled has been challenged for its authenticity, the words of "Willie Lynch" are part of the blueprint for White supremacy:

> In my own bag here, I have a full-proof method for controlling Black slaves. I guarantee every one of you that if installed correctly, it will control slaves for at least 300 hundred years. My method is simple. Any member of your family or your overseer can use it. … Don't forget, you must pitch the old Black males against the young Black males, the young Black male against the old Black males. You must use the dark skin slaves vs. the light skin slaves and the light skin slaves vs. the dark skin slaves. You must use the female vs. the male and the male vs. the female. You must also have your white servants and overseers distrust all Blacks, but it is necessary that your slaves trust and depend on you. They must love, respect and trust only us. (Lynch, 2008, p. 8)

These intentional ideological philosophies play a major role in perpetuating negative images of Black males that instill fear in people based on implicit racial bias. These deep-rooted biases are grounded in a historical perspective that begins with White supremacy. While many of these theories and the resulting reasoning have been denounced, White supremacy has continued to systematically maintain the power structure that has led to continuation of racism and discriminatory practices.

The ideological factor of White supremacy is complex and strategic in denouncing people of color and influencing how Blacks are viewed. These complex strategies include use of the media, information systems, and accepted norms of social behavior set by the majority. As these systems have penetrated the lives of Black people, they have had a major impact on how Blacks view themselves and each other. The impact on the individual, family, and community includes indoctrinated attitudes or internalized racism, self-fulfilling prophecies, inferiority complexes, and internalized self-hatred. All of these factors lead to the "permissible" killing of unarmed Black males by law enforcement officers.

The media's influence

The media is perhaps one of the most powerful tools of influence in America. American television news is flooded with criminalized images of Blacks, particularly Black males. According to William Drummond (1997), a journalism professor at the University of California, Berkeley, news media often project images of Black males as aggressive, violent, and lawless. The media is strategic not only in what it presents but also in the timing and frequency of that presentation.

The media also distorts facts, selectively focusing on specific information that may present a deviant image and using strong language to describe Black males. During the April 2015 Baltimore uprising and the condemnation of rioters, for example, Black males were described as "thugs," but Whites from the University of Kentucky who rioted that same month after a national basketball championship loss were described as "fans." These observations are similar to observations in the aftermath of Hurricane Katrina that caused devastation to the people and city of New Orleans, Louisiana, in 2005. Blacks were described as "looting" for food but Whites were described as "finding" food. This double standard is applied to all Blacks, but specifically to Black males.

The evening of June 17, 2015, in Charleston, South Carolina, was marked by the mass murder of nine Black persons, shot and killed during Bible study. When the White male suspect, Dylann Roof, was arrested for the murders, he was described as the perpetrator of a hate crime and a domestic terrorist, but his mental health almost immediately became the primary question in media accounts of the murders. The descriptions of Roof echoed many of the sentiments expressed in the Willie Lynch letter ("Negroes have lower IQs, lower impulse control, and higher testosterone levels in general. These three things alone are a recipe for violent behavior"). The media's depiction of Roof reinforced White supremacist ideals.

Black males are primarily denigrated for petty criminal offenses and perceptions of deviance. Trayvon Martin was wrongfully assumed to be a perpetrator of home invasions while walking in his neighborhood; after his death, he was described as having used marijuana. Eric Garner was approached by police for selling loose cigarettes, and he was accused of resisting arrest. Michael Brown was said to have engaged in shoplifting and bullying a store owner, then defying police orders. Tamir Rice was approached by police for playing with what turned out to be a toy BB gun. Walter Scott was stopped by police for a broken tail light and later charged with being delinquent on child support payments. Officers found a legal knife on the person of Freddie Gray when they made what has been described as an illegal arrest. Roof, a murder suspect, was nearly equitably compared to the Black male homicide victims.

The impact of this distortion on individual, community, and family life is seriously detrimental. Blacks are offered distressingly few positive images of self, often leading to self-fulfilling prophecies, including violent and criminal imagery that contributes to volatile internal and external relationships. Failure to educate children of all races regarding Black history can lead to an inferiority complex for Blacks and distorted perceptions of Blacks by others. In the face of inferiority complexes among Blacks, families and communities develop perceptions of helplessness and hopelessness. The inability to envision oneself as a valuable part of American society can lead to subconscious self-hatred, supporting indoctrinated attitudes that subconsciously support ideals of White supremacy. When Blacks become indoctrinated by internalized racism, they begin to see other Blacks as perpetrators of society's evils, rather than victims of White supremacy. These distorted perceptions also contribute to a lack of compassion and empathy on the part of non-Blacks, blocking effective transformative change for individuals, families, and the community at large.

Perceptions of Black males

Police officers' perceptions of Black males are the result of a dialogical feedback loop, initiated by concepts of White supremacy, followed by antisocial attitudes, a cultural of poverty-induced values, and violent practices by Black males toward authority figures and others. Law enforcement professionals escalate use of force to incapacitate real and/or perceived threats. Black males have experienced disparate contact with police and policing strategies, subsequent police misconduct, and their representation in the criminal justice system.

Scientific theories have been proposed to explain Black inferiority and to justify dehumanization of the Black race. Late 19th- and early 20th-century thought was influenced by Cesare Lombroso's theories of criminal anthropology, which supported the practice of eugenics (Ferrero, 1911). The theories described supposed inherent deviant characteristics of Blacks, Native Americans, and Hispanics and offered support for their designation as crime prone and best suited for punishment and reproductive control. Although these scientific theories have been denounced, their negative impact prolonged the devaluation of Black people, particularly Black men. Black males are still perceived as aggressive, violent, and disproportionately involved in criminal activity, even though White males are involved in criminal activity at a higher rate, based on arrest and prison/jail sentencing records (Alexander, 2010). The disproportionate representation of Black males in the criminal justice system reinforces the criminogenic perception.

Law enforcement officers have been cleared of charges of violence and murder when they articulate this negative perception in their defense testimonies. For example, Ferguson Police Department Officer Darren Wilson's description of the equally statured Michael Brown was that he felt like a child in the grip of "Hulk Hogan" and that Michael Brown's eyes revealed him to be a demon possessed with the intent to inflict harm (Weismann, 2014). The inclusion of the universal defense of Black males as a perceived and/or real threat is an integral factor in the legal defense of officers involved in the death of unarmed Black males.

Law enforcement's biased perceptions, practices, and accounts of their contact with Black males involving lethal intervention (1) perpetuate society's generalized culture of racist perceptions of Black males, (2) increase the institutionalization of lethal force against Black males, and (3) draw attention away from evidence of systemic racism, discrimination, and White supremacy. Local law enforcement represents the most visible form of government; inasmuch as the government has served the interests of White social advantage, their perceptions of "threatening" Black males must be analyzed for racial biases that are rooted in society's overtly racial past (Gabbidon & Greene, 2012). Judith Butler (1993) noted that these justifications of extreme use of force against violent Black males as serialized through media spectacle worked to limit White visibility of racial oppression. Butler (1993) argued that these incidents of excessive force calm White society's insecurity and paranoiac fear of Black males.

Theoretical framework

The Baltimore uprising had a profound effect on multiple levels of the authors' lives. All of the authors live in or have lived in, and teach or have taught in, the city of Baltimore. Clearly this event was very personal to each of us; we were all shaken by the experience. The authors can best be described as scholar-practitioners who are active at their respective institutions and in their communities, including Baltimore city and surrounding counties. Urie Bronfenbrenner's ecological perspective serves as the supporting framework for this investigation, involving analysis of microsystems, macrosystems, and mezzosystems of individuals within the social environment. According to Hepworth, Rooney, Rooney, Strom-Gottfried, and Larsen (2010), the microsystem focuses on individuals and how they relate to and interact with the system, the mezzosystem focuses on how groups or peers interact within the system or environment, and the macrosystem examines the impact of systems on organizations and communities.

Methodology

The unit of analysis for this article was the group of eight Black American faculty with close connections to the Baltimore city uprising. Five teach at Morgan State University in Baltimore, one teaches at a community college in the Baltimore area, and two live and teach in New York State. The authors range from young adult to mature adult; there are four women and four men. They represent Anthropology, Criminology/Criminal Justice, Psychology, Public Health, Sociology, Social Work, and Theology, and they have been involved in academia for a combined 71 years.

To understand the impact of the uprising, each author answered questions that were generated using Bronfenbrenner's ecological perspective. The responses are included not as a reflection of each individual's specific response per se, but as a summary of responses. Three questions were posed to the participating scholars:

(1) From the viewpoint of the Black scholar, what was the impact of the recent events?
(2) To what extent have the recent events influenced pedagogical and community work by Black scholars?
(3) In light of recent events, what can be done to improve policies and strengthen your academic discipline?

Responses

This section presents a brief summary of the responses by the authors to the three questions that examined the impact of the recent events, the influence of the events on their work in their communities and workplaces, and the impact of the events on their academic disciplines. These questions were designed to reflect views of the micro- (individual/personal level), mezzo- (groups), and macro- (broader community) impacts of the events on the lives of each author.

Question 1: From the viewpoint of the Black scholar, what was the impact of the recent events?

NCPH stated that the recent documentation of police brutality has forced Black scholars "over the cliff," so to speak:

> We can never again educate rising scholars based on the heavy Eurocentric practice of describing the criminal justice system without describing, in detail, its inherent flaws that impact our lives, personally, and undoubtedly affects the lives of our students who represent young men and women of color and others, who have been at the mercy of criminal justice system. Our scholarship has often been one that addresses the inequities in the system but must address educating students with a sense of urgency—the urgent need for them to help to amend the flaws of the system that could save lives and improve upon the life chances/quality of life for all people on U.S. soil. An academic career requires commitment to service, scholarship, and teaching. The three now mean reinvigorating our existing commitment to advocacy, research, and pedagogical approaches that does not ignore how we too are connected to the very ills of the system that threatens life chances. This especially involves university students who attend HBCUs and other institutions that have historically enrolled students who may not have otherwise been afforded a college education and are from locales like Baltimore city.

MMS recalled the words of W. E. B. Dubois:

> I have two warring ideals about the uprising that have yet to be reconciled. As a scholar, I must embrace the concept of "Writing is fighting!" The other side of me leans toward being an activist and a community organizer with little time or tolerance for rhetoric. I must do something, or we will continue to be assaulted as a people.

CBB stated,

> As a Black scholar, the impact of the recent events has inspired me to continue gathering the facts involving police shootings for increased scholarly writing and research. Doing research is one of my passions. In this way, I can expand the knowledge base in this particular area.

NRW stated that the major impact of this event is the blatant message that Black and poor lives do not matter:

> Our children have to live in a city with a failing school system, lack of recreational activities, lack of employment, and lack of resources. The subconscious, now conscious, message that our children and the people of Baltimore simply don't matter. I have seen this in some of the city's neighborhoods that were economically failing and observed how the city will choose which areas they will revitalize. It is not an impossible thing to change. For many of us who remember 20 years ago, cities like Atlanta were dangerous and failing. And now Atlanta is seen as the Black Mecca! It can be done, it's just a choice not to be done. Our children have to live in neighborhoods with abandoned houses, vacant buildings, dilapidated school systems in which they recently could not drink the water. Within the past 20 years, every 5–6 years, the Baltimore city school system gets a new CEO and thus a new administration. Every administration has a different agenda for the school system; therefore, the education system fails to stabilize because the structure is always changing. It is circumstances such as these that make our children feel hopeless and helpless.

KNT stated that as a Black scholar, former police officer, and an anthropologist of race and crime, the documented death of unarmed Black males has been quite significant, quite disturbing:

> I understand how structural violence of the state, both historically and contemporary, actively supported by White society, has led to disadvantage and ruined Black communities politically, culturally, and economically. This continuous assault on Black American life includes extrajudicial killings during the height of lynching season; the massive importation of crack cocaine and guns; the construction of disinvested ghetto communities for dwelling and unjustifiable shootings and assaults by police officers. Moreover, as an African American male scholar, the social justice end to my teaching and research has been to bring the underlying causes of disorganized and ghettoized communities into view and to therein find solutions. In so doing, I hope to recruit

and train students who are both culturally sensitive and particularly Black to become police officers. Moreover, and generally, I hope to train college students to become change agents as global citizens, irrespective of the careers within or beyond the criminal justice system. It is imperative that we have culturally sensitive police services available to our communities, because we have to deal with the real effects of past and present forms of state-sponsored violence which has left disorganized communities in its wake. The challenge of these recent deaths of unarmed Black males has compromised my efforts to cause students to see policing as an important service, profession they should aspire for.

BDS mentioned that the Baltimore uprising magnified conditions in underserved urban communities throughout the United States:

Not uncommon, people feel marginalized and hopeless, which manifests into anger and violence. Far too often, people of color, particularly Black Americans in poor communities, are devalued and treated with disdain based on assumptions and stereotypes about their worthiness. In Baltimore in particular, there is a depletion of resources such as neighborhood centers, high school dropout rates, high rates of unemployment and intergenerational poverty, and perceived disrespect by law enforcement; this becomes an incubator for civil duress. Essentially, the Baltimore uprising was reflective of denied justice, enforced poverty, inadequate education, and feelings of despair influenced the outcry demonstrated.

LB stated that the Baltimore uprising both antedates and postdates the April 27 uprising:

It started when activists and citizens took to the streets to protest the death of Michael Brown at the hands of Darren Wilson. The Baltimore Uprising has changed the political narrative completely by effecting police reforms, altering the destiny of local politicians, and spurring discussion of urban issues and police brutality in the 2016 presidential race. The Baltimore Uprising is a continuation of Black resistance to White supremacist terrorism going back to slave ship rebellions and insurrections waged by enslaved Black folk, such as the 1739 Stono Rebellion or the New Orleans Uprising in 1811.

Question 2: To what extent have the recent events influenced your workplace and community relations?

NCPH stated that, while writing the collaborative paper, the loose establishment of The Race and Criminology/Criminal Justice Consortium began to form, where she garnered help from student assistants:

We (student assistants and myself) identified race and justice experts (esp. professors) whose guidance will be employed to address police training, police/community relations, race and crime, police brutality, and racism and the criminal justice system. Policy that addresses these issues is expected to be shaped by the interworkings of the consortium.

CBB stated that it is incumbent on the Black church, in particular, to take an activist stance and outreach approach to the current issues. This would involve formulating strategies for effective community change emanating from a socially aware clerical leadership:

Undoubtedly, the civil rights movement had a profound effect on clergymen whose use of their pulpits was a means by which they could make proclamations to the Black community. It is evident there is a need for an increased awareness of the consequences of poverty in urban communities. Therefore, I have become more active in the church where I attend services to become a part of groups that discuss teaching our youth the importance of academic achievement.

NRW stated,

Asa human services professor at a predominantly White institution, I am active in educating my students who will become future human service practitioners, social workers, and addiction counselors to the reality of the communities and people that they will work with. It is important for me to point out these issues of systematic racism and social injustice so that my students not only learn to be culturally competent, but also learn to be empathetic to the plight of marginalized populations as well as an advocate and change agent. I am also involved in a sorority where the main purpose is community services, as well as being involved in the community as a mentor and board member of various nonprofits. At this time, I want to be more involved in the community and make transformative change. There are lots of nonprofits, fraternities and sororities, community organizations helping the community, but it's not necessarily creating transformative change. I want to be involved to the extent that Baltimore becomes transformed and change is seen across the city.

KNT said:

My research, which is qualitatively based, requires students to conduct field assignments in the very communities targeted with police force. This compromises the ability to use real-life examples from Black communities as an extension of the classroom. The shootings as of late have increased the very danger of students, whom many look like and are from communities similar to the sites of the unjustifiable and extrajudicial shootings of Black males by police officers. It limits the content of our instruction to abstract discourse and allows for an unnatural delinking of content and real life. As a qualitative researcher, it is important that we naturalize the logics of agency and social justice by being able to access real communities. This is of particular importance if we are to achieve the academies' putative held goal, which is to produce cosmopolitan citizens.

BDS said:

Although I am not currently teaching, I have used social media as a platform to address salient issues that impact our community. As such, I have become actively involved with increasing awareness and facilitating discussion that make entities like Facebook a mechanism to participate in activism through dialogue, signing petitions, and encouraging others to become less apathetic and to become involved with challenging the status quo. Also I have become involved with attending events associated with Black Lives Matter, Black Men Matter, and Black Women Matter movements that examine the intersection of race, gender, and social class and the extent to which lives are affected and strategies are discussed on how to effectuate change. I have become more engaged personally in activism, teaching using social media.

IM stated that he was very upset and angry at the lack of response from his college toward the incident in Baltimore, as well as any incidents examining issues of social justice:

At my institution there are only five Black professors, and at times, I think we are overwhelmed with addressing these issues. It seems we have to be the ones to raise the social and political activism flag for the entire campus. When I reviewed responses from other schools regarding the incidents in Baltimore, I was shocked that we didn't mention anything on our website. I wasn't asking for a rally for Freddie Gray or anyone else; I wanted to know why wouldn't they acknowledge this incident? Not for me, but for the number of Black and Latino students who come to this predominately White institution from downstate (Bronx, Manhattan, Brooklyn, etc.) who fit into the category of a Freddie Gray. Did the students feel the school understood them? I'm still baffled … because the mission of the college states that education elevates human dignity and, to me, no response allows issues such as these to persist.

LB reported that the Baltimore uprising led him to develop the #BaltimoreUprising Community Healing Research Project, which involved Morgan State students:

[We are] surveying 110+ residents at the epicenter of the Uprising to determine levels of PTSD in the aftermath of the events of April 27. It also led to a grant-writing effort examining the health effects of police brutality on young Black men as a response to the April 27 Uprising.

He has been invited to speak all around the city on issues related to Baltimore's long history of apartheid policies that led to the April 27 uprising.

Question 3: In light of the recent events, what can be done to improve policies and strengthen your academic discipline?

NCPH described The Race and Criminology/Criminal Justice Consortium as a tool to address policy concerns and strengthen the discipline in a way that will positively impact the community at large and the law enforcement community specifically:

The vision for the consortium is that it can be a go-to source of empirically tested recommendations to strengthen knowledge about how the practices of old, can be used to inform the practices of the present, and improve upon the practice of law enforcement in the future.

MMS stated:

We need to do three things at least. First, commit to training our youth (students) to be activists and change agents. We must have brown bag workshops, call in guest speakers, identify policies that are dangerous to disempowered people, etc. We must also caution that with any conflict there will be casualties. Second, social work has done a disservice if we continue to teach people how to cope with injustice, we must take clear risks and never become complacent. We have an ethical obligation to serve the disenfranchised and the marginalized; however, we spend a disproportionate amount of time emphasizing coping techniques for trauma and depression without seriously tackling the structural inequalities and systemic failures. Third, social work must lead the movement and form alliances with other disciplines to facilitate change. We cannot do this by ourselves. It does not mean we cannot do anything. At our national meetings [i.e., CSWE, NASW], we must develop sessions of how we as a profession can combat this growing feeling of disconnectedness among our poor and sick. We must have some directives and hold schools accountable, just like we hold schools accountable for implemented academic standards. We ought to ask, What have you done since your last site visit to eradicate poverty?

CBB said,

What I feel is needed for community change is a serious dialogue between church and civic officials to address problems of race/ethnicity, economics, education, and poverty. I believe that policies can be strengthened by a concerted effort on everyone's part—clergy, city, state, police, and governmental officials. Unless there is a line of communication, there will be no solution to the problems. Academically, there is a relationship between religion and society. Study of the intersection of religion as it relates to race and class can also broaden perceptions about the role religion and the church play in the lives of Black Americans.

NRW stated,

As educators, we have to put the pressure on our local and city government to stabilize the education in Baltimore. While I understand the purpose of unions, the unions have many positives, but negatives as well. Unions protect teachers and administrators who are not doing their jobs and are not committed to educating our children. CEOs for the school system have been allowed to come, fully change structures of the system, and then leave, often leaving the system in a state of chaos. Schools continue to close and positions are often eliminated often or changed, and therefore, those teachers, staff, and administrators don't have the opportunity to perfect their craft as educators because they fear either losing their job or knowing that their position may completely change. The first major policy change needs to be the school system. It is known that, when school systems are failing, crime and violence goes up! Education is the backbone of this city; without this our city will continue to fail. My academic discipline is human services and psychology. We need to continue to teach cultural diversity to our students who are future practitioners and teach students how to make transformative change through advocating on a local and national level, teaching students how to create effective programming for disenfranchised communities, and teach students to use research to impact change.

KNT said,

It is my belief and experience as an African American police officer that one's biography and socialization matters. If there is no exposure to diversity (except of the negative and stereotypical type) in the dominant society (rural, suburban, and White), which is where we recruit most of our police force, state violence will proceed unabated. It is my belief that most police officers are not willing participants in state violence, yet their backgrounds and police academy training cause them to view minorities as inherently criminal and violent. Therefore, it is my thought that we should conduct research to see if officers from diverse environments have less incidents of police brutality against minorities versus those who come from homogenous white communities. Anecdotally, I have collected evidence that officers who come from racially and economically diverse communities have higher degrees of tolerance and therefore engage in less violence against minorities. If this is the case, I think we should explore placing police academies on HBCU campuses or other ethnically diverse environments. In addition, tie the certification of basic policing to 4-year college degrees where police recruits can receive training in other academic areas that would bring into view the underlying factors of inner-city, urban crime and historical and contemporary inequality, namely, structural violence of the state.

BDS provided suggestions based on the Baltimore uprising:

While systemic change may not occur immediately, I do believe that concerted efforts should be made to address contributing factors that stand to destroy lives and communities. First, I believe that empirically tested measures to screen police officers should be considered. Greater emphasis should be placed on increased training to help police officers to work with culturally diverse and marginalized groups. Furthermore, greater attention is needed to focus on critical thinking, challenging assumptions, and better conflict resolution. Too often, tensions arise because of poor communication based on implicit bias against groups based on different attributes. As social work educators, we must be diligent in our efforts to prepare our students to develop macro-practice skills such as advocacy, mediation, and community organizing. Infusing service-learning assignments such as community asset mapping and hosting "Community Appreciation Day" events are opportunities to help students recognize the intersection of micro-, mezzo-, and macro-practice when working with their clients. Also, greater emphasis is needed to forge partnerships with community-based agencies to provide professional development training to ensure that attention is not only focused on service delivery, but to help social work professionals in agencies to become more engaged with the communities they are based. Last, more social workers must begin to consider transferring their knowledge and skills into becoming involved with the political process and teaching strategies on how to combat social injustice in grassroots organizations and faith-based institutions.

LB reports:

The most important thing that can be done to improve policies and strengthen the discipline of Public Health is to have a strong understanding of history, historical trauma, and the previous policies that helped to inflict genocidal trauma on the Black community throughout the history of the United States. This is the only way to appreciate the scale of the damage done and to effectuate policies and actions that would help undo the damage caused by White supremacy and improve the health outcomes of Black people in the United States.

Discussion

While the Rodney King beating spurred the first examinations of police-involved violence and death of unarmed Black males in recent history, public policy, police training, and general community practices have not led to significant changes in the treatment of Black males in the criminal justice system and in society at large. There are countless incidents in which Black males have been under siege and encountered the danger of being profiled, targeted to be arrested, or incarcerated. Increasingly, many, including professors and parents, have galvanized and joined forces with national and local organizations, along with Black media, to form a national movement to address the problem of community and police violence. Movements such as "Black Lives Matter" have illuminated the pervasive problem of police brutality and the extent to which Black families have historically faced overt racism and discrimination, spawned by the premises of White supremacy. We agree with many scholars who argue that many view police brutality as warranted because of preconceived negative perceptions of Black males as "prototypical criminals" (Chaney & Robertson, 2013; Peffley & Hurwitz, 2013; Tonry, 2011). Instead, Black males should be viewed as victims.

When assessing the incidents of police-involved homicide, it is imperative that the characteristics of the police, citizens, and their interactions be examined. Violence is acknowledged as a developmental process in which the decisions of the people and police, alike, can be used to predict whether there is likely to be a violent interaction (Binder & Sharf, 1980). With limited information on the background of police departments and communities and insufficient data, there is difficulty in examining police use of deadly force. Although recommendations have been made for a national deadly force reporting system, to include information regarding the totality of police-involved homicides, citing civilians and police as victims (Geller & Scott, 1992), no such system exists. There is, to date, no policy mandate to confirm the total number of justified or unjustified homicides by law enforcement (Klinger, 2012).

Although the present examination has been interdisciplinary, a unifying theme is the collective recognition of the responsibility to advance the body of knowledge about the problem and to provide strategies to effectuate positive outcomes. We present the following recommendations.

Transformative change

The reality of death of unarmed Black males by law enforcement officials requires continuous transformative change to affect law, policy, policing, and other institutionalized systems. Transformative change requires people of color and others to unite. In order for change to take place, all subjugated people must work from a position of compassion and empathy, education and strategy, communalism not individualism, and love not hate.

Trust between the community and the police

Black victims of police violence and other citizens believe that they are not being told in police reports "what really happened." According to Van Maanen's assessment (1980), officers are concerned about their reputations and are influenced by their role and social position. These factors lead to partial accounts of what actually happened during a police-involved shooting and injury or death of a civilian. The community's response to unfair, harsh, and biased treatment by the criminal justice system generally and law enforcement particularly leads to weaker support of the system, negative evaluations, and poor encounters with criminal justice professionals, resulting in secondary deviance (Brunson & Miller, 2006; Stewart, 2007).

Examination of the problem by those with a lived experience

Although work by experts such as Sherman (1986, 1992; 2013) on evidence-based policing has been cited, more police officers and scholars with lived experience should be part of the critique. Continuing Sherman's work, the following questions should be assessed: First, how can the police act more effectively and justly against violence in society? Second, how can we better understand and reduce the violence committed against police? Third, what accounts for the wide variations in police use of violence, and what can we learn? The authors of this article, based on their lived experience, provide solutions such as strengthening compulsory education in the inner city, training youth to take part in activism, training law enforcement officials, and instituting police training on Black campuses.

Conclusion

Writing this article has been a journey for all of us. We coupled our lived experience with our professional responsibilities and produced a document that gives hope and ideas for the future. As we engaged in writing this article, we reflected on our personal struggles with this topic, along with our connections to the epicenter of the uprising. The expository discourse of our own experience allowed us to show our truth about where we stand in the quest for liberation. If the situation is to change, we must teach students to be activists engaged for the cause. We must teach them that they have an obligation to be the educated representatives of their neighborhoods and communities. Academics must not succumb to hopelessness and fear, even though the dominant class would have us cower and submit to egregious police brutality and lawlessness; we must deliver and keep the promise of our forefathers.

This article forced us to examine activism in communities (as well as in our social and political circles) that are systematically and unfairly oppressed through race-based policies; it also forced us to be active voices in organizing activities that will enlighten and educate our brothers and sisters who are disconnected from the politics of the world in which we live. Most of all, this article taught us to pull together, a demonstration of *Harambee*. By combining ideas and efforts, we are powerful in the struggle.

References

Adler, J. S. (2007). Shoot to kill: The use of deadly force by the Chicago police, 1875–1920. *Journal of Interdisciplinary History*, *38*, 233–254. doi:10.1162/jinh.2007.38.2.233

Alexander, M. (2010). *The new Jim Crow: Mass incarceration in the age of colorblindness.* New York, NY: New Press.

Binder, A., & Fridell, L. (1984). *Lethal force as a police response.* Washington, DC: National Institute of Justice.

Binder, A., & Scharf, P. (1980). The violent police-citizen encounter. *Annals of the American Academy of Political and Social Science, 452,* 111–121. doi:10.1177/000271628045200111

Brunson, R. K., & Miller, J. (2006). Young black men and urban policing in the United States. *British Journal of Criminology, 46*(4), 613–640. doi:10.1093/bjc/azi093

Butler, J. (1993). Endangered/endangering: Schematic racism and white paranoia. In R. Gooding-Williams (Ed.), *Reading Rodney King/reading urban uprising* (pp. 15–22). Chicago, IL: University of Chicago Press.

Carlton-LaNey, I. (1999). African American social work pioneers' response to need. *Social Work, 44,* 311–321. doi:10.1093/sw/44.4.311

Chaney, C., & Robertson, R. V. (2013). *Racism and police brutality in America.* New York, NY: Springer.

Dottolo, A., & Stewart, A. (2008). "Don't ever forget now, you're a Black man in America": Intersections of race, class and gender in encounters with the police. *Sex Roles, 59,* 350–364. doi:10.1007/s11199-007-9387-x

Drummond, W. (1997, May 31). Media blamed for negative stereotypes of Black males. *New York Amsterdam News,* 13.

Dubois, W. E. B. (1935). *Black reconstruction in America, 1860–1880.* New York, NY: Harcourt Brace.

Elicker, M. K. (2008). Unlawful justice: An opinion study on police use of force and how views change based on race and occupation. *Sociological Viewpoints, 24,* 33–49.

Ferrero, G. L. (1911). *Criminal man, according to the classification of Cesare Lombroso.* New York, NY: G.P. Putnam's Sons.

Franklin, J. H. (1989). *Race and history: Selected essays 1938–1988.* Baton Rouge, LA: Louisiana State University Press.

Franklin, J. H., & Moss, A., Jr. (2000). *From slavery to freedom: A history of African Americans.* New York, NY: McGraw Hill.

Gabbidon, S. L., & Greene, H. T. (2012). *Race and crime.* Thousand Oaks, CA: Sage.

Geller, W. A., & Scott, M. (1992). *Deadly force: What we know–A practitioner's desk reference on police-involved shootings.* Washington, DC: Police Executive Research Forum.

Gottdiener, M., & Hutchison, R. (1994). *The new urban sociology.* New York, NY: McGraw-Hill.

Hepworth, D. H., Rooney, R. H., Ronney, G. D., Strom-Gottfried, K., & Larsen, J. A. (2010). *Direct social work practice: Theory & skills* (8th ed.). Belmont, CA: Brooks & Cole.

Higginbotham, A. L., Jr. (1996). Bondage, freedom & the constitution: The new slavery scholarship and its impact on law and legal historiography: Keynote address: The ten precepts of American slavery jurisprudence: Chief Justice Roger Taney's defense and Justice Thurgood Marshall's condemnation of the precept of black inferiority. *Cardozo, 17,* 1695.

Jones, R. E. (2006). Examining linkages between race, environmental concern, health, and justice in a highly polluted community of color. *Journal of Black Studies, 36,* 473–496. doi:10.1177/0021934705280411

Klinger, D. A. (2012). Back to basics: Some thoughts on the importance of organized skepticism in criminology and public policy. *Criminology & Public Policy, 11*(4), 637–640. doi:10.1111/capp.2012.11.issue-4

Lynch, W. (2008). *The Willie Lynch letter and the making of a slave.* Chicago, IL: Lushena Books.

Peffley, M., & Hurwitz, J. (2013). Persuasion and resistance: Race and the death penalty in America. In H. T. Greene & S. Gabbidon (Eds.), *Race and crime: A text/reader* (pp. 355–366). Thousand Oaks, CA: Sage.

Schiele, J. (2007). *Human services and the Afrocentric paradigm.* New York, NY: Routledge.

Sherman, L. (1986). Policing communities: What works? In A. J. Reiss, Jr. & M. Tonry (Eds.), *Communities and crime* (pp. 343–386). Chicago, IL: University of Chicago Press.

Sherman, L. (1992). Attacking crime: Police and crime control. In M. Tonry & N. Morris (Eds.), *Modern policing* (p. 605). Chicago, IL: University of Chicago Press.

Sherman, L. (2013). Targeting, testing and tracking police services: The rise of evidence based policing, 1975–2025. In M. Tonry (Ed.), *Crime and justice crime and justice in America, 1975–2025* (Vol. 42, pp. 377–451). Chicago, IL: University of Chicago Press.

Stampp, K. (1956). *The peculiar institution: Slavery in the ante-bellum South.* New York, NY: Knopf.

Stewart, E. A. (2007). Either they don't know or they don't care: Black males and negative police experiences. *Criminology & Public Policy, 6,* 123–130. doi:10.1111/cpp.2007.6.issue-1

Tonry, M. (2011). *Punishing race: A continuing American dilemma.* New York, NY: Oxford University Press.

Van Maanen, J. (1980). Beyond account: The personal impact of police shootings. *Annals of the American Academy of Political and Social Science, 452,* 145–156. doi:10.1177/000271628045200114

Weismann, J. (2014, November 25). "Like a demon": Read Darren Wilson's description of shooting Michael Brown. *The Slatest.* Retrieved from http://www.slate.com/authors.jordan_weissmann.html

"I can't breathe": A case study—Helping Black men cope with race-related trauma stemming from police killing and brutality

Samuel R. Aymer

Silberman School of Social Work, Hunter College, City University of New York, New York, New York, USA

ABSTRACT

It is impossible for individuals to survive without the ability to breathe. Eric Garner, an unarmed Black man, uttered "I can't breathe" during an arrest by the police, who placed him a chokehold and caused his death (Goldstein & Schweber, 2014). Seeing this inhuman image on videotape pierced the consciousness of the nation. The grand jury failed to indict the police officer who killed Mr. Garner, and this sparked civil protests, which birthed the notion "Black Lives Matter" (Owens, 2015). Protestors chanted "I can't breathe" to decry this injustice. This underscored literally and metaphorically how difficult it is for Black men to thrive in a hostile environment where their civil rights are denied. This article addresses the killings of unarmed Black men by the police, arguing that such killings are motivated by factors including how race, racism, and gender contribute to the "othering" of their humanity. Ideas from Critical Race Theory, the nexus among policing, criminality and racial profiling, critical consciousness, relational theory, and narrative therapy will provide a foundation for understanding the racialized experiences of Black men in America—where multiple forms of injustices exist—and where police killings are viewed as lawful. Highlighting practice themes from a case vignette involving an adolescent Black male engaged in psychotherapy will explicate how racial profiling by the police triggered race-based traumatic stress. The vignette will illuminate the implications for psychotherapeutic work with Black men who have been affected by race-based traumatic stress stemming from "living while Black."

As a historical fact, violence against Black people in the context of American history occurred during enslavement, Jim Crow, and the civil rights movement. Men, women, and children endured physical, psychological, sexual, and emotional terror during these periods (Leary, 2005; Petersen & Ward, 2015). The discourse of racial oppression in America cannot be disentangled from White supremacy, a worldview proclaiming White racial superiority and Black inferiority (Alexander, 2010; hooks, 1995; Madhubuti, 1990). The work of hooks (1995) delineates that White supremacy is a global system of domination affecting Black people in America and throughout the diaspora. Regarding such a claim, Alexander (2010) posits that "[f]aith in the idea that people of the African race were bestial, that whites were inherently superior, and that slavery was, in fact, for Blacks' own good, served to alleviate the white conscience and reconcile the tension between slavery and the democratic ideals espoused by whites in the so-called New World" (p. 26). Because the premise of White supremacy was largely built upon faith and a negative belief system about Black people's humanity, Alexander declares that its legacy and ideology have persisted far beyond its historical relevancy vis-à-vis American life.

In addition, Critical Race Theory (CRT is a paradigm that has its roots in the legal profession and has gained traction in other disciplines) provides a foundation for understanding that violence against Black people stems from a larger narrative, explicating that any evaluation of contemporary racism and/or racial oppression must take into account the influences that White supremacy has had on the American psyche (Crenshaw, Gotanda, Peller, & Thomas, 1995). Crenshaw et al. go on to suggest that an important facet of CRT is that race and racial oppression (historically or contemporary) cannot be divorced from the ethos of White supremacy, which permeates all aspects of human institutions (e.g., social, legal, health, political, and cultural entities) aimed at promoting the welfare of our society. And the penetration of White supremacy throughout such institutions has prevented Black people from realizing full equal rights as citizens under the law. West (1993 summarizes this point by noting that "Black people have always been in America's wilderness in search of a promised land" (p. 25). An important inference from West's observation is that Black people have always fought to gain justice and protection through persistent nonviolent protests intended to effect social change and disrupt White supremacy. Opposition to civil rights activities has historically resulted in state-sanctioned violence (e.g., hosing down Black people with water, setting dogs on them, firing strategic or random shots at them, and homicides) by law enforcement (Leary, 2015). The presence of militarized police to control protesters (triggered by the killing of Michael Brown) in Ferguson, Missouri, in 2014 evokes painful memories of watching television footage of protests in the 1960s. The nexus between historical and contemporary practices of state-sanctioned violence against Black people can be examined though the following six CRT domains: (1) CRT recognizes that racism is endemic to American life; (2) CRT expresses skepticism about the dominant legal claims of neutrality, objectivity, color blindness, and meritocracy; (3) CRT challenges ahistorism and insists on a contextual historical analysis of the law; (4) CRT insists on the recognizing of the experiential knowledge of people of color and our communities of origin in analyzing law and society; (5) CRT is interdisciplinary and eclectic; and (6) CRT works toward the end of eliminating racial oppression as part of the broader goal of eliminating oppression in general (Lawrence, Matusda, Delgado, & Crenshaw, 1993, p. 6). Aspects of these domains can provide a backdrop for exploring how race and gender (with respect to Black men) are understood and examined through the lenses of institutionalized sociopolitical structures in American society.

The killing of Michael Brown, Eric Garner, Tamir Rice, Akai Gurley, Kajieme Powell, John Crawford, Amadou Diallo, and other unarmed Black men by police between 1999 and 2015 is a arguably akin to lynching, a racialized form of terror authorized by the law that occurred during the late 19th and early 20th centuries (Petersen & Ward, 2015). Gratuitous violence and deaths from lynching in America were omnipresent; the practice induced terror in Black men and ended their lives. The literature indicates that lynching and brutality perpetuated social control over Black people, specifically men (Johnson, 1982; Leary, 2015; Petersen & Ward, 2015). Emmett Till, a 14-year-old Black boy who allegedly flirted with a White women and was brutalized and killed by a mob of White males, is one example of how violence was used to ensure that Black men did not move beyond their social location relative to Whites—particularly in encounters involving White women that could be construed as sexual or intimate. As the killing and dehumanization of Emmett Till was considered to be the norm during the era of lynching, his killers were acquitted (Baker, 2006).

Lynching ruptured family ties as Black men had to flee for their lives (Johnson, 1982). Researchers suggest that lynching was conceptualized as a spectator sport by parents and children, who watched while Black male bodies (and women) were tortured and killed (Tolnay & Beck, 1995). A fundamental question that can be raised regarding this form of racial violence against Black men is: What was the role of law enforcement and the government in 1955 when Emmett Till was murdered? Evoking Emmett Till and the practice of lynching does not imply that policing in the 21st century is akin to White supremacist activities. The point, however, is that ongoing fatalities and violence due to how unarmed Black men are policed in America are palpable and elicit historical memories of how the practice of lynching affected Black men (Alexander, 2010, hooks, 1995; Leary, 2015; Petersen & Ward, 2015). An important premise of CRT is that historical antecedents provide context for how we analyze the effects of contemporary racial oppression on multiple levels within our society. Police killings and violence appear to be a consistent and persistent inescapable truth for Black men: Such killings and violence are unwarranted; such killings appear to be lawful; dead Black men bodies are left on street corners in American cities (similar to how Black bodies were left hanging on trees during the era of lynching) for hours after they are shot by the police (Von Drehle, 2015); law enforcement tactics led to shooting a Black man in the back as he attempted to flee (Von Drehle, 2015), and finally police tactics caused significant injuries to the spinal cord of a Black man who died in police custody (Owens, 2015). These acts of police violence and killing are emblematic of why Black (male) lives may not matter, and they seem to evoke echoes of lynching, especially, because accountability of such types of unlawful police practices is lacking.

The racialized experiences of Black men

To be male and Black in America means that one must contend with omnipresent occurrences of racial and gender profiling on multiple levels (e.g., being arrested while Black, shopping while Black, driving while Black) of society. According to Ramirez, McDevitt, and Ferrell (2000), "racial profiling is defined as any police-initiated action that relies on race, ethnicity, or national origin rather than behavior of an individual or information that leads the police to a particular individual who has been identified as being, or having, engaged in criminal activity" (p. 3). This summary brings into focus what it means to "live while Black and male"—how racial profiling by the police in America undercuts the quality of life and physical well-being of this group. Racial profiling works against the interests of Black men, and we know from the "Person in Environment" paradigm that it is important for people to feel there is a "goodness of fit" between themselves and the environment, an important hallmark of social work (Germain & Gitterman, 1995). Moreover, Spencer, Fegley, Harpalani, and Seaton's (2004) research stresses that maturation and growth are impeded when the social environment fails to nurture and value the needs of the individual. Black men are disproportionately profiled in society, and this cultivates an indelible stain of marginalization, causing others to devalue their dignity.

According to the criminology literature, racial profiling is predicated on the following: the labeling perspective, conflict theory, and the colonial model (Gabbidon, 2003). The labeling perspective is an outgrowth of a longstanding belief system that Black people are criminals, despite the lack of empirical data to substantiate such a claim. Captured in literature as "Blackaphobia" (Gabbidon, 1994, p. 347), the notion speaks to several factors, including stereotypic assumptions that an entire group is inclined to commit crimes. The labeling perspective can generate a sense of alienation and construct a narrative of "othering" with regard to Black men, whose subjective experiences with the police are fraught with distrust and anxiety. Rich and Gray's (2005) findings reveal that the policing of Black men was viewed by participants as harassing and often stemmed from racial profiling. The labeling perspective can also be understood in the context of CRT discourse in that racism is inextricably linked to the myriad ways in which race, racism, and racial oppression complicate the lives of Black people in America. Although labeling affects both Black men and women, pronounced suspiciousness and scrutiny pervading police officers' encounters with Black men raise the question of why these men are always perceived as potential criminals who should be handled in inhumane ways.

Conflict theory is based on an understanding of how dominant social groups advance their status and power to strengthen their benefits (Quinney, 1980). Although conflict is inevitable in human interactions and dynamics, conflict theory asserts that the power differential in human transactions is underlined by oppression, exploitation, and social control of others to sustain social order and uphold the rights of the privileged. Moreover, "conflict theory holds that law and the mechanisms of its enforcement are used by dominant groups in society to minimize threats to their interests posed by those whom they label as dangerous, especially minorities and the poor powerful group" (Petrocelli, Piquero, & Smith, 2003, p. 1). Societal negative projections of Black men (e.g., images of this group as thugs, thieves, criminals, uneducated) lay the foundation for why this group is perceived as a menace to society; thus, conflict theory can be used to understand why profiling is used to combat criminality.

Furthermore, driving while Black (DWB) and shopping while Black (SWB) are examples of profiling strategies aimed at Black men in their daily lives (Gabbidon, 2003; Lund & Kaufman, 2003). DWB means that Black men are routinely stopped and searched by police if they are driving an expensive car or if they happened to be in a neighborhood that is dissimilar from their own. Black men are also burdened by SWB, predicated on the presumption of wrongdoing without probable cause when they visit stores to purchase goods and services. Such practices essentially place Blacks under siege. Portrocelli, Piquero, and Smith (2003) point out that "economic and racial minorities are seen as a threat to the ruling class. In regard to all of this, conflict theory maintains that the privileged, acting on the perception of threat, will use the crime control apparatus of the state to restrain and limit those who threaten their interests" (p. 2). Concomitantly, Alexander's (2010) thesis on the New Jim Crow stresses that Whites invested in maintaining the social order, and this supported the war on drugs. And as a result, the war on drugs created another scheme for profiling the Black community and targeting Black men. Regardless of the type of profiling experienced by Black men, American society has always viewed this group as a threat. Alexander's historical account of "death slavery" notes that Whites were afraid of violent uprising by Blacks; they constructed images signifying that Blacks were "menacing and dangerous" (p. 28). Alexander adds that "the current stereotypes of Black men as aggressive, unruly predators can be traced to this period, when Whites feared that an angry mass of Black men might rise up and attack and rape their women" (p. 28).

Gabbidon (2003) indicates that the colonial paradigm can also be used to explain racial profiling in the policing of Black men. In citing Fanon (1963), who has advanced the notion of internalized colonialism, Gabbidon points out that such a worldview situates Black people in America as "other"—they are viewed as being "colonized in America" (p. 348). Black people's existence is built upon the idea that they are colonized, and their entitlement to equal treatment under the law is often denied, a theme that emerges when the judicial system attempts to indict police officers for killing unarmed Black men (Alexander, 2010; Gabbidon, 2003). This view of Black people is embedded in institutional structures, notably the police, who utilize aggressive tactics to regulate their lives (Alexander, 2010; Portrocelli et al., 2003). It should be noted that the Black man's inalienable rights were ignored when he was shot in his back in 2015. Such a use of brute force is consistent with leveraging control over those who have been deemed to have no legal and human rights. By definition, colonization means unequal power dynamics between those who are being colonized and their colonizers, so that controlling the movements and actions of Black men within in the context of DWB or SWB is another proactive strategy to reduce crime, protect property, and keep the privileged safe.

Case vignette: Stop-and-frisk in the therapeutic space

The case of Jamal is an exemplar of how a Black adolescent male was impacted by stop and frisk, which arguably is a precursor to police brutality and the killings of unarmed Black men. Jamal (a pseudonym) is a 16-year-old male who was referred to me, by his parents, for therapy as a result of his parent's concerns about his education. Awaiting Jamal's arrival to therapy was interrupted by a phone call from his father indicated that he could not attend the session; he had been stopped, frisked, and detained by the police. The tone and tenor of his father's voice via our phone conversation meant he was worried about his son's welfare. He alluded to feelings he held over the years concerning his son being stopped by the police. In expressing these concerns for his son, Jamal's father revealed he had been stopped and frisked by the police several times while he was driving. Empathic listening from me seemed to be useful in enabling him to talk about his struggles as a Black man who, like many, could not protect his son from the same racial profiling he faced

(Coates, 2015; Franklin, 2004). As expected, his preoccupation centered on the safety of his son: he remained concerned about the police harming his son while he was detained.

Jamal was on his way to therapy when the police stopped, frisked, and detained him. Although temporary, this derailed our work because Jamal refused to continue sessions; he was fearful he could be arrested again en route to my office. Staying in touch with his parents via phone kept me informed of how he was coping with his feelings of anger, agitation, and confusion. The manifestation of these emotions caused Jamal's parents to provide support to help him cope with the unjustified treatment he received from the police. After several brief phone contacts with Jamal, he agreed (five weeks after he was stopped and frisked by the police) to return to therapy.

The psychosocial impact of stop-and-frisk

Arriving 20 minutes before the session, Jamal seemed anxious, asking if we could start the session early. Acknowledging that he had been through a terrible situation with the police emphasized my concerns regarding his well-being. With a stoic and sad affect, Jamal nodded, "I was not doing anything, they just stopped me." He further remarked that the police pushed him, opened his backpack, and arrested him for no reason. He was detained with other Black adolescent males who also had been stopped and frisked. Jamal discussed his inability to sleep at night and anxiety about additional encounters with the police during sessions. He spoke of leaving New York after completing high school, a possible indication of an avoidant coping response that may have been in the service of self-preservation.

Subsequent therapy sessions focused on helping Jamal manage his feelings of being racially profiling by police officers and storeowners who profiled him as he entered retail outlets (SWB). He experienced SWB scrutiny when he was 15 years old while shopping in a department store in Manhattan. He did not share this incident with his parents or anyone else. Yet he readily spoke of the indignation he felt via therapy, using expletives to express his sense of powerlessness. Jamal mentioned unintended consequences such as death and brutality that could have occurred during his involvement with the police, demonstrating just how attuned he was to his precarious existence as a young Black male in America (Brunson & Miller, 2006; Carter, 2007; Coates, 2015). He also had trouble comprehending why he was stopped by the police when he was an A student who did not sag his pants and did not perceive himself as a "thug" or "thief." Grief and sadness engulfed him, so I encouraged him to share all the facets of his emotions and explored questions of social injustices in his encounter with the police.

Summary of assessment and psychotherapeutic processes

Assessment

Limited space permits only a summary of assessment issues and treatment processes. It appeared that Jamal's reluctance to meet with me for therapy dissipated due to the psychological injury he felt from the aggressive and unjust police interactions (Carter, 2007). Meeting with Jamal for weekly psychotherapy facilitated a good working alliance. He developed increased comfort in exploring his feelings about two core areas: His desire to seek employment after high school and the emotional aftermath of being stopped, frisked, and detained by the police. In agreement with Jamal, I invited his parents to attend several sessions to support his growth as well as to mend ruptures associated with their disapproval of his decision to seek employment after high school. Jamal's opposition to his parent's wishes for him to attend college was understood through the prism of adolescent development (Blos, 1962; Erikson, 1963; McKenzie, 2008). The developmental epoch of adolescent reflects the need to repudiate and resist parental influences in order to grow and mature. Initial reactions from Jamal's parents generated a sense of anxiety, inducing questions about identity, separation, and individuation from parents. Erikson (1963) posits that such reactions during adolescent are normative and consistent with this phase of human maturation. Of equal importance is the impact of race and ethnicity on the psychosocial development of young Blacks and adolescents of color. These young people are categorized as minority and, according to Phinney (1996), "minority status is the presence of negative stereotypes" (p. 924). What is important here is that although Black male adolescents have to cope with life-course developmental challenges, they must also deal with the toxins from racial oppression in the social environment that ultimately impinge on their positionality (Franklin, 2004).

The pressing issue for Jamal, however, was his difficulties managing symptoms related to his negative interactions with the police. A psychiatric consultation revealed that Jamal was actually experiencing trauma (centering on being chased by the police), irritability, nightmares, flashbacks, and intrusive thoughts. Likewise, qualitative interviews of other young Black men profiled by the police reveal that anxiety, despair, and fear tend to surround their lived experiences (Brunson & Miller, 2006; Rich & Grey). Such feelings can be understood as traumatic reactions stemming from racial profiling and police abuse, which underscores Herman's (1992) point that traumatic experiences trigger symptoms that are both physiological and psychological, and this weakens an individual's capacity to function. And, indeed, Jamal's traumatic symptoms (along with the aforementioned qualitative interviews of other young Black men) underlined the gravity of oppression in terms of how it punctured his psychological state, echoing Carter's (2007) statement that "the symptom manifestations of race-based traumatic stress include having reactions of intrusion (re-experiencing), avoidance (numbing) of stimuli associated with the trauma, and increased arousal or vigilance. In the case of racial discrimination, or racial harassment, the client's subjective appraisal of the experience is valid" (p. 84).

Central to Carter's thesis is that exposure to racism and racial harassment trigger anguish, terror, torment, and physical pain. In Jamal's case, the police manhandled him, causing physical pain to his right arm. In addition, Herman (1992) proposes that:

> Trauma events call into question basis human relationships. They breach the attachment of family, friendship, love, and community. They shatter the construction of the self that is formed and sustained in relation to others. They undermine the belief systems that give meaning to human experience. They violate the victim's faith in a natural or divine order and cast the victim into a state of existential crisis. (p. 51)

Ascertaining a psychiatric consultation coupled with my lived experiences as a Black man allowed me to understand Jamal's traumatic reactions as a psychological sequelae of enduring aggressive and unfair police actions. According to writers and clinicians (Butts, 2002; Carter, 2007), there is no diagnostic categorization in the *Diagnostic and Statistical Manual of Mental Disorder* explicating how racism and racist encounters damage the psychological health of Black people living in America. And Butts's (2002) keen observation of this omission implies that, "even in those instances in which African-Americans are objects of discrimination and describe symptoms consistent with PTSD, their symptoms may be dismissed or trivialized because of the view that the stressors are not catastrophic enough, according to the *Diagnostic and Statistical Manual of Mental Disorder* (DSM), to warrant a diagnosis PTSD" (p. 336). Seeking a psychiatric consultation from a culturally competent practitioner was precipitated by a change in Jamal's behavior, an effect that was validated by his personal account of his feelings following his stop-and-frisk ordeal. Moreover, using my lived experiences as a Black man who has been profiled engendered empathy and support for Jamal. In addition, a tenet of CRT is that the lived experiences of Black people within the context of their communities should not be subjugated in analyzing race and racism; instead, such experiences should be used to evaluate social forces that undermine the human rights of Black lives (Lawrence et al., 1993).

Psychotherapeutic processes

Utilizing an integrative approach to treatment proved to be beneficial in an effort to improve Jamal's psychosocial functioning. Aspects of narrative therapy, relational factors, and critical consciousness development were employed in psychotherapeutic work with him. Narrative therapy suggests that all human beings possess a story that has multiple authors (Carr, 1998). Saying that our lives are storied and have multiple perspectives means that it is critical important to develop insights and meanings about who we are in relation to self, family, and the macrostructure of which we a part.

This encapsulation of (Carr's 1998) viewpoint holds true for Jamal on a multiplicity of levels. The basis of his troubles with law enforcement officers is rooted in biased attitudes that society has embraced about Black men. And of course Jamal had his own construction of himself, another narrative that intersects with the ones noted previously. As per Carr's frame, I helped Jamal to "externalize the problem" (p. 491), so that he could comprehend that his injurious experience with the police was rooted in a much larger sociopolitical context. As an intervention, externalizing the problem helped Jamal dispel the idea that there was something inherently problematic about his persona that provoked violent police behaviors, a point he alluded to upon his return to therapy. In addition, Jamal was encouraged to give voice to his feelings and concerns to lessen his traumatic reactions. The therapeutic hope was for Jamal to be less symptomatic so that he could feel better about himself and reconnect to his friends and his community. Notwithstanding this setback, he demonstrated a strong determination to reclaim his autonomy; an indication of this was the comfort he regained that allowed him to return to therapy. In affirming Jamal's emotions, my therapeutic expectation was to help him feel a sense of control over this facet of his life.

Jamal's narrative (as a dangerous young Black man) is authored by society. What it pointed to, as I noted in an earlier article (Aymer, 2013), is that "[s]hared vulnerability means that many African Americans have some level of psychological consciousness about the potential physical and psychic danger of living in a society that has a history of racial animus toward them" (p. 133). That Jamal had appropriated his good academic standing, his lack of interest in wearing sagging pants, and his view of himself as a nonthug or thief illustrated that he was acutely aware of how marginalized images of Black men lead to risks and vulnerability (Brunson & Miller, 2006). A critical consciousness and a cognitive and affective process helped Jamal grasp how internalized oppression affected him (Watts, Griffith, & Abdul-Adil, 1999). The aforementioned notion of labeling perspective (e.g., Blackaphobia) advanced by Gabbidon (2003) underscores that society's stereotypic perceptions of Black people as criminals lead to negative internalization, and this could explain to some degree why the issue of "Black male respectability" was important to him. Unlike his contemporaries, he might escape the pernicious effects of racial profiling. By using the lens of critical consciousness, psychoeducation was employed to shift his cognitive process away from believing he could lessen racism, oppression, and racial animus by simply modifying his physical appearance or believing his academic prowess would be transparent to others. Jamal's emphasis on such a positioning was a precaution against racial harassment, a lesson he may have learned from his parents. The goal was to help him develop what Du Bois (1953) refers to as "double consciousness": the importance of recognizing how historical and contemporary racial oppression have shaped multiple self-states in Black people in America, as well as the quintessential emotional struggles to coexist in a society that devaluates this group.

Helping Jamal loosen societal stereotypes of him as a young Black man fostered exploration of his subjective truths. Jamal used his cognitive and affective capacities to process how his feelings of marginality were influenced by larger institutional factors (as opposed to how he dressed or behaved), which underlined the saliency of using narrative processes to develop critical consciousness, which supports the observation by Watts et al. (1999) that "oppression is the principal target of critical oppression" (p. 287). Jamal felt empowered, and he reported that the process alleviated feelings of self-blame (e.g., questioning why he was profiled and believing he could have thwarted such an act by behaving in a particular fashion). Thomas, Davidson, and McAdoo (2008) note that "[h]aving a critical awareness of racism is being cognizant of the dynamics and nuances of racist and unfair treatment" (p. 285).

Conclusion

The aim of this article was to focus on unjust and aggressive policing culminating in killings and fatal injuries of unarmed Black men. In doing so, it was crucial to invoke and address historical state-sanctioned violence against and killings of Black people in America. Critical Race Theory has established that the liberation of Black people in America cannot occur without interrogating and analyzing how the horrific reality of enslavement, centuries of discrimination, and unequal treatment have affected this group. Critical discussions and analyses of racial oppression must be located in a historical context to understand the precursors to manifestations of contemporary social injustice. To this end, I argue that the current killings of unarmed Black men should be analyzed through the lens of how America has treated Black men throughout history, reflecting on the legacy of lynching when violence and killings were employed to control this group. I point out how this form of control is also illustrative of how society places Black men at the margins by constructing stereotypic images of them as dangerous and prone to criminality. That these men are perceived as suspects as opposed to citizens in the context of Driving While Black or Shopping While Black illuminates why a criminal justice policy such as random stop-frisk-search has infiltrated society's notion of how law and order should be maintained, especially in the context of policing Black (male) bodies.

The second part of the article discusses a case vignette involving a Black adolescent male who presented symptomatology due to his experience of being stopped, frisked, and detained by the police. Why is the presentation of this case relevant to the discourse about unjust policing in the 21st century? My observation has been that critical discussions about this social problem have focused primarily on reforming the police and criminal justice system. Unquestionably, it is logical to focus on these issues to effect systemic change. Yet it is equally useful to expose and attend to the psychological aftermath of police violence sustained by unarmed Black men (Rich & Grey, 2005). For instance, in Newtown, Connecticut (children living in this town were shot and killed by a mass murderer while they were at school), a horde of mental-health experts were brought in to work with surviving children and interviewed by the media, exposing the sequelae of individual and community trauma (pertaining to the mental health of children, their families, teachers, etc.) Unlike this type of media coverage, discussions of police killings of unarmed Black men are usually devoid of any exploration of how racial profiling, brutality, and racial harassment by police and other entities (SWB-store owners) causes traumatic reactions and possibly posttraumatic stress disorder in this population. Thus, it is hoped that this case vignette provides a framework for increasing knowledge of how racial profiling by the police (particularly as it relates to aggressive and abusive policing of unarmed Black men) can mar an individual's psychosocial functioning. Jamal's case shows the potency of racial oppression, particularly as it obstructs the humanity and worth of Black men living in America. Furthermore, the case raises the following themes: (1) It is counterproductive to pathologize (i. e., perceiving this group as crazy) Black men who are attempting to cope with the psychological wounds of racial oppression; (2) it is helpful to understand their pain within the realm of the ubiquitous reality of marginality and its psychosocial consequences; and (3) it is beneficial for Black men to reauthor their narratives a self-development process that can counteract the daunting effects of internalized oppression and can lead to self-empowerment.

Finally, psychotherapeutic work with Jamal was effective. His symptoms diminished considerably, The supportive and empathic space created in our work provided emotional safety for Jamal; he enhanced his adaptive coping, and this alleviated his anxiety, anger, and confusion about being profiled by the police. It was my professional assessment that although the police incident imprinted him, he worked through his feelings—and this enabled him to complete high school and follow through with his plan to leave New York City.

References

Alexander, M. (2010). *The new Jim Crow: Mass incarceration in the age of colorblindness*. New York, NY: New Press.

Aymer, S. R. (2013). An Afrocentric approach to working with African American families. In E. P. Congress, & M. J. Gonzalez (Eds.), *Multicultural perspectives in social work practice with families* (pp. 129–159). New York, NY: Springer.

Baker, C. (2006). Emmett Till, justice, and the task of recognition. *Journal of American Culture, 29*(2), 111–124. doi:10.1111/j.1542-734X.2006.00323.x

Blos, P. (1962). *On adolescence: A psychodynamic interpretation.* New York, NY: Free Press.

Brunson, K., & Miller, J. (2006). Gender, race and urban policing: The experience of African American youth. *Gender & Society, 20*(4), 531–552. doi:10.1177/0891243206287727

Butts, H. F. (2002). The black mask of humanity. Racial/ethnic discrimination and post-traumatic stress disorder. *Journal of the American Academy of Psychiatry, 30*(3), 33–339.

Carr, A. (1998). Michael White's narrative therapy. *Contemporary Family Therapy, 20*(4), 485–503. doi:10.1023/A:1021680116584

Carter, R. (2007). Racism and psychological and emotional injury: Recognizing and assessing race-based traumatic stress. *Counseling Psychologist, 35*(1), 13–105. doi:10.1177/0011000006292033

Coates, T. (2015). *Between the world and me.* New York, NY: Spiegel & Grau.

Crenshaw, K., Gotanda, N., Peller, G., & Thomas, K. (Eds.). (1995). *Critical race theory: The key writings that formed the movement.* New York, NY: New Press.

Du Bois, W. E. B. (1953). *The souls of Black folk.* Greenwich, CT: Fawcett Publications.

Erikson, E. H. (1963). *Childhood and society* (2nd ed.). New York, NY: Norton.

Fanon, F. (1963). *The wretched of the earth.* New York, NY: Grove-Weidenfield.

Franklin, A. J. (2004). *From brother hood to manhood: How Black men rescue their relationships and dreams from the invisibility syndrome.* Hoboken, NJ: John Wiley & Sons, Inc.

Gabbidon, S. L. (1994). Blackaphobia: What is it? And who are its victims? In P. R. Kedia (Ed.), *Black on Black crime: Facing facts—challenging fiction* (pp. 232–244). Lima, OH: Wyndam Hall.

Gabbidon, S. L. (2003). Racial profiling by store clerk and security personnel in retail establishments: An exploration of "Shopping while Black." *Journal of Contemporary Criminal Justice, 19*(3), 345–364. doi:10.1177/1043986203254531

Germain, C. E., & Gitterman, A. (1995). *The life model of social work practice: Advances in theory and practice* (2nd ed.). New York, NY: Columbia University Press.

Goldstein, J., & Schweber, N. (2014, July 18). *Man's death after chokehold raised old issue for the police. New York Times*, p. A1.

Herman, J. L. (1992). *Trauma and recovery: The aftermath of violence from domestic abuse to political terror.* New York, NY: Basic Books.

hooks, b. (1995). *Killing rage: Ending racism.* New York, NY: Henry Holt.

Johnson, J. E. (1982). The Afro-American family: A historical overview. In B. N. Bass, G. E. Wyatt, & P. Powell (Eds.), *The Afro-American family: Assessment, treatment and research issues* (p. 285–290). New York, NY: Harcourt, Brace Jovanovich.

Lawrence, C., Matusda, M., Delgado, R., & Crenshaw, K. (1993). Introduction. In M. Matsuda, C. Lawrence, R. Delgado, & K. Crenshaw (Eds.), *Words that would: Critical Race Theory, assaultive speech, and the First Amendment* (p. 6). Boulder, CO: Westview Press.

Leary, J. G. (2005). *Post traumatic slave syndrome: America's legacy of enduring injury and healing.* Milwaukee, OR: Uptone Press.

Lund, R. J., & Kaufman, R. L. (2003). Driving while Black: Effects of race, ethnicity and gender on citizens' self-reports of traffic stops and police actions. *Criminology, 41*(1), 196–220.

Madhubuti, H. R. (1990). *Black men: Obsolete, dangerous? The African American family in transition: Essays in discovery, solution and hope.* Chicago, IL: Third World Press.

McKenzie, T. T. (2008). *Theory and practice with adolescents: An applied approach.* Chicago, IL: Lyceum Books.

Owens, M. D. (2015, February). Enough is enough: Thousands of protestors gathered last December harnessing the moments of the new civil rights movement. *Essence, 96*, 1–3.

Petersen, N., & Ward, R. (2015). The transmission of historical racial violence: Lynching, civil rights–era terror, and contemporary interracial homicide. *Race & Justice, 5*(2), 114–143. doi:10.1177/2153368714567577

Petrocelli, M., Piquero, A. R., & Smith, M. R. (2003). Conflict theory and racial profiling: An empirical analysis of police traffic stop data. *Journal of Criminal Justice, 31*(1), 1–11. doi:10.1016/S0047-2352(02)00195-2

Phinney, J. S. (1996). When we talk about American ethnic groups, what do we mean? *American Psychologist, 51*(9), 918–927. doi:10.1037/0003-066X.51.9.918

Quinney, R. (1980). *Class, state, and crime* (2nd ed.). New York, NY: Longman.

Ramirez, O., McDevitt, J., & Ferrell, A. (2000). *A resource guide on racial profiling data collection systems: Promising practices and lesson learned.* Washington, DC: U.S. Department of Justice.

Rich, W. A., & Grey, C. M. (2005). Pathways to recurrent trauma among Black men: Traumatic stress, substance abuse and the "code of the stress." *American Journal of Public Health, 35*(5), 816–824. doi:10.2105/AJPH.2004.044560

Spencer, B. M., Fegley, S., Harpalani, V., & Seaton, G. (2004). Understanding hyper masculinity in context: A theory driven analysis of urban adolescent males' coping responses. *Research in Human Development*, *1*(4), 229–257. doi:10.1207/s15427617rhd0104_2

Thomas, H., Davidson, W., & McAdoo, H. (2008). An examination of the young empowered sisters (YES) program: Promoting cultural assets among African American girls through a culturally relevant school based intervention. *Journal of Black Psychology*, *34*(3), 281–308. doi:10.1177/0095798408314136

Tolnay, S. E., & Beck, E. M. (1995). *A festival of violence: An analysis of Southern lynchings, 1882–1930*. Urbana, IL: University of Illinois Press.

Von Drehle, D. (2015, April). Line of fire: An unarmed Black man shot by a police officer-and this time a video records the killing, where the debate on racism and law enforcement goes from here. *Time*, *185*(4), 24–28.

Watts, R. J., Griffith, D. W., & Abdul-Adil, J. (1999). Sociopolitical development as an antidote for oppression: Theory and action. *American Journal of Community Psychology*, *27*(2), 255–271. doi:10.1023/A:1022839818873

West, C. (1993). *Race matters*. New York, NY: Vintage Books.

Hands up—Don't shoot: Police shooting of young Black males: Implications for social work and human services

Sharon E. Moore[a], Michael A. Robinson[b], A. Christson Adedoyin[c], Michael Brooks[d], Dana K. Harmon[e], and Daniel Boamah[a]

[a]Raymond A. Kent School of Social Work, University of Louisville, Louisville, Kentucky, USA; [b]School of Social Work, University of Georgia, Athens, Georgia, USA; [c]Department of Social Work, Samford University, Birmingham, Alabama, USA; [d]Human Development & Services, North Carolina A&T State University, Greensboro, North Carolina, USA; [e]Department of Human Development and Family Studies, Child Development Research Center, The University of Alabama, Tuscaloosa, Alabama, USA

ABSTRACT

Police shootings of young Black males that ultimately result in their death have become an all-too-common occurrence in this country. The deaths of Michael Brown and Eric Gardner have highlighted police relations with this population. Before viable solutions can be established, a number of areas need to be addressed that relate to the historical context in which police relations with this group exist that impact current relations between the police and young Black males, why their lives are seemingly given less value by society than those of their White counterparts, the role that spirituality and religiosity play that may help to make connections between them and the police, and the benefit of the Black church in fostering amicable police relations with young Black males. This article addresses these issues and concludes with recommendations for how the social work and human services professions, along with the Black church and police, can be responsive and proactive in addressing this social problem.

> Wherever there is a human being, I see God-given rights inherent in that being, whatever may be the sex or complexion.—William Lloyd Garrison (2010)

In the aftermath of a police shooting of yet another unarmed Black teenager, the United States is presently witnessing one of the largest public protests and outpourings of social activism since the Civil Rights Movement. Police shootings of young Black males that ultimately result in their death have become an all too common occurrence in this country. Most recently on August 9, 2014, the shooting death of Michael Brown, an unarmed Black teenager by police officer Darren Wilson in Ferguson, Missouri, and the consequent public outcry caused a rustling effect across the nation. Staggering statistics are superfluous regarding unarmed young Black males who have died as a result of being shot by police officers in this country. For instance, Gabrielson, Jones, and Sagara (2014) reported that between 1980 and 2012, of the 41 teens age 14 and younger killed by police, 27 were Black, eight were White, four were Hispanic, and only one was Asian. On average, Blacks killed by police were 30 years of age compared to 35 for Whites (Gabrielson et al., 2014). The chances of a young Black male being killed by police are 21 times greater than their White counterpart. Furthermore, between 2010 and 2012, young Black males between ages 15 and 19 were killed by police at a rate of 31.17 per million, compared to only 1.47 per million White males in that same age range (Harris, 2014).

Since its inception, the United States has obligated itself to "uniting" all citizens by granting human rights to all who reside here. According to the Declaration of Independence:

> We hold these truths to be self-evident, that all men are created equal, that they are endowed by their Creator with certain unalienable Rights, that among these are Life, Liberty and the pursuit of Happiness" (Charters of Freedom, n.d.)

It is troubling that not all citizens have a right to a full and opportune life. In light of the lethal history between U.S. police and young Black males and the recent deaths of unarmed Black males by police, an exigent call has gone out by many for solutions to address this problem (Ghitis, 2014). Before viable solutions can be established, a number of questions beg answers. Among them are the following: In what historical context do police relations with this group exist and how does that context impact current police relations with this population? Why are the lives of young Black males seemingly given less value by society than their White counterparts? What role does spirituality and religiosity play in the lives of young Black males in helping to make connections between them and the police? How is the Black church beneficial and strategically important in fostering amicable relations between the police and young Black males? Finally, what can the social work and human services professions do to be responsive and proactive to this social problem? The authors of this article do not propose to have all of the answers to these inquiries but address these questions in an effort to increase the knowledge base about this social problem and to assist social workers, law enforcement agencies, and other helping professionals in their efforts to reduce if not eradicate the prevalence of this phenomenon.

Who are young Black males and what are their life experiences?

It is important to note that young Black males are diverse in ethnicity, sexuality, attitudes, and disposition but are unified by a socially constructed category based on their skin tone, place of ancestral origin, and their collective American experiences. The United States Census Bureau defines "Black" as a person having origins in any of the Black racial groups of Africa (US Census, 2011). This typically includes people of African American heritage (Blacks in America with ties to slave ancestry from Sub-Saharan Africa) as well as immigrants from Sub-Saharan African countries and Afro-Caribbean countries. For the purpose of this study, the authors borrow from lifespan developmental theorists and define young Black males as being those between the ages of 13 and 40. This time frame is crucial for them because it is in this period that they develop a personal identity, form intimate loving relationships, and begin to make significant contributions to society through a career and family formation (Erikson, 1959; Uzzell, 2008).

The role of the Black male in America has been constructed through history from the early periods of slavery. Black males were stripped of their identity and classified as subhuman/servant/owned, thereby reducing their status to property (Kitano, 1985). Black males were subjected to harsh tactics to make them submissive as a means of maintaining social control (Majors & Gordon, 1994). According to Majors and Gordon, the power and status of Black males in their families were taken away from them, and in most cases their families were removed as well. Ultimately the Black male was identified as only fit for working and breeding. The post–slavery era has seen some rights restored to Blacks males, yet many of the institutions and the ideologies that govern them have not changed. Young Black males' inclusion into mainstream society is often viewed as a privilege, not a right, accorded by the Constitution. This may be because the Constitution was not written to protect young Black males nor were social institutions mandated to protect them.

Their culture is viewed as substandard, and they are required to adapt to Eurocentric cultural institutions if they dare to be part of U.S. society. They commonly wrestle with divergent ascribed societal definitions. To the greater degree they have been pejoratively defined as one or more of the following:

A Gangsta—A "gansta" is a child who grew up in an arduous environment. He was generally exposed to traumatic events during his childhood, most of them violent. He has often lost many of his family members and close friends to violence and is struggling to keep what is important to him in the only way he knows how (violence or crime). Generally this person was never given a chance to succeed because of early circumstances that were out of his influence (Payne, 2006).

A Thug—He is a child dedicated to gathering the attention of those around him, with multiple shows of bravado. He will sometimes perform minor acts of theft and will often try to mimic the actions and words of other thugs seen in music videos. He may live in the inner city or suburbs but will refuse to participate in any hard-core criminal activity (Anderson et al., 2003).

A Traitor—Often known as an "Oreo." This is any young Black male who after showing signs of intelligence is willing to pursue his potential as an intellectual human being. He will speak using correct grammar and will enjoy reading and learning. He has sometimes shown tendencies of hatred toward those of his own skin color due to previous ridicule (Swanigan, 2012).

A Martyr—He may make reference to how Black people are still enslaved by White people, blaming every non-Black person for anything that goes wrong in his life. He often makes requests for reparations for slavery and assures people of his hatred for "The Man." He continues to make radical statements calling for mass acts of violence or the refusal to eat certain foods (Marable, 1998).

A Vagrant—Upon realizing the paradoxes in all the previously stated paths, this man has chosen to do what he wants. He will often spend hours in thought on the question of "Who am I?" (Cooper, 2013).

Many Black youth feel that the privileges that characterize a typical youth of White middle-class family background in the United States are unobtainable (Staples, 1982). Staples added that, at the very onset of teenage life, young Black males are more likely to have encounters with the justice system that negatively impact their quality of life in both the short and long term. They are also more likely to be incarcerated because of disproportionate policies and practices of law enforcement that target Black males (Warde, 2012). Young Black males are likely to be concentrated in urban areas, be high school dropouts, have a high unemployment rate, and experience social and often physical isolation that negatively impacts them socially and economically (Majors & Gordon, 1994). The collective impact of these factors places them at a disadvantage in relation to their White counterparts and other young males of different races. For instance, the unemployment rate for young Black males continues to be significantly higher than their peers. According to the Department of Labor in October 2014, the national unemployment rate of people 16 years of age was 5.8%, yet Blacks were at 10.9% compared to Whites at 4.8%, Asians (not seasonally adjusted) at 5.0%, and Hispanics at 6.8% (Bureau of Labor Statistics: U.S. Department of Labor, 2014).

Regardless of how society views this population, young Black males offer a unique perspective (Mcdaniel, Diprete, Buchmann, & Shwed, 2011). Moreover, although the pressure to thrive while grappling with their life circumstances makes young Black males very susceptible to depressive symptoms (Whooley et al., 2002) they demonstrate a level of resilience belied by popular beliefs (Mcdaniel et al., 2011). Despite living in a system of inequities, young Black males shed stereotypes and cultural pathology, all despite still not being understood. Hence, this group is extremely resilient and has an ability to thrive, excel, and exist in a culture that is biased against them. Most live productive lives, have great strength and survival skills, and go on to make meaningful contributions to society in spite of the challenges they face.

Their presence is invaluable, and they make unique inputs to the nation and to the world. Young Black males serve in the military, and just like their peers of other races they make life sacrifices to defend their country. They serve as frontline workers in various professions, as employees and business owners, as doctors and engineers, community activists, politicians, and teachers, among others. There is no doubt that young Black males have excelled in a plethora of areas and that their impact has resonated throughout society. Successful young Black males positively impact the general public socially and economically. As athletes, they are responsible for generating billions of dollars annually in television advertisements and the sale of athletic wear and through the overall profits of college and professional athletics that pay the salaries of owners, coaches, support staff, and administrators of university sports and professional franchises. As entertainers, they pay for the services of agents, musical accompanists, lawyers, and many other people who work in this arena, and collectively, as business entrepreneurs who make billions of dollars, they contribute to the salaries of employees and others who help run their businesses (Evans, 2006). They have made substantial impacts to the world's cultural landscape through music and the clothing industry by setting trends and creating styles. Perhaps the most valuable role that they play in society is that of role models and leaders to the next generation of young Black males. It is therefore crucial for the benefit of this nation and society at large that young Black males be given the fundamental rights of other young males. They have continually proven that they have the capability and capacity to succeed if given the opportunity to do so (Bimper, Harrison, & Clark, 2013; McGee & Martin, 2011).

What follows next is a discussion of the historical context in which police relations with young Black males exist and how this has impacted current police relations with this population.

The historical context of police relations with African American males

Slave Patrols and Night Watchers were instituted during the era of slavery to control the movement and behavior of slaves (Kappeler, 2014). The first Slave Patrol was said to have been established in 1704 with the purpose of stopping any form of slave revolt (Nelson, 2000). These patrollers were made up of adult White males who walked the streets to monitor slaves. These practices became widespread throughout the nation and especially in southern states. They were also sanctioned by state laws such as those enacted in Virginia in 1705 that allowed for whipping and mutilation by slaveholders as punishment for crimes committed by slaves and the 1723 Maryland law that allowed Africans who struck a White person to be punished by having their ear cut off (Nelson, 2000).

The Reconstruction Era that followed the Civil War did not see a reduction in the violence against African American males. It is argued that the plight of young Black males actually worsened, especially in southern states, as vigilante groups and lynch mobs attacked African Americans with fewer external constraints from law enforcement and local governments. These former Confederate governments did not provide protection for African Americans, and in some situations, they created a nonprotective environment by passing a series of "Black Codes" that economically and socially disenfranchised African Americans (Nelson, 2000). In some instances, police joined local White mobs to attack Black communities. For instance, a congressional investigation into the summer of 1917 mob attacks and killings of Black residents in East St. Louis revealed that the local police participated (Nelson, 2000). These acts of violence continued into late 19th century even as formal police forces began to emerge in various cities and counties in the United States (Sidney, 1983).

At the turn of the century into the early 20th century, police brutalities began to incite public riots as other segments of society began to organize to fight against what was seen as injustice. It is estimated that from 1882 to 1930 roughly 3,000 African Americans (mostly males) were lynched (Fritzgerald, 2007). Lynching became a common punishment given to those who challenged the oppressive culture. It was also used as a tool to draw a color line between Black and White males. When Black males were accused of raping White women, they were typically hanged by mobs with their genitals mutilated as a public statement to maintain color lines. However, when a Black woman reported having been raped by a White man, he usually was not persecuted or punished. The governmental judicial institutions that include the police and the courts were constructed by default to enforce such oppressive acts toward Black males. Predominantly all White police forces, juries, and government officials usually resulted in the incrimination of young Black males and the acquittal of White counterparts for the same crime. As a result, despite historic accounts of White men sexually assaulting Black females, 90% of persons in the United States convicted of rape from 1930 to 1976 and executed were Black men (Fritzgerald, 2007).

Throughout this period, many young Black men served the United States military only to face a malicious culture that treated them as second-class citizens. For instance, in the summer of 1917, in the city of Houston, Texas, a group of White policemen assaulted and arrested two Black servicemen of the Third Battalion of the Twenty-Fourth Infantry for not obeying Jim Crow laws (Shapiro, 1988). By the end of the 1930s, grassroots organizations like the Association of Southern Women for the Prevention of Lynching and the NAACP had intensified their campaign against lynching and drawn international attention to the issue. Yet this period also marked the expansion of urban policing, which coincided with increased reports of police brutality across the nation.

Brutality against young Black males by police has continued into the 21st century. There now exists a systemic culture of oppression and marginalization of them that transcends all socio-economic classes and permeates every social institution (excluding their families and the African American church) including law enforcement (Cornileus, 2012). As a result, young Black males are profiled as criminals, deviant, unapproachable, and to be greatly feared. This profile often is a determinant to how they are treated by police (Bell, Hopson, Craig, & Robinson, 2014; Hutchinson, 1996) as evidenced by 1999 shootings of Amadou Diallo in New York City, whose body was riddled with 19 bullets by four police officers for resembling a serial rapist while he was standing in front of his house (Cooper, 1999); in 2000, Richard L. Holtz, a naked unarmed murder suspect who was killed with a barrage of 27 bullets in a motel hallway for allegedly threatening six police officers (McFadden, 2000); and Ousmane Zongo, age 43, who in 20013 was confronted and killed by a police officer in New York City during a raid on a counterfeit-CD ring in which Zongo was not involved. Relatives of Mr. Zongo sued the city and were awarded $3 million. The judge in the trial of the officer who shot him (and was convicted of criminally negligent homicide but did not serve jail time) said he was "insufficiently trained, insufficiently supervised and insufficiently led" (Brick & Confessor, 2006). In 2006, Sean Bell, an unarmed 23-year-old New York City man scheduled to be married later that day, died in an onslaught of 50 bullets fired by a group of five police officers who believed that he had a gun. He had been celebrating his upcoming wedding with two friends.

According to a Department of Justice report (2011), six days after Hurricane Katrina, James Brissette, age 17, and Ronald Madison, age 40, a mentally ill person, were killed for no apparent reason by police officers on Danziger Bridge in New Orleans; Eric Garner (2014), age 43, died from being choked by a New York police officer for allegedly selling untaxed, loose cigarettes, with the officers subsequently not indicted by a grand jury for his death, and John Crawford III, age 22, was shot and killed in a Beavercreek, Ohio, Walmart while holding a toy air rifle that he had just picked up from a shelf (*Washington Post*, 2014). These killings result in mistrust of the police by members of the African American community and in particular leave negative feelings toward police among many young Black males (Britton, 2000; Freyer, 2014). Kappeler (2014) asserted that modern U.S. police departments' foundational roots and driving ideologies are influenced by slave era policies. It is therefore not erroneous to assume that police do not always exercise enforcement and justice uniformly with all groups in this society, and young Black males are among those who often become victims of such injustice compared to young White males.

We now consider spirituality and religiosity as a buffer against a person's ability to kill another.

Spirituality in the African American community and in the lives of young people

Spirituality is a distinct but confluent domain of human life. Burkhardt (1989, p. 72), who published the first formal concept analysis of spirituality, defined spirituality or "spiriting" as a process of "unfolding the mystery through harmonious interconnectedness that springs from inner strength." All persons have a physical, social, psychological, emotional, and spiritual dimension that collectively make up the total self (Agullar, 1997). Spirituality gives a person a sense that there is something greater than self and helps an individual understand that they are not the center of the universe, but rather inextricably connected to all other humans (Alexander & Moore, 2008).

Historically, spirituality has been at the center of African American community life and folk experience (Billingsley & Caldwell, 1991; Taylor & Chatters, 1991) and is a prominent component of African American culture because it permeates nearly every domain of African American life. Spirituality has and still serves as a personal and communal source of liberation, solace, hope, meaning, and forgiveness as it relates to social, political, and economic injustices (Mattis, 2002).

African Americans have used their spiritual convictions to subvert White, racist, and patriarchal hegemony; construct subjectively meaningful personal, racial, and gender identities; agitate for social justice; and maintain a sense of community (Long, 1997). Researchers who examined the role of spirituality in the lives of young people have found that among adolescents, spirituality promotes personal well-being and mitigates against negative behaviors and outcomes. In their work with a sample of sixth-grade, urban African American youth, Jagers and Mock (1993) found that a spiritual orientation was associated with fewer reported acts of delinquency and with an increased focus on such prosocial values as cooperation, empathy, and justice. Stevenson, Herrero-Taylor, Cameron, and Davis (2002) have found that African American adolescent males who hear, and presumably internalize, messages about spirituality tend to engage in greater levels of anger control and fewer acts of overt aggression than their counterparts. These findings suggest that spirituality plays a crucial role in promoting prosocial attitudes and behaviors among African American youth. Spirituality has also been found to promote personal well-being and mediate negative outcomes for African American adults.

The social sciences and American society as a whole have viewed African Americans in unacceptably simplistic ways, and research on the role of spirituality in the lives of African Americans among the social sciences has remained limited and disjointed. There is very little appreciation that the African American community comprises people of myriad cultures, ideologies, attitudes, and experiences. This has contributed to an ambivalent and simplistic approach to the study of African American religiosity and spirituality. Thus, the question that remains and needs to be addressed is why social work has done a poor job in studying the role of spirituality in the lives of African Americans. This is a crucial question because it provides researchers an opportunity to study social work's treatment of African American people relative to their spiritual life. The question also calls for researchers to examine the ways in which the field of social work must reposition itself if it is to do an effective job of examining African American life and appropriately responding to the chasm that exists between law enforcement and young Black males.

The interface of religiosity and police shootings of young Black males

For the current study, the authors' conceptualization of religion subscribes to the three-dimensional (organizational, nonorganizational, and subjective religiosity) domains of religion among African Americans posited by Taylor, Mattis, and Chatters (1999). Therefore, from the aforementioned three dimensions of religious involvement, the authors succinctly define religiosity among African Americans as the voluntary membership and regular participation within a formal religious group (church, mosque, or temple), coupled with a personalized practice of religious rituals (meditations, prayers, scripture reading, etc.) and strict adherence to religious values and perceptions. It is therefore not surprising that many studies have reported that compared to other races, African Americans have higher participation rates, allegiance, and social connectedness to religious organizations, otherwise called the Black church (Lincoln & Mamiya, 1990; Moore & Collins, 2002; Moore, 2011; Taylor et al., 1999; Williams, Griffith, Young, Collins, & Dodson, 1999).

Mattis (2002, p. 101) additionally affirmed that among African Americans, "religiosity is associated with organized worship." Furthermore, being religious has been identified as the medium, or conduit, for expressing one's spirituality (Frazier & Hansen, 2009; Mattis, 2002). Undeniably, organized religion has been identified as one of the major bastions of African Americans. For this study, the authors contend that the spirituality (a micro-, or private, perspective) and religiosity (a macro-, or formally organized, perspective) of young Black males provides ample interventional support to address the challenges of police shooting and law enforcement brutality to which young Black males are disproportionately exposed.

We now examine the role of the Black church in reducing police violence against young Black males.

The Black church's involvement in violence reduction against young Black males

For young Black males perennially exposed to police shooting and brutality, the Black church has been pinpointed as an indispensable institution that enhances positive youth development and "develop[s] a moral compass for adulthood" (Williams, 2003, p. 20), provides collective coping (Constantine, Donnelly, & Myers, 2002), offers a center for a sense of control and a place to reduce violence-related strains and stresses (Jang & Johnson, 2003, 2004), and above all serves as a mediator, or go-between, between the police and young Black males (Braga, Hureau, & Winship, 2008; Brunson, Braga, Hureau, & Pegram, 2014). Conversely, studies have reported that police officers utilize religious coping mechanisms to overcome critical stress incidents such as minority distrust and occupational hazards (Clark-Miller & Brady, 2013; Morash, Haarr, & Kwak, 2006). Therefore, a partnership and reciprocal professional relationship exist between some members of the clergy and police.

More specifically, the partnership of Black church leaders and police departments in Boston (such as "police-clergy neighborhood walks" in the famous "Operation Ceasefire" or "Boston Miracle" of the 1990s) also undergirds the important role that the Black church can play in reducing shooting violence that affects young Black males (Braga et al., 2008, p. 171). In the wake of the recent police shooting of Michael Brown in Ferguson, Missouri, Banks (2014) reported that signatures of African American church leaders were collected to jointly release press statements condemning the police shooting of yet another young Black male. The Banks (2014) report also indicated that Black church leaders encouraged the African American community to financially support Michael Brown's family in defraying the legal expenses of prosecuting the case.

It is, therefore, not surprising to observe that the mobilization, organization, and restoration roles that Black churches have continued to provide from the era of slavery to today persist among African Americans (Lincoln & Mamiya, 1990; Moore, 1991, 2011; Williams et al., 1999). Literature addresses the many religiously driven interventions to address social problems that assail young Black males. For instance, Adedoyin and Salter (2013) chronicled vital roles played by Black churches in addressing suicidal-shooting–related incidents and prevention strategies among young Blacks. In addition, the Black church was featured prominently in working with police departments nationwide to mitigate the problem of youth violence and gangsterism (Brunson, et al., 2014; Marsal, 2009). It is not uncommon to observe a working partnership between the leadership of the Black church and law enforcement agencies to reduce violence. What follows are recommendations for reducing police shootings of young Black males. These prescribed proposals are intended to help police, members of the Black church, and social workers address this issue.

Recommendations for violence reduction by police in relation to young Black males

The following recommendations are made in an effort to provide viable proactive measures that can be used to decrease the likelihood of lethal encounters between police and young Black males:

(1) *Cultural Sensitivity Training*—The United States is now an extremely diverse place occupied by people who have differing cultural backgrounds. Culture includes the shared collective worldview, language, foods, music, art forms, religious traditions, styles of communication, and modes of dress and body postures of a group that must be experienced to be fully appreciated. Having a theoretical knowledge of cultural differences is not enough. Culture must be experienced within the context of a particular people. Obtaining a law enforcement

degree usually requires a suite of courses that include the introduction and overview of the criminal justice system, theories of crime and punishment, and an introduction to the courts and correctional system. Other requirements may include elective and specialized courses in ethics, law enforcement operations, capital punishment, violent crime, and domestic violence. In many degree programs, internships are not part of the degree requirement (Stephenson, 2012; Werth, 2011). Hence, police can graduate from a law enforcement degree program without ever having hands-on community experience prior to being employed in law enforcement. This has often proven problematic or even deadly because "rookie" police sometimes enter a community and engage with individuals about whom they have little to no cultural understanding (Stephenson, 2012; Taiping, 1997). The authors investigated national law enforcement curricula and found no courses on spirituality among academic programs. This is an important point because, as previously stated, embracing spirituality enables a person to make the link between themselves and others. Perhaps the incidence of police shootings of unarmed young Black males would be positively impacted if during their academic preparation police were taught the value of being spiritually related to others. It is hoped that the culture of fear and disdain of young Black males (Brunson & Weitzer, 2009) would begin to dissipate among many within the ranks of law enforcement as a result of the introduction of courses on spirituality within law enforcement core curricula. The ultimate goal of exposing police to courses on spirituality would be to help them connect to the humanity of young Black males, which may cause them to be less likely to use deadly force in situations where it is not warranted such as when a male is not armed.

Social work is a profession that is concerned with the well-being of all people and especially those who are vulnerable and oppressed. Social workers can provide cultural immersion experiences specific to the life experiences and needs of young Black males as part of law enforcement training with the hope of changing negative perceptions that some police have about young Black males. They can also facilitate round table discussions between the African American community and police department officials and officers on police policies regarding the use of deadly force. This will provide education for community residents on policing procedures, policies, and strategies and will also provide a forum for discussions on how police interact with young African American males and alternative ways for police to interact with this population in their patrol areas. It must be noted that not all social workers who take diversity training are experts on relating to or knowledgeable enough about young Black males to provide in-depth cultural diversity training to police. The authors suggest that only those who have a working knowledge about young Black males are positioned to educate others.

(2) *Enhanced Law Enforcement Curricula*—Law enforcement curricula should include courses on protecting human rights and understanding cultural bias which can be taught to police by social workers. Police should also be required to take mandatory annual continuing education courses on the use of deadly force within the African American community. These courses will hopefully encourage police to recognize biases they may have when policing young African American males. A focus of the continuing education will be to teach alternative methods of policing within the African American community.

(3) *Proactive Intervention Strategies*—It is incumbent upon African American churches to take a proactive role by specifically targeting to young Black males' topics such as police relations and appropriate cordial responses to law enforcement personnel when encounters occur. Those discussions can occur during sermons, Bible study, and other forums. As indicated earlier in the Boston study, intentionally building bridges between African American churches and police departments has been shown to improve relationships and reduce violence. Second, proactive programs (not when a crisis occurs such as the Ferguson case) involving police officers and young Black males should be organized to better acquaint young

Black males with police departments. Additionally, it is proposed that representatives or leaders among young Black males participate in community policing training provided by the local police department so that these males can pass on the information they learn to successive generations of young Black males. Similarly, it is suggested that police officers occasionally attend youth programs that are sponsored by and/or located in Black churches and neighborhood programs to understand changing community dynamics, current frustrations, and agreed-upon suggestions made by the community to address potential issues (LaMotte et al., 2010).

(4) *Utilizing Indigenous Helpers*—The establishment of networks of representative young Black male leaders, throughout the Black community, who would serve as intermediaries between the police and young Black males could prove beneficial. They could be equipped with Twitter, Facebook, a mobile help line, or other instant messaging devices that a distressed young Black male can call immediately when altercations, confrontations, or pursuit ensue that involve them and police officers. This instant messaging, or communication, can then be relayed by the young leader to a trusted police officer who can instantly reassure colleagues (or in the case of the police, they can call this intermediary to mediate) before a shooting or fatal actions are carried out. Although these points are not guarantees, they may at least close the current relational gaps between young Black males and police and offer a structured and available bridge that can be crossed in the event of a crisis situation that may deteriorate into a shooting.

(5) *Police Civility*—Police officers should work to be friendlier when patrolling the Black community. Greeting members of the community with a simple "hello" or stopping to have a spontaneous conversation with people who live in the Black community may produce favorable feeling toward officers. In a community, such as Ferguson, Missouri, and many others, where there has been a history of tension between officers and residents, this kind of police civility is important. Genuine and kind gestures can be pathways for changing negative perceptions among members of the Black community about police. Even in situations where police officers have to engage in stopping people, being courteous or considerate can offset the police disrespect many young Black males experience. Wadman and Ziman (1993) found that when police officers are civil and courteous, it can strengthen their interaction with those in the community and will be reciprocated. Essentially, the initial approach of officers toward young Black males needs to reflect a nonoffensive tone of voice and language and a show of respect. With some encounters police officers have with young Black males there might not be the possibility for such greetings and friendly tones, but it should be something they consider as a matter of practice. It is critical for police officers to appreciate that as crime or the fear of crime decreases in a community, favorable attitudes toward the police increase (Cao, Frank, & Cullen, 1996). Therefore, attention should also be given to the broader systemic issues that young Black males face. For example, as low-income communities are often conducive to crime (Websdale, 2001), improvement in the economic condition of its residents (which includes young Black males) could have an impact on the reduction of violence, and thus police-citizen relationships may improve.

Implications for social work practice and education

The authors raise a number of implications for social work education and practice given the media attention that current highly publicized police shootings have garnered. In regard to social work education, families and friends of victims of police shootings require a number of services to cope with the death of a loved one. Traditionally, social work programs offer courses on death, dying, and bereavement. These programs teach various interventions for clients who are coping with the death of a loved one; however, the tragic and untimely death of a young Black male at the hands of police officers raises other issues. This type of death presents a unique set of problems because of the constant media attention and the public debates that often occur surrounding the shooting, and if a trial ensues it is often highly publicized, as is the verdict. Consequently, media attention can lead to friends and families constantly reliving the tragic event over and over, thus compounding their grief. Additionally, social work programs that include a specialization in school social work should be at the forefront of grief education because faculty who teach these courses are primary in teaching social work students how to provide therapy to classmates of the shooting victims. Overall, the constant media attention surrounding police shootings underscore the need for social work educators to address this reoccurring social problem across the social work curriculum and to prepare social work students for the challenges faced by such deaths.

Due to the complexity of challenges facing Black males, and the interdependent nature of social and educational systems, efforts to improve educational, social, and political outcomes for these young men must be collaborative, entailing sustained partnerships with school districts, community partners, researchers, colleges and universities, policymakers, and other key stakeholders. To that end, social work courses that focus on community partnerships can focus on social work organizations such as the National Association of Social Workers (NASW) and National Association of Black Social Workers (NABSW) forming partnerships with local government and police agencies similar to Operation Cease Fire (Braga et al., 2008). These partnerships will have a goal of discussing ways to prevent unnecessary shootings and implementing new procedures that specifically address the problem. Clearly a renewed focus on educating students and practitioners on addressing this social problem is warranted.

The untimely death of young Black males by police shootings also has implications for social work practice and particularly for social workers who practice in the realm of social justice. Death by police shooting can lead to a distrust of law enforcement officers and the criminal justice system within the Black community; moreover, there is the issue of social justice and human rights violations. The NASW Code of Ethics clearly states that social workers challenge social injustice, and the Code of Ethics also states that social workers' primary goal is to help people in need and to address social problems (NASW, 1996, 2008). There is a need for social workers to stand up for these victims, fight for changes in policies that govern police shootings, and scrutinize poor policing procedures as well.

Conclusion

The United States has positioned itself as a world superpower, and most of its citizens think that it is among the greatest countries in the world (Tyson, 2014). It is a place where freedom of speech is a right and people can speak their thoughts without fear of reprisal and imprisonment; it is a culturally diverse society made up of a plethora of ethnic and racial groups that lend to a richness of worldviews and ways of being; and it is a place where at the grassroots level people are socially active and participate in activities designed to challenge inequities and injustice. The United States is also a democracy where in theory all citizens have an equal right to full participation in the social order and its governance, but in practice this is not so.

At this time in history, America is being urgently challenged to rethink the policies that govern those, namely the police, who are responsible for ensuring the safety of all members of its populace. The authors have made recommendations that can be used by human service professionals, police, the Black church, and those who are concerned with the plight of young Black males to ensure the safety and survival of this group and to stop the killing of unarmed individuals by police. In the words of Liu Xiaobo (2014) "hatred is corrosive of a person's wisdom and conscience; the mentality of enmity can poison a nation's spirit, instigate brutal life and death struggles, destroy a society's tolerance and humanity, and block a nation's progress to freedom and democracy."

References

Adedoyin, A. C. A., & Salter, S. N. (2013). Mainstreaming black churches into suicide prevention among adolescents: A literature review. *Ethnicity and Inequalities in Health and Social Care*, *6*(2/3), 43–53.

Aguilar, M. A. (1997). Re-engineering social work's approach to holistic health. *Health & Social Work*, *22*(2), 83–84. doi:10.1093/hsw/22.2.83

Alexander, R., & Moore, S. E. (2008). The benefits, challenges and strategies of African American faculty teaching at predominantly White institutions. *Journal of African American Studies*, *12*(1), 4–18. doi:10.1007/s12111-007-9028-z

Anderson, C. A., Berkowitz, L., Donnerstein, M., Edward, K., Huesmann, L., & Rowell, J., et al. (2003). The influence of media violence on youth. *Psychological Science in the Public Interest*, *4*, 81–110.

Banks, A. M. (2014, August 22). Ferguson letter from black clergy becomes interracial call for justice. *Religious News Service*. Retrieved from http://www.religionnews.com/2014/08/22/ferguson-letter-black-clergy-becomes-interracial-call-justice/

Bell, G., Hopson, M., Craig, R., & Robinson, N. (2014). Exploring black and white accounts of 21st-century racial profiling: Riding and driving while black. *Qualitative Research Reports in Communication*, *15*(1), 33–42. doi:10.1080/17459435.2014.955590

Billingsley, A., & Caldwell, C. H. (1991). The church, the family and the school in the African American community. *Journal of Negro Education*, *60*, 427–440. doi:10.2307/2295494

Bimper, A., Harrison, L., & Clark, L. (2013). Diamonds in the rough: Examining a case of successful black male student athletes in college sport. *Journal of Black Psychology*, *39*(2), 107–130. doi:10.1177/0095798412454676

Braga, A. A., Hureau, D., & Winship, C. (2008). Losing faith, police, black churches, and the resurgence of youth violence in Boston. *Ohio State Journal of Criminal Law*, *6*, 141–171.

Brick, M., & Confessor, N. (2006). *Suit is settled in 2003 killing of immigrant*. Retrieved from http://www.nytimes.com/2006/07/21/nyregion/21zongo.html?_r=3&ref=ousmanezongo&

Britton, N. J. (2000). Examining police/black relations: What's in a story? *Ethnic and Racial Studies*, *23*(4), 692–711. doi:10.1080/01419870050033685

Brunson, R., & Weitzer, R. (2009). Police relations with Black and White youth in different urban neighborhoods. *Urban Affairs Review*, *44*(6), 858–885. doi:10.1177/1078087408326973

Brunson, R. K., Braga, A. A., Hureau, D. M., & Pegram, K. (2014). We trust you, but not that much: Examining police–black clergy partnerships to reduce youth violence. *Justice Quarterly*, *4*(2), 98–123.

Bureau of Labor Statistics: U.S. Department of Labor. (2014). *News release*. Retrieved from http://www.bls.gov/news.release/pdf/empsit.pdf

Burkhardt, M. (1989). Spirituality: An analysis of the concept. *Holistic Nursing Practice*, *3*(3), 69–77. doi:10.1097/00004650-198905000-00011

Cao, L., Frank, J., & Cullen, F. T. (1996). Race, community context and confidence in the police. *American Journal of Police*, *15*(1), 3–22. doi:10.1108/07358549610116536

Charters of Freedom. (n.d.). *The Declaration of Independence*. Retrieved from http://www.archives.gov/exhibits/charters/declaration_transcript.html

Clark-Miller, J., & Brady, H. C. (2013). Critical stress: Police officer religiosity and coping with critical stress incidents. *Journal of Police and Criminal Psychology*, *28*(1), 26–34. doi:10.1007/s11896-012-9112-8

Constantine, M. G., Donnelly, P. C., & Myers, L. J. (2002). Collective self-esteem and Africultural coping styles in African American adolescents. *Journal of Black Studies*, *32*(6), 698–710. doi:10.1177/00234702032006004

Cooper, F. R. (2013). We are always already imprisoned: Hyper incarceration and black male identity performance. *Boston University Law Review*, *93*(3), 1185–1204.

Cooper, M. (1999, February 5). Officers in Bronx fire 41 shots, and an unarmed man is killed. *The New York Times*. Retrieved from http://www.nytimes.com/1999/02/05/nyregion/officers-in-bronx-fire-41-shots-and-an-unarmed-man-is-killed.html?pagewanted=all

Cornileus, T. H. (2012). "I'm a black man and I'm doing this job very well": How African American professional men negotiate the impact of racism on their career development. *Journal of African American Studies*, *17*(4), 444–460. doi:10.1007/s12111-012-9225-2

Erikson, E. (1959). *Identity and the life cycle*. New York, NY: W. W. Norton.

Evans, M. (2006). Black-owned firms on the rise: Companies grew 25 percent in Nassau, 28 percent in Suffolk, according to a Census Bureau survey. *Newsday*, April 19, A32.

Frazier, R. E., & Hansen, N. D. (2009). Religious/spiritual psychotherapy behaviors: Do we do what we believe to be important? *Professional Psychology: Research and Practice*, *40*(1), 81–87. doi:10.1037/a0011671

Freyer, J. (2014). Holder discusses police mistrust outside Ferguson. *Associated Press Top News Package*, August 20. Retrieved from http://www.salon.com/2014/08/20/holder_discusses_police_mistrust_outside_ferguson/

Fritzgerald, S. (2007). *Police brutality: Opposing viewpoints*. Detroit, MI: Greenhaven Press.

Gabrielson, R., Jones, R. G., & Sagara, E. (2014). *Deadly force, in black and white*. Retrieved from http://www.propublica.org/article/deadly-force-in-black-and-white

Garrison, W. L. (2010). *Powerful quotes to uplift black men.* Retrieved from http://praisephilly.com/57321/powerful-quotes-to-uplift-black-men/

Ghitis, F. (2014). *Police shootings in U.S. out of hand.* Retrieved from http://edition.cnn.com/2014/12/01/opinion/ghitis-police-shootings/index.html

Harris, J. (2014). *Too poor to pay for peace of mind.* Retrieved from http://www.theroot.com/articles/culture/2014/11/mental_health_care_still_lacking_for_th ose_in_poverty.html

Huffington Post. (2014). *Eric Garner.* Retrieved from http://www.huffingtonpost.com/news/eric-garner/

Hutchinson, E. O. (1996). *The assassination of the Black male image.* Riverside, NJ: Simon & Schuster.

Jagers, R., & Mock, L. (1993). Culture and social outcomes among inner-city African American children: An Afrographic exploration. *Journal of Black Psychology, 19*, 391–405. doi:10.1177/00957984930194002

Jang, S. J., & Johnson, B. R. (2003). Strain, negative emotions, and deviant coping among African Americans: A test of general strain theory. *Journal of Quantitative Criminology, 19*(1), 79–105. doi:10.1023/A:1022570729068

Jang, S. J., & Johnson, B. R. (2004). Explaining religious effects on distress among African Americans. *Journal for the Scientific Study of Religion, 43*(2), 239–260. doi:10.1111/j.1468-5906.2004.00230.x

Kappeler, V. E. (2014). *A brief history of slavery and the origins of American policing.* Retrieved from http://www.plsonline.eku.edu/insidelook/brief-history-slavery-and-origins-American-policing

Kitano, H. H. L. (1985). *Race relations* (3rd ed.). Englewood Cliffs, NJ: Prentice-Hall.

LaMotte, V., Ouellette, K., Sanderson, J., Anderson, S., Kosutic, I., Griggs, J., & Garcia, M. (2010). Effective police interactions with youth: A program evaluation. *Police Quarterly, 13*(2), 161–179. doi:10.1177/1098611110365689

Lincoln, C. E., & Mamiya, L. H. (1990). *The black church in the African American experience.* Durham, NC: Duke University Press.

Long, C. (1997). Perspectives for a study of African American religion in the United States. In T. Fulop, & A. Raboteau (Eds.), *African American religion: Interpretive essays in history and culture* (pp. 23–35). New York, NY: Routledge.

Majors, R. G., & Gordon, J. U. (1994). *The American black male: His present status and his future.* Chicago, IL: Nelson-Hall.

Marable, M. (1998). Black fundamentalism: Farrakhan and conservative black nationalism. *Race & Class, 39*, 1–22. doi:10.1177/030639689803900401

Marsal, E. S. (2009). Spirituality as a protective factor against female gang membership. *Journal of Human Behavior in the Social Environment, 19*(3), 231–241. doi:10.1080/10911350802694584

Mattis, J. (2002). African American women's definition of spirituality and religiosity. *Journal of Black Psychology, 26* (1), 101–122. doi:10.1177/0095798400026001006

Mcdaniel, A., Diprete, T. A., Buchmann, C., & Shwed, U. (2011). The black gender gap in educational attainment: Historical trends and racial comparisons. *Demography, 48*(3), 889–914.

McGee, E., & Martin, D. (2011). From the hood to being hooded: A case study of a black male Ph.D. *Journal of African American Males in Education, 2*(1), 46–65.

McFadden, R. D. (2000, December 10). Police identify unarmed man shot to death by officer. *The New York Times.* Retrieved from http://www.nytimes.com/2000/12/10/nyregion/police-identify-unarmed-man-shot-to-death-by-officers.html

Moore, S. E. (2011). African American megachurches and community empowerment: Fostering life in dry places. *Journal of African American Studies, 15*(2), 129–132. doi:10.1007/s12111-011-9180-3

Moore, S. E., & Collins, W. L. (2002). A model for social work field practicums in African American churches. *Journal of Teaching in Social Work, 22*(3–4), 171–188.

Moore, T. (1991). The African-American church: A source of empowerment, mutual help, and social change. *Prevention in Human Services, 10*(1), 147–167. doi:10.1300/J293v10n01_09

Morash, M., Haarr, R., & Kwak, D. (2006). Multilevel influences on police stress. *Journal of Contemporary Criminal Justice, 22*(1), 26–43. doi:10.1177/1043986205285055

National Association of Social Workers. (1996, 2008). *Code of ethics.* Retrieved from http://www.socialworkers.org/pubs/code/default.asp

Nelson, J. (2000). *Police brutality.* New York, NY: W.W. Norton.

Payne, Y. A. (2006). "A gangster and a gentleman": How street life–oriented, U.S.-born African men negotiate issues of survival in relation to their masculinity. *Journal of Men and Masculinities, 8*, 288–297. doi:10.1177/1097184X05282072

Shapiro, H. (1988). *White violence and black and black response: From reconstruction to Montgomery.* Amherst, MA : University of Massachusetts Press.

Sidney, H. L. (1983). *Policing a class society: The experience of American cities, 1865–1915.* New Brunswick, NJ: Rutgers University Press.

Staples, R. (1982). *Black masculinity: The black male's role in American society.* San Francisco, CA: Black Scholar Press.

Stephenson, F. (2012). Good cop, better cop. *Research (Michigan Technological University)*, 16–18.

Stevenson, H. C., Herrero-Taylor, T., Cameron, R., & Davis, G. Y. (2002). Mitigating instigation: Cultural phenomenological influences of anger and fighting among "big-boned" and "baby-faced" African American youth. *Journal of Youth & Adolescence, 31*(6), 473–485. doi:10.1023/A:1020267221683

Swanigan, P. (2012). Much the same on the other side: The boondocks and the symbolic frontier. *Children's Literature, 40*, 28–48. doi:10.1353/chl.2012.0019

Taiping, H. (1997). Police use of deadly force and experience: Rookie v. veteran. *Justice Professional, 10*(2), 127–141. doi:10.1080/1478601X.1997.9959458

Taylor, R., & Chatters, L. (1991). Religious life. In J. S. Jackson (Ed.), *Life in black America* (pp. 105–123). Newbury, Park, CA: Sage.

Taylor, R. J., Mattis, J., & Chatters, L. M. (1999). Subjective religiosity among African Americans: A synthesis of findings from five national samples. *Journal of Black Psychology, 25*(4), 524–543. doi:10.1177/0095798499025004004

The United States Department of Justice (2011). *New Orleans police officers convicted of civil right violation in Danziger bridge case.* Retrieved from http://www.justice.gov/opa/pr/new-orleans-police-officers-convicted-civil-rights-violations-danziger-bridge-case

The Washington Post. (2014). *Ohio Wal-Mart surveillance video shows police shooting and killing John Crawford III.* Retrieved from http://www.washingtonpost.com/news/post-nation/wp/2014/09/25/ohio-wal-mart-surveillance-video-shows-police-shooting-and-killing-john-crawford-iii/

Tyson, A. (2014). *Most Americans think the U.S. is great, but fewer say it's the greatest.* Pew Research Center. Retrieved from http://www.pewresearch.org/fact-tank/2014/07/02/most-americans-think-the-u-s-is-great-but-fewer-say-its-the-greatest/

United States Census Bureau. (2011). *The black population: 2010 census brief.* Retrieved from http://www.census.gov/prod/cen2010/briefs/c2010br-06.pdf

Uzzell, K. (2008). The healthy psychosocial development of Black males: The relationship between wellness and racial identity development. *Dissertation Abstracts International, A: The Humanities and Social Sciences, 68*(12), xiv–76. ProQuest, Ann Arbor MI, 2008.AAI3293686.

Wadman, R. C., & Ziman, S. M. (1993). Courtesy and police authority. *FBI Law Enforcement Bulletin, 62*, 23–23.

Warde, B. (2012). Black male disproportionality in the criminal justice systems of the USA, Canada, and England: A comparative analysis of incarceration. *Journal of African American Studies, 17*(4), 461–479. doi:10.1007/s12111-012-9235-0

Websdale, N. (2001). *Policing the poor: From slave plantation to public housing.* Boston, MA: Northeastern University Press.

Werth, E. P. (2011). Scenario training in police academies: Developing students' higher-level thinking skills. *Police Practice & Research, 12*(4), 325–340. doi:10.1080/15614263.2011.563970

Whooley, M., Kiefe, C., Chesney, M., Markovitz, J., Matthews, K., Hulley, S. (2002). Depressive symptoms, unemployment, and loss of income: the CARDIA study. *Archive of Internal Medicine, 162*, 2614–2620.

Williams, D. R., Griffith, E. E., Young, J. L., Collins, C., & Dodson, J. (1999). Structure and provision of services in Black churches in New Haven, Connecticut. *Cultural Diversity and Ethnic Minority Psychology, 5*(2), 118–133. doi:10.1037/1099-9809.5.2.118

Williams, O. A. (2003). Effects of faith and church involvement on African American female adolescents. *Michigan Family Review, 8*(1), 19–27.

Xiaobo, L. (2014). *Liu Xiaobo quotes.* Retrieved from http://www.brainyquote.com/quotes/authors/l/liu_xiaobo.html

Index

Note: **Boldface** page numbers refer to figures, page numbers followed by "n" denote endnotes.

For Product Safety Concerns and Information please contact our EU representative GPSR@taylorandfrancis.com
Taylor & Francis Verlag GmbH, Kaufingerstraße 24, 80331 München, Germany

www.ingramcontent.com/pod-product-compliance
Ingram Content Group UK Ltd.
Pitfield, Milton Keynes, MK11 3LW, UK
UKHW050754180926
475701UK00007B/1042
9780367234973